Voices of the
African American Experience

Voices of the African American Experience

VOLUME 2

Edited by Lionel C. Bascom

GREENWOOD PRESS
Westport, Connecticut • London

Library of Congress Cataloging-in-Publication Data

Voices of the African American experience / edited by Lionel C. Bascom.
   3 v. cm.
   Includes bibliographical references and index.
   ISBN 978-0-313-34347-6 (set) — ISBN 978-0-313-34349-0 (vol. 1) —
ISBN 978-0-313-34351-3 (vol. 2) — ISBN 978-0-313-34353-7
(vol. 3) 1. African Americans—History—Sources. I. Bascom, Lionel C.
   E184. 6. V65   2009
   973′.0496073—dc22   2008056155

British Library Cataloguing in Publication Data is available.

Library of Congress Catalog Card Number: 2008056155

ISBN: 978-0-313-34347-6 (set)
       978-0-313-34349-0 (vol 1)
       978-0-313-34351-3 (vol 2)
       978-0-313-34353-7 (vol 3)

First published in 2009

Greenwood Press, 88 Post Road West, Westport, CT 06881
An imprint of Greenwood Publishing Group, Inc.
www.greenwood.com

Printed in the United States of America

∞

The paper used in this book complies with the
Permanent Paper Standard issued by the National
Information Standards Organization (Z39.48-1984).

10 9 8 7 6 5 4 3 2 1

Contents

VOLUME 2

VOLUME 3

43. Common Sense in Common Schooling: a sermon by Alex. Crummell, Rector of St. Luke's Church, Washington, D.C., September 13, 1886

As pastor of St. Luke's Episcopal Church in Washington, D.C., from 1879 to 1898, Alex Crummell gives a critique of the trends in African American educational facilities during this time. His belief is that the educators need to educate their students in practical trades and industrial arts. He also criticizes U.S. trade unions for their exclusion of blacks.

That the soul should be without knowledge is not good.—Prov. 9:12

To-morrow morning we shall witness the reopening of the public schools and the beginning of another year's school session. As the training and instruction of our children is a matter of very great interest and importance, I am glad of the opportunity to say a few words upon the whole subject of Common-School education.

I need not pause to explain the special significance of the text. It is so plain and apparent that even the youngest can readily take it in, and you, who are their elders, have years ago become familiar with its point and power.

It has had during the last few years a special and peculiar influence upon us as a people. Rarely in the history of man has any people, "sitting in the region and shadow of death"—a people almost literally enveloped in darkness—rarely, I say, has any such people risen up from their Egyptian darkness with such a craving for light as the black race in this country. It has been almost the repetition of the Homeric incident:—

Dispel this gloom—the light of heaven restore—

Give me to see, and Ajax asks no more.

Almost universal ignorance was the mental condition of the race of the previous to emancipation. Out of millions of people, not more than 30,000 were allowed an acquaintance with letters. To-day, hundreds of schools are in existence, and over a million of our children are receiving the elements of common-school education.

The point of interest in this grand fact is that this intellectual receptivity was no tardy and reluctant faculty. Albeit an ignorant people, yet we did not need either to be goaded or even stimulated to intellectual desire. There was no need of any compulsory laws to force our children into the schools. No; the mental appetite of the Negro was like the resurrection of nature in the spring-time of the far northern regions. To-day, universal congelation and death prevail. To-morrow, the icy bands of winter are broken and there is a sudden upheaval of dead, stolid rivers. The living waters rush from their silent beds and sweep away formidable barriers, and spread abroad over wide and extensive plains.

This craving of the appetite for letters and knowledge knows no abatement. Everywhere throughout the nation there still abides this singular and burning aptitude of the black race for schools and learning.

I am proud of this vast and ardent desire of the race; for the brain of man is the very first instrument of human achievement. Given, a cultivated and elastic brain, and you have the possibility of a man, and, with other qualifications and conditions, the probability of almost a demi-god. Take away the trained and cultivated intellect, and you get the likelihood of an animal, and, possibly, of a reptile.

But while I rejoice in the wide spread of lettered acquaintance among us, I cannot close my eyes to a great evil which has been similtaneous with the increase of our knowledge. This evil is becoming so alarming that I feel it a duty to call the attention of both parents and children to it. The evil itself I call Disproportion! It is that which we mean when we have an excess of somewhat that is pleasing, with a loss of what is convenient and substantial. We are all apt then to say that it is "*too much of a good thing*." The like one-sidedness discovers itself among us in our common-school education. Too many of our parents are ruining their children by this error.

They crave an excess of one kind of education, and at the same time neglect important elements of another and quite as important a kind. This sad fact suggests as a theme for consideration to-day "Common Sense in Common Schooling." The subject presents itself in the two topics, *i.e.*, the *excess* and the *defect* in the training of our youth.

(1.) Education as a system in our day divides itself into two sections, which are called, respectively, the higher and the lower. The former pertains to classical learning, *i.e.*, Latin and Greek, Science, and Art, in which latter are included music, drawing, and painting. It is with regard to the higher education that I feel called upon to express my fears and to give my counsel.

I fear we are overdoing this matter of higher learning. Everywhere I go throughout the country I discover two or three very disagreeable and unhealthy facts. I see, *first* of all, (*a*) the vain ambition of very many mothers to over-educate their daughters, and to give them training and culture unfitted for their position in society and unadapted to their prospects in life. I see, likewise, too many men, forgetful of the occupations they held in society, anxious to shoot their sons suddenly, regardless of fitness, into literary characters and into professional life. This is the first evil. (*b*) Next to this I have observed an ambition among the youth of both sexes for aesthetical culture; an inordinate desire for the ornamental and elegant in educational to the neglect of the solid and practical. And (*c*), thirdly, to a very large extent school children are educated in letters to a neglect of household industry. Scores of both boys and girls go to school. That is their life business and nothing else; but their parents neglect their training in housework, and so they live in the streets, and during the first twelve or fourteen years of their life are given to play and pleasure. And (*d*), lastly, our boys and girls almost universally grow up without trades, looking forward, if they do look forward, many of them, to being servants and waiters; and many more I am afraid, expecting to get a living by chance and hap-hazard.

Doubtless some of you will say that the colored people are not the only people at fault in these respects; that the American people, in general, are running wild about the higher culture—are neglecting trades and mechanism, and are leaving the more practical and laborious duties of life to foreigners. Grant that this is the case; but it only serves to strengthen the allegation I make that we, in common with American people, are running into an excessive ambition for the higher culture to the neglect of industrial arts and duties. I go into families. I ask parents what they are preparing their children for, and the answer I frequently receive is: "Oh, I am going to send my son to college to make him a lawyer, or the daughter is to go to the East or to Europe to be made an accomplished lady." Not long ago I met an old acquaintance, and, while talking about the future of her children, I inquired:

"What are you going to do with—I will call him 'tom?"

Tom is a little fellow about fourteen years old; by no means a genius; more anxious about tops and taffy and cigarettes than about his books; never likely, so far as I can see, to set the Potomac on fire. Her answer was that his father purposed sending him to college to make him a lawyer. On another occasion I was talking to a minister of the Gospel about his daughters, and *he* was anxious to send his two girls to Belgium to be educated for society! Not long ago an acquaintance of mine told me that his sons should never do the work he was doing. He was going to educate one to be a doctor, another to be a lawyer, and the third he hoped to make a minister. I must give him the credit that when I pointed out the danger of ruining his sons by this over-education, and that this sudden rise from a humble condition might turn them into lazy and profligate spendthrifts, he listened to me, and I am glad to say he took my advice. He is now giving them his own trade, and I think they are likely to become quiet and industrious young men.

Let me not be misunderstood. I am not only *not* opposed to the higher culture, but I am exceedingly anxious for it. We *must* have a class of trained and superior men and women. We *must* have cultured, refined society. To live on a dead level of inferiority, or to be satisfied with the plane of uniform mediocrity, would be death to us as a people.

Moreover we need, and in our blood, the great molders and fashioners of thought among us. To delegate the thinking of the race to any other people would be to introduce intellectual stagnation in the race; and when thought declines then a people are sure to fall and fade away.

These, then, are the most sufficient reasons for a large introduction among us of the highest training and culture. But this is no reason or excuse for disproportion or extravagance. Culture *is* a great need; but the greater, wider need of the race is industry and practicality. We need especially multitudinous artizans, and productive toil, and the grand realizations of labor, or otherwise we can never get respect or power in the land.

And this leads me next to the other topic, viz, the employments and occupations of industrial life. Here we encounter one of the most formidable difficulties of our civil life in this country. The state of things in this regard is an outrage upon humanity! And I protest, with all my might, against the mandate of the "Trades' Unions," which declare "You black people must be content with servant life!" I say that this race of ours should demand the right to enter every avenue of enterprise and activity white men enter. They should cry out, too, against our exclusion from any of the trades and businesses of life. But with all this remember that no people can *all*, or even many of them, become lawyers, doctors, ministers, teachers, scholars! No people can get their living and build themselves up by refined style and glittering fashion or indulgence in belle-lettres.

No people can live off of flowers, nor gain strength and robustness by devotion to art.

And it is just this false and artificial tendency which is ruining colored society almost everywhere in the United States. It is especially so in the large cities. The youth want to go to school until they are nineteen or twenty years of age. Meanwhile, the book-idea so predominates that duty and industry are thrown into the shade. Mothers and fathers work hard to sustain their children. After awhile the children look with contempt upon their unlettered, hard-handed parents, and regard them as only born for use and slavish toil. Is this an exaggeration? Have you not seen some of those fine young ladies, whose mothers sweat and toil for them in the wash-tub or cook in the kitchen, boasting that they can't hem a pocket handkerchief or cook a potato? Have not you seen some of these grand gentlemen who forget the humble parents who begot them, forget the humble employments of those parents, turn up their noses at the ordinary occupations of the poor race they belong to, and then begin the fantastic airs of millionaires, while they don't own ground enough to bury themselves in?

You say, perchance, "Such girls and boys are 'sillies,'" and that their brainless folly is no reason why the higher education should not be given in all the schools. It is just here I beg to differ with you. I maintain that parents should exercise discrimination in this matter. They have no right to waste time and expense upon incapable girls and boys. They have no right to raise up a whole regiment of pretentious and lazy fools to plague society and to ruin themselves. They have no right to send out into the world a lot of young men and women with heads crammed with Latin, Greek, and literature; with no heart to labor; with hands of baby softness; interested only in idleness, and given to profligacy and ruinous pleasure. And just this, in numerous cases, is the result of this ambitious system of education in this land. We are turning out annually from the public schools a host of fine scholars, but not a few of them lazy, inflated, senseless, sensual! Whole shoals of girls hating labor, slattern in habits and at the same time bespangled with frippery, devoted to dress, and the easy prey of profligate men! And lots of young men utterly indifferent to the fortunes of their families and the interests of their girls, but scores of them throughly unprincipled and profligate!

They live for to-day, but the life they live is for sensual delight, and the culture they have gained is spent in skillful devices to administer to the lusts of the flesh. This I am constrained to say is the result of the higher education in well nigh half of the colored youth who graduate from high schools and colleges, and it is ruinous to our people.

You ask me the remedy for this great evil. MY answer is by avoidance of the excess which I have pointed out and the adoption of the ordinary common-school education. Shun disproportion. Hold on to the higher education, but use it only in fit and exceptional cases. If you have a son or a daughter burning with the desire for learning, give that child every possible opportunity. But you see the condition I present, viz, that it *burns* with intellectual desire. But how often is this the case? The difficulty in the matter is that parents themselves are to blame for the miscarriage of their children's education. Everybody now a days is crazy about education. Fathers and mothers are anxious that their children should shine. However ordinary a boy or girl may be the parents want them to be scholars. The boy may be a numbskull, the girl a noodle. The fond parent thinks the child a prodigy; stimulates its ambition, gives it indulgence, saves it from labor, keeps it at school almost to its majority and then, at last, it finds out that the child has no special talent, dislikes labor, is eager for pleasure, dress, and display, is selfish and cruel to its parents, unable to earn its own living, and expects father and mother to drudge for its support and vanity. I am sure that you all know numerous cases of such failure and ruin.

And it all comes from a neglect of a few plain common-sense rules which belong naturally to the subject of education.

Let me briefly set before you some of these rules:

First of all, secure for your children an acquaintance with reading writing, arithmetic, and geography. When well grounded in these studies, which is ordinarily at 12 or 13, then ascertain whether your children are fitted for the higher branches. If you yourself are educated, form your own judgement; if not, get the advice of a well-qualified friend, or the opinion of your minister, or take counsel of the child's schoolmaster. If convinced that the child gives promise of superiority, keep it at school, give it the best opportunities, and labor hard to make your child a thorough scholar.

(2) On the other hand, if you find your child has but ordinary capacity, take it from school and put it at an early day to work. If you don't you will not only waste time but you are likely to raise up a miserable dolt or a lazy dandy. Such a child, brought up to fruitless inactivity, dawdling for years over unappreciated culture, will, likely as not never want to work for his living, may turn out a gambler or a thief, and in the end may disgrace your name or break your heart. Don't keep your children too long at school; don't think too much about the book and so little about labor. Remember that the end of all true education is to learn to do duty in life and to secure an honorable support and sustenance.

And here (3) let me press upon you the importance of training your children in industrial habits *at home* during the period of their school life. Going to school should never prevent a girl from learning to sew, to cook, to sweep, bed-making, and scrubbing the floor; nor a boy from using a hammer, cleaning the yard, bringing in coal, doing errands, working hard to help his mother, or to assist his father. Home work, moreover, is the natural antidote to the mental strain, and oftentimes the physical decline which, in these days, comes from the excess of study, which is the abnormal feature of the present school system.

From labor health, from health contentment flows.

If you begin your child's school life by the separation of books and learning from manual labor, then you begin his education with poison as the very first portion of his intelligent life! He had better a deal be ignorant and industrious than lettered and slothful, and, perchance, a beggar! Laziness and learning are as incongruous as a "jewel in a swine's snout," and few things are so demoralizing to the young. Witness the large numbers of lettered youth and young men, fresh from schools, academies, and colleges, who fill the jails and prisons of the country, and then think of the large and more skillful numbers outside who ought, in justice, to be companying with those *within*. Nothing is more contemptible than the crowds of these danda-

dandaical "clothes-bags," for they deserve no better title, one sees in our large cities, who have, indeed, the varnish of the schools and literature, but who lack common sense, full of vanity and pretense, poisoned with lust and whisky, and, while too proud and too lazy to work, get their living by vice and gambling. This abuse of learning, however, is not confined to men. Alas! that it must be acknowledged, we have all over the land scores of cultured young woman in whose eyes labor is a disgrace and degradation, who live lives of lazy cunning or deception, and plunge determinedly into lust and harlotry. And the poor old fathers and mothers who toiled so painfully for their schooling, and hoped such great things for their daughters, have been cast down to misery and despair, or else have died broken-hearted over their daughters shame and ruin. And in every such case how sad the reflection: "O, that I had been wise with my child! O, that I had scouted her false notions about style and elegance! O, that I had been more anxious to make her industrious and virtuous! Then all this anguish and distress would never have fallen upon me!" Such cases of folly have their lessons for all of us who are parents. May Almighty God make us both wise in our generation, and prudent and discreet with our children.

The words I have spoken this day have sprung from two or three deep convictions which I am sure are thoroughly scriptural and true, and which, I think, may rightly close this discourse:

1. The first of these is that children are neither toys nor playthings, such as are embroidery and jewels and trinkets. They are moral spiritual beings, endowed with conscience and crowned with the principle of immoratality. You may toy and play with your trinkets, but you are accountable to God for the soul, the life, the character, and the conduct of your child. Hence duty and responsibility are the two paramount considerations which are to be allied with the entire training of your children, whether at home or in their school life.

2. Children are trusts for the good and health of society and the commonwealth. The law don't allow you to poison the air with filth and garbage, and for the simple reason that as a householder you are a trustee for your fellow-creatures. But in regards of your children you are, in a far higher sense, a trustee for your fellow-creatures around you. What right have you to send forth from your threshold a senseless fool, full of learning it may be, but with no sense, no idea of responsibility for anybody, impudent to old people, a rowdy in God's Church, a rioter, a gambler, a rake? Ought not the culture you have toiled to give him serve to make him modest, a mild-mannered man, a stay to his humble toilsome parents, a useful man in society, a thrifty and productive citizen in the community? And was it not your duty, all his life long, to strive to realize such a large and high-souled being as the fruit of your family life and training?

Or, if perchance it is a girl, what right have you to send forth into the world a lazy, impertinent creature, bedecked and bejeweled indeed; full perchance, of letters and accomplishments, but with no womanly shame; brazen with boldness; lazy as a sloth, and, yet, proud, pretentious, crazy for ruinous delights; swept away by animal desires; alien from domestic duties, and devoted to pleasure? Go to, now. Is this the fruit of your vineyard? When God and man, too, look that it should bring forth grapes, will you only thrust upon us such wild grapes?

You have no such right! You are a trustee for society, and you should take a pride in rearing up ornaments for society—"Sons," as the psalmist describes them, "who may grow up as the young plants;" "daughters, as the polished corners of the temple." Just such, I am proud to say, as I see in many of your own families is this church, whose children are intelligent, scholarly, and, at the same time, virtuous, modest, obedient, and industrious. God's holy name be praised for such children, such parents, such godly families! May God, for Jesus' sake, multiply them a hundred fold in all our communities!

3. Join to this, thirdly, the most solemn of all considerations, *i.e.*, that your children are the servants of the most high God. All souls are says the Almighty. God made them and sent them into the world. He it is who places living souls in the family, in human society, in the nation, in the church, for His own honor and glory. Not for mere pastime, for trifling, or for pleasure are human beings put amid the relations of life. We are all God's property—our children and ourselves—for God's service and His praise. Beloved, accept this grand prerogative of your human existence; train your children for godly uses in this world; train their minds by proper schooling; their bodies by industry; their immortal souls by teaching, catechising, and family devotion, so that they may glorify God in their bodies and their spirits; and then God will give you family order and success in this world; your children honor and blessing by the Holy Ghost, and everlasting light shall be the inheritance of your seed, and your seeds' seed from generation to generation on earth, and glory, honor, and peace, at the last, in the Kingdom of Heaven above!

Source: Library of Congress, Rare Book and Special Collections Division, Daniel A. P. Murray Pamphlets Collection.

44. The Wonderful Eventful Life of Rev. Thomas James, by himself, 1887

This is an excerpt from an autobiography by Rev. Thomas James, a minister in the African Methodist Episcopal (AME) Church, who writes about his life from slavery to the ministry to the anti-slavery movement in New York and Massachusetts. The narrative is an account of how he ran a camp for free and refugee African Americans in Kentucky during the Civil War.

The story of my life is a simple one, perhaps hardly worth the telling. I have written it in answer to many and oft repeated requests on the part of my friends for a relation of its incidents, and to them I dedicate this little volume.

The Author

Rochester, [N.Y.] Feb. 15, 1886.

I was born a slave at Canajoharie, this state, in the year 1804. I was the third of four children, and we were all the property of Asa Kimball, who, when I was in the eighth year of my age, sold my mother, brother and elder sister to purchasers from Smith-town, a village not far distant from Amsterdam in the same part of the state. My mother refused to go, and ran into the garret to seek a hiding place. She was pursued, caught, tied hand and foot and delivered to her new owner. I caught my last sight of my mother as they rode off with her. My elder brother and sister were taken away at the same time. I never saw either my mother or sister again. Long years afterwards my brother and I were reunited, and he died in this city a little over a year ago. From him I learned that my mother died about the year 1846, in the place to which she had been taken. My brother also informed me that he and his sister were separated soon after their transfer to a Smithport master, and he never heard of her subsequent fate. Of my father I never had any personal knowledge, and, indeed, never heard anything. My youngest sister, the other member of the family, died when I was yet a youth.

While I was still in the seventeenth year of my age, Master Kimball was killed in a runaway accident; and at the administrator's sale I was sold with the rest of the property, my new master being Cromwell Bartlett, of the same neighborhood. As I remember, my first master was a well-to-do but rough farmer, a skeptic in religious matters, but of better heart than address; for he treated me well. He owned several farms, and my work was that of a farm hand. My new master had owned me but a few months when he sold me, or rather traded me, to George H. Hess, a wealthy farmer of the vicinity of Fort Plain. I was bartered in exchange for a yoke of steers, a colt and some additional property, the nature and amount of which I have now forgotten. I remained with Master Hess from March until June of the same year, when I ran away. My master had worked me hard, and at last undertook to whip me. This led me to seek escape farm slavery. I arose in the night, and taking the newly staked line of the Erie canal for my route, traveled along it westward until, about a week later, I reached the village of Lockport. No one had stopped me in my flight. Men were at work digging the new canal at many points, but they never troubled themselves even to question me. I slept in barns at night and begged food at farmers' houses along my route. At Lockport a colored man showed me the way to the Canadian border. I crossed the Niagara at Youngstown on the ferry-boat, and was free!

Once on free soil, I began to look about for work, and found it at a point called Deep Cut on the Welland Canal, which they were then digging. I found the laborers a rough lot, and soon had a mind to leave them. After three months had passed, I supposed it safe to return to the American side, and acting on the idea I recrossed the river. A farmer named Rich, residing near Youngstown, engaged me as a wood chopper. In the spring I made my way to Rochesterville and found a home with Lawyer Talbert. The chores about his place were left to me, and I performed the same service for Orlando Hastings. I was then nineteen years of age. As a slave I had never been inside of a school or a church, and I knew nothing of letters or religion. The wish to learn awoke in me almost from the moment I set foot in the place, and I soon obtained an excellent chance to carry the wish into effect. After the opening of the Erie canal, I obtained work in the warehouse of the Hudson and Erie line, and found a home with its manager, Mr. Pliny Allen Wheeler. I was taught to read by Mr. Freeman, who had opened a Sunday-school of his own for colored youths, on West Main street, or Buffalo street, as it was then called. But my self-education advanced fastest in the warehouse during the long winter and spring months, when the canal was closed and my only work consisted of chores about the place and at my employer's residence. The clerks helped me whenever I needed help in my studies. Soon I had learning enough to be placed in charge of the freight business of the warehouse, with full direction over the lading of boats. I became a member of the African Methodist Episcopal Society in 1823, when the church was on Ely street, and my studies took the direction of preparation for the ministry. In 1828

I taught a school for colored children on Favor street, and I began holding meetings at the same time. In the following year I first formally commenced preaching, and in 1830 I bought as a site for a religious edifice the lot now occupied by Zion's church. In the meantime the Ely street society had ceased to exist, its death having been hastened by internal quarrels and by dishonesty among its trustees. On the lot already mentioned I built a small church edifice, which was afterwards displaced by a larger one, the latter finally giving way to the present structure on the same site. I was ordained as a minister in May, 1833, by Bishop Rush. I had been called Tom as a Slave, and they called me Jim at the warehouse. I put both together when I reached manhood, and was ordained as Rev. Thomas James.

Two years before the last mentioned event in my life, Judge Sampson, vice-president of the local branch of the African Colonization Society of that day, turned over to me a batch of anti-slavery literature sent him by Arthur Tappan. It was these documents that turned my thoughts into a channel which they never quitted until the colored man became the equal of the white in the eye of the law, if not in the sight of his neighbor of another race. In the early summer of 1833 we held the first of a series of anti-slavery meetings in the court house. The leading promoters of that meeting were William Bloss, Dr. Reid—whose widow, now in the 86th year of her age, still lives in Rochester—and Dr. W. Smith. There was a great crowd in attendance on the first night, but its leading motive was curiosity, and it listened without interfering with the proceedings. The second night we were plied with questions, and on the third they drowned with their noise the voices of the speakers and finally turned out the lights. Not to be baulked of his purpose, Mr. Bloss, who was not a man to be cowed by opposition, engaged the session room of the Third Presbyterian church; but even there we were forced to lock the doors before we could hold our abolition meeting in peace. There we organized our anti-slavery society, and when the journals of the day refused to publish our constitution and by laws, we bought a press for a paper of our own and appointed the three leaders already named to conduct it. It was printed fort-nightly and was called *The Rights of Man*. I was sent out to make a tour of the country in its interest, obtaining subscriptions for the paper and lecturing against slavery. At LeRoy I was mobbed, my meeting was broken up, and I was saved from worse treatment only by the active efforts of Mr. Henry Brewster, who secreted me in his own house. At the village I next visited, Warsaw, I was aided by Seth M. Gates and others, and I was also well received at Perry. At Pike, however, I was arrested and subjected to a mock trial, with the object of scaring me into flight from the place. At Palmyra I found no hall or church in which I could speak. Indeed the place was then a mere hamlet and could boast of but half a dozen dwellings. My tour embraced nearly every village in this and adjourning counties, and the treatment given me varied with the kind of people I happened to find in the budding settlements of the time. In the same fall I attended the first Anti-Slavery State Convention at Utica.

In 1835 I left Rochester to form a colored church at Syracuse. Of course I joined anti-slavery work to the labor which fell upon me as a pastor. In the city last named the opponents of the movement laid a trap for me, by proposing a public discussion of the leading questions at issue. I was a little afraid of my ability to cope with them alone, and therefore, quietly wrote to Gerrett Smith, Beriah Green and Alvin Stewart for help. When the public discussion took place, and these practiced speakers met and answered the arguments of our opponents, the representatives of the latter—the leading editor and the foremost lawyer of the place—left the church in disgust, pleading that they had a good case, but did not expect to face men so well able to handle any question as the friends of mine I had invited. After their retreat from the hall, the two champions of slavery stirred up the salt boilers to mob us, but we adjourned before night, and when the crowd arrived at the edifice they found only prayer meeting of the church people in progress, and slunk away ashamed. I was stationed nearly three years at Syracuse, and was then transferred to Ithaca, where a little colored religious society already existed. I bought a site for a church edifice for them, and saw it built during the two years of my stay in the village. Thence I was sent to Sag Harbor, Long Island, and, finally to New Bedford, Massachusetts.

It was at New Bedford that I first saw Fred. Douglass. He was then, so to speak, right out of slavery, but had already begun to talk in public, though not before white people. He had been given authority to act as an exhorter by the church before my coming, and I some time afterwards licensed him to preach. He was then a member of my church. On one occasion, after I had addressed a white audience on the slavery question, I called upon Fred. Douglass, whom I saw among the auditors, to relate his story. He did so and in a year from that time he was in the lecture field with Parker Pillsbury and other leading abolitionist orators. Not long afterwards a letter was received from him by his fellow church members, in which he said that he had cut loose from the church; he had found that the American Church was the bulwark of American slavery. We did not take the letter to mean that Mr. Douglas had repudiated the Christian religion at the same time that he bade good-by to the churches.

It was soon after this that great excitement arose in New Bedford over the action of Rev. Mr. Jackson, a Baptist minister, who had just returned from a Baltimore clerical convention, which sent a petition to the Maryland Legislature in favor of the passage of a law compelling free Negroes to leave the state, under the plea that the free colored men mingling with the slaves incited the latter to insurrection. Rev. Mr. Jackson was a vice-president of that convention and a party to its action. Printed accounts of the proceedings were sent to me, and at a meeting called to express dissent from the course taken by the minister named and his brethren, I introduced a resolution, of which the following is a copy: "*Resolved,* That the great body of the American clergy, with all their pretensions to sanctity, stand convicted by their deadly hostility to the Anti-Slavery movement, and their support of the slave system, as a brotherhood of thieves, and should branded as such by all honest Christians."

The tone and tenor of this resolution now carry an air of extravagant injustice, but there was at that time only too much truth in the charge it contains. The resolution was tabled, but it was at the same time decided to publish it, and to invite the ministers of the town to appear at an adjourned meeting and defend their course, if they could. Nearly thirty ministers of New Bedford and vicinity appeared at the next meeting, and with one voice denounced the obnoxious resolution and its author. The result was that a strong prejudice was excited against me, a prejudice that was increased by an event which took place soon afterwards—the whole due to the fact that the respectable and wealthy classes, as well as the lower orders, at the time regarded abolitionists with equal aversion and contempt. The conscience of the North had not yet been fairly awakened to the monstrous wrong of human bondage.

On my journey homeward from a visit to New York City, I met Mr. Henry Ludlam, his wife, two children and a slave girl, from Richmond, Va., all bound for New Bedford to spend the summer with Captain Bunbar, father-in-law of the head of this party of visitors. I said that I met them, but the meeting consisted only in this, that they and I were on board the same train, but not in the same car. I was in the "Jim Crow" car, as colored persons were not permitted to enter the others with white people, and the slave girl was sent to the same car by the same rule. I talked with her, and, as I was in duty bound to do, asked her to come to my church during the stay of the family in New Bedford. After some weeks had passed and she did not come, I took with me a colored teacher and another friend to call on her and learn, if we could, why she did not attend the services. Her master or owner met us at the door and gave us this answer: "Lucy is my slave, and slaves don't receive calls." In short, he refused to let us enter the house, whereat we took advice from friends, and applied to Judge Crapo for a writ of *habeas corpus*. The judge sent us about our business with the advice not to annoy Mr. Ludlam, who was entitled to hospitable treatment as a visitor and guest. Instead of taking this advice, we journeyed to Boston, and were given by Judge Wilds the writ his judicial brother in New Bedford had denied us. We had Sheriff Pratt and the writ with us when we made our next call on the slave girl's master. The latter at first refused even the sheriff leave to see the girl, and finally proposed to give bail for her appearance before the judge. The sheriff turned to me inquiringly when this proposal was made, and I answered: "Mr. Sheriff, you were directed to take the person of the girl Lucy, and I call upon you to do your duty." Thus we got possession of the girl, but not before her owner had obtained leave for a few minutes' private conversation with her. In this talk, as we afterwards learned, he frightened Lucy by telling her that our purpose was an evil one, and obtained her promise to display a handkerchief from the room in which she would be confined as a signal for the rescue he promised her. We took the girl to a chamber on the upper floor of the residence of the Rev. Joel Knight, and the evening we prepared to lie down before the door. Lucy displayed the handkerchief as she had promised, and, when we questioned her about it, answered: "Master told me to do it; he is coming to take me home." At this we quietly called together twenty men from the colored district of the place, and they took seats in the church close at hand, ready for any emergency. At one o' clock in the morning Ludlam appeared on the scene, with a backing of a dozen men, carrying a ladder, to effect a rescue. The sheriff hailed them, but they gave no answer, whereat our party of colored men sallied forth, and the rescuers fled in all directions. The entire town was now agog over the affair. So many took sides against us, and such threats were made, that the sheriff was forced to call to his aid the local police, and, thus escorted, the girl was placed aboard the cars for Boston. The other party, to the number of 150 men, chartered a train by another route, with the design of overpowering the sheriff's posse in the streets of Boston; but so large a force of officers was called out by the sheriff that the slaveholder's friends gave up the idea of carrying out their design. Lucy was brought before Judge Wilds, who postponed the hearing until the following Saturday, and meanwhile invited us privately to bring the girl to his home in the course of the day, as he wanted to talk with her. This we did, and the judge told Lucy what her rights were; that by the laws of Massachusetts she was free—her case was not covered by the fugitive slave law—and that if she wanted her freedom she should have it. If, however, she chose to return to her master she could do so; "but," added the judge, "after what has happened, he will probably sell you on your return with the family to a slave state." She asked for her freedom, and received it the next day, when the case was heard in open court. The Sunday night following word was received at the colored church where we were holding services that our enemies were trying to kidnap the girl. That broke up the meeting; the colored people rallied, and the attempt failed. Lucy's master was forced to return to his slave home without his human chattel. The girl afterwards married, had children, and, I believed, live happily among the people of her own color at the North.

One of the earliest cases in which I became interested as a laborer in the anti-slavery cause was that of the Emstead captives. The slaver Emstead was a Spanish vessel which left the African coast in 1836 with a cargo of captive blacks. When four days out the captives rose, and, coming on deck, threw overboard all but two of the officers and crew. The two they saved to navigate the vessel; but instead of taking the vessel back to the coast they had just left, as they were directed by the blacks, the two sailors attempted to make the American main, and the vessel finally drifted ashore near Point Judith, on Long Island Sound. The Spanish Minister demanded the surrender of the blacks to his government. They were taken off the ship and sent to Connecticut for trial. Arthur Tappan and Richard Johnson interested themselves in the captives, and succeeded in postponing their trial for two and a half years. Two young men were meanwhile engaged to instruct the captives, and when their trial at last came they were able to give evidence which set them free. They testified that they had been enticed on board of the slaver in small parties for the ostensible purpose of trade, and had then been thrown into the hold and chained. There were nearly one hundred of the captives, and on their release we tried hard, but vainly, to persuade them to stay in this country. I escorted them on shipboard when they were about to sail from New York for their native land.

After a stay of two years at New Bedford I took charge of a colored church in Boston, and left that to give nearly all my time of lectures and addresses on the anti-slavery issue. It was during this period that I took an active interest in the case of Anthony Burns, a runaway slave, who reached Boston as a stowaway in 1852. His former master learned that Burns had found a home in Boston, and made two futile attempts, with the aid of government officials, to recapture him. They made a third trial of it with such precautions as they thought would surely command success. A posse of twenty five United States Deputy Marshals was collected in Richmond, Washington, Philadelphia and New York, and secretly sent to Boston. They lined the street in the vicinity of the shop in which Burns was employed. Several of them followed him when he emerged from the door, and at the corner of Hanover and Cambridge streets they surrounded, captured and ironed him, telling the crowd which was fast collecting that he was accused of breaking into a jewelry store. The marshals succeeded in getting their prisoner into the court-house before the true state of the case became known to the crowd. A call was at once issued for a meeting of our Anti-Slavery Vigilance Committee, and word was sent to Theodore Parker, Wendell Phillips, and other noted leaders, to attend and give advice as to the wisest course to take under the circumstances. It was at first proposed to buy or ransom Burns, and representatives of the committee accordingly offered $1,300 for him. But the marshals would not take it. They said they would let Boston people see the law—the fugitive slave law—could be executed in spite of their opposition. Two companies of marines from the navy yard were called out to support the marshals. But the people gathered from all quarters; they came in swarms from points as far as Lowell, and it was determined at all hazards to prevent the return of the fugitive to slavery. A beam sixty feet long was procured, and at nine o'clock that night was used as a battering-ram against the court house doors. An incident which happened just before this attempt to force an entrance into the court-house added fuel to the fierce fire of excitement. One of the court attendants who found himself outside the building tried to re-enter it, but received a deadly slash from a sword in the hands of a guard, who mistook the character of the man. The victim of this ghastly mistake ran but a few rods before he fell, bleeding and lifeless. The doors gave way at the first thrust of the beam, and we entered to find ourselves in the midst of the two armed companies already mentioned. We gave the soldiers warning that they would get but one fire before all would be over with them, and at this threat they gave up trying actively to interfere with us. But although it had proved easy to break into the court house, it was not so easy to get at the prisoner. The marshals had him with them in an underground cell. The passage to it was narrow, the doors were strong, and we could for the moment do nothing. We finally hit upon a plan to bring the marshals to reason by threatening to starve them out. When they found that not even a glass of water could be sent in to them they began to talk of terms, offering to take the $1,300 we had in the first instance proposed to give them for their prisoner. We declined the proposition, but now offered them $300 for their trouble. This they consented to take, with the provision that they should be allowed to convey the prisoner unmolested to Richmond, Va., and then return him quietly to Boston, in order that they might be able to say they had succeeded in taking their man out of the state. We made them give a bond in the sum of $10,000 that they would abide by the agreement, and use Burns well while they had him in their hands. It was all done, as people say, according to contract. Benjamin F. Butler said to me at the time—he was then the Democratic collector of the port—"James," these were his characteristic words, "I had rather see the court house, niggers and all, blown up to the seventh heaven than see a slave taken out of the city of Boston." When Burns was taken to the wharf guarded by a large force of marshals and from fifteen to twenty companies of militia, every store along the streets traversed was hung with crape. At one point a black coffin suspended from a wire level with the third story windows was drawn back and forth. Boston was in mourning over the disgrace of even in appearance surrendering as a slave a human being who had once set foot on its soil.

Another case in which I was equally interested was that of the fugitive slaves, William and Ellen Craft. The latter, who had hardly a tinge of African blood in her veins, and who could not in color be distinguished from a white person, was housekeeper for a rich southern planter, and the former, who was quite black, was her husband. In August, 1851, the master and his family departed for a watering place, leaving Ellen in charge of the mansion during their absence, and putting money enough in her hands for the temporary needs of the household. Soon after the departure of the family, Ellen put on men's clothing, and with husband set out on foot at night for the North and freedom! In the morning they stopped at a public house, Ellen representing herself as a planter's son, with a servant—her husband—to attend her. She carried her arm in a sling, and told the clerk she could not use it when he asked her to register their names. In this manner they made their way north, and finally to Boston. Their master at last obtained trace of them, and one day arrived at Boston to recover his human property. He called upon the judge of the proper court for the necessary order, but the judge, pleading pressure of business, directed the applicant to call again later in the day. In the interval the judge notified the abolitionists, and they held a meeting the same evening to decide what to do in the case. They came to the conclusion that as the writ or process issued in conformity with the fugitive slave law was civil, and not criminal, there would be no means of serving it upon the fugitives if the latter kept within the domicile and locked the doors. The Crafts acted upon this advice, and were secretly supplied with food by their abolitionist friends during their confinement within doors. The master was thus prevented from recovering possession of them, but he remained in the city and lingered about the neighborhood in which the fugitives were self-confined until the Boston boys annoyed and pestered him to such a degree that he was forced to ask police protection. He obtained it only on a promise to leave the city, but broke his word and was again persecuted by the boys so persistently that he was forced to leave Boston. The fugitives were not again molested, for they quietly removed to Montreal as soon as their prosecutor was fairly out of the way.

Still another case in which I was concerned was that of a runaway slave girl who was seized in Boston and taken to the court house, where a hearing was obtained for her by the opponents of the fugitive slave law. Our counsel had little hope of gaining anything but time by the proceeding, and arranged a signal by which we who were gathered outside the court room—for the proceedings took place with closed doors—might understand that the case had gone against us. When the decision was given the lawyer started for the door in feigned disgust, and it was partially opened for his exit he gave the signal by raising his hand. Instantly a huge colored man named Clark thrust an iron bar between the door and its frame, so that it could not be closed, and we rushed in, to the terror of the court attendants. We took the girl from their hands, and, placing her in a closed carriage, drove her to Roxbury. Three other carriages were driven from the court house in other directions at the same moment, in order to baffle any attempt at pursuit. The crowd of colored people collected in front of the court house on the occasion included a large number of women, each of them armed with a quarter of a pound of Cayenne pepper to throw into the eyes of the officers should the latter come to blows with their friends. The girl was kept in her hiding place a fortnight, and then as the excitement had abated, safely sent to Canada.

In relating the rescue of the slave girl Lucy, I mentioned the fact that we colored people were in those days obliged to ride in a second class or "Jim Crow" car, even in New England. The same separation was enforced on steamboats and stagecoaches, colored people being compelled to ride on the outside of the latter. It was hard to make headway against the rules of the railroad and steamship companies, because they would only sell us half-fare tickets, and on these we could not demand seats with white people I finally procured two first class or full fare tickets by having a white man buy them for me. A colored friend and myself quietly took seats in the corner of the regular passenger coach. The brakemen did not see us until just before the time for the train to start. Then one of them, approaching us, said: "You have made a mistake." "No," was our answer, as we held up the tickets But the man persisted, "You can't ride in here; you know that." My answer was: "You advertise a fare of nine shillings from New Bedford to Boston, and I have this ticket as a receipt that

I have paid the money." He reiterated: "You can't ride here, and I want you to go out." "No," was my answer, "I have bought and paid for this ticket and have the same right here as other people." The ticket agent was called in, and tried to persuade us to leave the car. "Our rules," he said, "forbid your occupation of seats in this car. We want no trouble, and you had better go out peaceably." "We want none," answered I, "and shall make none, but we propose to stay where we are." They sent in trainmen, baggageman, and hackmen; we resisted passively, and three seats to which we clung as they were dragging us along were torn up before they got us out. I obtained a warrant from Judge Crapo, and had them arrested at once. The hearing took place the same day, and on the following morning the judge handed down a long written opinion. He ruled that custom was law, and by custom colored people were not allowed to ride in the company of white people.

Furthermore railway corporations had the right to make their own regulations on such a subject, and consequently we had no cause of action, I paid the costs and gave notice of appeal to the Supreme Court. When the case was heard at Boston the court decided that the word "color," as applied to persons, was unknown to the laws of the commonwealth of Massachusetts, and that the youngest colored child had the same rights as the richest white citizen. No company chartered as a common carrier had a right to enact regulations above the laws of the state. The decision of Judge Crapo was reversed, and I was given $300 damages besides. That broke up the practice of consigning colored railway passengers to "Jim Crow" cars.

I had somewhat similar experience on the steamer plying between New Bedford and Nantucket. They would sell only blue or second-class tickets to colored persons, who were thus prevented from entering the cabin with white people. When I asked for a full fare ticket it was refused me, but they offered to sell me a blue one. This I would not take, and I went on board without a ticket. I visited the cabin and other parts of the boat forbidden to colored passengers, but no trouble occurred until the ticket gatherer made his rounds. I told the man that I had no ticket, but would pay the regular fare, not half fare. The captain began by taking the hat from my head and locking it up in his office. Next, he told me that I could pay half fare or be put off the boat at her next landing place. He was in such haste to carry out his threat, that he retarded the steamer's headway in sight of a port at which she was not to stop, had a boat lowered over the side and ordered me to enter it. I refused and he swore. "You have men enough to put me ashore if you choose," said I, "but I want the right of redress." At this he ordered the boat raised, and the steamer proceeded to her destination with me still on board. When we came within sight of Nantucket he sent a servant to me with my hat, but I refused to take it. I went ashore with a handkerchief tied about my head. It was well advertised before evening that I would at my lecture—I was already booked to speak there that night—tell the story of my treatment on the boat. When the bells were calling people to the lecture hall, the captain's clerk came to me with the message that that officer wanted to see me; but I sent back word that I would say all I had to say to him at the lecture. After the lecture three ladies presented me a new hat, in accepting which I remarked that Captain Nottfinney was welcome to wear my old one, left in his hands. I went back on the same boat without a ticket, for they still refused to sell me a full fare one; but no one asked for my ticket, and no one said a word to me, although I went where I pleased on the boat.

While stationed at Boston I made the acquaintance of Rev. Mr. Phileo and his wife, the latter being that Prudence Crandall who was sent to a Connecticut jail for teaching a school for colored children at Canterbury Green. As I remember, a special session of the legislature was called by the governor for the express purpose of passing a law to cover such cases, and under the law thus enacted she was sent to jail. She was engaged at the time to the young preacher. He married her in jail, and when she was his wife, claimed and obtained her release. The social persecution to which she had been subjected before her imprisonment was renewed on her release, and she and her husband left the place, never to return to it.

I returned to Rochester in 1856, and took charge of the colored church in this city. In 1862 I received an appointment from the American Missionary Society to labor among the colored people of Tennessee and Louisiana, but I never reached either of these states. I left Rochester with my daughter, and reported at St. Louis, where I received orders to proceed to Louisville, Kentucky. On the train, between St. Louis and Louisville, a party of forty Missouri ruffians entered the car at an intermediate station, and threatened to throw me and my daughter off the train. They robbed me of my watch. The conductor undertook to protect us, but, finding it out of his power, brought a number of Government officers and passengers from the next car to our assistance. At Louisville the government took me out of the hands of the Missionary Society to take charge of freed and refugee blacks, to visit the prisons of that commonwealth, and to set free all colored persons found confined without charge of crime. I served first under the orders of General Burbage, and then under those of his successor, General Palmer. The homeless colored people, for whom I was to care, were gathered in a camp covering ten acres of ground on the outskirts of the city. They were housed in light buildings, and supplied with rations from the commissary stores. Nearly all the persons in the camp were women and children, for the colored men were sworn into the United States service as soldiers as fast as they came in. My first duty, after arranging the affairs of the camp, was to visit the slave pens, of which there were five in the city. The largest, known as Garrison's, was located on Market Street, and to that I made my first visit. When I entered it, and was about to make a thorough inspection of it, Garrison stopped me with the insolent remark, "I guess no nigger will go over me in this pen." I showed him my orders, whereupon he asked time to consult the mayor. He started for the entrance, but was stopped by the guard I had stationed there. I told him he would not leave the pen until I had gone through every part of it. "So," said I, "throw open your doors, or I will put you under arrest." I found hidden away in that pen 260 colored persons, part of them in irons. I took them all to my camp, and they were free. I next called at Otterman's pen on Second Street, from which also I took a large number of slaves. A third large pen was named Clark's, and there were two smaller ones besides. I liberated the slaves in all of them. One morning it was reported to me that a slave trader had nine colored men locked in a room in the National hotel. A waiter from the hotel brought the information at daybreak. I took a squad of soldiers with me to the place, and demanded the surrender of the blacks. The clerk said there were none in the house. Their owners had gone off with "the boys" at daybreak. I answered that I could take no man's word in such a case, but must see for myself. When I was about to begin the search, a colored man secretly gave me the number of the room the men were in. The room was locked, and the porter refused to give up the keys. A threat to place him under arrest brought him to reason, and I found the colored men inside, as I had anticipated. One of them, an old man, who sat with his face between his hands, said as I entered: "So'thin' tole me last night that so' thin' was a goin' to happen to me." That very day I mustered the nine men into the service of the government, and that made them free men.

So much anger was excited by these proceedings, that the mayor and common council of Louisville visited General Burbage at his headquarters, and warned him that if I was not sent away within forty-eight hours my life would pay the forfeit. The General sternly answered them: "If James is killed, I will hold responsible for the act every man who fills an office under your city government. I will hang them all higher than Haman was hung, and I have 15,000 troops behind me to carry out the order. Your only salvation lies in protecting this colored man's life." During my first year and a half at Louisville, a guard was stationed at the door of my room every night, as a necessary precaution in view of the threats of violence of which I was the object. One night I received a suggestive hint of the treatment the rebel sympathizers had in store for me should I chance to fall into their hands. A party of them approached the house where I was lodged protected by a guard. The soldiers, who were new recruits, ran off in affright. I found escape by the street cut off, and as I ran for the rear alley I discovered that avenue also guarded by a squad of my enemies. As a last resort I jumped a side fence, and stole along until out of sight and hearing of the enemy. Making my way to the house of a colored man named White, I exchanged my uniform for an old suit of his, and then, sallying forth, mingled with the rebel party, to learn, if possible, the nature of their intentions. Not finding me, and not having noticed my escape, they concluded that they must have been misinformed as to my lodging place for that night. Leaving the locality they proceeded to the house of another friend of mine, named Bridle, whose home was on Tenth street. After vainly searching every room in Bridle's house, they dispersed with the threat that if they got me I should hang to the nearest lamp-post. For a long time after I was placed in charge of the camp, I was forced to forbid the display of lights in any of the buildings at night, for fear of drawing the fire of rebel bushwhackers. All the fugitives in the camp made their beds on the floor, to escape danger from rifle balls fired through the thin siding of the frame structures.

I established a Sunday and a day school in my camp and held religious services twice a week as well as on Sundays. I was ordered by General Palmer to marry every colored woman that came into camp to a soldier unless she objected to such a proceeding. The ceremony was a mere form to secure the freedom of the female colored refugees; for Congress had passed a law giving freedom to the wives and children of all colored soldiers and sailors in the service of the government. The Emancipation Proclamation, applying as it did only to states in rebellion, failed to meet the case of slaves in Kentucky, and we were obliged to resort to this ruse to escape the necessity of giving up to their masters many of the runaway slave women and children who flocked to our camp.

I had a contest of this kind with a slave trader known as Bill Hurd. He demanded the surrender of a colored woman in my camp who claimed her freedom on the plea that her husband had enlisted in the federal army. She wished to go to Cincinnati, and General Palmer, giving me a railway pass for her, cautioned me to see her on board the cars for the North before I left her. At the levee I saw Hurd and a policeman, and suspecting that they intended a rescue, I left the girl with the guard at the river and returned to the general for a detail of one or more men. During my absence Hurd claimed the woman from the guard and the latter brought all the parties to the provost marshal's headquarters, although I had directed him to report to General Palmer with the woman in case of trouble; for I feared that the provost marshal's sympathies were on the slave owner's side. I met Hurd, the policeman and the woman at the corner of Sixth and Green streets and halted them. Hurd said the provost marshal had decided that she was his property. I answered—what I had just learned—that the provost marshal was not at his headquarters and that his subordinate had no authority to decide such a case. I said further that I had orders to take the party before General Palmer and proposed to do it. They saw it was not prudent to resist, as I had a guard to enforce the order. When the parties were heard before the general, Hurd said the girl had obtained her freedom and a pass by false pretenses. She was his property; he had paid $500 for her; she was single when he bought her and she had not married since. Therefore she could claim no rights under the law giving freedom to the wives of colored soldiers. The general answered that the charge of false pretenses was a criminal one and the woman would be held for trial upon it. "But," said Hurd, "she is my property and I want her." "No," answered the general, "we keep our own prisoners." The general said to me privately, after Hurd was gone: "The woman has a husband in our service and I know it; but never mind that. We'll beat these rebels at their own game." Hurd hung about headquarters two or three days until General Palmer said finally: "I have no time to try this case; take it before the provost marshal." The latter, who had been given the hint, delayed action for several days more, and then turned over the case to General Dodge. After another delay, which still further tortured the slave trader, General Dodge said to me one day: "James, bring Mary to my headquarters, supply her with rations, have a guard ready, and call Hurd as a witness." When the slave trader had made his statement to the same effect as before, General Dodge delivered judgment in the following words: "Hurd, you are an honest man. It is a clear case. All I have to do, Mary, is to sentence you to keep away from this department during the remainder of the present war. James, take her across the river and see her on board the cars." "But, general," whined Hurd, "that won't do. I shall lose her services if you sent her north." "You have nothing to do with it; you are only a witness in this case," answered the general. I carried out the order strictly, to remain with Mary until the cars started; and under the protection of a file of guards, she was soon placed on the train en route for Cincinnati.

Among the slaves I rescued and brought to the refugee camp was a girl named Laura, who had been locked up by her mistress in a cellar and left to remain there two days and as many nights without food or drink. Two refugee slave women were seen by their master making toward my camp, and calling upon a policeman he had then seized and taken them to the house of his brother-in-law on Washington street. When the facts were reported to me, I took a squad of guards to the house and rescued them. As I came out of the house with the slave women, their master asked me: "What are you going to do with them?" I answered that they would probably take care of themselves. He protested that he had always used the runaway women well, and appealing to one of them, asked: "Have I not, Angelina?" I directed the woman to answer the question, saying that she had as good a right to speak as he had, and that I would protect her in that right. She then said: "He tied my dress over my head Sunday and whipped me for refusing to carry victuals to the bushwhackers and guerillas in the woods." I brought the women to camp, and soon afterwards sent them north to find homes. I sent one girl rescued by me under somewhat similar circumstances as far as this city to find a home with Colonel Klinck's family.

Up to that time in my career I had never received serious injury at any man's hands. I was several times reviled and hustled by mobs in my first tour of the district about the city of Rochester, and once when I was lecturing in New Hampshire a reckless, half-drunken fellow in the lobby fired a pistol at me, the ball shattering the plaster a few feet from my head. But, as I said, I had never received serious injury. Now, however, I received a blow, the effects of which I shall carry to my grave. General Palmer sent me to the shop of a blacksmith who was suspected of bushwhacking, with an order requiring the latter to report at headquarters. The rebel, who was a powerful man, raised a short iron bar as I entered and aimed a savage blow at my head. By an instinctive movement I saved my life, but the blow fell on my neck and shoulders, and I was for a long time afterwards disabled by the injury. My right hand remains partially paralyzed and almost wholly useless to this day.

Many a sad scene I witnessed at my camp of colored refugees in Louisville. There was the mother bereaved of her children, who had been sold and sent farther South lest they should escape in the general rush for the federal lines and freedom; children, orphaned in fact if not in name, for separation from parents among the colored people in those days left no hope of reunion this side the grave; wives forever parted from their husbands, and husbands who might never hope to catch again the brightening eye and the welcoming smile of the help-mates whose hearts God and nature had joined to theirs. Such recollections come fresh to me when with trembling voice I sing the old familiar song of anti-slavery days:

Oh deep was the anguish of the slave mother's heart
When called from her darling forever to part;
So grieved that lone mother, that broken-hearted mother
In sorrow and woe.
The child was borne off to a far-distant clime
While the mother was left in anguish to pine;
But reason departed, and she sank broken-hearted
In sorrow and woe.

I remained at Louisville a little over three years, staying for some months after the war closed in charge of the colored camp, the hospital, dispensary and government stores. In 1865 the colored people of Kentucky were called upon for the first time to celebrate the Fourth of July. I spoke to General Palmer about it, and he, approving the idea, issued a proclamation for the purpose. There was but a single voice raised against it, and that, strange as it may seem, was the voice of a colored Baptist preacher named Adams. But the slave holders had always pursued the policy of buying over to their interest a few unworthy colored ministers who took an active part in the peaceful political revolution which placed the local government of the District of Columbia in loyal hands. In 1878 I was appointed by Bishop Wayman a missionary preacher for the colored churches of Ohio. While engaged in this missionary work I was driven out of Darke county by a terrorizing band of ruffians, who called themselves regulators, and many of whom were from the Kentucky side of the river. A number of leading white citizens were treated in like manner by the same band. In 1880, when the exodus from the South began, I labored under the direction of the Topeka Relief Association in behalf of the homeless throngs of colored people who flocked into Kansas. In the following year this relief was discontinued, and we organized in southern Kansas an agricultural and industrial institute, of which I became general agent. The institute of which Elizabeth L. Comstock was an active advocate, is still in existence, and has done a noble work in the education of people of color. My last charge was the pastorate of the African Methodist Episcopal Church at Lockport. Between three and four years ago both my eyes became affected by cataracts, and I now grope my way in almost complete blindness.

My home is again in the city of Rochester, where I began my life work. In 1829 I married in this city a free colored girl, and by her had four children, two of whom are now married and living at the West. My first wife died in 1841. Sixteen years ago I married again. My wife was a slave, freed by Sherman at the capture of Atlanta and sent north with other colored refugees. I first met her in the State of Pennsylvania. She is the companion of my old age. Two children—my daughter, who is in the fifteenth year of her age, and my son, who is verging on his twelfth year, are the comfort and joy of our household. With them I sing the old "Liberty Minstrel" songs, which carry me back to the days when the conscience of the North was first awakened to the iniquities of slavery. Blessed be God that I have lived to see the liberation and the enfranchisement of the people of my color and blood!

You ask me what change for the better has taken place in the condition of the colored people of this locality in my day. I answer that the Anti-Slavery agitation developed an active and generous sympathy for the free colored man of the North, as well as for his brother in bondage. We felt the good effect of that sympathy and the aid and encouragement which accompanied it. But now that the end of the Anti-Slavery agitation has been fully accomplished, our white friends are inclined to leave us to our own resources, overlooking the fact that social prejudices still close the trades against our youth, and that we are again as isolated as in the days before the wrongs of our race touched the heart of the American people. After breathing for so considerable a period an atmosphere surcharged with sympathy for our race, we feel the more keenly the current of neglect which seems to have chilled against us even the enlightened and religious classes of the communities among which we live, but of which we cannot call ourselves a part.

Oh! deep was the anguish of the slave mother's heart,
When called from her darling for ever to part;
So grieved that lone mother, that heart-broken mother,
In sorrow and woe.
The lash of the master her deep sorrows mock,
While the child of her bosom is sold on the block;
Yet loud shrieked that mother, poor heart-broken mother,
In sorrow and woe.
The babe in return, for its fond mother cries,
While the sound of their wailings together arise;
They shriek for each other; the child and the mother,

In sorrow and woe.
The harsh auctioneer, to sympathy cold,
Tears the babe from its mother and sells it for gold,
While the infant and mother loud shriek for each other,
In sorrow and woe.
At last came the parting of mother and child—
Her brain reeled with madness—that mother was wild;
Then the lash could not smother the shrieks of that mother
Of sorrow and woe.
The child was borne off to a far distant clime,
While the mother was left in anguish to pine;
But reason departed, and she sank broken-hearted,
In sorrow and woe.
That poor mourning mother, of reason bereft,
Soon ended her sorrows and sank cold in death:
Thus died that slave mother, poor heart-broken mother,
In sorrow and woe.
Oh! list ye kind mothers to the cries of the slave,
The parents and children implore you to save;
Go! rescue the mothers, the sisters and brothers,
From sorrow and woe.

(Scene in the nether world-purporting to be a conversation between the ghost of a Southern slaveholding clergyman and the devil!)

At dead of night, when others sleep,
Near Hell I took my station;
And from that dungeon, dark and deep,
o'erheard this conversation:
"Hail, Prince of Darkness, ever hail,
Adored by each infernal,
I come among your gang to wail,
And taste of death eternal."

"Where are you from?" the fiend demands,
"What makes you look so frantic?
Are you from Carolina's strand,
Just west of the Atlantic?
"Are you that man of blood and birth,
Devoid of human feeling—
The wretch I saw, when last on earth,
In human cattle dealing?
"Whose soul with blood and rapine stain'd,
With deeds of crime to dark it;
Who drove God's image, starved and chained,
To sell like beasts in market?
"Who tore the infant from the breast,
That you might sell its mother?

Whose craving mind could never rest
Till you had sold a brother?
"Who gave the sacrament to those
Whose chains and handcuffs rattle?
Whose backs soon after felt the blows,
More heavy than thy cattle?
"I'm from the South," the ghost replies,
"And I was there a teacher;
Saw men in chains, with laughing eyes:
I was a Southern Preacher!
"In tasseled pulpit, gay and fine,
I strove to please the tyrants,
To prove that slavery is divine,
And what the Scripture warrants.
"And when I saw the horrid sight
Of slaves by torture dying,
And told their masters all was right,
I knew that I was lying.
"I knew all this, and who can doubt
I felt a sad misgiving
But still, I knew if I spoke out
That I should lose my living.
"They made me fat—they paid me well—
To preach down abolition.
I slept—I died—I woke in Hell—
How altered my condition!
"I now am in a sea of fire,
Whose fury ever rages;
I am a slave, and can't get free
Through everlasting ages.
"Yes! when the sun and moon shall fade,
And fire the rocks dissever,
I must sink down beneath the shade,
And feel God's wrath forever."
Our Ghost stood trembling all the while—
He saw the scene transpiring;
With soul aghast and visage sad,
All hope was now retiring.
The demon cried, on vengeance bent,
"I say, in haste, retire!
And you shall have a Negro sent
To attend and punch the fire."

Louisville, Kentucky, July 8th, 1865.
Rev. Thomas James, now of the Military Police of this Department, is hereby
continued in charge of the HOME FOR THE COLORED REFUGEES, in the city
of Louisville. His authority to manage the same, subject to the following and such

other rules as may hereafter be prescribed, is to be regarded as only subordinate Headquarters of the Department.

1. Said Thomas James will have charge of the Home and of all the property and furniture therein, and of all the property which may be committed to his care by freed men and women.
2. He will receive into the House only such persons as need temporary assistance; will give all such whatever advice or assistance in finding homes and employment that may be in his power. He will superintend contracts they may make for employment or service, and encourage all to industry and good conduct.
3. No guards or other persons will be allowed to enter said house without his permission.
4. Said James is authorized and directed to establish a Sabbath and Day School in connection with said house, and to make and enforce proper rules for the government of said schools.
5. He will make such rules for the government of the house and the conduct of the inmates as he may deem proper with reference to police, and will read his rules every Sabbath day once to the occupants of the house.
6. Said Thomas James will keep a record of the number of men women and children received into the house each day, No. Sick, No. Deaths, No. discharged and No. remaining over, and such other facts as will give a correct view of his operations.

John M. Palmer, Maj.
General Commanding.
Source: Rochester, N.Y. 1887. Third edition, Rochester, N.Y.: Post-Express Printing Company, 1887. Library of Congress, Rare Book and Special Collections Division, Daniel A.P. Murray Pamphlets Collection.

45. A memorial souvenir of Rev. J. Wofford White, Pastor of Wesley M.E. Church, Charleston, S.C., who fell asleep, January 7th, 1890, aged 33 years, 1890
GEORGE C. ROWE CLINTON

George C. Rowe Clinton, an African American minister in Charleston, South Carolina, writes two poems in memory of J. Wofford White, pastor of Wesley M.E. Church in Charleston in 1890.

GOD'S MESSENGER

How beauteous, how grand, on the crest of the mountain,
Are the feet of the messenger, servant of God;
The King's representative, bringing good tidings,
Of peace and full pardon, to publish abroad.
How gentle his accents, how winsome and tender
He tells all that wonderful story of love;
Of love so amazing,—magnificent wonder—
Transcending our knowledge, and pointing above.
So he led forth the flock which to him God had given,
Forth into the nourishing pastures of green;

On the right of the beautiful mountain of Zion,
To the bright living waters, the life-giving stream.
He led them with care in the path of the righteous,
In ways whither conflict and discord must cease;
Where, walking in love, in the footprints of Jesus,
They enter His kingdom through pathways of peace.
And ofttimes he entered the Valley of Shadows
With those whom he loved, to give counsel and cheer;—
To show that in darkness existeth no shadow,
That ev'n in the valley, King Jesus is near.
Yes, near, and His presence dispelleth the darkness,
His radiance in glory outrivals the sun;
When they who trust Him droop in physical weakness,
He gives strength to complete the full course well-begun.
These lessons which often he taught to another,
Were welcomed from others when the closing hours came;
With the courage of faith he greeted each brother,
And welcomed each message they brought
in His Name.
The messenger came at the dawn of the morning:
"The Master hath need of thee, come, come away!"
Like a tired little child, his eyes gently closing,
He slept, to awake in the bright realms of day.
'tis finished! The battle of life now is ended;
A victor he stands on the glorified shore!
'tis finished! The victory for which he contended
Is won; and he reigneth with Christ evermore!
We greet thee, dear Brother! Watch, watch, we are coming!
Though here on the nether shore longer we wait!
But watch Brother White, we shall meet in the morning,
With triumph we'll enter the Beautiful Gate!
How beauteous, how grand, on the crest of the mountain
His feet, who God's message hath published abroad;
And, bright as the morning, the crown now adorning,
The brow of our Brother in the palace of God!

January 7th, 1890.

Source: Charleston, S. C.: Walker, Evans & Cogswell Co., Printers, 1890. Library of Congress, Rare Book and Special Collections Division, Daniel A. P. Murray Pamphlets Collection.

46. What the Southern Negro is Doing for Himself, June 1891
SAMUEL J. BARROWS

In this statement, *Atlantic Monthly* contributor Samuel J. Barrows summarized the progress of the African American in American society. He pointed out that there were new leaders in this community to whom many young scholars could look for inspiration. In addition, he illustrated that the black man had a community of support, which had provided opportunities for business, education, and collaboration of creative expression.

For twenty-six years the Negro has had his freedom, and now the question is, What use has he made of it? I have just returned from an extended trip through the South, arranged and made solely for the purpose of getting an answer to the question, What is the colored man doing for himself? I have traveled through Virginia, the Carolinas, Georgia, Alabama, Mississippi, Louisiana, returning through Tennessee, the District of Columbia, and Maryland. In the course of this journey, covering 3500 miles, I have visited schools, colleges, and industrial institutions in most of the large centres of the South, from Baltimore to New Orleans. I have gone through the Black Belt, inspected the agricultural districts, visited farms and cabins, and have seen every phase of Negro life, from the destitution of the one-room cabin to the homes of the comfortable and prosperous, and every degree of social standing, from the convicts in the chain gang in the New Orleans Parish prison and the Birmingham mines to ministers, lawyers, doctors, and bankers on the top round of the social ladder. As a result of this observation and experience, I have some interesting evidence as to what the Negro is doing for himself.

Under slavery the Negro was mainly a plantation laborer. Freedom found him where slavery left him. While there has been some transmigration to the South and North, the shifting of population since the war has not been great. The Negro and his descendants remain pretty much in the places where they lived when the war closed. Three courses were open to him as a free man: first, to rent his own labor; secondly, to rent and work the land of his former master; thirdly, to buy and work a farm for himself. All these courses have in turn been accepted. As a simple farm laborer the Negro has small opportunity to accumulate. His wages do not average over fifty or sixty cents a day. Two tendencies are observable in the agricultural districts of the South: one is the exceptional aggregation of immense farms under white ownership, worked by Negro laborers; the other is the segmentation of the old plantations into small farms let out to Negro tenants. In Georgia, for example, one white farmer owns 20,000 acres of land, and employs a vast number of Negroes. But in the districts I have visited the breaking up of the old plantations into small farms has been the more common process. All through the Black Belt and the adjacent country, plantations have been cut up and rented to Negroes in "one-mule farms" of from twenty-five to thirty acres each. Other things being equal, the step from the position of a man who simply lets out his own labor to the position of one who hires a field for its exercise is a step in advance. It furnishes conditions which stimulate intelligence, self-interest, and power of self-help; it is the roadway towards earning a farm and a home. Great numbers of Negroes have taken this initiative. But the transition is not easily made. Farms are not to be had for the asking. The Negro was not a capitalist. He was without credit, and his capacity for managing his own affairs was distrusted. He has had to contend, and is still contending, with an onerous system of commercial oppression which keeps him down. This is the mortgage system, or the lien on the crop, which prevails very extensively in the Black Belt. The colored man who hires twenty-five or thirty acres of land pays at the lowest one bale of cotton, worth about $50; or sometimes he pays as much as two or two and a half bales, equivalent to $100 or $125 rent. When we know that land can be bought at from five to seven dollars an acre, we see that the rent in some cases equals half the value of the farm. If the Negro raised all his own corn, meat, and vegetables, he would still be able to make progress, but he is dependent for clothes and much of his provisions upon the storekeeper. As he cannot buy with ready money, he mortgages his crop, paying twenty and twenty-five per cent, and in exceptional cases one hundred per cent, interest on the amount of his bill. It matters not that he does not begin to draw his goods for three months after the contract is made; he pays interest just the same on the whole amount from the beginning. Add to this that the Negro is charged in the first instance three or four prices for what he buys, and it can easily be seen that when the crop is all gathered little or nothing of it belongs to him. "I go to Pennsylvania," said a colored farmer, "and can buy sugar for six and a half cents a pound, but in North Carolina it is eleven cents. The merchant is making a vast profit." The colored race has emerged from civil bondage. The next step will be to come out of a bondage which is financial.

To know, therefore, what the colored man is doing for himself we must know the conditions from which he has to rise. These are hard enough, but not beyond the capacity of the Negro to break through them, as is shown in thousands of instances. Thus in Virginia and Kentucky and Tennessee the condition of things is much better than further south, and the colored man, in spite of these obstacles, is rapidly becoming a farmowner and householder. "In North Carolina," said Bishop Moore, "our people are buying land wherever they can get it." Land ranges from ten to fifteen dollars an acre, in some places running as low as eight dollars. The bishop himself has a little farm of thirty-three acres, near Salisbury, that cost thirty-four dollars an acre. "I am so anxious to see my race improve," he said, "that I should like to have a great deal more done, but in view of the small wages we get for labor we are doing pretty well." In Tennessee, experts assured me that the colored people are buying land throughout the country, and the mortgage system does not prevail extensively. As we go south and enter the Black Belt, the conditions vary with the fertility of the soil, the intelligence of the people, and the degree of education. A great difference is sometimes apparent in different counties in the same State. Thus in Lee County, Georgia, the people are largely laborers, working for wages. But in Marion County fifty per cent of the people own homes, and some of them have large plantations. In Sumter and Terrell counties, they likewise live mostly on farms. In the latter county, I was told that in a small city of 10,000 nearly all the colored people own their homes, and live in cabins or houses varying in size from one room to eight. The same difference is seen in Alabama. In Russell County the blacks are much behind those of Pike County, where there are better schools and more freedom from the mortgage system. In Bullock County, much government land has been preempted by the Negroes. In one section of that county the colored people are prosperous, one man of exceptional thrift owning 300 acres, twelve good mules, and four horses, and raising his own meat and potatoes. In Coffee County, the people are just beginning to rent their homes. In Elmore County, many have farms of fifty acres. In Macon County, not much land is owned. In Barbour County, land is mainly rented, but there are many who have stock. In the southern part of Randolph County, about half of the blacks own their land. In one township of Lee County, nearly all the colored people own their homes. At Notasulga, about half the people have farms ranging from twenty-five to one hundred and fifty acres. Here I learned of one prosperous woman farmer, who raises three or four bales of cotton, as well as potatoes, chickens, and cows. In the vicinity of Birmingham, farms are owned ranging from fifty to two hundred acres.

The home-buying that is going on in the agricultural districts is going on also in the cities. In Montgomery, street after street is owned by colored people. In

Chattanooga, one third of the colored people own their homes. Suburban lots range in cost from $350 to $400. A cottage costs in the neighborhood of $600 to $650. In Birmingham, colored people pay $10 or $12 a month rent. A number of householders have gardens with two or three acres of land. Some were fortunate enough to purchase land before the prices went up, and have profited by the rise.

The Negro is also venturing as a tradesman. In all the large cities, and even in the smaller towns, in the South, he is hanging out his sign. Two young men have engaged in the grocery business at Tuskegee, Alabama. Their credit is good at the bank, and I was told that they were doing more for their race by their industry and thrift than could be done by any amount of talk. The colored grocers in Birmingham are sharing the prosperity of this thriving city. Near a little place which I visited in the Black Belt, a colored school-teacher, who got his education with hand and brain at Tuskegee, had bought for $225 a lot of land, and established a grocery store. At Tuscaloosa, the livery stable man who drove me owns several horses and carriages, and is doing well. Thus, in whatever direction one goes, he can find Negroes who are rising by force of education and of character. The influence of such schools as Hampton, Atlanta, and Tuskegee is felt all through the South in the stimulus given to industrial occupations. Tuskegee has turned out a number of printers, who have made themselves independent, and get patronage from both white and colored customers. One has a printing office in Montgomery. Another has opened an office in Texas. The growth of journalism and the gradual reduction of illiteracy among the colored people will make a way for many printers. In all the mechanical trades, colored men are finding places as blacksmiths, wheelwrights, masons, bricklayers, carpenters, tinsmiths, harnessmakers, shoemakers, and machinists. In Washington, colored brickmakers are earning from four to five dollars a day. Hod-carriers receive $1.50. A boy trained in the industrial department of Atlanta University has built a schoolhouse in Alabama on contract. This boy can earn $2.50 a day with his hands and tools, and is besides a college graduate.

In slavery times there was no stimulus to Negro inventiveness. Before the war, an application made at the United States Patent Office for a patent for a Negro inventor was denied, on the ground that he was a slave. With industrial education and diversified mechanical pursuits, the Negro brain is becoming adaptive and creative. The records of the United States Patent Office make no distinction between white and colored inventors. It is impossible to furnish statistics, therefore, showing how much the colored man has done in this direction. The chief of the issue division surmises that there may be between five and ten thousand colored patentees, but this estimate has no reliable basis, being derived simply from the casual reports of attorneys in paying their fees. A colored assistant examiner in the Patent Office department has, however, placed at my service a list of some fifty patents taken out by colored people, which show the scope of their inventive genius. In the list of things represented are an improved gridiron, a locomotive smokestack, a cornstalk harvester, a shield for infantry and artillery, a fire extinguisher, a dough kneader, a cotton cultivator, life-preserving apparatus, a furniture caster, a biscuit cutter, a rotary engine, a printing press, a file holder, a window ventilator for railroad cars, an automatic switch for railroads, and a telephone transmitter. The electric inventions are said to have a good deal of merit, and have been assigned to a prominent company. In Birmingham, a colored inventor is making money out of his patent.

With the purchase of homes and the accumulation of property, the colored people are gradually changing their condition of living. It is seen at its worst in the miserable one-room cabins of the country districts, and in the alley population of such cities as Washington and Baltimore. In the Black Belt, the typical home is a rude log cabin, without windows, and with one door and a stick chimney. The door is usually kept open during the day, in fair weather, to admit light, which at night is furnished by a pine knot. Into such cabins a whole family is frequently crowded. In Alabama, I heard of twenty-five persons living in three rooms. The genial climate permits a good deal of outdoor living, and the babies need no sand yards to be made for their benefit. The mother sets them out on the ground, and lets them roll. Bad as the one-room cabin is, it is not so bad as the tenement house in the slums of the great cities. The Negro, too, can rival the Chinaman in practicing economy. Sixty cents a week, spent in pork, meal, and syrup, will keep him well alive. At Athens, Georgia, a colored man testified in court that "a man can live mighty good on thirty-five cents a week."

The social evolution of the Negro can be seen even by the casual observer. A house with a window, even if closed with a shutter, is an improvement over one which has only a door, and a double-room house is an improvement over one with a single room. The influence of new ambition is seen later in the growth of the cabin into a two-story house, and at the dinner table in a more varied bill of fare. At Pensacola, where the wages received for loading vessels are unusually good, the laborer is prosperous, and a colored censor said, deprecatingly: "The live 'most too high as far as eating is concerned; some of them eat as fine food as millionaires." A Methodist bishop told me that in Montgomery $24,000 was spent annually on excursions. The Negro is surely learning how to earn his dollar, but he has not learned how to spend it. He is buying his experience dear. The patent-medicine vender and the sewing-machine peddler draw no distinctions in regard to color, and the black often insists on spending his money as foolishly as his white brother. In one little country cabin stood a wooden clock worth about $1.25, for which a woman had paid $10, giving new sarcasm to the proverb that "time is money." Yet the Negro's knowledge of what a dollar will buy is growing.

New social ambitions are manifest even in the humblest cabins. The illustrated newspaper furnishes decoration for the walls. The old people can admire the pictures, and the younger ones can read the text. The cheap chromo follows, until by and by the evolution of taste produces a house such as one I visited in Washington, in which three beautiful copies of celebrated Madonnas were hanging on the walls. In the cities social development is going on more rapidly, though here we also find greater social degradation. With all their destitution, the people in the country cabins are not tempted by the liquor saloons.

The social progress of the Negro is well illustrated by two historic cities,—the federal capital at Washington and the former capital of the Confederacy at Montgomery. The casual traveler, who sees the alley districts and the settlements around the railroads, forms no better idea of the social development of the Negro than he does of Northern whites, if he confines his inspection to similar localities. In Montgomery, under the guidance of Dr. Dorsette, a colored physician and a respected citizen, I had an opportunity to see the homes of the colored people at their best. In some of the streets, the whites occupy one side, and the blacks the other. Occasionally the colors alternate, like the squares on a checkerboard. It is not easy externally to tell one from the other. The interiors of these homes, especially of the younger and more progressive people, are comfortably and tastefully furnished. The rooms are as high as those of their white neighbors, well carpeted and papered, while the piano or the cabinet organ suggests loftier musical tastes than that of the plantation banjo. While in most respects the movement or development of the white and colored races runs on parallel lines, in music they seem to be going in opposite directions. Though I traveled all through the South, in urban, suburban, and agricultural districts, from Baltimore to New Orleans, the only banjo I heard was played in Atlanta by a white man. Returning to Boston, one of the first sights which met my eyes was that of a fashionable young lady carrying the instrument the Negro is discarding. I was twice serenaded at Tuskegee, once by a brass band, once by a string band, and I slept well after both performances. In New Orleans, I was astounded at the strange phenomenon of a colored hand-organ grinder. Whether this represents a state of musical development or degeneracy, as compared with the banjo, I will not undertake, in the present state of Northern fascination, to decide. It is estimated that there are from 250 to 300 pianos and cabinet organs in the homes of colored people in Montgomery.

The pride of the colored people in buying these homes and furnishing them is a healthful form of domestic ambition, requiring sacrifice and resolute concentration of purpose. A fine house on a corner lot was shown me which had been bought with the savings of a hackman. Even in the poorer districts it is interesting to note the ambition to improve. "I have seen these houses grow," said the doctor. "There is one in which lives an old woman. She began with one room, then built on another; then finished off one, and now has just finished off the other. It has taken her some time, but she has done it."

Immediately after the war I lived at the national capital. Thousands of destitute blacks from Virginia and further south had settled in the barracks around the city. They owned little more than the clothes on their backs, and most of these had been given to them. The change in these districts is remarkable. Large numbers of people live in their own homes. There is not much squalor outside of the alley population. Even the poorest houses have some comforts and show some endeavor to improve. A similar story may be told of Baltimore.

Standards among the negroes are becoming as varied as among the whites. In some districts I was informed that a colored man had very little standing with his own people unless he had a trade or profession. It is inevitable, too, that cliques and affiliations should be formed, with the advantage and disadvantage which come from such social differentiation. Two aristocracies are appearing in the colored race,—the aristocracy of culture and the aristocracy of wealth. Fortunately, at present, in the younger generation culture and prosperity are moving together. The colored man's standard of wealth is relatively much smaller than that of the white man. There are no Negro millionaires that I know of; but there is growing up a class of men with fortunes ranging from $15,000 to $100,000. This accumulation has been going on in recent years with increasing rapidity. The colored people in North Carolina are said to have amassed more in the last five years than they did in the twenty years preceding. In most of the States, there are no data from which the amount of taxes paid by the Negroes can be separated from that paid by the whites, or the valuation of their property ascertained. It is one good result of the Fourteenth Amendment that no distinction is made in law between property owned by whites and that owned by blacks. Georgia is the only State in which the comptroller is able to furnish the figures for 1890. The amount of taxes paid by the whites in that State was

$1,599,977.75; by the colored people, $48,795.13. The property of whites was assessed at a valuation of $404,287,311; the property of blacks, at a valuation of $12,332,003. The Census Bureau at Washington has the material for making these comparisons in the different States, and as the question is now one of sociology, and not of politics, it is to be hoped that the figures which illustrate the progress of the Negro may be published. The total valuation of Negro property in the South has been given as $150,000,000 or $200,000,000. There are those who maintain that the colored man does not receive full credit for what he is paying. In North Carolina, a daily Democratic paper claimed, about two months ago, that the colored people are paying about three times the tax they are credited with by actual statistics.

There are conspicuous cases of individual prosperity in nearly all the large centres and in the agricultural districts. Thus, in Montgomery, Alabama, a colored barber, originally a slave, has accumulated property amounting to $75,000 or $100,000. An ex-slave in Mississippi has bought one of the plantations that formerly belonged to Jefferson Davis. The colored people of Maryland are said to possess property to the amount of $9,000,000. In Baltimore, there are several colored men worth $15,000 each, three or four worth from $40,000 to $60,000, and the estate of a Negro recently deceased was appraised at $100,000. In Washington, also, colored men have profited by the rise of real estate, and a few are possessed of ample fortunes. These instances might be greatly multiplied from my notes.

The subject of Negro education is vast and absorbing. Among its varied aspects two are of special and correlative interest: first, What is education doing for the Negro; secondly, What is the Negro doing for education? In this paper I can refer only to the latter topic. But these questions cannot be absolutely separated. No man "receives an education" who does not get a good deal of it himself. The student is not so much inert material; he reacts on the forces which impress him. The Negroes are showing their awakened and eager interest in education by the zeal with which they are embracing their opportunities. Everywhere I found in colleges, normal institutes, and district schools fresh, live interest. In some sections, the eagerness of the colored people for knowledge amounts to an absolute thirst. In Alabama, the state superintendent of education, a former Confederate major, assured me that the colored people in that state are more interested in education than the whites are. Nothing shows better this zeal for education than the sacrifices made to secure it. President Bumstead, of Atlanta University, asks, "Where in the history of the world have so large a mass of equally poor and unlettered people done so much to help themselves in educational work?" This challenge will long remain unanswered. The students of Atlanta University pay thirty-four per cent of the expenses of that institution. A letter from the treasurer of Harvard College informs me that about the same proportion of its expenses is paid from tuition fees. If we compare the wealth represented by the students of Harvard with that represented by the colored students of Atlanta, we shall find how large a sacrifice the latter are making in order to do so much. It must be remembered, also, that at Harvard tuition fees and other expenses are mostly paid by parents and guardians; at Atlanta they are paid by the students themselves, and to a large degree by personal labor. President Bumstead calculates that for every million dollars contributed by the North at least a half million is contributed by the colored people for educational purposes. Though it is difficult to get the material for such large and general totals, it is easy to furnish a vast number of facts illustrating the truth that in the very process of getting his education the Negro is learning the lesson of self-help. Among the denominational colleges, the Livingston Institute at Salisbury, North Carolina, is a good illustration of this capacity for self-help. It receives no state aid. The colored people of the Zion Methodist Episcopal church give $8000 towards the support of this school. The students give towards their own support not less than $6000 more. The president, Dr. Price, one of the ablest colored orators of the South, is a conspicuous example of what the colored man can do for himself.

Another remarkable illustration is furnished by the Tuskegee Normal School. This institution was started in 1881 by a Hampton graduate, Mr. Booker T. Washington, on a state appropriation of $2000. It has grown from 30 pupils to 450, with 31 teachers. During the last year 200 applicants had to be turned away for want of room. Fourteen hundred acres of land and fourteen school buildings form a part of the equipment. While friends of education, North and South, have generously helped its growth, the success of the school is due largely to the executive ability of Mr. Washington and his officers. General Armstrong says, "I think it is the noblest and grandest work of any colored man in the land." All the teachers are colored. Of the fourteen school buildings, eight have been erected, in whole or in part, by the students. The school is broadly unsectarian. It is teaching the colored people the dignity of labor and how to get out of debt. It is an agricultural and industrial school combined. Its stimulating and renovating influence is felt all through the Black Belt.

One of the most important results of the excellent work done by Hampton, Atlanta, and Tuskegee is seen in the radiating influence they exert through the country in stimulating primary education. In most of the communities of the lower Southern States, the money derived from local taxation is not sufficient to keep the school more than three months in the year, and the pay of teachers is poor. The interest of these communities is so quickened by a good teacher that the people raise money to extend the school time and supplement the pay of the teacher. A few examples taken from many will illustrate. In one district in Alabama, the school time was thus extended by private subscription from three months to seven. In Coffee County, the teacher's salary was increased from ten to twenty-five dollars a month. In many cases the raising of this extra sum means a good deal of self-denial. As the State makes no appropriation for school-houses, most of the schools in the Black Belt are held in churches, which gives rise to sectarian jealousy and disturbance. To overcome these difficulties and build school-houses, additional sacrifice is required. In a district of Butler County, Alabama, the children formed a "one cent society." They brought to the teacher a penny a day. About thirty dollars was raised to buy land, and the school-teacher, a colored girl, helped to clear it and burn the brush. In one township, where the school fund is sufficient for seven or nine months, the teachers are paid thirty-five dollars a month. In Lee County, the people "supplement" for an assistant teacher. One district school which I visited, eighteen miles from Tuskegee, taught by a graduate of its institute, well illustrated the advantage of industrial education. Having learned the carpenter's trade at the normal school, he was able, with the help of his pupils, to build a fine new school-house. The girls often do better than the men. One, who teaches about twenty-five miles from Tuskegee, has now a good two-story school building with four rooms. She has two assistant teachers, who live with her in the building. She has revolutionized that section of the country. A Hampton student whom I met once applied for a school in his district, as he wished to learn to read and write. He was told that there was not a sufficient number of children. Then he offered to give a school building, if the town would furnish a teacher. With the aid of his father he carried out the plan, and established a good school. Samuel Smiles might easily make a library of books on Self-Help out of thousands of individual examples furnished by the colored people.

The interest in education is seen also in the self-denial and sacrifice which parents make to keep their children at school. This sacrifice falls chiefly on the mothers. A student told me that two thirds of the younger scholars at Tuskegee were sent by their mothers. Very often the mother is a widow. She may get twenty dollars a month, or eight, or only four, for her labor. Out of this small sum she sends to college and clothes her boy or girl. "I know mothers," said a student, "who get three dollars a month, and out of that pay one dollar for the rent, and yet send their children to school." To do this they will wash all day and half the night. Said a colored clergyman in Chattanooga: "Sometimes, when I go about and see how hard many of these mothers work, I feel almost inclined to say, 'You ought to keep your child at home;' but they hold on with wonderful persistence. Two girls graduated from Atlanta University. Their mother had been washing several years to keep them in school. She came up to see them graduate. She was one of the happiest mothers I ever saw." At Selma University, some of the students walk from ten to fifteen miles a day in going to and from the university.

There is one education which the children get; there is another which they give to their parents. The influence of the normal school reacts on the home life. The boys and girls at Hampton and Tuskegee are taught to keep house. They are not satisfied to live in the old way, when they go home. "I have seen," says Professor Washington, "the influence of the daughter so potent, when she got home, that the father has torn down the old house, and built another and better one."

The result of higher education is seen in the rise of a professional class. I remember the time when a colored doctor was a curiosity even in Washington; but colored physicians, lawyers, journalists, college professors, dentists, educated clergymen, and teachers are now to be found in all the large cities of the South. In Montgomery, Dr. Dorsette has built up a thriving practice. He has erected a three-story brick building, on the lower floor of which are two stores, one of them a large and well-equipped drug store. A hall above is used for the accommodation of colored societies. In Birmingham, there are two practicing physicians, one dentist, and one lawyer. At Selma, the practicing physician is a graduate of the university. There is also a pharmacist, owning his drug store, who studied at Howard University. There are six colored lawyers and seven colored physicians in Baltimore. The professional men command the confidence and support of their own people.

Journalism is growing slowly. There are now about fifty-five well established Negro newspapers and journals. Thirty-seven are in the Southern States; seven are monthlies and two are semi-monthlies. The aggregate weekly circulation of all is about 805,000 copies. There are other ephemeral journals, not included in this list. The largest circulation, 15,000, is claimed for the Indianapolis Freeman.

The colored people are determined to have their churches, and they subscribe, in proportion to their means, large sums to sustain them. Last year the Zion Methodist Episcopal church in North Carolina raised $84,000 to support its religious institutions. This amount represents but one State and but one denomination. The churches built reflect fairly the social standard of the people. In the comparatively new city of Birmingham, there are seven comfortable colored churches, ranging in cost from $2000 to $15,000. In Washington, two churches cost nearly $30,000 each, and the money has been raised almost exclusively by the colored people. In Baltimore, there are forty-four colored churches, holding a large amount of property. The old-time preacher still fills the pulpit in many communities, and the old slaves are loath to give up the hysteric emotionalism of revival preaching. The younger and progressive Negroes are breaking away from it, and demanding preachers whose intelligence and education secure respect. They are giving up, too, the old slave melodies. Modern Protestant hymnology is substituted. The universities and theological schools are meeting the demand for better preachers. The colored people are also ambitious to pay their preachers as much as the whites pay theirs. In Montgomery, one colored preacher has a salary of $1200 a year with a parsonage. In another city in Alabama, $1800 is paid.

The standard of morality is rising, also. There is more respect for property now that the Negro is learning what mine and thine mean. An eminent judge of Louisiana assured me that intoxication among the colored people is the principal cause of crime, but that crime does not exist to the same extent that it formerly did. Marriage, he said, had changed largely the condition of their society. The Negroes are seeking to make this a matter of importance, so that their rights of property may be respected. The temperance movement makes headway. In Methodist conferences in North Carolina, and possibly elsewhere, no one is admitted to the ministry who uses liquor or tobacco.

The colored people do more towards taking care of their unfortunate classes than is generally realized. With all the destitution that exists, there is almost no mendicancy. When one considers how much is done in the North for hospitals, homes, and institutions of every sort, and how little in the South, it is apparent that aid must come from some other quarter. The colored orphan asylum established by Mrs. Steele in Chattanooga is, I am told, the only Protestant colored orphan asylum south of Washington. What, then, becomes of orphan children? They are adopted. I have met such children in many homes, and their love and respect for their foster parents refute the charge that the Negro is incapable of gratitude. Thus the colored people have instinctively and of necessity adopted the placing-out system for orphans, which, other things being equal, is the best disposition that can be made of them.

In other respects the colored people have developed a laudable disposition to take care of their own poor. In addition to the Odd Fellows, Masons, and Knights of Pythias, benevolent and fraternal organizations are multiplying. The city churches are feeling a new impulse to such work. Brotherhoods, Good Samaritan societies, and mutual benefit organizations are established. Members of these organizations are allowed a regular stipend when sick. In New Orleans, the colored people have started a widows' home, and have collected enough money to buy a piece of ground and to put up a respectable building. In Montgomery, I visited the Hale Infirmary, founded by the late Joseph Hale and his wife, leading colored citizens. It is a large two-story building, especially designed by the son-in-law of the founder for hospital purposes. Such gifts and such organizations show that there is a disposition among the colored people to adopt the practices of a higher order of society. It is charged that the Negro imitates the vices of the white; it is often overlooked that he also imitates his virtues. A good illustration of practical Christianity was given by the Young Men's Christian Association at Tuskegee, in building, last year, a little house for an old colored woman. A colored teacher paid the cost of the lumber, and the young men gave the labor. They are planning more work of this kind. One interesting case of Negro generosity shows the reverses of fortune which followed emancipation. An ex-slave in Louisiana bought a farm, paid for it, and became prosperous. Not long after his old master came to him in a state of destitution. The Negro took him in, kept him for a week, and gave him a suit of clothes on his departure.

Under slavery the Negroes were not organized, except in churches. The organic spirit must have time for growth. Cooperation has made no great headway. In various States and counties the Farmers' Alliance is attracting attention, many of the Negroes hoping to find relief through it from the bondage of the mortgage system. Small stock companies for various purposes exist in a number of cities. A little has been done in the way of building associations. There is one at Atlanta, with branches and local boards elsewhere; others at Tuskegee, Montgomery, Selma, Baltimore, and Washington. In Baltimore there are three or four such associations, but the German organizations, managed by white people, have had much more of their patronage. A daily paper of Charlotte, North Carolina, in speaking of the loan associations there, said that the colored shareholders were outstripping the white. It was noticeable that they paid more promptly. A penny savings bank, chartered under state law, was organized at Chattanooga about ten months ago. It has already one thousand depositors, the amounts ranging from two cents to one thousand dollars. The white as well as the colored children are being educated to save by this bank. In Birmingham, a similar institution was opened last October, and has about three thousand depositors. A school savings bank or postal savings bank system, as recommended by the Mohonk Negro conference, would be of great benefit to the colored people.

A full report of what the colored man is doing for himself within the old slave States can be given only when the census reports are elaborated, or when such a thorough record of his progress is made in every State as Dr. Jeffrey A. Brackett has made for the State of Maryland. All that has been attempted in this article is to give such indications and evidence as can readily be obtained by one who travels through the South, on this mission, with his eyes and ears open.

To sum up, then, the facts which show what the Negro is doing for himself, it is clear that the new generation of Afric-Americans is animated by a progressive spirit. They are raising and following their own leaders. They are rapidly copying the organic, industrial, and administrative features of white society. They have discovered that industrial redemption is not to be found in legislative and political measures. In spite of oppressive usury and extortion, the colored man is buying farms, building homes, accumulating property, establishing himself in trade, learning the mechanic arts, devising inventions, and entering the professions. Education he sees to be the pathway to prosperity, and is making immense sacrifices to secure it. He is passing into the higher stages of social evolution. In religion the "old-timer" is giving way to the educated preacher. Religion is becoming more ethical. The colored people are doing much to take care of their own unfortunate classes. The cooperative spirit is slowly spreading through trades unions, building associations, and benevolent guilds. In no way is the colored man doing more for himself than by silently and steadily developing a sense of self-respect, new capacity for self-support, and a pride in his race, which more than anything else secure for him the respect and fraternal feeling of his white neighbors.

Samuel J. Barrows.

Source: Boston: *The Atlantic Monthly*, Vol. 67, pp. 805–815, June, 1891. Copyright © 1999, by the Rector and Visitors of the University of Virginia. Courtesy of The University of Virginia Library.

47. In memoriam: Sarah Partridge Spofford: born November 10, 1823, departed May 11, 1892, Substance of address by Rev. R. R. Shippen at the funeral service, May 13, 1892

The following eulogy and poetry memorialized Sarah Partridge Spofford, the wife of Ainsworth Rand Spofford, the Librarian of Congress, and Daniel A. P. Murray's patron. Murray was a staff member of the Library of Congress in 1871 and an authority on African-American materials at the Library. He was also a prolific author.

The Blessed Memory Of Sarah Partridge Spofford abides in the hearts of her relatives and friends. Single-hearted and self-reliant from childhood, she was a rare example of a refined and amiable nature, combined with marked independence of character. Her perceptions were intuitively keen, her sense of justice unerring, her loyalty to duty and to friendship never failing. To a most delicate and sensitive physical organization she united an intellectual strength, a power of will, and a persistent endurance, which were the admiration of all who knew her. Although long a martyr to bodily infirmity in some form, suffering during the first half of her life from distressing head-aches, and for the latter half from a bronchial malady which proved incurable, she bore all with a patience, a courage, and a constancy which kept her always cheerful and uncomplaining. Her useful and devoted life was dedicated to good of others—always forgetful of herself, ever thoughtful of her family and friends.

Her last days were not darkened by long or painful illness. Only eight days after she took to her bed, her pure spirit was released. The death-angel came swiftly, and spared her that which she most dreaded—a slow, lingering, suffering decline. She was conscious and cheerful until half and hour before the close, when she appeared to fall into a deep sleep, broken only by the difficult breathing which betokened the rapid progress of pneumonia.

To those who mourn the loss of one of the purest souls which the earth held, her life of fortitude and resignation remains a precious example. In the words of one of the best of women, who knew and loved her—"She was so wise, so true, so good, so noble, we shall always think of her as one of the saints—the most precious of the saints." To her who never, in word or thought, praised herself, it may matter little what tribute of gratitude or praise her memory wins from others. But to those who knew the sweetness and the strength of her nature, and the virtues that shone in her daily life, no words can adequately express the love and admiration which her gentle character inspired.

On a beautiful afternoon in May a simple memorial service was held at her late residence, which was wholly filled by her friends, sincere mourners at her departure from the world. Robed in white and garlanded with pure and fragrant flowers brought by loving hands, she seemed to lie in a tranquil and pleasant sleep. As the procession moved to the suburban cemetery of Rock Creek, she was borne to rest amid arching trees in the green foliage of spring, while a flood of sunlight poured its gentle beams on the white marble tomb.

After selections from Scripture: "In addition to these words of Holy Writ for our instruction and consolation, let me read to you these lines by Mrs. Stowe:

Still, still with Thee, O God,when morning breaketh,
When the bird waketh,and the shadows flee;

Fairer than morning, lovelier than the daylight,
Dawns the sweet consciousness, I am with Thee.

****

When sinks the soul, subdued by toil, to slumber,
Its closing eye looks up to Thee in prayer;
Sweet the repose beneath thy wings o'ershading,
But sweeter still to wake and find Thee there.
So shall it be at last in that bright morning,
When the soul waketh, and life's shadows flee;
Oh, in that hour, fairer than daylight dawning,
Shall rise the glorious thought, I am with Thee.

"Also these words of Whittier:

God giveth quietness at last!
The common way once more is passed
From pleading tears and lingerings fond,
To fuller life and love beyond.
Fold the rapt soul in your embrace,
Dear ones familiar with the place!
While to the gentle greetings there
We answer here with murmured prayer.
What to shut eyes hath God revealed?
What hear the ears that death has sealed?
What undreamed beauty passing show
Requites the loss of all we know?
O, silent land to which we move!
Enough if there alone be love.
And mortal need can ne'er outgrow
What it is waiting to bestow!
O, pure soul! from that far off shore
Float some sweet song the waters o'er;
Our faith confirm, our fears dispel,
With the dear voice we loved so well!

"Sweetly our dear friend seems to sleep. After life's weariness she is at rest and in peace. So God giveth to his beloved sleep. She has exchanged the limitations of time and sense for the fuller freedom and larger life beyond. We linger amid the shadows of mortality and walk in the dark valley. Not for her, but for ourselves we need to pray.

"We would not indulge in vain eulogy. She herself would forbid it. The best words at the preacher's command would indeed seem inadequate to the thought of those who knew and loved her. Not for her sake, but for our own, it is well to take to heart the lesson of her life. In the relations of home, of church, and of society she was loyal, sweet, and true. Borne up by a devout religious faith, to it she bore her full testimony and witnessed a good confession.

"I always love to think of the sweet flowers we lay upon the casket as speaking not only of our mortality—fading as the flower, here to-day and gone to-morrow—but repeating for us Jesus' lesson of the lily; of the Heavenly Father's unfailing love and care, and reminding us that He who from the ice and desolation of the winter time brings the fresh spring bloom, can from the seeming death of the grave bring the souls of his children into new life in His nearer presence, in a home of larger love, and a garden of unfading flowers.

"The event that brings us hither draws all hearts tenderly together. Opinions that separate are superficial. The deep experiences of life and death bring us face to face with the great spiritual qualities that summon profoundest faith. Would that our faith *in* Jesus might give us the faith *of* Jesus in the immortal hope and the goodness of God. Besides his words of duty and brotherhood, these are the two primal and grand faiths of His gospel: that in the House of many Mansions the world beyond is real and sure, and we are in the keeping of a good Father who doeth all things well, our best Friend forever.

"Not by multitude of deeds, but by high quality of life, we best serve God and man. In brief ministry Jesus manifested the divine quality of character that is transforming the world. With fidelity and sweetness our dear friend completed her work and finished her course. As tenderly we say farewell, let it be with devout gratitude for memories unspeakably fragrant and precious."

Dr. E. M. Gallaudet read, with deep feeling, this selection from the "Elegiac Stanzas" of Wordsworth:

O, for a dirge! But why complain?
Ask rather a triumphal strain
When virtue's race is run;
A garland of immortal boughs
To bind around the Christian's brows,
Whose glorious work is done.
We pay a high and holy debt;
No tears of passionate regret
Shall stain this votive lay;
Ill-worthy, brothers, were the grief
That flings itself on wild relief,
When Saints have passed away.
Was ever Spirit that could bend
So graciously?-that could descend,
Another's need to suit,
So promptly from her lofty throne?
In works of love, in these alone,
How restless, how minute!
Then hushed be every thought that springs
From out the bitterness of things;
Her quiet is secure;
No thorns can pierce her tender feet,
Whose life was, like the violet, sweet,
As climbing jasmine, pure.
Thou takest not away, O Death!

Thou strik'st—and absence perisheth,
Indifference is no more;
The future brightens on our sight;
For on the past hath fallen a light
That tempts us to adore.

Source: Washington, D.C.: s.n., 1892. Library of Congress, Rare Book and Special Collections Division, Daniel A.P. Murray Pamphlets Collection.

48. A Noble Life: Memorial Souvenir of Rev. Jos. C. Price, D.D, 1894
GEORGE C. ROWE CLINTON

George C. Rowe Clinton, an African American minister, wrote this speech in the form of a poem for Joseph C. Price, deceased president of Livingstone College in Salisbury, North Carolina.

A star arose at close of night:
'tis dark before the dawn;
A brilliant star, a righteous light,
Foretoken of the morn—
The day when the oppressor's hand
Should palsied be throughout the land.
A man of influence and power,
Who laid himself with grace,
Upon the altar of his God,
An offering for his race.
E'er prodigal of strength and thought,
And from his race withholding nought.
He cried: "If I'd a thousand tongues,
And each a thunderbolt;
I'd turn them on in mighty power,
Like an electric volt;
I'd send them forth with lightning pace—
To help and elevate my race!
With purpose firm he lived his creed,
And toiled with might and main,
Each day more clearly saw the need—
Despising worldly gain—
He counted not his life too dear
To spend in raising mortals here.
The manly form now prostrate lies;
The flashing eye is dim;
The hand oft raised for principle,
Touched by the monster grim,

Is laid upon the quiet breast,
The life-work finished—entered rest.
The tongue of fire is silent now;
The loving heart is still;
The mind surcharged with burning thought,
Yet loyal to God's will—
Has ceased to plan for mortals here,
Is active in another sphere.
A sense of loss our hearts shall feel:
Hushed is the sweet voice now;
While we shall miss his thrilling words.
To God we humbly bow;
And thank Him for the sacrifice
So freely made by Joseph Price.
His task on earth was finished soon;
Life's battle nobly won.
He rests from labor ere the noon,
His life race fully run.
He watches still the conflict here,
And perfect love has cast out fear.
He is not dead; but gone to join
The host from care set free!
He is not dead; his spirit lives
Where joys immortal be!
Where noble souls are victors crowned;
Where perfect love at last is found.
Now glorified amid the host,
Whose names in honor stand;
Phillips and Garnet, Garrison,
And all that noble band—
Lincoln and Sumner—heroes brave,
Who sought to free and help the slave.
Yes, there within the pearly gates,
They wait for you and me;
Those men who planned that from the curse
Our people might be free;
Rejoicing in the broadening day
When shadows dark should flee away.
Our hero was a patriot true,
A messenger of truth:
Whose words of faith and hope rang out
Inspiring age and youth.
His life will inspiration give—
Through coming time his influence live!

Rest in peace, beloved brother,
Holy influence will not cease;

Memory of the just is blessed—
Rest in peace, then, rest in peace!
—G.C.R.

Source: Charleston, S.C.: s.n., 1894. Library of Congress, Rare Book and Special Collections Division, Daniel A. P. Murray Pamphlets Collection.

49. Light beyond the Darkness, 189-(?)
FRANCES E. W. HARPER

As a freed African American woman from Baltimore, Frances E.W. Harper expressed belief in racial cooperation and harmony through her poetry. She refuted the call for black revenge against white society.

From the peaceful heights of a higher life
I heard your maddening cry of strife;
It quivered with anguish, wrath and pain,
Like a demon struggling with his chain.
A chain of evil, heavy and strong,
Rusted with ages of fearful wrong.
Encrusted with blood and burning tears.
The chain I had worn and dragged for years.
It clasped my limbs, but it bound your heart.
And formed of your life a fearful part;
You sowed the wind, but could not control
The tempest wild of a guilty soul.
You saw me stand with my broken chain
Forged in the furnace of fiery pain.
You saw my children around me stand
Lovingly clasping my unbound hand.
But you remembered my blood and tears
'mid the weary wasting flight of years.
You thought of the rice swamps, lone and dank,
When my heart in hopeless anguish sank.
You thought of your fields with harvest white,
Where I toiled in pain from morn till night;
You thought of the days you bought and sold
The children I loved, for paltry gold.
You thought of our shrieks that rent the air-
Our moans of anguish and deep despair;
With chattering teeth and paling face,
You thought of your nation's deep disgrace.
You wove from your fears a fearful fate
To spring from your seeds of scorn and hate;

You imagined the saddest, wildest thing,
That time, with revenges fierce, could bring
The cry you thought from a Voodoo breast
Was the echo of your soul's unrest;
When thoughts too sad for fruitless tears
Loomed like the ghosts of avenging years.
Oh prophet of evil, could not your voice
In our new hopes and freedom rejoice?
'mid the light which streams around our way
Was there naught to see but an evil day?
Nothing but vengeance, wrath and hate,
And the serpent coils of an evil fate-
A fate that shall crush and drag you down;
A doom that shall press like an iron crown?
A fate that shall crisp and curl your hair
And darken your faces now so fair,
And send through your veins like a poisoned flood
The hated stream of the Negro's blood?
A fate to madden the heart and brain
You've peopled with phantoms of dread and pain,
And fancies wild of your daughter's shriek
With Congo kisses upon her cheek?
Beyond the mist of your gloomy fears,
I see the promise of brighter years.
Through the dark I see their golden hem
And my heart gives out its glad amen.
The banner of Christ was your sacred trust,
But you trailed that banner in the dust,
And mockingly told us amid our pain
The hand of your God had forged our chain.
We stumbled and groped through the dreary night
Till our fingers touched God's robe of light;
And we knew He heard, from his lofty throne,
Our saddest cries and faintest moan.
The cross you have covered with sin and shame
We'll bear aloft in Christ's holy name.
Oh, never again may its folds be furled
While sorrow and sin enshroud our world!
God, to whose fingers thrills each heart beat,
Has not sent us to walk with aimless feet,
To cover and crouch, with bated breath
From margins of life to shores of death.
Higher and better than hate for hate,
Like the scorpion fangs that desolate,
Is the hope of a brighter, fairer morn
And a peace and a love that shall yet be born;

When the Negro shall hold an honored place,
The friend and helper of every race;
His mission to build and not destroy.
And gladden the world with love and joy.

Source: Chicago: Donohue and Henneberry, 189-?. Library of Congress, Rare Book and Special
Collections Division, Daniel A.P. Murray Pamphlets Collection.

50. Excerpted from *Afro-American encyclopedia, or, the thoughts, doings, and sayings of the race: embracing addresses, lectures, biographical sketches, sermons, poems, names of universities, colleges, seminaries, newspapers, books, and a history of the denominations, giving the numerical strength of each. In fact, it teaches every subject of interest to the colored people, as discussed by more than one hundred of their wisest and best men and women, 1895*

COMPILED AND ARRANGED BY JAMES T. HALEY

This is a profile of Bishop Henry Turner, a leader of the African Methodist Episcopal Church, one of the most influential African American religious organizations.

Bishop Henry M. Turner of the A.M.E. Church, who has stood for many years as one of the foremost representatives of the negro race in this country, has attracted attention of late by his advocacy of the return of the black man to his native land. His published views on this subject have been extensively discussed, and because of the bishop's prominence and his reputation as a student of the Afro-American problem, have had great weight attached to them.

The bishop is himself an interesting personality. He was born in Newberry, S. C., in 1834. His parents were free, but while a boy he was "bound out" to a slave owner and worked side by side with slaves in the fields until his fifteenth year. Then, tiring of the hard labor and ill treatment, and with restless longings for something higher than the farm hand's fate, he ran away from his master and entered the service of a firm of attorneys in Abberville, S. C., where John C. Calhoun once practiced law. His employers, attracted by his aptitude, especially in spelling, taught him the elementary English branches, and in the intervals of his duties as office boy he read law, often pouring over his books late at night, when his "bosses" had gone home.

At twenty years of age young Turner became a liscensed minister of the M. E. Church, South. After a few years of itinerant service, during which his fame as an eloquent preacher spread through the surrounding country, he determined to go to Africa as a missionary. About the same time he transferred his allegiance to the A. M. E. Church, and entered Trinity College, in Baltimore, where he studied for four years, completing the courses in divinity, Latin, Greek and Hebrew.

Source: Nashville, Tenn.: Haley & Florida, 1895. Documenting the American South, University of North Carolina at Chapel Hill, 2000. Electronic edition available at: http://docsouth.unc.edu/church/haley/haley.html.

51. Sermon preached by Rev. G. V. Clark, at Second Congregational Church, Memphis, Tenn., Sunday morning June 16, 1895

Rev. Clark, pastor of the Second Congregational Church in Memphis, Tennessee, in the late 1890s, delivered a stirring reminder to his congregation that God's plan, not man's, was the most important rule in their lives. By illustrating ambition for the Lord's work, Clark argued, African Americans could overcome the inherent discrimination of post—Civil War America. This notion by Clark was very much in line with the position of Booker T. Washington.

Clark's church, founded in 1868, is was one of the most famous African American churches in the South; its affiliation with LeMoyne-Owen College made Clark quite influential with black students during the turn of the century.

There is a noble ambition in every successful individual or race. Some one has said, "I am charged with ambition. The charge is true and I glory in its truth. Let that ambition be a noble one and who shall blame it."

Rev. G. V. Clark

"I set before you an open door, and no man can shut it."—Rev. iii. 8.

The application of the truth in the text was to the church in Philadelphia, in Asia Minor. Then to all the Christian world. The door opened is emblematic of the opportunities presented to the church. In other words, it was a setting before the church her mission—henceforward the church would not be so handicapped as before. Oppositions, such as had proved an obstacle before, would cease; unbelief would not be so stubborn and unreasonable; the gospel and its messengers would have easier access to the world, Jews and Gentiles. We notice, too, that the opening is by Christ, the great head of the church. Behind the church is his authority. None can, therefore, resist successfully her authority, nor question with propriety her right to teach truth. The principles to be promulgated are two, namely: Love to God supremely, and to our neighbors as ourselves. The latter command, however, seems to be regarded by men and races after they have reached the zenith of power, as antiquated and abrogated. It is neither antiquated nor abrogated, I boldly declare. The declaration of all the world to the contrary, rich or poor, high or low, of whatever race, country or nationality, do not alter the fact. Putting this truth in a little different form, Christ said, "They that are strong ought to bear the infirmities of the weak." This the Lord means his church shall do, and if she does not do this, for this is a cardinal principle of practical Christianity, then I think he will set aside the church in her present form, purifying her, and bring her forth clad in new, cleaner garments. It is a burning shame that herein her robes are verily stained with guilt. This idea of helpfulness to the weaker is not to be understood as of limited application, but of universal force. A principle binding alike on church and state. It is intended to be placed as a foundation stone for governmental, as well as ecclesiastical righteousness and equity. Moreover, the divine blessing invariably attends the efforts of that people who make it the rule of their lives, and the theme of their discussion, and the object of their every endeavor to do unto others just as they wish to be done by. Christ calls this the fulfillment of the royal law. Creeds, nationality, learning, sciences, philosophy, splendidly equipped armies and navies, with power to successfully resist the invasions of all foes, by wading in their blood, all sink into insignificance when compared with this great and all important principle. All else is worthless in the sight of God when this is wanting. The open door, or opportunities, presented the church of Christ, in the text, carries with it great responsibilities. There is no work necessary to the highest development of the race, or the purity and happiness of mankind that is not here offered through the church, a mission, higher in degree and broader in extent than was ever committed to mortals before. The length, breadth, height and magnitude of this trust hath not yet been fully comprehended, I fear, by even the wisest and best of men. This is due, in part, to inherited prejudices infused into the Christian life, and part, also, from environment. If once the church gets a clear understanding and a just conception of her high calling, much, if not all, that now obstructs her entrance into that "open door" will vanish as mist before the rising sun. To this end I join the poet who said:

"To her my tears shall fall,
To her my prayers ascend,
To her my cares and toils be given,
Till toils and cares shall end."

In this commission the church is to know no race distinction nor condition, but to preach Christ to both Jew and Gentile, bond and free, African and Caucasian, rich and poor, ignorant and learned, all, as equally under necessity to repent and believe in order to receive salvation.

To preach is not sufficient, as practice speaks much louder than words. Sectarianism, the caste spirit and the like are blots on the escutcheon of Christians, by whomsoever practiced. It must be renounced and denounced, else the grand opportunity offered by the "open door" will be closed and barred eternally. It was not until Peter had his house-top vision, and the church held her first council at Jerusalem, did the meanness and exclusiveness of caste and race antagonism appear to these primitive saints. This was an excrescence produced and made to develop on the body of Christ's bride, the church, by the blind hate and racial exclusiveness among the first followers of Christ. As in those days, this evil, with others, hindered the church and caused the rejection of many churches by the Lord, so will it continue to do to races and religions who refuse to practice this spirit as required by Christ, the author of our religion.

Thus I have given you some thoughts on the primary application of this Scripture teaching. I desire now to call attention to a secondary consideration in this connection. There is a warning which comes to us, of this most enlightened age of the world's history, in the rise of four of the greatest nations known to the world, namely: the Greeks, Romans, Hebrews and Anglo-Saxons. Let us consider each in the order mentioned. I assume to begin with that God had a mission of a far-reaching purpose in bringing each of these races into historical notice. That mission I believe was to glorify and serve God. I can conceive no divine purpose in raising up a nation which does not have for its object the purest, most perfect obedience and service of which that people is capable. We know the Greeks were once the foremost race of antiquity, successful alike on the field of battle and in the sphere of arts and letters. Their skill as sculptors stands unsurpassed by any race of past ages. They left to the world monuments of their genius and high achievements, showing their exquisiteness of touch and delicacy of taste. The literary quality of their writings and public addresses show a very advanced stage of scholarship. Their poetry will never cease to be the wonder, and claim the admiration of the literary world. Their philosophers are acknowledged by the great men of this age, who are esteemed as learned, as master minds. To say all this is but to proclaim the Greeks a highly intellectual, artistic people. This is but the verdict of many centuries. It would be but partial praise to say all I have in their behalf and fail to say that they were great educators. When carried as captives from their native land as prisoners of war it was a most common thing for them to be brought as tutors in royal palaces, and among the nobility. This was a result of an eagerness always to learn something new. In war they were aggressive, heroic and skillful. Their language as a vehicle of communication is most admirable in lucidity and laconicalness. In all of this you readily see what the Greeks gave the world showing their mental possibilities. But there is one more thing to mention which shows the spirit of a great race. It is that they were possessed of love of personal liberty. No encroachment upon this sacred ground was ever allowed to the state by them. Their idea of government was that the state existed for the individual and not the individual for good of the state. Having said so much, all of which is true, one may ask why they were not retained and perpetuated. Great warriors, artists, scholars and lovers of individual liberty in a race, are not the chief element to qualify a race or individual for permanence of existence before God. They were lacking in the first and chief essential. God is seeking an ideal people. The Greeks were not that people. Had they religion? The answer is yes. The Apostle Paul declared they were too religious. Gods were more easily found among Athenians than men. Their religion, like all paganism, proved more degrading than elevating. The relation between Jehovah and man was served by the nation rejecting him for carnal things called gods. More still, the relation between man and man was predominated by a debasing, sensual gratification which destroyed all their noble aspirations. Having reached, therefore, the summit of their glory in material and intellectual achievements, and declining more and more rapidly, at the same time, in morality and spiritual discernment, God wrote on the walls of the nation's hall of revelry, "Thou art weighed in the balances and found wanting." Thus their doom came. They achieved greatness in everything but one, and that was *true godliness*. No nation can be truly great without it. The door that was once opened to them finally closed and that forever.

The Romans we next notice before the "open door" of opportunities. Through many vicissitudes this great race passed from a mere clannish state on up into a monarchy, and the world's first great republic. From first to last, however, they were doomed to utter extinction because, mainly, they fell short of the divine ideal of greatness. The Romans possessed, notwithstanding, many noble traits or qualities necessary to produce greatness. They surpassed the Greeks in some respects while they fell behind them in some others. While the former exalted culture, the latter put stress upon unity and order. By diplomacy they succeeded in forming helpful alliances such as afforded them great advantages in times of war. Under her splendidly equipped armies, on sea and land, she became the mistress of the world. The Greeks with all their greatness became subject to Rome. The zenith of her glory was reached about the transition period from a republic to a monarchy. From that time, owing to her vanity and vices, she steadily declined. Before, however, her downfall came she was allowed to contribute something substantial to the world's progress. I mention such as her arts, sculpture, massive architecture, royal highways, a magnificently organized government, matchless orators and statesmen, and a language both exquisite and expressive. By means of these the world is in advance of what it was prior to the rise of the Romans into power and supremacy over the world. For hundreds of years she wielded the scepter. And, mark you, I believe under the controlling hand of God, great blessings to mankind have resulted from the contributions of this race. Their greatness none can dispute. But for one needful indispensable virtue, which Rome lacked, she might to-day still be in the ascendency among nations. This falling short was that they failed to have, as a nation, the religion requiring supreme love to God, and love for "our neighbors as ourselves." On every other achievement without love as the chief element, was written, "weighed and found wanting." This is the central thought in the divine mind and must be with nations. The displacement of this ruling people was an act of God rather than the superior forces of enemies. For the crime of ungodliness Rome, like Greece, was set aside. She failed to enter the "open door." Their love of country, learning and the domestic relation could not save them from ruin.

Let us take another highly favored race for our consideration. These people were more than any other blessed of God. I refer to the Hebrews, the descendants of Abraham. If God could be charged with partiality because he seemed kinder and more considerate of one race than another, it would be because of His great patience and love for Israel. The story of how the race began and developed under Divine providence is fully known to all. Sacred and secular history have most fully recorded the facts. There was doubtless a far reaching purpose in the mind of God in thus blessing and forbearing with his chosen yet most rebellious children. That purpose I conceive to be to raise up if possible an ideal race. It seemed at times that God would in them accomplish greater results than in any other race. He came nearer exhausting his goodness in helping this nation than with any other. They sprung from faithful Abraham, developed in their government, into families, tribes and ultimately a nation. In it all was the hand of God revealed.

Now as to results. They were a means of direct communication from God to the world. The best code of laws, many of the most beautiful characters of men, women, and finally the world's Redeemer came of that race. To them, as to no other, we are indebted through God for that book, the Bible. It is at once unique, instructive and the only authorized record of God, Christ and the future state, good and bad. The oracles of God were committed to these people to be transmitted to the world. This old world is a better one because they lived and wrought. But like Greece and Rome they were found wanting. Having been elevated to the highest distinction they doomed themselves to a mighty fall. The same old charge of, "I have somewhat against thee," was laid at their door. That old sentence, "thou art weighed in the balances and found wanting" was written on the nation's walls. This, however, was not done until they had many times been warned and entreated to repent. God finished in and with them his work just so far as they were willing. The door swung open before them for 2,500 years. They were free to enter and were plead with to enter. Their final opportunity came. The chances are forever gone now. As a nation, they are without a country, shepherds without sheep. You say their downfall was due to their rejection of Christ, but I say to you the crucifixion of the Messiah was but the culmination of an evil heart of centuries of growth. Yea, it was as much a breaking of the Golden Rule, the sin against their fellowman, as a sin against God. In the fall of Jerusalem the national crash came.

Take still another race, now on trial. I name to you the Anglo-Saxons. In the unfolding of the divine will and providence, as manifested in rearing up of nations, this race comes into history with great promise of permanency. They seem to possess more great qualities than any other hitherto noticed. It is a race of great energy, intelligence, virtue, and courage. The great men and women of the race that adorn the pages of history with a halo of glory exceed all others. From this race have sprung great poets, artists, statesmen, warriors, scholars, reformers, geniuses, philanthropists and devout Christians. Such a race is destined, under God, to a great future. Their foundation is extensive and firm. But one thing, however, can cause their downfall. That one thing, too, seems now to threaten the overthrow, namely, the sin against man, especially the weaker brother. Around this class of human beings God seems to desire to throw protection and encouragement. Diametrically opposed to this (herein is the Golden Rule summed up) is the declaration of the Anglo-Saxons to the effect that all races in the way of their civilization must go to the wall. That means a merciless declaration of war on others. This spirit, let them remember, is irreconcilably at war with the very spirit and genius of Christianity. This spirit and genius are to bring back man to his Creator. That race that is in harmony with this principle grasps in one hand the Almighty, and in the other humanity. Thus there is an uplifting through first and second causes.

The great danger to this race lies in its prosperity and supremacy over the weaker races. When they forget that all they are, or might be, is due to divine favor only, and it seems they are forgetting in the United States, then will come the beginning of the end. If the advantages enjoyed by them but be ascribed to God's blessing, and used to promote his glory and the welfare of his little ones, the Anglo-Saxons will perpetuate their own supremacy and reflect glory upon the name of the God of nations. The failure to deal justly by their brethren will as surely send them into oblivion as that night follows day. The sentence against them in that event will be, "Inasmuch as ye did it not to one of the least of these ye did it not to me." These shall go away to everlasting punishment. The door of opportunity is open before this race. The most honored and blessed of God are such as not only honor him, but who serve their fellowmen best. What a high trust is here committed! The race seems, however, to be committed firmly to their boasted pride and arrogance, regardless of the warning which the fate of the Greeks, Romans and Hebrews experienced will afford.

Has this race of blood and cruelty reached the pinnacle of its glory? Is it in a state of sure, imperceptible decline? Have we reached the beginning of a disgraceful end in the history of this hitherto greatest race known to historians? Should this be the case, then what? I answer, as one of them, it appears to me that the Divine purpose is to place the colored American on trial, as he has the races referred to, and is now doing with the above named race. There are some distinguishing characteristics of this, my race, which if called of God, into the service of mankind, will put a distinctive stamp upon history never before made prominent. These characteristics are: docility, patience under adversity, as shown under American slavery, musical, imaginative, imitative, great endurance in toil, forgiving, lovers of domestic life, religious. The race, moreover, is unequalled in natural oratory. Such a race must have a future.

It is barely possible that the Divine purpose in permitting American slavery was to raise up on this continent a future people, who, catching all that is good of

Anglo-Saxon civilization, and by the use of his imitative genius, assimilate it with his own native qualities, and so produce the ideal race which God is seeking. Certain it is that while none can prove this position as the true one, yet none can disapprove it. All I mean is that it is possible. The door is open before us. By the righteous use of the endowments which the race possesses, recognizing them as from God, a civilization distinctively our own will be the country's blessing and salvation. The world, too, will feel a quickening impulse from such a leavening influence. I realize that the American colored man is without a past, such as is the boast of Anglo-Saxons. There was a time when no race was any better off than we are. They had to begin. So must we make a beginning. All contemporary races have a bloody record to confront them. The colored race is to make its conquests with a sheathed sword. This is an age wherein the peace man, as did the Lord Jesus Christ, is to contend against sin and error with righteousness and the sword of the Spirit, which is the word of God. Therefore that race which approaches most nearly the divine ideal will endure longest and accomplish most for the world's highest welfare. The crown is not to the most intellectual or warlike domineering race, but to the one serving God and man best. Now, I would not have any race serve God less, but I would have my own serve him best. A failure to do this cannot be substituted by one nor all other noble qualities. A holy competition for the Divine favor and honor will greatly accelerate the speed of the race in striving for the goal.

Mark you, hearer, that every other nation yet fully tried has been rejected of God, not for what they were but for what they were not. Each one contributed something to mankind's betterment, but so far as they were concerned it all meant nothing. Greece gave the world culture; Rome, law and order; the Hebrews, revelation and the Savior; the Anglo-Saxon, science, social order and the most advanced civilization. It is left to some race to yet give that best obedience which God requires, namely; give supremacy to God in head and heart and to place our neighbors deep down in the citadel of our heart or affections. I would therefore appeal to the colored American to let the zeal of God and an impartial love for our fellowmen, of all races and conditions, friends and foes, be the all-absorbing passion of daily life. If you really love your race, if you would have it stand on the very summit of the world's elevation, if you would have it without a peer or parallel in the galaxy of the greatest of nations, then let this love for both Divine and human burn on the altar of your heart. With such God is most well pleased. Therefore, seize the opportunity and save the race from degradation and irrevocable ruin. Such is the burden of my heart.

Source: Afro-American encyclopedia, or, the thoughts, doings, and sayings of the race:embracing addresses, lectures, biographical sketches, sermons, poems, names of universities, colleges, seminaries, newspapers, books, and a history of the denominations, giving the numerical strength of each. In fact, it teaches every subject of interest to the colored people, as discussed by more than one hundred of their wisest and best men and women. Compiled and arranged by James T. Haley. Nashville, Tenn.: Haley & Florida, 1895. Documenting the American South, University of North Carolina at Chapel Hill, 2000. Electronic edition available at: http://docsouth.unc.edu/church/haley/haley.html.

52. The Atlanta Compromise, 1895
BOOKER T. WASHINGTON

Booker T. Washington (April 5, 1856 to November 14, 1915) was an influential political leader, educator, and author whose autobiography, *Up From Slavery*, remains widely read. This is an address Washington gave to a predominantly white audience at the Cotton States and International Exposition in Atlanta, Georgia, on September 18, 1895.

Mr. President and Gentlemen of the Board of Directors and Citizens:

One-third of the population of the South is of the Negro race. No enterprise seeking the material, civil, or moral welfare of this section can disregard this element of our population and reach the highest success. I but convey to you, Mr. President and Directors, the sentiment of the masses of my race when I say that in no way have the value and manhood of the American Negro been more fittingly and generously recognized than by the managers of this magnificent Exposition at every stage of its progress. It is a recognition that will do more to cement the friendship of the two races than any occurrence since the dawn of our freedom. Not only this, but the opportunity here afforded will awaken among us a new era of industrial progress. Ignorant and inexperienced, it is not strange that in the first years of our new life we began at the top instead of at the bottom; that a seat in Congress or the state legislature was more sought than real estate or industrial skill; that the political convention or stump speaking had more attractions than starting a dairy farm or truck garden.

A ship lost at sea for many days suddenly sighted a friendly vessel. From the mast of the unfortunate vessel was seen a signal, "Water, water; we die of thirst!" The answer from the friendly vessel at once came back, "Cast down your bucket where you are." A second time the signal, "Water, water; send us water!" ran up from the distressed vessel, and was answered, "Cast down your bucket where you are." And a third and fourth signal for water was answered, "Cast down your bucket where you are." The captain of the distressed vessel, at last heeding the injunction, cast down his bucket, and it came up full of fresh, sparkling water from the mouth of the Amazon River.

To those of my race who depend on bettering their condition in a foreign land or who underestimate the importance of cultivating friendly relations with the Southern white man, who is their next-door neighbor, I would say: "Cast down your bucket where you are"—cast it down in making friends in every manly way of the people of all races by whom we are surrounded.

Cast it down in agriculture, in mechanics, in commerce, in domestic service, and in the professions. And in this connection it is well to bear in mind that whatever other sins the South may be called to bear, when it comes to business, pure and simple, it is in the South that the Negro is given a man's chance in the commercial world, and in nothing is this Exposition more eloquent than in emphasizing this chance. Our greatest danger is that in the great leap from slavery to freedom we may overlook the fact that the masses of us are to live by the productions of our hands, and fail to keep in mind that we shall prosper in proportion as we learn to dignify and glorify common labor, and put brains and skill into the common occupations of life; shall prosper in proportion as we learn to draw the line between the superficial and the substantial, the ornamental gewgaws of life and the useful. No race can prosper till it learns that there is as much dignity in tilling a field as in writing a poem. It is at the bottom of life we must begin, and not at the top. Nor should we permit our grievances to overshadow our opportunities.

To those of the white race who look to the incoming of those of foreign birth and strange tongue and habits for the prosperity of the South, were I permitted I would repeat what I say to my own race, "Cast down your bucket where you are." Cast it down among the eight millions of Negroes whose habits you know, whose fidelity and love you have tested in days when to have proved treacherous meant the ruin of your firesides. Cast down your bucket among these people who have, without strikes and labor wars, tilled your fields, cleared your forests, built your railroads and cities, and brought forth treasures from the bowels of the earth, and helped make possible this magnificent representation of the progress of the South. Casting down your bucket among my people, helping and encouraging them as you are doing on these grounds, and to education of head, hand, and heart, you will find that they will buy your surplus land, make blossom the waste places in your fields, and run your factories. While doing this, you can be sure in the future, as in the past, that you and your families will be surrounded by the most patient, faithful, law-abiding, and unresentful people that the world has seen. As we have proved our loyalty to you in the past, in nursing your children, watching by the sick-bed of your mothers and fathers, and often following them with tear-dimmed eyes to their graves, so in the future, in our humble way, we shall stand by you with a devotion that no foreigner can approach, ready to lay down our lives, if need be, in defense of yours, interlacing our industrial, commercial, civil, and religious life with yours in a way that shall make the interests of both races one. In all things that are purely social, we can be as separate as the fingers, yet one as the hand in all things essential to mutual progress.

There is no defense or security for any of us except in the highest intelligence and development of all. If anywhere there are efforts tending to curtail the fullest growth of the Negro, let these efforts be turned into stimulating, encouraging, and making him the most useful and intelligent citizen. Effort or means so invested will pay a thousand percent interest. These efforts will be twice blessed—blessing him that gives and him that takes.

There is no escape through law of man or God from the inevitable:

The laws of changeless justice bind Oppressor with oppressed; And close as sin and suffering joined We march to fate abreast.

Nearly sixteen millions of hands will aid you in pulling the load upward, or they will pull against you the load downward. We shall constitute one-third and more of the ignorance and crime of the South, or one-third its intelligence and progress; we shall contribute one-third to the business and industrial prosperity of the South, or we shall prove a veritable body of death, stagnating, depressing, retarding every effort to advance the body politic.

Gentlemen of the Exposition, as we present to you our humble effort at an exhibition of our progress, you must not expect overmuch. Starting thirty years ago with ownership here and there in a few quilts and pumpkins and chickens (gathered from miscellaneous sources), remember the path that has led from these to the inventions and production of agricultural implements, buggies, steam-engines, newspapers, books, statuary, carving, paintings, the management of drug stores and banks, has not been trodden without contact with thorns and thistles.

While we take pride in what we exhibit as a result of our independent efforts, we do not for a moment forget that our part in this exhibition would fall far short of your expectations but for the constant help that has come to our educational life, not only from the southern states, but especially from northern philanthropists, who have made their gifts a constant stream of blessing and encouragement.

The wisest among my race understand that the agitation of questions of social equality is the extremist folly, and that progress in the enjoyment of all the privileges that will come to us must be the result of severe and constant struggle rather than of artificial forcing. No race that has anything to contribute to the markets of the world is long in any degree ostracized. It is important and right that all privileges of the law be ours, but it is vastly more important that we be prepared for the exercise of these privileges. The opportunity to earn a dollar in a factory just now is worth infinitely more than the opportunity to spend a dollar in an opera-house. In conclusion, may I repeat that nothing in thirty years has given us more hope and encouragement, and drawn us so near to you of the white race, as this opportunity offered by the Exposition; and here bending, as it were, over the altar that represents the results of the struggles of your race and mine, both starting practically empty-handed three decades ago, I pledge that in your effort to work out the great and intricate problem which God has laid at the doors of the South, you shall have at all times the patient, sympathetic help of my race; only let this be constantly in mind, that, while from representations in these buildings of the product of field, of forest, of mine, of factory, letters, and art, much good will come, yet far above and beyond material benefits will be that higher good, that, let us pray God, will come, in a blotting out of sectional differences and racial animosities and suspicions, in a determination to administer absolute justice, in a willing obedience among all classes to the mandates of law. This, coupled with our material prosperity, will bring into our beloved South a new heaven and a new earth.

Source: Afro-American encyclopedia, or, the thoughts, doings, and sayings of the race:embracing addresses, lectures, biographical sketches, sermons, poems, names of universities, colleges, seminaries, newspapers, books, and a history of the denominations, giving the numerical strength of each. In fact, it teaches every subject of interest to the colored people, as discussed by more than one hundred of their wisest and best men and women. Compiled and arranged by James T. Haley. Nashville, Tenn.: Haley & Florida, 1895. Documenting the American South, University of North Carolina at Chapel Hill, 2000. Electronic edition available at: http://docsouth.unc.edu/church/haley/haley.html.

53. The higher education of the colored people of the South, remarks of Hugh M. Browne, of Washington D.C., 1896

While Hugh M. Browne saw the value of practical education, from the elementary level to higher education for African Americans living in Liberia and the southern United States, this is also a cautionary tale about the mis-education of black men who could easily have found themselves out of touch with the reality of being black when slavery was not a distant memory anywhere in the world.

In my invitation to take part in the discussion of the higher education of the colored people of the South, your Vice-President indicated that the fact that I had lived in Liberia would enable me to speak as one having authority. I am not sure that I understand just what Dr. Wayland meant by this hint,—whether he wished me to give an account of Liberia, the republic which began with an imported college, and has not yet established a common school; nor been able, although maintained financially by friends in the United States, to prevent this college from falling into the condition which Mr. Cleveland calls "innocuous desuetude,"—or whether, possessing himself a knowledge of the retrograding effects of higher education upon that republic, he predicates therefrom the position which I shall take in this discussion. If the latter, he is perfectly right. No man whose judgement is worth accepting can live one week in Liberia without becoming a radical advocate of the now celebrated ratio of 16 to 1,—not between gold and silver money, for Liberia has neither, but between higher and industrial education. I mean that, in the matter of the education of my people, one part of industrial is worth, in weight, volume, and potential energy, sixteen parts of the best literary or higher education the world has ever seen. After much thought and prayerful consideration, I have arrived at the conclusion that the Great Creator has permitted the foundation and existence of Liberia in order to give to the world a striking and forcible object-lesson on the folly of attempting to prepare an undeveloped race for the "ceaseless and inevitable struggle and competition of life" by higher education.

In the time allotted, it is impossible to enter into anything like a full presentation of this object-lesson. Happily, this is not necessary for this Association. If, therefore, I can succeed in presenting what a friend of mine once called "a brief epitome of a brief syllabus," it will be hint sufficient to you gentlemen who are wise in matters relating to social evolution.

Zadig, when required to explain his perfect description of the king's horse, which he had never seen, said:—

Wandering through the paths which traverse the wood, I noticed the marks of horse—shoes. They were all equidistant. "Ah!" said I, "this is a famous galloper." In a narrow alley, only seven feet wide, the dust upon the trunks of the trees was a little disturbed at three feet and a half from the middle of the path. "This horse," said I to myself, "had a tail three feet and a half long, and, lashing it from one side to the other, he has swept away the dust." Branches of the trees meet overhead at the height of five feet, and under them I saw newly-fallen leaves; so I knew the horse had brushed some of the branches, and was, therefore, five feet high. As to his bit, it must have been made of twenty-three carat gold, for he had rubbed it against a stone, which turned out to be a touchstone, with the properties of which I am familiar by experiment. Lastly, by the marks which his shoes left upon the pebbles of another kind, I was led to think that his shoes were of fine silver.

A nineteenth-century Zadig travelling in Liberia—the people having been swept out of existence—could, by a similar retrospective prophecy, describe what manner of man the Americo-Liberian was. His description would be something like this: He was a man who, in every line of life, was a non-producer. All that he possessed came as a gift, either from another race, or from the wild products of nature. A man who had simply used some of the effects of civilization, without ever manipulating the causes which produce these effects. A man who had memorized the higher education of another race, without ever realizing the fact that knowledge is power. He was like the hello-girl in the central office of a telephone system who uses the phone many times in the day, but knows nothing of the induction coil, the variable contact of the carbon and platinum buttons, and the effect of this contact on the strength of the current passing through it. She simply uses a completed instrument which she can neither repair nor reproduce.

When asked to explain this true description of a man whom he had never seen, the nineteenth century Zadig would answer:—

In my journey through Liberia I find a few iron implements used by civilized races, but I find no remains of an iron foundry of factory; and the iron ore, though plentiful, rests undisturbed. I find some manufactured cotton wares, but I find no remains of a cotton gin or mill, and the cotton plant is only found in its wild state. I find rubber manufactures, but no remains of the rubber-factory, and the wild rubber-trees have never been tapped. I find ground coffee, but no remains of the pulping-house or pulper; yet the country is overrun with wild-coffee trees of the finest quality. I find cans which contain all kinds of vegetables, but I find no trace whatever of a truck garden or canning factory. I find leather articles, but no remains of a cattle ranch, slaughter-house, or tannery. I find gold coins, but these bear the stamps of other countries; and the rich deposits of gold throughout the country have not been disturbed. I do not find the slightest evidence of the existence of a railroad or a wagon road, nor are there any indications that the streams were ever used as water-ways. I find a few official records, but among these no other evidence of an income to the republic than that derived from import and export duties; and the exports are uncultivated, raw products, furnished by the uncivilized tribes, and exported by white men residing in the country. I do not find one article bearing the stamp of a Liberian manufacture. I find a college in a sad state of decay, but I find no trace whatever of a common school.

I am not slandering Liberia in this "retrospective prophecy." I am but hinting at facts to which I called the attention of her people while in that country, and pleaded with them at the peril of my life for a change from a dependent to an independent existence; from a delusive imitation of civilization to a real living civilization; from a memorized knowledge of higher education to that bread-winning, resource-developing industrial knowledge which is a power unto the salvation of both soul and body and which alone can help and undeveloped people to help themselves. I pleaded and labored in that country for industrial education, as I have never pleaded for God's protection and guidance for myself or labored for my own existence. After studying the country and the condition of the people, I formulated a plan of education for Liberia quite similar to that which has been made famous by Tuskegee. In the letter to the interested white friends in America accompanying this plan occur such passages as the following, which I now quote to show my position on the question we are now discussing thirteen years ago, while in Liberia, and my position to-day while laboring in the cause of education in this country.

There is too much at stake in the trail which Liberia is making for any one connected with her, be that connection ever so remote, to be indifferent to the most indifferent of her concerns; but to neglect or unwisely order the education of her youth is to sound he death knell before she has reached her majority.

There is not royal road to civilization for the negro; nor does he need such. He needs now, in Liberia, an industrial institute, common primary schools, and a crops of well-trained and experienced foreign teachers, and these black or white, only that they believe in the brotherhood of man, and, above all, are such as think it not a sin to work.

It was a serious mistake when the affairs and control of the college were committed to the charge of the trustees in Liberia. A board of trustees, composed principally of unlearned and illiterate men, is no more prepared to conduct the affairs of a college than is a canal boatman to direct safely over the Atlantic one of our great streamers. I don't believe it possible to step out of slavery into such positions,—the distance is too great, and the steps between the two stages too necessary to the securing and maintaining the latter.

Nor do I think it just in those who desire to see a race *rise* undertake to raise it, as so many of our friends have done since the war. Give the negro the opportunity to grow into such positions and he will stand firm, think correctly, act wisely; but make him the holder of such positions and you expect no more fruit from him than one does perfume from the artificial flower. We must *grow*, and those who direct our growth must themselves be *grown*.

This country needs an institution which will put within the reach of the children of the masses, of the Americo-Liberians and of the natives, a common school education coupled with some trade,—mental improvement and muscular development of distinct money value.

They need the knowledge which skillfully grapples with the difficulties attendant on the development of a new country by a poor and untrained people,—an education which not only trains the mind how to observe and think properly, but which prepares one to intelligently understand the various duties and avocations of life, and enables him to earn a competent livelihood. The child crawls before it walks, and the young nation must struggle first in the rougher roads of material development before she essays to tread the higher paths of purely intellectual culture. For the present, provision for higher education should be made only for exceptional cases of talent and merit. Indeed, it would probably be well if this arrangement were permanent; for, after all, only those of exceptional talent and merit succeed in the walks of higher culture.

Liberia needs thousands of intelligent farmers and skilled artisans. Through these must education show its power and attract the people to its ways. The rising generation here must be taught self-reliance and independence. They must be made producers, who shall bring to markets of the world the products, wares, and manufactures of properly conducted farms, workshops, and manufactories. The institution for this country at present is at Hampton. And I have underscored Hampton four times.

These quotations indicate the conviction which my loyalty to race, wide observation, and experience all unite to confirm,—namely, that a people's education should fit them to succeed in the condition and environment in which their lot is cast.

Let us now come nearer home than Liberia. And let us be perfectly frank and outspoken. The trial of the negro before the bar of nations on the question of his title to the brotherhood of man is too near the jury-stage for sentimentality and weak excuses. The time has arrived for plain speaking and acting, for the presentation of substantial evidence of facts.

The same serious mistake made in Liberia, namely, substituting higher for industrial education, was made in the South. There we had the same disregard of the fact that a wilderness exist between Egypt and Canaan in the progress of a race or people. When we reached the opposite shore of our Red Sea, at the close of the late Rebellion, the majority of our saintly white friends of the North, and the colored men who had ear of the nation at that time, believed that we placed our feet upon the land of Canaan. They, therefore, fed us on the milk and honey of that land.

And to us, in our ignorance, this food was sweeter than manna, though the latter was supercharged with the proper nutriment and came directly from heaven. Now that they and we are beginning to realize that the land was not Canaan, but the shores of a wild, rugged, unexplored wilderness, we are both also discovering that the diet of Canaan does not produce the bone and sinew necessary for the journey.

We were given the higher education of the advanced white man, whose race has fought the good fight in the wilderness and is now concerned about the improvement of Canaan; and with this misfit training we have gone to our people in the wilderness, only to discover that we possess the *outfit of leisure* where the *outfit of labor* is needed.

No, my friends, neither man nor race steps from Egypt to Canaan, they journey there through undiscovered roads. The wedding garment of that land is of the crazy-quilt pattern, made of pieces of experience gathered only on this journey. I am, therefore, singing daily, not of "arms and men," but of the sweet uses of this wilderness, where necessity prepares us to win in the struggle for life, and God prepares us to win in the struggle for the life of others. And the burden of my song is that an education and Christian services, which are not adapted to our present condition and environment, are of no more value to us than is a pair of skates to a boy who lives in Madeira.

We have been sent to the Greek and Latin authors, but they do not teach us to bridge the streams we meet nor how to bring bread from the untilled soil. We need schools which put the hoe in one hand and a book on farming in the other; a hammer in one hand and a book on carpentry in the other; a broom in one hand and a book on housekeeping in the other. Christian scientific industrial training is the highway in the wilderness for us. Every circumstance at present makes this way so clear that wayfaring men, though fools shall not err therein, and those colored men who do err are the fools whom the Good Book recommends should be left to perish in their folly.

Labor, though the taste for it is acquired, is the true means of development. That it required, under God's providence, two centuries and a half to introduce us to a mild form of this means, in the South land of this country, is to me a very significant fact. If we will come to a familiar acquaintance and saving knowledge of labor, we must do so by educating our children to cherish labor as the pearl of great price, and to sell all else to purchase it. We must eradicate the idea that labor is degrading, by training our children to labor, and industrial education alone does this.

I favour the industrial, because the higher or purely literary education is not in touch with out present condition and those parts of our environment with which we are in correspondence. Among others, this higher education produces these three effects which are inimical to the progress of any race or people in our present condition:—

First, This purely literary education produces an unmarketable article, thus entailing upon the race three total losses; namely, the cost of its production, the anticipated selling price, and saddest of all, the expense of carrying this article in stock. The avenues of employment which require higher education are to-day over-crowded with white men; among the supply is greater than the demand, and is still increasing. Nor is their higher education a new thing. It is the result of natural growth, and rests upon an *experience* with the *letter* which now celebrates not its birthdays, but its centennials.

Colored men deceive themselves when they fancy color prejudice the obstacle which closes against us the avenues in which higher education reaps its harvest. That which closes these avenues tightest is our lack, of that factor of proficiency which is acquired only from experience. And this is the factor which our present condition and environment do not furnish. The whites will not let us practised upon. I am thoroughly convinced that the best way to established this factor amongst, us in this country, is to extract the greatest possible life from those parts of our environment with which we are at present in correspondence.

Second, This purely literary education puts the average colored man out of touch with our people. The young white man, squandering the wealth of his parents, because he was reared out of touch with the causes which accumulated that wealth presents to my mind no sadder or more demoralizing picture in the social life of this country than the young colored squandering the knowledge of the university, because his people were reared out of touch with the concrete causes which produced that formulated, abstract knowledge.

This purely literary training does not touch the present social condition of our people in sufficient vital points. Its trend is toward the abstract, while we are wrestling with the coarser forms of concrete. The formulated knowledge of the book is but the experience of those who have succeeded in the struggle with the concrete, and can be of little developing value to one whose study of it is divorced from the concrete. When we step out of these seminaries of higher education, we are quite like the girl who thought she was a cook because she had memorized the better part of a scientific course on cooking. When thus equipped she finally entered the kitchen, it was only to discover that the old cook did not understand her theories and scientific terms, and she herself did not know a rolling-pin from a cullender— hence each was disgusted with the other.

We are just learning to manipulate the causes of the higher civilization; the knowledge of the effects if this civilization, therefore, will not help us, and one equipped therewith is out of touch with us.

We form the working masses engaged in fields of unskilled labor the world over, even in Africa. The educated men and women who will help us succeed, round by round, to the top of the ladder, must bring us their learning in our own language. Herein lies the difference between the average college-bred man amongst us and our distinguished educator, Booker T. Washington: the former speaks to us *brokenly* in a foreign language, while the latter speaks to us *plainly* in our own language.

Harvard University honored the race which built her, when she honored Booker T. Washington. I have never known the white race to hesitate in their sanction and praise of men, whatever their color or creed, when they find them storing up energy, the motions arising from which produce social efficiency.

Third, This purely literary training puts the average colored man out of touch with himself. I don't believe any man, white or black, can in the first generation of hid intellectual life, digest and assimilate the present prescribed course of higher education.

Physically, there is but one way to obtain the full corn in the ear, and that is to give the seed the condition and environment essential to its daily growth. The seed thus provided for gradually and slowly takes in, digests, and assimilates each day its daily bread, and build up first the blade, then the ear, and after that the full corn in the ear. It is none the less true of the metal development of a people,—they must receive mental food gradually and orderly, first that which pertains to the blade stage, then that which pertains to the ear stage, and after that, that which pertains to the full-corn-in-the-ear stage. To supply all this while in the blade stage produce the worst form of mental indigestion, and a resemblance to an educated man which is ludicrous and yet self-satisfied. In this connection, I do not hesitate to declare that if one should analyze the efforts put forth under this unnatural training, he will find that they aim rather at the impossible task of changing the Ethiopian's skin than at the possible and God ordained one improving the condition of that skin; and in the name God and humanity, what else can the harvest be than impracticability and discontent? Knowledge, like food, is a power to its possessor only when it is assimilated. There can be very little harmony among the "internal relations" of that man whose head is overloaded with indigested knowledge while his empty stomach is wrestling with the petition, "God us this day our daily bread."

A man educated out of touch with himself is like poor little David clothed in the mighty armor of Saul. I rejoice, though, that the time has come when we are learning, even though slowly, that there is at the present stage of our progress more virtue in the sling than there is in the mightiest of such armors.

In conclusion, I am not opposing higher education in itself, I am opposing it at a stage in a people's history when it destroys efficiency and power. I am pleading for an education specially adapted to the circumstances and conditions of a specific case. I am beseeching our benevolent white friends to look upon us in the terrific plants, and not as so much clay to be cast into various forms by the potter. I am not asking a change in the system of education which the white man has built up. I am, out of the fullness of my heart, begging that it be kindergartenized when brought among us. I am claiming that the best way to teach the young idea of an undeveloped people how to shoot it to practise it in shooting the seed corn into the furrow and striking the nail upon the head with the hammer.

I see no reason for blaming the white man for the results of my own inactivity. Nor do I look with alarm upon restrictions placed upon my desire to continue in this inactivity. I do know that his former history gives every assurance that when Ethiopia shall unfold her arms and stretch forth her hands in the rivalry of life he will admit her "on a footing of equality of opportunity." The altruistic feeling of his civilization will demand this as truly as it demanded the abolition of slavery the world over. The height to which we shall rise in true civilization depends upon the energy and wisdom with which we shall stretch forth her hands in this rivalry.

Source: Library of Congress, Rare Book and Special Collections Division, Daniel A. P. Murray Pamphlets Collection.

54. Supreme Court of the United States in Plessy vs. Ferguson 163 U.S. 537, 1896

When and how racial segregation began in America remains an open debate. While some southern states erected legal barriers that restricted the movement of African Americans immediately after slavery ended in 1863, other states erected de facto barriers that effectively controlled the movement of blacks. For many decades well into the twentieth century. It is clear that while blacks and whites lived and worked in much the same way after slavery as during it in the South, an extensive system of social and economic segregation enforced by widespread hostility towards blacks reigned in many parts of the nation in the 1880s and 90s. When northern troops left the South decades after those hostilities that had sparked the Civil War, old patterns of racial divides resurfaced.

Every southern state had enacted black codes immediately after the war to keep the former slaves under tight control. When these laws were voided by the Union, white southerners began exploring other means to maintain their supremacy over blacks. Southern legislatures, for example, enacted criminal statutes that invariably prescribed harsher penalties for blacks than for whites convicted of the same crime, and erected a system of peonage that survived into the early twentieth century.

In 1878, the United States Supreme Court ruled that the states could not prohibit segregation on railroads, streetcars, or steamboats. Twelve years later, the Court approved a Mississippi statute requiring segregation on intrastate carriers. In doing so the Court acquiesced in the South's solution to race relations.

In the best known of the early segregation cases, *Plessy v. Ferguson* (1896), Justice Billings Brown asserted that distinctions based on race did not violate the Thirteenth or Fourteenth Amendments, two Civil War amendments passed to abolish slavery and secure the legal rights of the former slaves.

Although the phrase "separate but equal" is not present in the decision, the Court's ruling in *Plessy* approved legally enforced segregation as long as the law did not make facilities for blacks inferior to those of whites. In his now famous dissent, Justice Harlan protested that states could not impose criminal penalties on citizens simply because they wished to use the public highways and common forms of transportation.

Justice Brown delivered the opinion of the Court.

This case turns upon the constitutionality of an act of the General Assembly of the State of Louisiana, passed in 1890, providing for separate railway carriages for the white and colored races ...

The constitutionality of this act is attacked upon the ground that it conflicts both with the Thirteenth Amendment of the Constitution, abolishing slavery, and the Fourteenth Amendment, which prohibits certain restrictive legislation on the part of the States.

1. That it does not conflict with the Thirteenth Amendment, which abolished slavery and involuntary servitude, except as a punishment for crime, is too clear for argument ...

The proper construction of the Fourteenth Amendment was first called to the attention of this court in the Slaughter-house cases, ... which involved, however, not a question of race, but one of exclusive privileges. The case did not call for any expression of opinion as to the exact rights it was intended to secure to the colored race, but it was said generally that its main purpose was to establish the citizenship of the negro; to give definitions of citizenship of the United States and of the States, and to protect from the hostile legislation of the States the privileges and immunities of citizens of the United States, as distinguished from those of citizens of the States.

The object of the amendment was undoubtedly to enforce the absolute equality of the two races before the law, but in the nature of things it could not have been intended to abolish distinctions based upon color, or to enforce social, as distinguished from political equality, or a commingling of the two races upon terms unsatisfactory to either. Laws permitting, and even requiring, their separation in places where they are liable to be brought into contact do not necessarily imply the inferiority of either race to the other, and have been generally, if not universally, recognized as within the competency of the state legislatures in the exercise of their police power. The most common instance of this is connected with the establishment of separate schools for white and colored children, which has been held to be a valid exercise of the legislative power even by courts of States where the political rights of the colored race have been longest and most earnestly enforced ...

So far, then, as a conflict with the Fourteenth Amendment is concerned, the case reduces itself to the question whether the statute of Louisiana is a reasonable regulation, and with respect to this there must necessarily be a large discretion on the part of the legislature. In determining the question of reasonableness it is at liberty to act with reference to the established usages, customs and traditions of the people, and with a view to the promotion of their comfort, and the preservation of the public peace and good order. Gauged by this standard, we cannot say that a law which authorizes or even requires the separation of the two races in public conveyances is unreasonable, or more obnoxious to the Fourteenth Amendment than the acts of Congress requiring separate schools for colored children in the District of Columbia, the constitutionality of which does not seem to have been questioned, or the corresponding acts of state legislatures.

We consider the underlying fallacy of the plaintiff's argument to consist in the assumption that the enforced separation of the two races stamps the colored race with a badge of inferiority. If this be so, it is not by reason of any-thing found in the act, but solely because the colored race chooses to put that construction upon it. The argument necessarily assumes that if, as has been more than once the case, and is not unlikely to be so again, the colored race should become the dominant power in the state legislature, and should enact a law in precisely similar terms, it would thereby relegate the white race to an inferior position. We imagine that the white race, at least, would not acquiesce in this assumption. The argument also assumes that social prejudices may be overcome by legislation, and that equal rights cannot be secured to the negro except by an enforced commingling of the two races. We cannot accept this proposition. If the two races are to meet upon terms of social equality, it must be the result of natural affinities, a mutual appreciation of each other's merits and a voluntary consent of individuals ... Legislation is powerless to eradicate racial instincts or to abolish distinctions based upon physical differences, and the attempt to do so can only result in accentuating the difficulties of the present situation. If the civil and political rights of both races be equal one cannot be inferior to the other civilly or politically. If one race be inferior to the other socially, the Constitution of the United States cannot put them upon the same plane ...

Justice Harlan, dissenting.

While there may be in Louisiana persons of different races who are not citizens of the United States, the words in the act, "white and colored races," necessarily include all citizens of the United States of both races residing in that State. So that we have before us a state enactment that compels, under penalties, the separation of the two races in railroad passenger coaches, and makes it a crime for a citizen of either race to enter a coach that has been assigned to citizens of the other race ...

In respect of civil rights, common to all citizens, the Constitution of the United States does not, I think, permit any public authority to know the race of those entitled to be protected in the enjoyment of such rights. Every true man has pride of race, and under appropriate circumstances when the rights of others, his equals before the law, are not to be affected, it is his privilege to express such pride and to take such action based upon it as to him seems proper. But I deny that any legislative body or judicial tribunal may have regard to the race of citizens when the civil rights of those citizens are not involved. Indeed, such legislation, as that here in question, is inconsistent not only with that equality of rights which pertains to citizenship, National and State, but with the personal liberty enjoyed by every one within the United States ...

The white race deems itself to be the dominant race in this country. And so it is, in prestige, in achievements, in education, in wealth and in power. So, I doubt not, it will continue to be for all time, if it remains true to its great heritage and holds fast to the principles of constitutional liberty. But in view of the Constitution, in the eye of the law, there is in this country no superior, dominant, ruling class of citizens. There is no caste here. Our Constitution is color-blind, and neither knows nor tolerates classes among citizens. In respect of civil rights, all citizens are equal before the law. The humblest is the peer of the most powerful. The law regards man as man, and takes no account of his surroundings or of his color when his civil rights as guaranteed by the supreme law of the land are involved. It is, therefore, to be regretted that this high tribunal, the final expositor of the fundamental law of the land, has reached the conclusion that it is compe-tent for a State to regulate the enjoyment by citizens of their civil rights solely upon the basis of race.

In my opinion, the judgment this day rendered will, in time, prove to be quite as pernicious as the decision made by this tribunal in the Dred Scott case ... The present decision, it may well be apprehended, will not only stimulate aggressions, more or less brutal and irritating, upon the admitted rights of colored citizens, but will encourage the belief that it is possible, by means of state enactments, to defeat the beneficent purposes which the people of the United States had in view when they adopted the recent amendments of the Constitution, by one of which the blacks of this country were made citizens of the United States and of the States in which they respectively reside, and whose privileges and immunities, as citizens, the States are forbidden to abridge. Sixty millions of whites are in no danger from the presence here of eight millions of blacks. The destinies of the two races, in this country, are indissolubly linked together, and the interests of both require that the common government of all shall not permit the seeds of race hate to be planted under the sanction of law. What can more certainly arouse race hate, what more certainly create and perpetuate a feeling of distrust between these races, than state enactments, which, in fact, proceed on the ground that colored citizens are so inferior and degraded that they cannot be allowed to sit in public coaches occupied by white citizens? That, as all will admit, is the real meaning of such legislation as was enacted in Louisiana ...

If evils will result from the commingling of the two races upon public highways established for the benefit of all, they will be infinitely less than those that will surely come from state legislation regulating the enjoyment of civil rights upon the basis of race. We boast of the freedom enjoyed by our people above all other peoples. But it is difficult to reconcile that boast with a state of the law which, practically, puts the brand of servitude and degradation upon a large class of our fellow-citizens, our equals before the law ...

I am of opinion that the statute of Louisiana is inconsistent with the personal liberty of citizens, white and black, in that State, and hostile to both the spirit and letter of the Constitution of the United States. If laws of like character should be enacted in the several States of the Union, the effect would be in the highest degree mischievous. Slavery, as an institution tolerated by law would, it is true, have disappeared from our country, but there would remain a power in the States, by sinister legislation, to interfere with the full enjoyment of the blessings of freedom; to regulate civil rights, common to all citizens upon the basis of race; and to place in a condition of legal inferiority a large body of American citizens, now constituting a part of the political community called the People of the United States, for whom, and by whom through representatives, our government is administered.

Source: Court proceedings argued April 18, 1896. Decided May 18, 1896. Copyright © Jerry Goldman, Justia & Oyez.

55. Address of Booker T. Washington, delivered at the alumni dinner of Harvard University, Cambridge, Massachusetts, after receiving the honorary degree of "Master of Arts," June 24, 1896

In this speech, Negro leader Booker T. Washington responded to the increasing improvement between the black and white races. However, he advised that collaboration between the races would reap positive results for humanity in general. This address was reprinted in the pages of *The Colored American* with an introduction written by Thomas J. Calloway.

First in the history of America, a leading American University confers an honorary degree upon a colored man. Harvard has been always to the front in ideas of liberty, freedom and equality. When other colleges of the North were accepting the Negro as a tolerance, Harvard has been awarding him honors, as in the case of Clement G. Morgan of recent date.

Her present action, therefore, in placing an honorary crown upon the worthy head of Mr. Washington, is but a step further in her magnanimity in recognizing merit under whatever color of skin.

The mere announcement of this event is a great testimony to the standing of Mr. Washington, but to any black person who, as I did, saw and heard the enthusiasm and applause with which the audience cheered the announcement by President Eliot, the degree itself was insignificant. The Boston Lancers had conducted Gov. Wolcott to Cambridge, and 500 Harvard graduates had double filed the march to Sanders' Theatre. It was a great day. Latin orations, disquisitions, dissertations and essays in English were delivered by selected graduates, clad in stately and classic cap and gown. Bishops, generals, commodores, statesmen, authors, poets, explorers, millionaires and noted men of every calling, sat as earnest listeners. President Eliot had issued 500 diplomas by handing them to representatives of the graduates in bundles of twenty to twenty-five. Then came the awarding of honorary degrees. Thirteen were issued. Bishop Vincent and General Nelson A. Miles, Commander of the U.S. Army, being among the recipients. When the name of Booker T. Washington was called, and he arose to acknowledge and accept, there was such an outburst of applause as greeted no other name except that of the popular soldier-patriot, General Miles. The applause was not studied and stiff, sympathetic and condoling; it was enthusiasm and admiration. Every part of the audience from pit to gallery joined in, and a glow covered the cheeks of those around me, proving that sincere appreciation of the rising struggle of an ex-slave and the work he has accomplished for his race.

But the event of the day was the alumni dinner, when speeches formed the most enjoyable bill of fare. Two hundred Harvard alumni and their invited guests partook of their annual dinner. Four or five speeches were made, among them one from Mr. Washington.

At the close of the speaking, notwithstanding Senator Henry Cabot Lodge, Dr. Minot J. Savage and others had spoken, President Eliot warmly grasped Mr. Washington by the hand and told him that his was the best speech of the day.

Anent the conferring of the degree and the toast, the papers have been unusual in favorable comment. Says the Boston Post:

"In conferring the honorary degree of Master of Arts upon the Principal of Tuskegee Institute, Harvard University has honored itself as well as the object of this distinction. The work which Prof. Booker T. Washington has accomplished for the education, good citizenship and popular enlightenment in his chosen field of labor in the South, entitles him to rank with our national benefactors. The University which can claim him on its list of sons, whether in regular course or *honoris causa*, may be proud.

"It has been mentioned that Mr. Washington is the first of his race to receive an honorary degree from a New England University. This, in itself, is a distinction. But the degree was not conferred because Mr. Washington is a colored man, or because he was born in slavery, but because he has shown, by his work for the elevation of the people of the Black Belt of the South, a genius and a broad humanity which count for greatness in any man, whether his skin be white or black."

The Boston Globe adds: "It is Harvard which, first among New England colleges, confers an honorary degree upon a black man. No one who has followed the history of Tuskegee and its work, can fail to admire the courage, persistence and splendid common sense of Booker T. Washington. Well may Harvard honor the ex-slave, the value of whose services, alike to his race and country, only the future can estimate."

The correspondent of the New York Times kindly remarks: "All the speeches were enthusiastically received, but the colored man carried off the oratorical honors, and the applause which broke out when he had finished, was vociferous and long-continued."

Most of the papers have printed his cut, and congratulations have come from every source.

The grandest feature of the whole thing, is that the fame and honor that are coming thus to Mr. Washington, do not spoil him. Twelve months in the year, night and day, he works for Tuskegee—his heart and love. No vacation, no rest; his life is one unceasing struggle for his school. This is the secret of his power. Here is the lesson to be learned.—

Thos. J. Calloway, in The Colored American.

BOSTON, June 24th, 1896

MR. PRESIDENT AND GENTLEMEN:—

It would in some measure relieve my embarrassment if I could, even in a slight degree, feel myself worthy of the great honor which you do me to-day. Why you have called me from the Black Belt of the South, from among my humble people, to share in the honors of this occasion, is not for me to explain; and yet it may not be inappropriate for me to suggest that it seems to me that one of the most vital questions that touch our American life, is how to bring the strong, wealthy and learned into helpful touch with the poorest, most ignorant, and humble and at the same time, make the one appreciate the vitalizing, strengthening influence of the other. How shall we make the mansions on yon Beacon street feel and see the need of the spirits in the lowliest cabin in Alabama cotton fields or Louisiana sugar bottoms? This problem Harvard University is solving, not by bringing itself down, but by bringing the masses up.

If through me, an humble representative, seven millions of my people in the South might be permitted to send a message to Harvard—Harvard that offered up on death's altar, young Shaw, and Russell, and Lowell and scores of others, that we might have a free and united country, that message would be, "Tell them that the sacrifice was not in vain. Tell them that by the way of the shop, the field, the skilled hand, habits of thrift and economy, by way of industrial school and college, we are coming. We are crawling up, working up, yea, bursting up. Often through oppression, unjust discrimination and prejudice, but through them all we are coming up, and with proper habits, intelligence and property, there is no power on earth that can permanently stay our progress."

If my life in the past has meant anything in the lifting up of my people and the bringing about of better relations between your race and mine, I assure you from this day it will mean doubly more. In the economy of God there is but one standard by which an individual can succeed—there is but one for a race. This country demands that every race measure itself by the American standard. By it a race must rise or fall, succeed or fail, and in the last analysis mere sentiment counts for little. During the next half century and more, my race must continue passing through the severe American crucible. We are to be tested in our patience, our forbearance, our perseverance, our power to endure wrong, to withstand temptations, to economize, to acquire and use skill; our ability to compete, to succeed in commerce, to disregard the superficial for the real, the appearance for the substance, to be great and yet small, learned and yet simple, high and yet the servant of all. This, this is the passport to all that is best in the life of our republic, and the Negro must possess it, or be debarred.

While we are thus being tested, I beg of you to remember that wherever our life touches yours, we help or hinder. Wherever your life touches ours, you make us stronger or weaker. No member of your race in any part of our country can harm the meanest member of mine, without the proudest and bluest blood in Massachusetts being degraded. When Mississippi commits crime, New England commits crime, and in so much, lowers the standard of your civilization. There is no escape—man drags man down, or man lifts man up.

In working out our destiny, while the main burden and center of activity must be with us, we shall need, in a large measure in the years that are to come, as we have in the past, the help, the encouragement, the guidance that the strong can give the weak. Thus helped, we of both races in the South, soon shall throw off the shackles of racial and sectional prejudice and rise, as Harvard University has risen and as we all should rise, above the clouds of ignorance, narrowness and selfishness, into that atmosphere, that pure sunshine, where it will be our highest ambition to serve MAN, our brother, regardless of race or previous condition.

Source: Library of Congress, Rare Book and Special Collections Division, Daniel A.P. Murray Pamphlets Collection.

56. How shall the colored youth of the South be educated?, 1897
A. D. MAYO

In this essay, A. D. Mayo, an African American minister from Massachusetts, addressed the educational status of African Americans in the rural South. He wrote that the focus of education should center on industrial arts schools, staffed by well-trained African American teachers, for such schools would provide a solid education of political and social advancement for rural Southern blacks.

Next to the preservation of the Union the most notable result of the great Civil War was the emancipation of more than six millions of Negroes and their sudden and perilous elevation, in defiance of all historic precedents, from the lowest to the highest position in modern civilizations,—complete legal citizenship of the United States. For more than thirty years the people of the old fifteen slave states have been wrestling with the problem of bringing the actual condition of these new citizens into conformity with their legal civic status as recorded in the Constitution and laws of every American commonwealth. By common consent the only lever that can lift this nation within a nation to its final position in American life is found in that group of agencies which, "working together for good," is know as education. The present essay is an attempt to outline the educational status of the American negro citizen in our Southern states, and to suggest some of the more evident and imperative methods by which the great educational movement of the colored race, begun with its emancipation in 1865, can now be reorganized in the light of past experience and carried forward to a successful issue.

But first let me indicate the point of view from which this observation and estimate are taken.

1. I trace the direct hand of God's providence in the removal of this people from the darkness of pagan barbarism and bondage in the "dark continent," amid the comparative darkness of Christendom three hundred years ago, to a new continent, destined to become the seat of the world's chief republic. No other portion of this race, either in Africa or elsewhere, has at any time been so favored by divine Providence as in this calling out of Egypt, at the beginning of a forty years in the wilderness, in the journey toward the land of promise.

2. I trace the hand of God through the two hundred and fifty years of the life of this people in the English colonies and the southern United States before its final emancipation, a generation ago. I have no apologies for its darker shades, and make no claim for the "peculiar institution" as a missionary enterprise. But this I see: While the masses of the European peoples, without exception, came up to their day of deliverance through a thousand years of war, pestilence and famine, which destroyed as many as now live on that continent, this people was trained for civilization through a prolonged childhood under the direction and by the consent of the superior class in the most progressive nation on earth. This is the only people that

has made the passage from barbarism to civilization without passing through a wilderness dominated by the three furies of the prayer-book,—"sword, pestilence and famine." Up to 1860 it never strewed the continent with its bones or watered its fields with its blood in war. Its people never died in thousands, like every European people, by famine. And so well were they guarded against pestilence that no people on earth has so increased and multiplied, until to-day we behold a nation three times as numerous as the American republic under the presidency of George Washington.

3. When at last the republic, like every great people, was called upon to make the grand decision whether it was indeed one nation or a confederacy of thirty nations which one of the number could sever, this people was providentially so placed that neither the Union nor the confederacy could boast that it had received the greater aid at its hands. Among the three million soldiers and sailors of the Union, at most were found not more than a quarter of a million of colored fighter and workers. But until the close of the great conflict the confederacy received the aid of probably five millions of the colored people, in raising supplies, carrying on the home life, and working in the various ways whereby the effective strength and number of its armies was prodigiously increased. And it was no small gain for the freedmen that, when peace and freedom came, every generous and thoughtful family in the South acknowledged a debt of gratitude to them and laid no charge against them for what had happened. Meanwhile, the North and the nation, which had liberated the slaves as an act of civil war, felt bound by every consideration of justice and humanity to do its uttermost for their protection and elevation.

4. And when the war cloud lifted and the six millions of this people stood up for the first "dress parade" of the grand army of freedmen, the whole civilized world looked on with amazement at what appeared. For during that period of less than three centuries the race had made a greater progress than any other people in the history of mankind. During those memorable years the African negro had learned the three fundamental lessons of civilization: How to work under intelligent supervision; the language and the religion of a civilized, Christian country. And that country was the world's foremost republic, and all the experiences of slave life had been during the years when it was growing from thirteen colonies to the United States of America. It was not remarkable, under those circumstances, that among these five or six millions was found a body of men and women who became the foremost leaders of the race, by the natural selection of superior intelligence, superior character, and superior executive ability. Freedom came to the Negro in a country by climate adapted to his condition; where good land was a drug in every market; so fertile that no family need starve; so sparsely populated that one of its states to-day could support the entire colored population of eight millions and still call aloud for millions more.

5. I do not discuss the wisdom or unwisdom of the last great act of this "strange eventful history"—the conferring on this people at once the world's highest opportunity—the supreme right of full American citizenship world's highest opportunity—the supreme right of full American citizenship, with all that belongs thereto. But I see that, under the same directing providence, even this, the most daring and perilous experiment in government recorded in history, awoke the entire country at once to the necessity and duty of providing that education for the coming generation without which freedom itself would have been only a mockery and a phantasm.

At once the national government stretched forth its hand to the two millions of colored children and youth. The great philanthropist, George Peabody, born and reared in the common schools of Massachusetts, a citizen of the South, a resident in and illustrious benefactor of the metropolis of the British empire, included the Negro children in the greatest personal gift at that time ever made for the education of a whole people. The board of Peabody trustees, the most distinguished body of men that ever served as a "common school board of education," under the presidency of Robert C. Winthrop, the descendant of Governor John Winthrop, the most illustrious of his great family, the model American citizen; through its right and left hand, Dr. Barnas Sears and Dr. J. L. M. Curry, invited the South to make its final effort to establish the common school for "every sort and condition" of its people. And, most wonderful of all the wonders of this era of miracles, the old master class of the South joined hands with the educational public of the North in the glorious enterprise of educating the children of its freedmen for the new American citizenship. All honor to the North and the nation for what it has done in giving to this people the greatest opportunity, to train its superior youth for the leadership of a nation. But we must not forget that for every dollar expended from the marvelous wealth of the richest nation and the wealthiest states of Christendom in behalf of the Negro, the sixteen states of the South, in the day of their poverty, have given four dollars for the education of these children in the new Southern common schools.

6. So here our "nation within a nation" stands to-day. The North and the republic have given the Negro personal emancipation and, as far as constitutions and laws can go, political freedom. But the only highway to the real use and enjoyment of complete American citizenship is the education of the head, the heart and the hand, which leads a people through the paths of peace and by the methods of a Christian civilization, up from every possible depth to every possible height of human achievement. The South has struck hands once and forever with the North and the nation, and in the establishment and support of the American common school, at a cost, during the past twenty-five years, of more than four hundred and eighty-three million dollars for its colored citizens,—has done such a work as no people under similar circumstances ever did before.

The only question now in order is: in view of what God and the Republic have done, what does this people propose to do for itself? What must this "nation within a nation" do to be saved?

I answer, without one word of hesitation: Turn its back upon the past. Return thanks to Almighty God that it now stands on the threshold of the world's highest position, sovereign citizenship in the world's greatest republic. Let it behold in this opportunity for the education of the two millions of its children and youth in the American common school, the final proof of the gracious providence that "thus far has let it on." Now let it gird up its loins, face the sunrise, and along this highway of civilization begin its upward march toward the future that can only be achieved through that education which is but another name for the Christian method of rising out of the lower places of the earth toward the sunlit summits that front the heavens and scan the horizon.

With the best light at my command I therefore hold that the absolute impending duty of the colored citizens of the South is to combine and by every practical method inaugurate a grand revival in behalf of the country and village common school.

The graded school for colored children and youth in the cities and larger towns in these states is now in a fair way to success. But it is in the vast majority of the common schools for the colored children and youth, in the open country and smaller villages, that the great field for educational work in the south is now found.

By the report of the National Bureau of Education for 1892–93 we learn that in sixteen states and the District of Columbia there are now (estimated) 2,630,331 colored children between the ages of five and eighteen. Of these 1,267,828 are enrolled in the common schools. The average daily attendance varies in different states; in Virginia one-half, in South Carolina a larger, in Maryland a smaller proportion; in the District of Columbia, where the colored schools are best, 11,000 of the 14,500 enrolled. It would probably be an approximate estimate to say that one-third the number of colored children in the South between five and eighteen are in average daily attendance on common schools, in session less than five and rarely four months in the year, during a period probably not exceeding four years in the life of the pupil. These children are under the instruction of 25,615 colored teachers.

"In the academies, schools, colleges, etc., for colored youth there are, as far as known, 10,191 male and 11,920 female students. In all these schools reported in 1892–93 there are 25,859 students. In the elementary departments of seventy-five of these institutions are 13,176 pupils; in the secondary 7,365; in the collegiate, 963; and in professional 924. In the collegiate department of these institutions only twenty-five per centage of colored illiteracy of persons above the age of ten in 1890 was found in Alabama; 69.1 per cent. During the twenty years from 1870 to 1890 the per centage of colored illiteracy was reduced from 85 to 60 per cent of the entire population. In Kentucky the colored school enrolment has reached 78 per cent of the colored youth of school age, while in nine states it falls below 60 per cent. Alabama, with the exception of three states, is giving education to the largest number of colored children in secondary schools. In the number of colored students in normal school courses in 1895 Alabama led the entire South, with 785; also in the number of colored students receiving industrial training, 3,427. It is estimated that the Hampton school in Virginia and the Tuskegee in Alabama now receive nearly one-half the entire sum contributed by the North for the education of the Southern Negro; more than three hundred dollars annually. But, with the best effort of the National Bureau of Education, owing to a chronic habit of neglect in forwarding school returns, these statistics of Negro education can be regarded as little better than a tolerable accurate approximation. Other estimates give in the entire South 162 schools of the secondary and higher type, with 37,000 students and 1,550 teachers. But at the highest estimate, of probably 800,000 colored children and youth in daily school attendance, not 50,000 will be found in any grade above the elementary and lower grammar schools.

If these institutions, especially those largely supported by the North for the secondary and higher schooling of the colored youth in all these states are wise in time and correctly gauge the drift of sentiment in the educational and religious public in the nation, they will at once do four things:—

1. With all possible dispatch consistent with existing arrangements they will relieve themselves of their elementary department and concentrate their work on the training of competent youth for leadership in all the positions where superior ability and character are in demand.

2. These institutions are waking up to the importance of giving better instruction and in many cases improving the quality of their teaching force.
3. They will co-operate, to the extent of their ability and with a heart in their co-operation, in the attempt to make sound industrial training for both sexes, not an annex to, but a permanent feature of their course of study and discipline.
4. They will discourage the attempt of some of our Southern educational missionary associations and home churches to force the sectarian parochial system of elementary schools upon the colored people.

With these four reforms these institutions can rely upon the continued favor of the friends of education throughout the country; at present for temporary supplies, and finally for substantial endowment, to establish them as the future collegiate and professional seminaries for this people.

So we are thrown back upon our fundamental position,—the almost absolute dependence of the colored people of the South upon the country district and village common school of the generation of children and youth now on the ground. More than ninety-five per cent of these two million six hundred thousand, from five to eighteen, will there receive the schooling that will largely determine their ability, twenty years hence, to become the American Macedonian phalanx, the chosen ten thousand on which our "nation within a nation" must depend for its direction in all public and private affairs.

Hitherto, this work of education, including a good deal of aid and comfort for the colored churches, has borne very largely upon the white people of both sections of the country. There are no very reliable statics of the amount of money contributed by the whole country to the schooling of the colored people during the past thirty-five years. It will probably not be very wide of the truth to say that from the outbreak of the Civil War not less than one hundred and ten million dollars has been paid for this purpose. Of this eighty-five million has been expended by the people of the South for the education of the colored children and youth in the common school, and not less than twenty-five million by the national government and churches and people of the states that remained in the Union in 1862.

Probably no hundred million dollars was never expended anywhere with better results. Nothing that has happened south of Mason and Dixon's line since the foundation of the government has been honorable to the leading class of the South as the voluntary contribution of the eighty-five million dollars, under the peculiar condition of the American common school for the children of their former bondmen.

But, as a grim old railroad president once remarked to me, as he very leisurely extracted a five-dollar fold coin from his vest pocket as his contribution to my ministry of education, I don't take much stock in trying to educate two million of Southern children by passing round a hat." Our nation within a nation must realize, as its educated leaders everywhere declare, that the present condition of affairs is temporary and cannot be prolonged without danger of a decided reaction, not only among the benevolent people of the North, but from the roundabout common sense of the American people. The conviction is abroad, even in a more dangerous form in the South than elsewhere, that a people, eight millions strong, virtually the reliable laboring class of a dozen great states, which from a condition of absolute poverty in 1865, in thirty years has gathered together $300,000,000 of taxable property; the church property of one religious denomination amounting to nine million dollars; the majority of its intelligent, moral and industrial people to-day handling more money than the settlers of New England during the first half-century of their occupation; its average church and social gatherings displaying a better style of dress than entire classes of people in all the states; with the sympathy of Christendom behind it; should not so largely as at present rely on the prodigious system of solicitation that makes every Northern city from June to October a lively imitation of a new administration. Ordinary even "sanctified" human nature, cannot forever endure this tremendous pressure.

It is useless to ignore or in any general way to attempt to resist this impression, or to evade the danger of its becoming more influential in certain sections of the country.

The question comes louder every year: "Why cannot the colored people themselves do more to build their own school system, which is practically their one reliance for the training of the generation of their children now on the ground? Why do their people of means so often ignore their own public schools and spend their money on expensive schools and seminaries elsewhere, or even inferior schools at home? And why do so many of these more prosperous families compel their most valuable school men and women, who are needed at their posts of home service, to wear out their lives in tramping from the Atlantic to the Pacific and from the Lakes to the Gulf, beseeching the gift of student aid, which, if applied in their home common schools, would give an additional month of instruction to fifty children instead of supporting one Common school pupil in a "university?"

I repeat,—I see no help in this emergency save by a great revival in behalf of the common school among the colored masses of all these states. That revival must be led by the teachers and the educational public,—that portion of this people which appreciates the situation and feels the tremendous issues impending on the response to the demand. No political party in state or nation, no system of evangelization in any or all of the churches; no new departure of private benevolence can meet the emergency. There is no other way under heaven known among men" whereby this nation within a nation "can be saved"; as far as its salvation concerns its earthly destiny, except by a great awakening among these eight millions aroused by their own trusted and most influential leaders; not a revival that comes as a cyclone and leaves a spiritual wreck in its wake; but an intelligent, far reaching, practical awakening of whole communities, counties, cities, states; "growing while men sleep"; extending from commonwealth to commonwealth; giving the partisan politician notice to be "up and doing" and every enemy of the common school a "fearful looking for of judgment," until it compels the "power that be" to provide for the training of the young American Negro for the momentous duties already thundering at the door.

"The way to resume specie payments is to resume," said Horace Greeley while the statesmen at Washington were pounding their solemn brows over the financial problem of twenty-five years ago. Booker T Washington, after his own vivid practical manner of speech, has told us the way in which this work was done in one case:

"Ten years ago a young man born in slavery found his way to the Tuskegee school. By small cash payments and work on the farm he finished the course with a good English education and a practical and theoretical knowledge of farming. Returning to his country home, where five-sixth of the citizens were colored, he still found them mortgaging their crops, living on rented land from hand to mouth, and deeply in debt. School had never lasted longer than three months, and was taught in a wreck of a log cabin by an inferior teacher. Finding this condition of things, the young man took the three months public school as a starting point. Soon he organ organized the older pupils into a club that came together every week. In these meetings the young man instructed as to the value of owning a home, the evils of mortgaging, and the importance of educating their children. He taught them how to save money, how to sacrifice—to live on bread and potatoes until they could get out of debt, beginning buying a home and stop mortgaging. Through the lessons and influence of these meetings the first year of this young man's work, these people built up by their contributions in money and labor a nice farm school-house that replaces the wreck of the cabin. The next year this work continued, and those people, out of their own pockets, added two months to the original three-months school term. Month by month has been added to the school term till it now lasts seven months every year. Already fourteen families within a radius of ten miles have bought and are buying homes, a large proportion have ceased to mortgage their crops and are raising their own food supplies. In the midst of all was the young teacher with a model cottage and a model farm as an example and a center of light for the whole community."

In all save exceptional cases, at first by private contributions, and ultimately by some method of local taxation, it may be possible to extend the common school in the country and village of the South even for two or three months; put the school-house in better repair, insist on a more competent teacher, and generally to lift up the entire business of country school-keeping to an assured and progressive condition.

Nowhere in this republic is an able, religious, tactful, dead-in-earnestyoung man or woman so powerful for good as the thousands of teachers in the colored schools of the sixteen states once called the South. Any state association of colored teachers in five years could place their state as far in advance of its present position in the people's common school as it is to-day beyond the old field-school of the grandfathers.

Now, if any reliable or competent man or woman would appear in any metropolitan city of the North or South, properly indorsed and supported, bringing the "good news" that five hundred country and village common schools districts of the colored people of any of these states would, this coming year, by voluntary contribution, raise each the sum of twenty-five dollars that would furnish the salary of one good teacher indorsed by a principal of a state normal school for one additional month's instruction for its thirty to fifty children, I believe an additional twelve thousand five hundred dollars could be raised in a month and all these fifteen to twenty-five thousand pupils receive two additional months of instruction from a teacher who teaches and does not "fumble" with his little consistency.

This proposition is no visionary theory of my own. During my entire ministry of education in the South, since 1880, I have never asked a Southern community to do what many other Southern communities, no better off than itself, had not successfully done. Hundreds of district schools in all these states are thus being improved by the voluntary contributions of their own people, often assisted from without. I am convinced that if this method of local aid were organized and thoroughly tried, with the indorsement of responsible educators in both sections, it would become not only a success, but one of the most poplar methods of giving aid and comfort where most needed by the colored people.

There is yet another reason for the inauguration of this people's grand revival in the interest of the children and youth of their nation within a nation.

The American people's common school is a public university of good manhood, good womanhood, good citizenship in a republican government and order of society. It is from beginning to end an arrangement "of the people, for the people, by the people," acting through a flexible majority, for educating the children in the great American art of living together; each pupil acquiring the mastery of his own mental, moral and executive faculty in preparation for a responsible and inspiring career of full American citizenship at the coming of legal manhood or womanhood. Here the people organize, support and, through responsible officials elected by a legislative school board, teach and train their own children. The pupil is neither a slave under a schoolmaster, nor the subject of a government his parents did not create and control. He is a "minor" citizen, in training for his "majority" in a miniature commonwealth, whose "rules and regulations" are the laws enacted or approved by a popular body and administered by a teacher responsible to the people for every act within his jurisdiction.

Here for this time the child steps out from the limited and exclusive life of the family, where he is often the "all in all," into the broad society of a little republic where no superiority in the wealth, ability, culture, social, personal or public positions of his family tells on his standing among his fellows. As in his future life, he stands for himself and rises or falls according to his own personal merit or demerit.

Another superiority of the American common school over all its rival is that it is no less a seminary for the adult people than for the adult people than for the children. Before the year 1860 several of the states of the South endeavored to put on the ground the public school system for the white race devised by Thomas Jefferson, at the time of its publication in some ways the broadest and most enlightened that had appeared in this or any land. Although the South was not lacking in good scholars, farsighted educational statesmen, and an increasing body of superior people, who realized the peril to the lower class of its population from the illiteracy that like a great pestilential slough, there as in Europe, festered at the bottom of society, there was never satisfactory or permanent result until the close of the war.

All these interesting experiments were finally stranded on the most dangerous reef in the old-time Southern order of society,—the lack of efficient local government. The old-time system of government in the wide, sparsely settled district of a Southern county was at best a government at long range, always in danger of falling into the hands of a court-house "ring" at the country town; in many ways the feeblest possible arrangement.

The most beneficent and powerful influence was the social and moral power exerted by the superior families,—one of the ablest and best of the aristocratic families in Christendom, held together by one central interest, the preservation of the social and political order of which it was the head. This arrangement did good service through the first half-century transition period of the republic and produced a state of affairs that some of its literary admires even now laud as the golden age of Southern American society. There was little vagrancy, for the colored folk were under the strict police control of the plantation; the poor white man of the district was an easy-going dependent; and the non-slave-holding farmer generally lived in a different portion of the state.

Thomas Jefferson early saw the peril of a such a condition and urged Virginia to adopt the New England system of town local government, which in a modified form, was afterwards extended to the new Northwest.

But that was then possible. The coming of emancipation found the vast rural districts of this section almost destitute of local government, with the drift of the civil war and the criminal and vagrant class of its six millions of freedmen afloat; with no effective labor laws to protect the children from the ignorance or greed of the patent or the tyranny of the corporation; no efficient vagrant law to save the open country from the nuisance and peril of the idle, vicious, depraved, often fiendish tramp who wandered about at his own wicked will until he ran against an indignant man with a shotgun or an infuriated mob, too crazy with drink and revenge to await the slow motion of a trial in a court, where a swarm of furious criminal lawyers were bound to move heaven and earth in defense of the most flagrant offender.

A potent cure of this and other disorders of the present rural Southern society is the building up of a more efficient style of local government; so that in every neighborhood may be found a body of people accustomed to public activity and administration; not merely voting in a fiercely contested election, but making and administering public ordinances for their own protection and the development of all the conditions of a well-ordered state.

This course must be the growth of a generation. But, meanwhile, as by a special political providence, the beginning of this great movement has already come to the Southern people in the establishment and administration of the people's country and village district school.

This school, although a part of the educational system of the state and still to a large extent dependent on the state for support, is in fact a little republic set up in a limited area of territory through the entire vast rural domain of these sixteen states. Here the people may and often do elect their own local board of school trustees, who administer the school law of the state and supervise the school which contains a representative of every style of family in the district. The school house becomes a little state house, the one centre of the local public life. Every family that sends a child in interested in it as in no political party, church or secret society. The goings-on therein are watched as nothing else is watched in the neighborhood. Its teacher is the "observers." Every good boy is known and encouraged; every bad boy is "spotted"; every superior girl aspiring to the dignity of a school mistress is "booked" for Tuskegee Hampton, Claflin or one of the one hundred and sixty-two superior institutions where she may be educated into all of which she is capable.

The people, already possessed of additional public influence, will more and more seek to have their way in this great pubic function. Here they are trained to act together for the most important public interest, the education of their own children. The public life that revolves about the little school house is of the most valuable and stimulating sort. It need have none of the vulgarity and ferocity of partisan political contest. It can dispense with the sectarian fury and superstitious fanaticism that too often make a devil's normal school of a quarrelsome church. It steers clear of the bitter rivalries of social ambition; for the child of the humblest mother may become the foremost leader of his race.

What a people's university can this school be made! It is set up in sight of every man's door, always waiting to be improved, able by the self-sacrifice and enlightens cooperation of its families to become anything good they demand. It is the most radical and powerful training school of young and old America for the new republic that we all will face with the rising sun in the twentieth century. It only needs that the people of every school district in all these states rise to the occasion; take the schools into their own hands: if the legislature will not permit them under the law, improve it by calling in the gospel of putting their own shoulder to the wheel, turning their backs to the politicians and doing the work themselves. Nobody will care or dare to resist any sensible, practical, persistent effort of the people in any country or village school district in the South to make its school the best in the country, in the state, in nation.

No Southern Legislature will permanently refuse to come to the relief of a country school system when the people are straining every nerve to make the best of a hard situation and send up a plea to the capitol for aid and encouragement for the children. And, better yet, any people of any state in the Union that goes on educating itself after this fashion, in the self-helping American way of doing business, as it can in the management of the people's common school, will sooner or later become a body politic that no statesman, even the cross-roads politician, can safely offend or ignore,—a constituency that will know just what it needs, and just how to get what it wants, in the direct, peaceful, obstinate American way. A people so trained will vote, and be apt to vote right, especially on education, and that vote will be counted. And every aspirant "in a strait" for an office will look that way, and every patriotic and thoughtful man will rejoice that this glorious right of suffrage, given to our "nation within a nation," has finally become a public blessing, the bulwark of the children's right to education in the people's common school.

The colored teachers must become the leaders in the great revival of the country district and village common school. The young colored man or woman graduate from any of the superior seminaries of the race, especially if his instruction has been a reality and not a sham, if he really knows what he has studied and can tell what he knows, and, beyond his function as a pedagogue, has a broad and generous outfit of intelligent, moral and executive manhood or womanhood, at once may become a missionary of the higher Christian civilization to the entire community.

The colored schools of the Southern country and village need a larger number of well qualified women teachers. The colored woman seems endowed by nature with a genius and faculty for the care of children. Amid all the discord and mutual political defamation of the last thirty years, the first Southern man in his sober senses, is yet to be found who has presumed in public to raise his voice against his colored "Mammy." Repeat that venerable name in the Congress of the United States and a freshet of eloquence will burst all the barriers that even Speaker Reed could pile up, and a score of "great statesmen" will again become a mob of juvenile wildcats in praise of a loving black "mammy" who sunk herself so deep down into their hearts that she could never be forgotten. Now send the granddaughter of that woman of the old time to a good school; help her to drink deep from the fountains of the new education, and put her in charge of the children in the country school house; and there will come a revival that will blossom like the flowery April that reigns in glory in the opening Southern spring.

Of course a great need of the Southern Negro youth is a training in the new industrial education.

I say "new industrial education." For after a very practical and effective style the colored citizen of the United States has graduated with respectable standing from a course of two hundred and fifty years in the university of the old-time type of manual labor. The South of to-day is what we see it, largely because the colored men and women at least during the past two hundred and fifty years, have not been lazy "cumberers of the ground," but the grand army of labor that has wrestled with nature and led these sixteen states "out of the woods" thus far on the high road to material prosperity.

But the new industrial education places the emphasis on the last word: Education. it teaches that all effective work done by the hand is first done by the soul. It is the man that works the hand, not the hand that works the man. No ordinary system of labor, however plodding, faithful and persistent, can develop the resources of the least American state, unless it is organized, supervised and directed by intelligence, character and trained executive ability.

The state of Massachusetts, more than two hundred and fifty years ago, "started business" on the bleak north-eastern Atlantic coast with two ideas:

1. That every man and woman should "work for a living."
2. That every boy and girl should be sent to school. The little state "fought it out on that line" for two hundred or more years before there was within its borders what we now call a school of industrial training. But during this time it had raised up a dozen generations of people of more than ordinary intelligence and habit of work as "steady-going" and persistent as the procession of the he seasons and days and hours and minutes of the revolving years. To-day the new Bay State is one of the richest in the world. The average wage-earning in the Commonwealth, including every man, woman and child is 73 cents a day,—nearly twice the amount of the average wage of the whole country; and the state earns $250,000,000 per year in excess of the average earning of that number of the American people. And, beside this, there is no especial lack of all that characterized our higher American civilization.

This does not mean that industrial education is useless. Massachusetts was the first state, twenty-five years ago, to move in the introduction of industrial drawing into every common school, and she challenges the republic to-day for the excellence of her school of skilled industry and the various useful ornamental arts. But her example does remind some of our education that a trained mind, a solid character, an intelligent purpose and a determined will behind the hand, are the creators of all the genuine progress in the material development of the republic.

The especial problem of industrial education in the South is: How shall the vast majority of its colored children and youth who cannot live in cities and can attend only the country district or village common school for a few months in the year and a few years in a lifetime be introduced to the wide field of intelligent and skilled labor in its different departments?

It is so evident that we are almost indignant that any man in his sober senses fail to see it, that unless within the coming twenty-five years the young men and women of this race do take up the mechanical and operative occupations, as they have not yet, they will be first invited and finally compelled to "take a back seat" in the ranks of the laboring and producing class.

I have no question that the South has in its colored population the material for one of the most valuable operative classes in the world; a source of boundless prosperity in the development now awaiting it. What is needed just now is a little less newspaper "thundering in the index" about the vast resources of the Southern country to attract a rush of undesirable immigration from abroad, and a good deal more work put in on the practical side of education to bring its own laboring people up to their native capacity as the enlightened and skilled working class which the South now demands.

The colored graduates of the one hundred and sixty schools of the secondary and higher education in the South, if fitly trained, can be sent forth as teachers to the open country and village schools, where the vast majority of the children are found, and in numerous ways can awaken a great interest in all that relates to improved farming, house-keeping, economical living, mechanical training and operative industry. And thus can they explode the most dangerous public fallacy that still holds captive multitudes of well-meaning but ill-informed people—that the education of the masses is only another name for laziness and "big head." They can inaugurate a movement in thousands of rural communities that will crowd the secondary schools with students, well prepared by a good English elementary training for that union of a thorough academical and industrial outfit which will come like a fertilizing flood upon the open country and lift the people above the stagnation and discouragement that now broods over entire regions of the South-land.

The time has come when the colored clergy of the South should be called to the aid of this greatest of needed revivals. The history of every denomination of Christian churches in America proclaims the fact that that, in exact proportion to the revival of popular intelligence, good schools, improved industry and moral reform in the affairs of this world, has been the growth of "pure and undefiled religion." The old-time Congregational and Presbyterian clergy of the eastern and middle states of the Union, whose church polity carried along, as upon a strong current, the establishment of schools for the whole people, were the prophets of the prosperity, power and beneficent influence of these churches in the republic. The great revival of interest in popular education in every American church, at present, is one of the most hopeful omens of the future and largely accounts for the fact that the American Christian church as a whole to-day gives to the world the most reasonable, truthful, moral and spiritual interpretation of the Christian religion ever given to any people in any land since the great Teacher lived and taught in Palestine.

And while all this is coming to pass, let every man and woman of the race who seeks the ultimate and highest good of our "nation within a nation" stand fast in his or her own place and watch and pray and work for that "good time coming," which always does come when zeal is married to wisdom and "righteousness and peace have kissed each other" in any great effort for the uplift of mankind. Let not the young men and women waste life in reckless and visionary efforts, or in the attempt to carry by assault the venerable fortress of prejudice and injustice that can only be reduced through a siege of starvation by the grand army of children and youth which is now organizing and drilling for a final campaign of education. Man at the best is slow and obstinate; and the barbarism which is the growth of ages of human ignorance, folly and sin will only yield the gradual but irresistible power of a growing enlightenment, a broader justice and a more profound and comprehensive love. Horace Mann used to say "the difficulty with me is that I am always in a hurry, while God is never in a hurry." Certainly, on the backward look, this people, least of all, has reason to rail against Providence; for never in the world before was a community so numerous, in three brief centuries, so tided over the period of transition from the depths of human abasement to the summit of human opportunity.

It will not be through any crisis of violence and tumult and conflict of races, classes and nationalities that the grand army of the American people, 75,000,000 strong, will attain to its complete organization and be marshalled on the field to confront the united ignorance, superstition, shiftlessness, vulgarity and vice of the world on some perhaps not far distant, eventful day to come. All that can be done at present, in the unity and patience of wisdom and love, to lift the masses of our people to a higher plane of intelligent and skilled industry, better home living, economy, solid prosperity and a wider and loftier view of the life, through the entire range of agencies included in that greatest of all words, Education, will hasten the day of deliverance from every private and public hindrance to the complete success of any class of the American people.

Through a whole week before the battle of Sedan, which closed the dismal era of the despotism of Napoleon III, the different armies of the German powers were silently and steadily marching, each by its own most available road, toward the concentration of the hosts for the decisive conflict. If the leaders and soldiers of any special division had become discouraged and demoralized and gone tramping off on its own account, it would have come to grief and there would have been no united Germany and no republican France to-day. Happily each division of that mighty army, in good faith, marched by others from above which it did not understand, "trusting in God and keeping its power dry." And when on the final morning, the fog lifted from above the doomed city, and the hills all around it were swarming with the combined soldiery of the coming German empire, all men understood that the beginning of a new era for Europe and mankind was at its dawn.

Even so, whenever I "can get into the quiet" of trust in God and hope for man, do I seem to hear the steady tramp of the gathering armies of the republic that is to be; each still a "nation within a nation," but all under orders from the Captain of Salvation up in the heavens; approaching that union of races which shall make the real American people the chosen of God for the leadership of mankind through centuries to come. My prayer to God is that through no "invincible ignorance" concerning the past, no frivolity, no madness of impatience or failure in the common ways of life, this "nation within a nation" may be diverted from its providential line of march and be found wandering through unknown regions to its own confusion and the postponing yet farther the final destiny of the land we love. For this republic is the land that has led this people forth out of the wilderness; and its starry flag is the banner under which we all may one day find ourselves looking upward together, hearing once more the last word of our great commander, "Let us have peace."

Source: Boston: *New England Magazine*, 1897. Library of Congress, Rare Book and Special Collections Division, Daniel A.P. Murray Pamphlets Collection.

57. "Lift Every Voice and Sing," or, "The Negro National Anthem"

JAMES WELDON JOHNSON AND JOHN R. JOHNSON

This song, "Lift Every Voice and Sing," was first written, titled, and deposited with the New England Conservatory of Music sometime between 1897 and 1900 by civil rights leader James Weldon Johnson and composer John Rosamond Johnson. It was sung for decades well into the twentieth century and throughout the Civil Rights era of the 1960s, particularly at rallies and demonstrations.

Lift every voice and sing
Till earth and heaven ring,
Ring with the harmonies of Liberty;

Let our rejoicing rise
High as the listening skies,
Let it resound loud as the rolling sea.
Sing a song full of the faith that the dark past has taught us,
Sing a song full of the hope that the present has brought us,
Facing the rising sun of our new day begun
Let us march on till victory is won.

Stony the road we trod,
Bitter the chastening rod,
Felt in the days when hope unborn had died;
Yet with a steady beat,
Have not our weary feet
Come to the place for which our fathers sighed?
We have come over a way that with tears have been watered,
We have come, treading our path through the blood of the slaughtered,
Out from the gloomy past,
Till now we stand at last
Where the white gleam of our bright star is cast.

God of our weary years,
God of our silent tears,
Thou who has brought us thus far on the way;
Thou who has by Thy might
Led us into the light,
Keep us forever in the path, we pray.
Lest our feet stray from the places, Our God, where we met Thee;
Lest, our hearts drunk with the wine of the world, we forget Thee;
Shadowed beneath Thy hand,
May we forever stand.
True to our GOD,
True to our native land.

Source: New York: Edward B. Marks Music Corporation, 1949.

58. Commentary on *The Progress of Colored Women*, by Mary Church Terrell, 1898
RICHARD T. GREENER

The question of women's rights surfaced with great force in the 1850s, and the ranks of this movement for American mothers, wives, and sisters swelled rapidly. A woman who was called Sojourner Truth, and sometimes called the American Sibyl, was the only visible representative of the black women in the United States by the time the movement celebrated its 50th birthday. This article appeared in the newspaper *The Colored American*.

The distance from Sojourner Truth to Mary Church Terrell is really more than the forty or fifty years of fight for political recognition for women. It is an infinitely greater distance, almost limitless space, between the centuries of debasement and degradation of a sex, and the meteor's flight of education, purity, aplomb, rare scholarly training and literary culture.

The cold type cannot give to those who simply read the following earnest words, full of suggestive thought, of pathos and deepest reflection, that warmth and color which the occasion itself furnished—the brilliant setting, the *entourage* of intellectuality which made this the finest meeting of a most notable assembly.

Nor can the ordinary reader perceive the severity of the test, which set this champion of her sex, in juxtaposition in forensic art, with such war-worn and battle-scarred veterans, as Miss Anthony, Mrs. Blake, Mrs. Shaw, Mrs. Foster, and with the able and eloquent representatives of Norway and Sweden.

Never have I seen a more profound impression nor felt myself more stirred at the romance of the American negro as exemplified in the deeper tragedy of the negro woman, who stands today not merely the forlorn hope of the race; but in her achievements and her attainments, in her sorrows, travailing, and aspirations, the highest type of the race—the portion, psychologically and physiologically, upon which its future mainly depends.

That the opportunity was afforded Mary Church Terrell, to sound the note, and sing so strong, beautifully and pathetically the refrain of her struggling sex, is a source of extreme gratification to those of us, who well know her advantages of training, travel and culture: but even we were surprised most agreeably, and delighted at the able treatment and the signal success of her womanly exposition, judged by its cordial reception and its evident effect upon the audience.

Such occasions rarely occur in a race's history and it is no small privilege to be permitted, as I am here, to call attention to one for the history of the race, whose annals unfortunately are only too brief and at best most imperfectly kept.

Source: Richard T. Greener. *The Colored American*, Washington, D. C.: February 19, 1898. Library of Congress, Rare Book and Special Collections Division, African American Pamphlet Collection.

59. A Century of Negro Migration
CARTER G. WOODSON

In 1889, President Benjamin Harrison opened up the Oklahoma Territory to homesteaders by proclamation. Intense race prejudice by the white immigrants and the rule of the mob prevented a larger number of Negroes from settling in that promising commonwealth. This is a brief history of a period well into the twentieth century by historian Carter Godwin Woodson.

The exodus to the west was mainly directed to Kansas and neighboring States, the migration to the Southwest centered in Oklahoma and Texas, pioneering Negro laborers drifted into the industrial district of the Appalachian highland during the eighties and nineties and the infiltration of the discontented talented tenth affected largely the cities of the North. But now we are told that at the very time the mining districts of the North and West are being filled with blacks, the western planters are supplying their farms with them and that into some cities have gone sufficient skilled and unskilled Negro workers to increase the black population more than one hundred per cent. Places in the North, where the black population has not only not increased but even decreased in recent years, are now receiving a steady influx of Negroes. In fact, this is a nation-wide migration affecting all parts and all conditions.

In spite of these interstate movements, the Negro still continued as a perplexing problem, for the country was unprepared to grant the race political and civil rights. Nominal equality was forced on the South at the point of the sword and the North reluctantly removed most of its barriers against the blacks.

Source: Washington, D.C: The Association for the Study of Negro Life and History, 1918. Copyright © 1918 by Carter Godwin Woodson.

60. An address by Booker T. Washington, prin., Tuskegee Normal and Industrial Institute, Tuskegee, Alabama: delivered under the auspices of the Armstrong Association, Lincoln Day exercises, at the Madison Square Garden Concert Hall, New York, N.Y., February 12, 1898

On February 12, 1998, Booker T. Washington, principal of the Tuskegee Normal and Industrial Institute in Tuskegee, Alabama, delivered a speech under the auspices of the Armstrong Association, Lincoln Day exercises, at the Madison Square Garden Concert Hall in New York City.

At this celebration, Washington advised African Americans to get training and employment in industrial and agricultural sciences, because he believed that would lead to a sense of accomplishment, self-respect, confidence, and recognition of African American manhood and citizenship.

Not long ago an old colored man in Alabama said to me: "I's done quit libin in de ashes; I's got my second freedom." That remark meant that, this old man, by economy, hard work and proper guidance, after twenty years of severe struggle, had freed himself from debt, had paid for fifty acres of land and built a comfortable house, was a tax-payer, that his two sons had been educated in academic and agricultural branches and that his daughter had received mental training in connection with sewing and cooking.

With a few limitations, here was an American Christian home the results of individual effort and philanthropy. This Negro had been given the chance to get upon his feet; that is all which any Negro in America asks for. What position in state, letters or commerce the offspring of this family is to occupy, must be left to the future and the capacity of the race. That the race may have a new birth—a new freedom, in habits of thrift, economy and industrial development, I take to be the meaning of this meeting.

If this be true, I believe that the second birth, this new baptism of the race into the best methods of agriculture, mechanical and commercial life and respect for labor, will bring blessings not less than those given us by our Great Emancipator, whose birthday we celebrate.

Freedom from debt, comfortable homes, profitable employment, intelligence, bring a self-respect and confidence, without which no race can get on its feet. During the years of slavery we were shielded from competition. To-day, unless we prepare to compete with the outside world, we shall go to the wall as a race.

Despite the curse of slavery, during those dark and bitter days, God was preparing the way for the solution of the race problem, along the line of industrial training. The slave master who wanted a house built or a suit of clothes made, went to a Negro carpenter or tailor. Every large slave plantation was, in a limited sense, an industrial school. On these plantations, thousands were taught common farming, others carpentry, others brick masonry, others sewing and cooking. Thus, at the beginning of our freedom, we found ourselves in possession of the common and skilled labor of the South. For twenty years after freedom, except in the case of Gen. Armstrong, our patron saint, whose name will go down in history linked with that of the immortal Lincoln, we overlooked what has been taking place on these plantations for more than two centuries. We were educated in the book, which was all right. But gradually those who learned to be skilled laborers during slavery, disappeared by death; then it was that we began to realize that we were training no colored youths to take their places. Then it was that another race from foreign lands began to take from us our birth-right—this legacy in the form of skilled labor, that was purchased by our forefathers at the price of 250 years in slavery. That we may hold our own in the industrial and business world, we must learn to put brains and skill into the common occupations about our doors, and we must learn to dignify common labor.

It is an easy matter to project the mental development of a race beyond its ability to supply the wants thereby increased.

In all parts of the country there should be a more vital and practical connection between the Negro's educated brain and his opportunity for earning his daily living. In the present condition of my race, that knowledge of chemistry will mean most which will make forty bushels of corn grow where only twenty bushels have grown; that knowledge of mathematics will be most helpful that will construct a three-room cottage to replace the one-room cabin; that literature most potent which will make the girl the thorough mistress of modern household economy. The race sees it, the race wants it; you must "push the button and we will do the rest." All this is not as an end, but as a means to the higher life. It is beyond our duty to set meets and bounds upon the aspirations and achievements of any race, but it is our duty to see that that foundation is fitly laid.

It is a hard thing to put much Christianity into a hungry man. There is one thing in which my race excels yours; when it comes to thinking you can excel us; in feeling we can excel you. I would not have my race change much in this respect, but I would have the man who likes to sing, shout and get happy in church on Sunday, taught to mix in during the week, with his religious zeal and fervor, habits of thrift, economy, and with land and a house of two or three rooms, a little bank account, just as the white man does.

Industrial development, coupled with religious and mental development, will bring a change in the civil and political status of the South. And this, if for no other reason, should enlist the active aid and sympathy of every patriotic citizen in the North. Those who revere the name of Lincoln should see to it that we do not fail in the reaping of the full fruit of his life and martyrdom. In this matter let us take high ground. The Negro that has learned to respect a white man, is ten fold greater than a white man who hates a Negro. I propose that the Negro shall take his place upon the high and undisputed ground of usefulness and generosity, and that he invite the white man to step up and occupy this position with him. From this position I would have the Negro forgive the past and adjust himself to the present. From this position

I would have him teach that no race can wrong another race without himself being dragged down. So long as my race is submerged in poverty and ignorance, so long, as with hooks of steel, will we drag down and retard the upward growth of the white man in the South. If the Negro's degradation tempts one to steal his ballot, remember that it is the one who commits the theft that is permanently injured. You owe it, not less to yourselves than to your white brethren in the South, that this load be lifted from their shoulders. Industrial training will help to do it. Strike a common interest in the affairs of life, and prejudice melts away.

A few weeks ago a black man of brains and skill, in Alabama, produced 261 bushels of sweet potatoes on a single acre of land; twice as much as any white man in that community had produced, and every one of the dozen white men who came to see how it was done, was ready to take off his hat to this black man. Not a bit of prejudice; against those 261 bushels of sweet potatoes.

It is along this line that we are to settle this problem, and along this line it is slowly but surely working itself out. But let us not be deceived. It is not settled yet. A recent close investigation teaches me that in the Black Belt of the South we have not more than touched the edges.

Says the Great Teacher, "I will draw all men unto Me." How? Not by force, not by law, not by superficial ornamentation. Following in the footsteps of the lowly Nazarene, we will continue, with your help, to work and wait till by the exercise of the higher virtues, by the products of our brains and hands, we shall make ourselves so important to the American people that they will accord us all the rights of manhood and citizenship by reason of our intrinsic worth.

Source: Library of Congress, Rare Book and Special Collections Division, Daniel A. P. Murray Pamphlets Collection.

61. The Progress of Colored Women, 1898
MARY CHURCH TERRELL

In this document, an address to the National American Women's Suffrage Association at the Columbia Theater in Washington, D.C., on February 18, 1898, for its fiftieth anniversary, activist Mary Church Terrell recounted her role as the founding president of the National Association of Colored Women's Clubs, a confederation of black women's service clubs dedicated to instilling racial pride. This group's goals included improving social and moral conditions in the African American community, and founding settlement houses for migrant women, orphanages, day nurseries, kindergartens, evening schools for adults, clinics, and homes for the aged. People attending the meeting included activists Susan B. Anthony, Isabella Beecher Hooker, Rev. Anna Shaw, Lillie Deverux, Mary Wright Sewell, and Carrie Chapman.

Fifty years ago a meeting such as this, planned, conducted and addressed by women would have been an impossibility. Less than forty years ago, few sane men would have predicted that either a slave or one of his descendants would, in this century at least, address such an audience in the Nation's Capital at the invitation of women representing the highest, broadest, best type of womanhood, that can be found anywhere in the world. Thus to me this semi-centennial of the National American Woman Suffrage Association is a double jubilee, rejoicing as I do, not only in the prospective enfranchisement of my sex but in the emancipation of my race. When Ernestine Rose, Lucretia Mott, Elizabeth Cady Stanton, Lucy Stone and Susan B. Anthony began that agitation by which colleges were opened to women and the numerous reforms inaugurated for the amelioration of their condition along all lines, their sisters who groaned in bondage had little reason to hope that these blessings would ever brighten their crushed and blighted lives, for during those days of oppression and despair, colored women were not only refused admittance to institutions of learning, but the law of the States in which the majority lived made it a crime to teach them to read. Not only could they possess no property, but even their bodies were not their own. Nothing, in short, that could degrade or brutalize the womanhood of the race was lacking in that system from which colored women then had little hope of escape. So gloomy were their prospects, so fatal the laws, so pernicious the customs, only fifty years ago. But, from the day their fetters were broken and their minds released from the darkness of ignorance to which for more than two hundred years they had been doomed, from the day they could stand erect in the dignity of womanhood, no longer bond but free, till tonight, colored women have forged steadily ahead in the acquisition of knowledge and in the cultivation of those virtues which make for good. To use a thought of the illustrious Frederick Douglass, if judged by the depths from which they have come, rather than by the heights to which those blessed with centuries of opportunities have attained, colored women need not hang their heads in shame. Consider if you will, the almost insurmountable obstacles which have confronted colored women in their efforts to educate and cultivate themselves since their emancipation, and I dare assert, not boastfully, but with pardonable pride, I hope, that the progress they have made and the work they have accomplished, will bear a favorable comparison at least with that of their more fortunate sisters, from the opportunity of acquiring knowledge and the means of self-culture have never been entirely withheld. For, not only are colored women with ambition and aspiration handicapped on account of their sex, but they are everywhere baffled and mocked on account of their race. Desperately and continuously they are forced to fight that opposition, born of a cruel, unreasonable prejudice which neither their merit nor their necessity seems able to subdue. Not only because they are women, but because they are colored women, are discouragement and disappointment meeting them at every turn. Avocations opened and opportunities offered to their more favored sisters have been and are tonight closed and barred against them. While those of the dominant race have a variety of trades and pursuits from which they may choose, the woman through whose veins one drop of African blood is known to flow is limited to a pitiful few. So overcrowded are the avocations in which colored women may engage and so poor is the pay in consequence, that only the barest livelihood can be eked out by the rank and file. And yet, in spite of the opposition encountered, the obstacles opposed to their acquisition of knowledge and their accumulation of property, the progress made by colored women along these lines has never been surpassed by that of any people in the history of the world. Though the slaves were liberated less than forty years ago, penniless, and ignorant, with neither shelter nor food, so great was their thirst for knowledge and so herculean were their efforts to secure it, that there are today hundreds of negroes, many of them women, who are graduates, some of them having taken degrees from the best institutions of the land. From Oberlin, that friend of the oppressed, Oberlin, my dear alma mater, whose name will always be loved and whose praise will ever be sung as the first college in the country which was just, broad and benevolent enough to open its doors to negroes and to women on an equal footing with men; from Wellesley and Vassar, from Cornell and Ann Arbor, from the best high schools throughout the North, East and West, Colored girls have been graduated with honors, and have thus forever settled the question of their capacity and worth. But a few years ago in an examination in which a large number of young women and men competed for a scholarship, entitling the successful competitor to an entire course through the Chicago University, the only colored girl among them stood first and captured this great prize. And so, wherever colored girls have studied, their instructors bear testimony to their intelligence, diligence and success.

With this increase of wisdom there has sprung up in the hearts of colored women an ardent desire to do good in the world. No sooner had the favored few availed themselves of such advantages as they could secure than they hastened to dispense these blessings to the less fortunate of their race. With tireless energy and eager zeal, colored women have, since their emancipation, been continuously prosecuting the work of educating and elevating their race, as though upon themselves alone devolved the accomplishment of this great task. Of the teachers engaged in instructing colored youth, it is perhaps no exaggeration to say that fully ninety per cent are women. In the back-woods, remote from the civilization and comforts of the city and town, on the plantations reeking with ignorance and vice, our colored women may be found battling with evils which such conditions always entail. Many a heroine, of whom the world will never hear, has thus sacrificed her life to her race, amid surroundings and in the face of privations which only martyrs can tolerate and bear. Shirking responsibility has never been a fault with which colored women might be truthfully charged. Indefatigably and conscientiously, in public work of all kinds they engage, that they may benefit and elevate their race. The result of this labor has been prodigious indeed. By banding themselves together in the interest of education and morality, by adopting the most practical and useful means to this end, colored women have in thirty short years become a great power for good. Through the National Association of Colored Women, which was formed by the union of two large organizations in July, 1896, and which is now the only national body among colored women, much good has been done in the past, and more will be accomplished in the future, we hope. Believing that it is only through the home that a people can become really good and truly great, the National Association of Colored Women has entered that sacred domain. Homes, more homes, better homes, purer homes is the text upon which our have been and will be preached. Through mothers' meetings, which are a special feature of the work planned by the Association, much useful information in everything pertaining to the home will be disseminated. We would have heart-to-heart talks with our women, that we may strike at the root of evils, many of which lie, alas, at the fireside. If the women of the dominant race with all the centuries of education, culture and refinement back of them, with all their wealth of opportunity ever present with them—if these women feel the need of a Mothers' Congress that they may be enlightened as to the best methods of rearing children and conducting their homes, how much more do our women, from whom shackles have but yesterday fallen, need information on the same vital subjects? And so throughout the country we are working vigorously and conscientiously to establish Mothers' Congresses in every community in which our women may be found.

Under the direction of the Tuskegee, Alabama, branch of the National Association, the work of bringing the light of knowledge and the gospel of cleanliness to their benighted sisters on the plantations has been conducted with signal success. Their efforts have thus far been confined to four estates, comprising thousand of acres of land, on which live hundreds of colored people, yet in the darkness of ignorance and the grip of sin, miles away from churches and schools. Under the evil influences of plantation owners, and through no fault of their own, the condition of the colored people is, in some sections to-day no better than it was at the close of the war. Feeling the great responsibility resting upon them, therefore, colored women, both in organizations under the National Association, and as individuals are working with might and main to afford their unfortunate sisters opportunities of civilization and education, which without them, they would be unable to secure.

By the Tuskegee club and many others all over the country, object lessons are given in the best way to sweep, dust, cook, wash and iron, together with other information concerning household affairs. Talks on social purity and the proper method of rearing children are made for the benefit of those mothers, who in many instances fall short of their duty, not because they are vicious and depraved, but because they are ignorant and poor. Against the one-room cabin so common in the rural settlements in the South, we have inaugurated a vigorous crusade. When families of eight or ten, consisting of men, women and children, are all huddled together in a single apartment, a condition of things found not only in the South, but among our poor all over the land, there is little hope of inculcating morality or modesty. And yet, in spite of these environments which are so destructive of virtue, and though the safeguards usually thrown around maidenly youth and innocence are in some sections withheld from colored girls, statistics compiled by men, not inclined to falsify in favor of my race, show that immorality among *colored women* is *not* so great as among women in countries like Austria, Italy, Germany, Sweden and France.

In New York City a mission has been established and is entirely supported by colored women under supervision of the New York City Board. It has in operation a kindergarten, classes in cooking and sewing, mothers' meetings, mens' meetings, a reading circle and a manual training school for boys. Much the same kind of work is done by the Colored Woman's League and the Ladies Auxiliary of this city, the Kansas City League of Missouri, the Woman's Era Club of Boston, the Woman's Loyal Union of New York, and other organizations representing almost every State in the Union. The Phyllis Wheatley Club of New Orleans, another daughter of the National Association, has in two short years succeeded in establishing a Sanatorium and a Training School for nurses. The conditions which caused the colored women of New Orleans to choose this special field in which to operate are such as exist in many other sections of our land. From the city hospitals colored doctors are excluded altogether, not even being allowed to practice in the colored wards, and colored patients—no matter how wealthy they are—are not received at all, unless they are willing to go into the charity wards. Thus the establishment of a Sanatorium answers a variety of purposes. It affords colored medical students an opportunity of gaining a practical knowledge of their profession, and it furnishes a well-equipped establishment for colored patients who do not care to go into the charity wards of the public hospitals.

The daily clinics have been a great blessing to the colored poor. In the operating department, supplied with all the modern appliances, two hundred operations have been performed, all of which have resulted successfully under the colored surgeon-in-chief. Of the eight nurses who have registered, one has already passed an examination before the State Medical Board of Louisiana, and is now practicing her profession. During the yellow fever epidemic in New Orleans last summer, there was a constant demand for Phyllis Wheatley nurses. By indefatigable energy and heroic sacrifice of both money and time, these noble women raised nearly one thousand dollars, with which to defray the expenses of the Sanatorium for the first eight months of its existence. They have recently succeeded in securing from the city of New Orleans an annual appropriation of two hundred and forty dollars, which they hope will soon be increased. Dotted all over the country are charitable organizations for the aged, orphaned and poor, which have been established by colored women; just how many, it is difficult to state. Since there is such an imperative need of statistics, bearing on the progress, possessions, and prowess of colored women, the National Association has undertaken to secure this data of such value and importance to the race. Among the charitable institutions, either founded, conducted or supported by colored women, may be mentioned the Hale Infirmary of Montgomery, Alabama; the Carrie Steel Orphanage of Atlanta; the Reed Orphan Home of Covington; the Haines Industrial School of Augusta in the State of Georgia; a Home for the Aged of both races at New Bedford and St. Monica's Home of Boston in Massachusetts; Old Folks' Home of Memphis, Tenn.; colored Orphan's Home, Lexington, Ky., together with others of which time forbids me to speak.

Mt. Meigs Institute is an excellent example of a work originated and carried into successful execution by a colored woman. The school was established for the benefit of colored people on the plantations in the black belt of Alabama, because of the 700,000 negroes living in that State, probably 90 per cent are outside of the cities; and Waugh was selected because in the township of Mt. Meigs, the population is practically all colored. Instruction given in this school is of the kind best suited to the needs of those people for whom it was established. Along with their scholastic training, girls are taught everything pertaining to the management of a home, while boys learn practical farming, carpentering, wheel-wrighting, blacksmithing, and have some military training. Having started with almost nothing, only eight years ago, the trustees of the school now own nine acres of land, and five buildings, in which two thousand pupils have received instruction—all through the courage the industry and sacrifice of one good woman. The Chicago clubs and several others engage in rescue work among fallen women and tempted girls.

Questions affecting or legal status as a race are also constantly agitated by our women. In Louisiana and Tennessee, colored women have several times petitioned the legislatures of their respective States to repeal the obnoxious "Jim Crow Car" laws, nor will any stone be left unturned until this iniquitous and unjust enactment against respectable American citizens be forever wiped from the statutes of the South. Against the barbarous Convict Lease System of Georgia, of which negroes, especially the female prisoners, are the principal victims, colored women are waging a ceaseless war. By two lecturers, each of whom, under the Woman's Christian Temperance Union has been National Superintendent of work among colored people, the cause of temperance has for many years been eloquently espoused.

In business, colored women have had signal success. There is in Alabama a large milling and cotton business belonging to and controlled entirely by a colored woman who has sometimes as many as seventy-five men in her employ. In Halifax,

Nova Scotia, the principal ice plant of the city is owned and managed by one of our women. In the professions we have dentists and doctors, whose practice is lucrative and large. Ever since the publication, in 1773, of a book entitled "Poems on Various Subjects, Religious and Moral," by Phyllis Wheatley, negro servant of Mr John Wheatley of Boston, colored women have from time to time given abundant evidence of literary ability. In sculpture we are represented by a woman upon whose chisel Italy has set her seal of approval; in painting, by Bougerean's pupil, whose work was exhibited in the last Paris Salon, and in Music by young women holding diplomas from the first conservatories in the land.

And, finally, as an organization of women nothing lies nearer the heart of the National Association than the children, many of whose lives, so sad and dark, we might brighten and bless. It is the kindergarten we need. Free kindergartens in every city and hamlet of this broad land we must have, if the children are to receive from us what it is our duty to give. Already during the past year kindergartens have been established and successfully maintained by several organizations, from which most encouraging reports have come. May their worthy example be emulated, till in no branch of the Association shall the children of the poor, at least, be deprived of the blessings which flow from the kindergarten alone. The more unfavorable the environments of children, the more necessary is it that steps be taken to counteract baleful influences on innocent victims. How imperative is it then that as colored women, we inculcate correct principles and set good examples for our own youth, whose little feet will have so many thorny paths of prejudice temptation, and injustice to tread. The colored youth is vicious we are told, and statistics showing the multitudes of our boys and girls who crowd the penetentiaries and fill the jails appall and dishearten us. But side by side with these facts and figures of crime I would have presented and pictured the miserable hovels from which these youth criminals come. Make a tour of the settlements of colored people, who in many cities are relegated to the most noisome sections permitted by the municipal government, and behold the mites of humanity who infest them. Here are our little ones, the future representatives of the race, fairly drinking in the pernicious example of their elders, coming in contact with nothing but ignorance and vice, till at the age of six, evil habits are formed which no amount of civilizing or Christianizing can ever completely break. Listen to the cry of our children. In imitation of the example set by the Great Teacher of men, who could not offer himself as a sacrifice, until he had made an eternal plea for the innocence and helplessness of childhood, colored women are everywhere reaching out after the waifs and strays, who without their aid may be doomed to lives of evil and shame. As an organization, the National Association of Colored Women feels that the establishment of kindergartens is the special mission which we are called to fulfill. So keenly alive are we to the necessity of rescuing our little ones, whose noble qualities are deadened and dwarfed by the very atmosphere which they breathe, that the officers of the Association are now trying to secure means by which to send out a kindergarten organizer, whose duty it shall be both to arouse the conscience of our women, and to establish kindergartens, wherever the means therefore can be secured.

And so, lifting as we climb, onward and upward we go, struggling and striving, and hoping that the buds and blossoms of our desires will burst into glorious fruition ere long. With courage, born of success achieved in the past, with a keen sense of the responsibility which we shall continue to assume, we look forward to a future large with promise and hope. Seeking no favors because of our color, nor patronage because of our needs, we knock at the bar of justice, asking an equal chance.

Source: Washington, D.C.: Smith Brothers, Printers, 1898. Library of Congress, Rare Book and Special Collections Division, Daniel A.P. Murray Pamphlets Collection.

62. The Literary souvenir, Volume 1, 1898
MISS ROSENA C. PALMER, MISS LIZZIE L. NELSON, MISS LIZZIE B. WILLIAMS … [ET AL.]

This is a collection of uplifting essays that deal with the African American experience, written by various African American women. They cover a wide variety of subjects, including temperance, stepping stones to higher things, diligence as the secret of success, and a college education. These kinds of essays were popular, particularly in black newspapers, sermons, and other communications aimed at instilling racial pride in communities where such was difficult to uphold because society thwarted any kind of self-respect or positive images of the Negro in America.

VIEWS OF THE YOUNG

by Anonymous

To say that this little volume is issued to no purpose would be false. The reasons on the part of the collector are manifold and therefore must be abridged.

I. *A stimulus to the authors*.

II. *An incentive to the readers*.

III. *Godly inspiration to the learner*.

Read your own thoughts over and over and those of your race; read them critically. Make comparisons, as you read, with the thoughts of other men and others races, and the improvement will be well worth the undertaking.

Many are averse to the publication of their thoughts because of failure to cope with others, who have had greater opportunities and a more extended experience. To those it may be said that the extremely doubtful and unduly reticent very seldom accomplish much in this life. The young people who have taken the risk, and have launched upon the literary sea, ought to be encouraged by an extended patronage. We pray heaven's benedictions upon them and their efforts for good unto their lives, end.

Intemperance is the most fruitful source of domestic strife, poverty, immorality, degradation, disease and crime, and every Christian is bound in loyalty of Christ to discontinue whatever is ruinous to the bodies and souls of men. It is hard for those who are advanced in life to begin new ways. The power of habit is strong. How often have we seen or heard of the wine cup being passed in social gatherings? It is the cause of many a man becoming a drunkard. In like way women who have a mistaken notion about hospitality, or who from some inability are unable to resist the persuasion that drink is necessary to strengthen, fall into habits that are not ladylike. She whom nature and religion mark out as the children's truest and most unselfish guardian is thus unfit for a mother's place. Parents sometimes bequeath to their children a hereditary taste for drink. Intemperance destroys life. In many instances intemperate persons are often picked up dead. There is no doubt that the liquor they drank was the cause of their death. It is said that seventy thousand intemperate persons die annually in this country. On this account no insurance can be taken on their lives, When this command was given to all "Thou shall not kill," it meant that life should not be taken by alcoholic drinks just as much as by arsenic, opium or any other way. Intemperance violates no civil law, but is the means of self destruction. We should do nothing to injure our health. God forbids any practice by which moral nature is degraded. Gospel temperance therefore requires us to keep our bodies pure. Some believe that drinking intoxicating liquor is a "lawful indulgence." But there is no law for this indulgence. There is a law of gospel temperance which should guard us against it. Some claim that a drink of liquor makes one feel good, but I cannot see how that is, for some shout, sing, fight, and swear; sometimes they are often helpless and senseless. This feeling amounts to nothing. It would be far better if they would find some other way of feeling good. The work of temperance exists almost wholly among men. But women ought to engage in it, for they are the real suffers from intemperance. Whose heart bears the burden of sorrow when the intoxicated husband enters the home? She bears the burden of poverty and disgrace. For instance, see what a wretched home the intoxicating cup makes for women, when it should be the centre of every attraction, but is a scene of madness and cruelty. The intoxicated husband is often inoffensive and kind until he reaches home; then the reign of the demon of his crazed brain commences. His amiable nature changes to fury. Children flee from the presence of their father, often the whole family is turned out of doors in the night and women often dragged by the hair. These scenes occur among the rich in the mansions as well as in dirty hovels. Alcoholic drink is no respecter of persons. What would a man think to see his wife or sister drinking in company with other women?

Bible in the mother tongue, but one man Wycliffe. No learned society discovered America, but one man Columbus. No great staff of generals led the French forces on to victory, but one woman Joan of Arc. To no assembly of philosophers do we owe the existence of our Howard to-day, but to the indomitable will and untiring energy of one man, General O. O. Howard. The same thing is true of every great step in the progress of mankind. Step by step gradually they increased. It is said some men are born great, some achieve greatness, some have greatness thrust upon them. In this day few are born great and still fewer are those who have honors cast upon them.

There are more ways than one to step higher. From the instructions of nature within us we are obliged to love virtue, justice and morality, to conquer self and allow no passion to become our master, to keep in mind the words of Carlisle, "Remember now and always that life is no idle dream but a solemn reality based upon and encompassed by eternity. Find out your task, stand to it; the night cometh when no man can work. The present alone is ours to do with as we will."

With the sped arrow and the spoken word past opportunities come not back. We have no time to lose. Opportunity has hair in front, behind she is bald; if once suffered to escape, you can never overtake her. As we enjoy and welcome the seasons as they come and go—so let us welcome and seize every opportunity that presents itself. As the years roll on each year we are stepping higher. Thus far our step has been firm and steady; from 1885 to 1895 have we labored dilligently and earnestly and can we not make our step still higher? The great future before us is full of complicated influences, the great problems of the country are to be solved. Great dragons red with blood are already upon the surface of the waters. This is a crisis when we know not who our neighbors are. Inmates are treated as strangers, and friends as enemies. The ocean has an intimate connection with the progress of nations.

In 1492 there was a young sea captain of Genoa who had spent the early part of his life upon the waves. He was enterprising, and ambitious not to conquer kingdoms, but to discover new realms; his greatest foe was ignorance. It was thought that to comply with his request was not only a loss of money, but a loss of life. If a century later with all the blaze of art, science and learning, the most learned men ridiculed the idea of the earth revolving around the sun, how could prejudiced priests during the time of Columbus believe that the unknown ocean could be crossed and the voyage when made would open to them inexhaustible treasure; But all was clear to the scientific mariner. We are not always understood by those we labor to assist. All great movements meet success through courage and sacrifice. Personal security, individual liberty, and constitutional freedom have been attained through untiring effort.

"DILIGENCE THE SECRET OF SUCCESS"

By Miss Frankie L. Ellington

"See'st thou a man diligent in his business, he shall not stand before mean men, he shall stand before Kings."

As we look above and around us upon the blue vaulted heavens, the stars, the moon, the sun, and the myriad of worlds that move in their appointed orbits, we behold a scene such as the aged Kepler beheld in telescopic visions when he gave utterance to the imperishable sentiment. "O God, I think thy thoughts after Thee."

We behold upon the earth, the trees, the flowers, the birds, the ants, the rivers, the rivulets, and the rills that empty themselves into old ocean's arms.

As we gaze into the bowels of the earth upon the hidden secrets and treasures there buried in untold ages, even while the morning stars sang together, we at once recognize the infinite wisdom and industry which placed them there for the convenience, comfort, and happiness of man.

The diligent man has snatched the lightning from the clouds and harnessed it, he has scaled the mountain and levelled it, he has blazed the forest and there built mansions and temples of worship and established laws and governments. He has measured the starry vaults and computed their time and distance, he has delved into the bowels of the earth for coal, iron, marble, brass and for such secrets of nature that give to us to-day the natural sciences which have not only beautified and adorned man but have made the close of the nineteenth century the most brilliant in arts and sciences, even surpassing the literary ages of Pericles, Augustus and Elizabeth. The thought and literature of which have been admired and studied through the generations even to our own enlightened time.

Says the accomplished philosopher Locke, "If heaven were to offer me truth in one hand, and the search after truth in the other, I would prefer the search after truth."

In all ages of the world the dilligent man alone has achieved success for us.

In the language of Pope, "who would have pearls must dive below." And the poet Longfellow bears out this magnificent idea when he says,

"In the broad fields of battle,
In the bivouac of life,
Be not like dumb driven cattle,
Be a hero in the strife."

Life is a battle, a warfare, and he is most who achieves most. But let us ask here, who does not admire even now the writing of Homer, Virgil, Livy and others of the past, of Shakespeare, Milton and Cowper of the middle present, of Addison and Irving of the still more recent present? Burk once said. "What shadows we are and what shadows we pursue. This is agnosticism and against the real and true purpose of life, for,

"Life is real, life is earnest,
And the grave is not its goal."

The magnificent and permanent achievements of the nineteenth century are the results of enlightened efforts. The astounding inventions and discoveries of Edison alone in electricity which have added so much to the comfort and happiness of man, show that we should always be up and doing, for God alone helps him who helps himself.

The moral, religious and intellectual structure reared under the guidance of the sainted Allen who among all men irrespective of color can proclaim the fatherhood of God and the brotherhood of man is an indisputable fact of the secret of success for this grand old church.

The results of negro brain virtue and diligence extend from ocean to ocean and even into the islands of the sea.

We point with pride and satisfaction to Douglas, Langston, Price and Dickens who were the tribunes of the people and who have registered their names among those immortal souls who were not born to die.

After thirty years of freedom our people by thrift and industry have acquired five hundred thousand dollars in property; and they are distinguished as theologicans, physicians, lawyers and prosperous merchants, and in short they are worthily filling every avenue of industry which leads to fame and distinction.

"Let us then be up and doing,
With a heart for any fate,
Still achieving, still pursuing,
Learn to labor and to wait."
for dilligence is the secret of success.

A COLLEGE EDUCATION NOT BEYOND THE REACH OF THE POOR

By Miss Ruth I. Carter

Our country has so developed in arts, sciences and literature that it now possesses an abundance of facilities in its increased numbers of educational men and women, colleges, seminaries and universities, so that a thorough college training is now in easy reach of all people, the poor as well as the rich.

During the days of Washington, Franklin and their contemporaries, many hundred would have contradicted the statement that a college education is not beyond the reach of the poor; but the achievements of many poor young men and women have proven the assertion since to be true.

Even in the days of the fathers those who were poor demonstrated the fact that wealth is not the only important factor to insure a college college training, but nothing short of will power.

He who wills to learn and to reach the highest possible attainment in this life, even though he is very poor, yet blessed with good health, will not stop shorter than the top round of the ladder. Nothing is more admirable in man than an indomitable will to acquire a Christian education. Let such a one continue striking, he will sooner or later reach the desired goal.

When Waites McIntosh of Arkausas, a native of our own S. C., married he knew but little about, books the same being a diligent reader of the Bible. But all along he persistently vowed that he was going to be a man, and he continued to study and to know. The news came to us last June on a printed program of Philander Smith College that Waites was one of the College graduates for that session. In spite of obstacles he passed on.

It was not dress he was after but a fertile mind. The expenses in many of our Colleges are so little yet the schools are good, that it is needless for a person to try to frame an excuse. If he or she is healthy and strong and has the will, success is sure.

Many of those who have lived before us and *shook* the world with power and ability were those who were no better off than some of those among us whose intention is to stop school as soon as they finish a Normal education. Be this far from you, from any of us. The education of Normal graduates is so poor nowadays that they cannot be considered any longer up stairs or at the top. Truly there is room at the top. But that means beyond the Normal course. Look around among College presidents and professors, and you will find those who will be able to corroborate this fact that a college education is not beyond the reach of the poor.

They have swallowed the pill themselves, and while it was once bitter and undergoing the ordeal it is now sweet, for they are reaping the fruits of their labor and are able to get more of the necessaries of life and receive the recognition of those who are in high life and the best society. They demand the respect of the "rich and well-to-do" because of this acknowledged ability.

If we have a desire to doubt that a college education is beyond the reach of the poor, refer to such men as Franklin, Lincoln. Douglas, J.D. Whittaker, Arnett and our worthy president W. D. Chappelle, and others, whom time will not permit me to mention.

Benjamin Franklin was one of the poorest boys of his day, but his poverty was no excuse; his aspirations were lofty. He continued to press forward and at last made a mark. Before his death he helped to draft the Declaration of Independence. In his eighty-second year he was a member of the Constitutional Convention, and at his death twenty thousand persons assembled to do honor to his memory.

Our Lord and Savior Jesus Christ was born very poor, and wandered about as the poorest of men; and we see that his poverty did not prohibit him from attaining great heights.

Let us think no longer that a poor boy or girl cannot receive a college education.

When we see the eminence that has been attained by the poorest boys and girls, is it not better to be born poor? We will repeat that a college education is not beyond the reach of the poor.

FAME

By Miss Estelle Thompson.

Fame is indeed something worthy of praise, and he who has reached the top of the ladder of fame ranks foremost among his fellow men. Yet vanity is a great vice and enters as a detriment into that which is good. Men struggle continually for earthly fame, but it is only an unreal thing or a passing shadow. To obtain the top-most round of this ladder, some of us struggle continually the greater part of our natural lives, and when we look at those who are said to be at the top we find them still looking forward to higher things; thus we find it all vanity. Fame acquired by goodness is very naturally freed from vanity. We therefore should aspire to that fame which is beyond this life. That fame which is permanent and into which the vice of vanity never enters. Why should vanity enter into that which we cannot control? The most renowned characters presented us by historians have, in the twinkling of an eye, woefully exchanged places with the most secluded of their race. Those renowned for wealth have been reduced to pauperism, those renowned for deeds have allowed vice to enter into their inmost hearts, and thus totally destroyed every sentiment of good. There seems to be a principle within the minds of men that at certain stages of life seems to exert itself toward some effort of human greatness. If it were not for this principle we would, doubtless, be surrounded by a stagnation of things. We would not have perhaps the many improvements and developments that we see around and about us. But may it not be truthfully said that even in these things we might write in large letters "All is Vanity." For all these things and the earthly glory they create, as well as the inventors and discoverers of them, must pass away from time. Once an old baron gave a grand banquet. In the midst of the festivities, in the midst of the wine and the music and the gay garlands, he requested the seer to write some inscription of the wall in memory of the occasion. The seer wrote, "This too must pass away." And where are they tonight, the gay retainers of that festive hall? Like the blooming rose, like the waxen candle's light, they have all passed away from time. How foolish that men have hazarded their lives, sacrificed the comforts of their homes, destroyed the peace of their country, and ruined their souls to all eternity, and all for an earthly name. And what has it profited them? In many instances little good has been done. And again would I not be asserting the truth, if I should say, that men live more for an earthly name, more that they might get a great name, than for the real good they might do their fellow-men. And you will find on a careful search that this unrestrained principle, or inflamed passion, works itself into every phase of human society. We have all felt its withering touch. But what profit is it to gain a great name I ask? One says, It makes the world respect you, and people speak well of you, they praise you to the skies. Everywhere you will be called a great statesman, philosopher, a great inventor and discoverer of something that will be of great use to the present condition of things. That all may be true, but what real good is it to you, when perhaps, in principle and character you may be far behind the most humble whose life may be actuated by the proper motives.

WORK WINS

By Miss Ruth A. Croft

Nothing has ever been accomplished in life without an effort. That effort is called work.

The question arise, what is work? To work is to overcome resistance. There are two kinds of work, mental and physical.

If we attempt to lift a ton weight, no matter how we fatigue ourselves we can not move it. Nothing is won: but if we try to lift a ten pound weight we can move it without any trouble. Something is won: therefore we work because we overcome resistance. When we try to learn a hard lesson and succeed. our mental powers overcome the resistance and we have won it.

Mental work has given us our presidents, our statesmen, our orators, our preachers and teachers; while physical work gave us our carpenters, farmers and machinists: all of these overcame resistance.

Look at the farmer, the most independent of men. What gave him his independence? Ask him and he'll say *work.*

What won the American independence? It was both mental and physical *work.*

For instance, take our state, what gave it its grandeur? It was *work.*

No one can ever say that *work* doesn't *win,* for it has won us our education and liberty.

To attain to any degree of eminence it requires earnest efforts. Thriftless individuals enjoy nothing in common with other men, because they have not energy enough.

If we want to advance in our studies or attain to any standard of excellence of character we must work. If the farmer wants an abundant harvest, he must work, else he will have no harvest.

If a man would make himself a scholar he must apply himself diligently to his books, for he can gain no superiority without work, for "there is no excellence without labor".

The adage: "Labor and perseverance conquer all things" is true.

Many boys and girls enter school with the intention of finishing the course of study outlined, but fail because they are not willing to work and persevere that they might win the object of their hope.

Those who have risen highest in science, invention and literature are those who labor hardest.

"The hand of the diligent shall rule." Those who have done much good are the men who had to work despite disadvantages.

The world's history is full of the triumphs of those who had to fight from beginning to end for recognition. Burns, the poet, was a day laborer. Rare Ben. Johnson was a brick-layer. Andrew Johnson, president of the United States, was a tailor. These men dreamed of their future greatness and did not stop in their efforts until they won a name in the world. They willed success and won it.

Then, classmates and friends, the road to human success lies along the old highway of steadfast work and well-doing, and they who are the most zealous and work in the truest spirit will be the most successful.

Then let us apply ourselves diligently and ernestly to whatever we may choose as our life work; for we all have a life work to perform.

If we are forced by circumstance to earn our daily bread, let us use every moment at our disposal to enrich the mind and remember that work wins.

ROUGH GOLD OR POLISHED BRASS

By Miss Alice B. McLeod

In the early civilization, when man was searching for wealth, he found many metals, each useful in its own way, but the most valuable was gold.

In his search, he also produced brass, which though not so costly and beautiful, is very valuable because of its hardness and usefulness.

Gold in the rough is not very attractive, because it is alloyed with other metals which cast a film over its beautiful color.

We who know nothing of metals would pass a piece of rough gold by, deeming it not worth our attention. while to highly polished brass we should be attracted. We would grasp at it eagerly, thinking we had found the true metal, when in realty we had thrown that aside and taken brass. Then would the truism of this adage be seen.

"All is not gold that glistens." Only an experienced eye could see beneath that rough covering the wealth, and spy out in the other the dross.

From time immemorial, there have been characters of gold and characters of brass, but never have such good illustrations of brass been given us as at the present. Indeed it will be no exaggeration to say that the nineteenth century is the age of brass. You think me pessimistic, but, indeed I am not. I reason from facts. This is the age when brass commands the highest premiums in our schools, societies, and even some churches. This is the age when political schemes are used in the church to secure sacred offices. This is the age when people are going wild over shiny trinkets, not noticing the real worth. This is the age when no value is placed on human life; when men throw aside essentials of true worth and toil on in search of glitter; when our law makers are simply "Nominative, *I*; Possessive, *My or Mine*; Objective, *Me*."

I dare not, and do not say there is no good in this age, because there is, but the good like Belshazzar has been "weighed in the balances and found wanting."

Prospectors looking for gold have thrown aside huge masses of black ore as useless, and toiled on in search of glitter, when in reality the black masses were worth more than all the glitter obtained.

So it is in life. We have thrown aside as useless chances for doing good or making ourselves felt in the world, and when we think of them now we say, Oh! If I had only grasped those opportunities, how different it might have been. Then it is we realize the truth and bitterness of the oft repeated quotation—

"Of all sad words of tongue or pen,
The saddest are these, 'It might have been.'"

Our young ladies feel it a greater sin to break one of the laws of fashion or conventionality than to break one of the Ten Commandments.

The young men think glitter will take with us, the ladies, so they polish the outside, and let the inside remain brass.

The time has come when there must be a choice, and now, dear reader, which will you choose, rough gold or polished brass? Think not for a moment we object to polished gold for we do not. That is beautiful and precious, and we would rather have it than rough gold. It is only the tendency to esteem brass more than gold, that we object to.

Let us not only select gold, but let us *be* gold. Let us not polish the manners, and let the heart go unpurified. Let us not white wash the outside of the house, and let the inside remain filthy. Let us remember that, "man looketh on the outward appearance, but the Lord looketh on the heart"

Gentle reader, please keep in mind that you are a "part of God's great plan." As such you must bravely fight for right, and "do the duty that lies nearest thee." In so doing, thou wilt lift thy race to a higher plane of civilization, and at the same time prepare thyself for living.

"Be what thou seemest: live thy creed,
Hold up to earth the touch divine;
Be what thou prayest to be made:
Let the Great Master's step be thine."

"Fill up each hour with what will last,
Buy up the moments as they go,
The life above when this is past,
Is but the ripe fruit of life below."

Anderson, S.C.

THE BLIND POET

By Miss Lottie C. Brooks

"His life was gentle; and the elements
So mix'd in him, that Nature might stand up,
And say to all the world. This was a man!"

These words of Shakespeare, the great dramatic genius of the sixteenth century, tend so beautifully to illustrate the life and character of a pure and noble man, that we can truthfully apply them to Milton, *"The Blind Poet."*

Among the names rendered illustrious by intellectual superiority, of which the world justly boasts, his stands out conspiciously prominent.

It is said that no one is fit to estimate a great man who does not himself belong to that class. If this be true, how few would dare venture to judge *"The Blind Poet."*

This celebrated author was born of Puritan parents in the year 1608 in London. His father was a scrivener. He came of an honest and honorable line, and was distinguished by the undeviating integrity of his life. His mother was a noble Christian woman, highly esteemed and beloved by all who knew her.

Their home in the very heart of old London was the abode of plenty, peace, culture and piety.

This family engaged in conversations which not gossip; but such conversations as would tend to elevate and culture the mind, tempered by that sweet cheerfulness which made the poet's home one of happiness.

Great was the influence of his home life on the development of his genius.

Young John was the pride and delight of his parents, although he was reared with a sister and a brother. But well might such a lad be the pride of his parents. He was remarkable for his beauty, sweet voice, engaging manner, and his musical and literary tastes.

He must have inherited his physical, spiritual, and intellectual traits, as well as his tendency to weak vision.

From early youth he was characterized by a lofty and elevated mind. His scholastic education began early under the direction of his father. At the age of twelve he was sent to St. Paul's grammar school.

He was a persevering, ambitious young man. By the time he was seventeen he was fully prepared for admission to Cambridge College.

His true devotion to study was unabated. After having spent seven years of close application to study, at Cambridge, he received his degrees, not only for his scholarship, but for his character; yea, he moulded such a character, that as long as the world lasts, he will be looked up to as a model for mankind.

Having finished his college career he spent five happy years of leisure at his father's home. At that time, if Milton had but known his future, his years of rest and leisure would have seemed to him but an interlude in a life that was destined to know the stormiest scenes.

About this time we find our poet depressed with grief, his angel mother having passed into the realms beyond. He decides to spend several years visiting foreign lands, especially France and Italy. Before he had traveled very extensively, troubles arose in England and he, being true to his country, returned home at once to serve her.

But, alas, how true it is that some men are *branded* as disturbers of peace because they dare to think for themselves. Sometimes centuries elapse before their worth is appreciated. *Such* was the case of Milton.

But in his character we find the noblest qualities combined in harmonious union; his mind was continually fixed on the Almighty Judge.

About the fiftieth year of his life he had the misfortune totally to lose his sight which had long been in process of decay. He felt the full force of this calamity, as is shown by several pathetic passages in his later works.

In very early life Milton exhibited a turn for poetical display. It appears as though he gravely resolved to be a great man and achieved it.

Few will now question whether Milton should be assigned a second place among his poetical brethren. His works are the richest treasures of the kind our language possesses; unless an exception be pleaded for the works of Shakespeare.

Although his works abound in passages of the noblest poetry, he has an insight into the human heart which places him beyond all competition among the other poets. His poetry though lofty is wavering. Milton's poetry is upborne by the power of native genius, elevated by all that tends to give force and dignity to the mind, and holds on a steadfast course.

His Mask of Comus is a composition of itself sufficient to place its author at the summit of English poetry.

His L'Allegro, Penserosa and Lycidas are all written in such exquisite strains that though he had left no other monuments of his genius, his name would have been immortal.

Paradise Lost, his greatest work, was composed while he sat in darkness, and though it was composed at a time of life when images of beauty and tenderness were beginning to fade, he adorned it with all that is most lovely and delightful in the physical and moral world. It will never cease to be admired while the world lasts. It is one of the noblest poems that ever wit of man produced in any age or nation. There was never anything so delightful as the music of Paradise Lost.

It may be doubted that the Creator ever created one altogether so wonderful as Milton, taking into view his many virtues, his super-human genius, his zeal for truth, true piety, true freedom and his eloquence in displaying it. He stood alone and aloft in his times. His immortal fame is perpetual.

And in the words of Wordsworth,

"His soul was like a star, and dwelt apart;
He had a voice whose sound was like the sea:
Pure as the naked heavens, majestic, free,
So did he travel on life's common way,
In cheerful godliness."

IF CHANCE ELEVATES INSTEAD OF MERIT, A FALL IS CERTAIN

By Miss Ellen L. Knights
"All things on earth rise but to fall, and flourish to decay."
When chance, not merit, contributes to a man's elevation, his fall may be considered certain. Hence, whatever fortune has raised to a height she has raised only that it may fall. If a man has been elevated to the very pinnacle of fortune, his foundation is not solid unless merit was the power that raised him. The loftiest pine is often agitated by the winds; the highest towers often rush to the earth with the heaviest fall; the lightning most frequently strikes the highest mountains; and those exalted by chance are most liable to the strokes of adversity. Whatever height you may reach, have the satisfaction of knowing that you have reached it on your merit. The lives of those elevated by chance are one long sham,—a perpetual make-believe. They deceive the world so persistently that after having deceived themselves, they deceive posterity in their tombs. In days of yore people were esteemed in proportion to their merit.

But oh. what changes have been brought about by time. Each passing year robs us of a share of what we possessed. Talent, beauty and health,—the most valuable possessions of human nature all fall a prey to the ravages of time. How often do persons obtain wealth by mere chance, which they dared not even hope for. But would that they could exclaim like those elevated on merit, "I have gained the palm but not without labor." So whatever chance shall bring to you, bear it with an equal mind, for you cannot control the vicissitudes of fortune, and when your certain fall has come you will cry out "what have I done or where am I fallen?" Merit is the surest way of attaining honor. The general elevation of the inward powers of the human mind to a pure human wisdom is the universal purpose of education. Everywhere humanity feels this want; everywhere it struggles to satisfy it with labor and earnestness: for want of it men live restless lives and at death cry out that they have not fulfilled the purpose of their being. Let silence guard that height that has been raised by merit.

"Leave its praises unexpressed,
Leave its greatness to be guessed."

But take the wings of fancy and ascend to Fortune's height. There touch thy dull goal of joyless gray and while awaiting thy destined fall hide thy shame beneath the ground. *"I have gained the palm, but not without labor."* How sweet is the reward of labor. The earnestness with which we strive for it is but a light labor when we compare it with those of ancient times, for knowledge is no more a fountain sealed. Drink deep until the sins of slander, spite, gossip and emptiness die. What a grand satisfaction accompanies that one who can say that he is making his way through the world by the force of his own merit. A chance may either raise or sink a soul where merit is wanting and it lieth in a direction that may not easily be seen. Its work, therefore, is sudden. Merit works slowly and surely, laying first a solid foundation upon which it builds. One may say the simple fact that chance has elevated me shows to the world that I have undergone no labor because from the foundation of the world there has been a tendency to look down upon labor. Oh, would he only reflect! Without man's labor God had created the world in vain. Merit is that divine principle which has filled the earth with all the comforts and joys possessed by it, and is undoubtedly the instrument of happiness wherever it is found. Merit is gained by the co-operation of labor and intellect. Intellect is the head, labor, the right hand. Take away the hand and the head is a magazine of knowledge and fire that is sealed up in eternal darkness. For the height to which fortune raises one has no foundation. Therefore he may find himself at the very pinnacle of fortune, but a dreadful fall is certain. For as he did not rise step by step he will not descend in that way. Low, indeed, must be the state of that person who is content to drift through the world on chance, who has no ambition, no object for which to strive. Is it the end and aim of all humanity to accumulate wealth? How much greater, how much more lasting are the riches of the mind? If man were created for no other purpose than that of hoarding up treasures, then there would be no necessity for an education. But God bestowed upon him that wonderful machine, the brain, with the purpose that it should be trained and cultivated. We sometimes covet the height attained by others, but oh, could we see the foundation of that height! Let us then consider merit as the chief motive cause in a successful elevation, and leave success to set the seal upon height attained. Talent and opportunity may form the sides of the ladder on which we mount, but let the rounds be made of merit, that it may stand the wear and tear heaped upon it by the world. Let merit have no substitute. Let us take the eagle as an object of emulation and grow eminent by the power of merit. If you claim to have been raised to a certain height by the force of your merit, much is expected of you and much should lie in your power. While we may not produce the principle of merit, yet we may enforce the practice, and your daily acts will be seen registered that posterity may know that true merit will stand when chance shall have rotted in oblivion.

Source: Library of Congress, Rare Book and Special Collections Division, Daniel A.P. Murray Pamphlets Collection.

63. A Negro Schoolmaster in the New South, 1899
W. E. BURGHARDT DuBOIS

Scholar W. E. B. DuBois began his academic career as a school teacher in the hills of Tennessee 1885–1888). He had been a student at Fisk in that state as a young man. DuBois went on to earn the first Ph.D. ever awarded to a black man in the United States. This is his rememberance of those early years in Tennessee.

First, there was a teachers' Institute at the county-seat; and there distinguished guests of the superintendent taught the teachers fractions and spelling and other mysteries,— white teachers in the morning, Negroes at night. A picnic now and then, and a supper, and the rough world was softened by laughter and song. I remember how.

There came a day when all the teachers left the Institute, and began the hunt for schools. I learn from hearsay (for my mother was mortally afraid of firearms) that the hunting of ducks and bears and men is wonderfully interesting, but I am sure that the man who has never hunted a country school has something to learn of the pleasures of the chase. I see now the white, hot roads lazily rise and fall and wind before me under the burning July sun; I feel the deep weariness of heart and limb, as ten, eight, six miles stretch relentlessly ahead; I feel my heart sink heavily as I hear again and again, "Got a teacher? Yes." So I walked on and on,—horses were too expensive,—until I had wandered beyond railways, beyond stage lines, to a land of "varmints" and rattlesnakes, where the coming of a stranger was an event, and men lived and died in the shadow of one blue hill.

Sprinkled over hill and dale lay cabins and farmhouses, shut out from the world by the forests and the rolling hills toward the east. There I found at last a little school. Josie told me of it; she was a thin, homely girl of twenty, with a dark brown face and thick, hard hair. I had crossed the stream at Watertown, and rested under the great willows; then I had gone to the little cabin in the lot where Josie was resting on her way to town. The gaunt farmer made me welcome, and Josie, hearing my errand, told me anxiously that they wanted a school over the hill; that but once since the war had a teacher been there; that she herself longed to learn,—and thus she ran on, talking fast and loud, with much earnestness and energy.

Next morning I crossed the tall round hill, lingered to look at the blue and yellow mountains stretching toward the Carolinas; then I plunged into the wood, and came out at Josie's home. It was a dull frame cottage with four rooms, perched just below the brow of the hill, amid peach trees. The father was a quiet, simple soul, calmly ignorant, with no touch of vulgarity. The mother was different,—strong, bustling, and energetic, with a quick, restless tongue, and an ambition to live "like folks." There was a crowd of children. Two boys had gone away. There remained two growing girls; a shy midget of eight; John, tall, awkward, and eighteen; Jim, younger, quicker, and better looking; and two babies of indefinite age. Then there was Josie herself. She seemed to be the centre of the family: always busy at service or at home, or berry-picking; a little nervous and inclined to scold, like her mother, yet faithful, too, like her father. She had about her a certain fineness, the shadow of an unconscious moral heroism that would willingly give all of life to make life broader, deeper, and fuller for her and hers. I saw much of this family afterward, and grew to love them for their honest efforts to be decent and comfortable, and for their knowledge of their own ignorance. There was with them no affectation. The mother would scold the father for being so "easy;" Josie would roundly rate the boys for carelessness; and all knew that it was a hard thing to dig a living out of a rocky side hill.

I secured the school. I remember the day I rode horseback out to the commissioner's house, with a pleasant young white fellow, who wanted the white school. The road ran down the bed of a stream; the sun laughed and the water jingled, and we rode on. "Come in," said the commissioner,—come in. Have a seat. Yes, that certificate will do. Stay to dinner. What do you want a month?" Oh, thought I, this is lucky; but even then fell the awful shadow of the Veil, for they ate first, then I—alone.

The schoolhouse was a log hut, where Colonel Wheeler used to shelter his corn. It sat in a lot behind a rail fence and thorn bushes, near the sweetest of springs.

There was an entrance where a door once was, and within, a massive rickety fireplace; great chinks between the logs served as windows. Furniture was scarce. A pale blackboard crouched in the corner. My desk was made of three boards, reinforced at critical points, and my chair, borrowed from the landlady, had to be returned every night. Seats for the children,—these puzzled me much. I was haunted by a New England vision of neat little desks and chairs, but, alas, the reality was rough plank benches without backs, and at times without legs. They had the one virtue of making naps dangerous,—possibly fatal, for the floor was not to be trusted.

It was a hot morning late in July when the school opened. I trembled when I heard the patter of little feet down the dusty road, and saw the growing row of dark solemn faces and bright eager eyes facing me. First came Josie and her brothers and sisters. The longing to know, to be a student in the great school at Nashville, hovered like a star above this child woman amid her work and worry, and she studied doggedly. There were the Dowells from their farm over toward Alexandria: Fanny, with her smooth black face and wondering eyes; Martha, brown and dull; the pretty girl wife of a brother, and the younger brood. There were the Burkes, two brown and yellow lads, and a tiny haughty-eyed girl. Fat Reuben's little chubby girl came, with golden face and old gold hair, faithful and solemn. 'Thenie was on hand early,—a jolly, ugly, good-hearted girl, who slyly dipped snuff and looked after her little bow-legged brother. When her mother could spare her, 'Tildy came,—a midnight beauty, with starry eyes and tapering limbs; and her brother, correspondingly homely. And then the big boys: the hulking Lawrences; the lazy Neills, unfathered sons of mother and daughter; Hickman, with a stoop in his shoulders; and the rest.

There they sat, nearly thirty of them, on the rough benches, their faces shading from a pale cream to a deep brown, the little feet bare and swinging, the eyes full of expectation, with here and there a twinkle of mischief, and the hands grasping Webster's blue-back spelling-book. I loved my school, and the fine faith the children had in the wisdom of their teacher was truly marvelous. We read and spelled together, wrote a little, picked flowers, sang, and listened to stories of the world beyond the hill. At times the school would dwindle away, and I would start out. I would visit Mun Eddings, who lived in two very dirty rooms, and ask why little Lugene, whose flaming face seemed ever ablaze with the dark red hair uncombed, was absent all last week, or why I missed so often the inimitable rags of Mack and Ed. Then the father, who worked Colonel Wheeler's farm on shares, would tell me how the crops needed the boys; and the thin, slovenly mother, whose face was pretty when washed, assured me that Lugene must mind the baby. "But we'll start them again next week." When the Lawrences stopped, I knew that the doubts of the old folks about book-learning had conquered again, and so, toiling up the hill, and getting as far into the cabin as possible, I put Cicero pro Archia Poeta into the simplest English with local applications, and usually convinced them—for a week or so.

On Friday nights I often went home with some of the children; sometimes to Doc Burke's farm. He was a great, loud, thin Black, ever working, and trying to buy the seventy-five acres of hill and dale where he lived; but people said that he would surely fail, and the "white folks would get it all." His wife was a magnificent Amazon, with saffron face and shining hair, uncorseted and barefooted, and the children were strong and beautiful. They lived in a one-and-a-half-room cabin in the hollow of the farm, near the spring. The front room was full of great fat white beds, scrupulously neat; and there were bad chromos on the walls, and a tired centre-table. In the tiny back kitchen I was often invited to "take out and help" myself to fried chicken and wheat biscuit, "meat" and corn pone, string beans and berries. At first I used to be a little alarmed at the approach of bed-time in the one lone bedroom, but embarrassment was very deftly avoided. First, all the children nodded and slept, and were stowed away in one great pile of goose feathers; next, the mother and the father discreetly slipped away to the kitchen while I went to bed; then, blowing out the dim light, they retired in the dark. In the morning all were up and away before I thought of awaking. Across the road, where fat Reuben lived, they all went outdoors while the teacher retired, because they did not boast the luxury of a kitchen.

I liked to stay with the Dowells, for they had four rooms and plenty of good country fare. Uncle Bird had a small, rough farm, all woods and hills, miles from the big road; but he was full of tales,—he preached now and then,—and with his children, berries, horses, and wheat he was happy and prosperous. Often, to keep the peace, I must go where life was less lovely; for instance. 'Tildy's mother was incorrigibly dirty, Reuben's larder was limited seriously, and herds of untamed bedbugs wandered over the Eddingses' beds. Best of all I loved to go to Josie's, and sit on the porch, eating peaches, while the mother bustled and talked: how Josie had bought the sewing-machine; how Josie worked at service in winter, but that four dollars a month was "mighty little" wages; how Josie longed to go away to school, but that it "looked like" they never could get far enough ahead to let her; how the crops failed and the well was yet unfinished; and, finally, how "mean" some of the white folks were.

For two summers I lived in this little world; it was dull and humdrum. The girls looked at the hill in wistful longing, and the boys fretted, and haunted Alexandria. Alexandria was "town,"—a straggling, lazy village of houses, churches, and shops, and an aristocracy of Toms, Dicks, and Captains. Cuddled on the hill to the north was the village of the colored folks, who lived in three or four room unpainted cottages, some neat and homelike, and some dirty. The dwellings were scattered rather aimlessly, but they centered about the twin temples of the hamlet, the Methodist and the Hard-Shell Baptist churches. These, in turn, leaned gingerly on a sad-colored schoolhouse. Hither my little world wended its crooked way on Sunday to meet other worlds, and gossip, and wonder, and make the weekly sacrifice with frenzied priest at the altar of the "old-time religion." Then the soft melody and mighty cadences of Negro song fluttered and thundered.

I have called my tiny community a world, and so its isolation made it; and yet there was among us but a half-awakened common consciousness, sprung from common joy and grief, at burial, birth, or wedding; from a common hardship in poverty, poor land, and low wages; and, above all, from the sight of the Veil that hung between us and Opportunity. All this caused us to think some thoughts together; but these, when ripe for speech, were spoken in various languages. Those whose eyes thirty and more years before had seen "the glory of the coming of the Lord" saw in every present hindrance or help a dark fatalism bound to bring all things right in His own good time. The mass of those to whom slavery was a dim recollection of childhood found the world a puzzling thing: it asked little of them, and they answered with little, and yet it ridiculed their offering. Such a paradox they could not understand, and therefore sank into listless indifference, or shiftlessness, or reckless bravado. There were, however, some such as Josie, Jim, and Ben,—they to whom War, Hell, and Slavery were but childhood tales, whose young appetites had been whetted to an edge by school and story and half-awakened thought. Ill could they be content, born without and beyond the World. And their weak wings beat against their barriers,—barriers of caste, of youth, of life; at last, in dangerous moments, against everything that opposed even a whim.

The ten years that follow youth, the years when first the realization comes that life is leading somewhere,—these were the years that passed after I left my little school. When they were past, I came by chance once more to the walls of Fisk University, to the halls of the chapel of melody. As I lingered there in the joy and pain of meeting old school friends, there swept over me a sudden longing to pass again beyond the blue hill, and to see the homes and the school of other days, and to learn how life had gone with my school-children; and I went.

Josie was dead, and the gray-haired mother said simply, "We've had a heap of trouble since you've been away." I had feared for Jim. With a cultured parentage and a social caste to uphold him, he might have made a venturesome merchant or a West Point cadet. But here he was, angry with life and reckless; and when Farmer Durham charged him with stealing wheat, the old man had to ride fast to escape the stones which the furious fool hurled after him. They told Jim to run away; but he would not run, and the constable came that afternoon. It grieved Josie, and great awkward John walked nine miles every day to see his little brother through the bars of Lebanon jail. At last the two came back together in the dark night. The mother cooked supper, and Josie emptied her purse, and the boys stole away. Josie grew thin and silent, yet worked the more. The hill became steep for the quiet old father, and with the boys away there was little to do in the valley. Josie helped them sell the old farm, and they moved nearer town. Brother Dennis, the carpenter, built a new house with six rooms; Josie toiled a year in Nashville, and brought back ninety dollars to furnish the house and change it to a home.

When the spring came, and the birds twittered, and the stream ran proud and full, little sister Lizzie, bold and thoughtless, flushed with the passion of youth, bestowed herself on the tempter, and brought home a nameless child. Josie shivered, and worked on, with the vision of schooldays all fled, with a face wan and tired,—worked until, on a summer's day, some one married another; then Josie crept to her mother like a hurt child, and slept—and sleeps.

I paused to scent the breeze as I entered the valley. The Lawrences have gone; father and son forever, and the other son lazily digs in the earth to live. A new young widow rents out their cabin to fat Reuben. Reuben is a Baptist preacher now, but I fear as lazy as ever, though his cabin has three rooms; and little Ella has grown into a bouncing woman, and is ploughing corn on the hot hillside. There are babies a plenty, and one half- witted girl. Across the valley is a house I did not know before, and there I found, rocking one baby and expecting another, one of my schoolgirls, a daughter of Uncle Bird Dowell. She looked somewhat worried with her new duties, but soon bristled into pride over her neat cabin, and the tale of her thrifty husband, the horse and cow, and the farm they were planning to buy.

My log schoolhouse was gone. In its place stood Progress, and Progress, I understand, is necessarily ugly. The crazy foundation stones still marked the former site of my poor little cabin, and not far away, on six weary boulders, perched a jaunty board house, perhaps twenty by thirty feet, with three windows and a door that locked. Some of the window glass was broken, and part of an old iron stove lay mournfully under the house. I peeped through the window half reverently, and found things that were more familiar.

The blackboard had grown by about two feet, and the seats were still without backs. The county owns the lot now, I hear, and every year there is a session of school. As I sat by the spring and looked on the Old and the New I felt glad, very glad, and yet—

After two long drinks I started on. There was the great double log house on the corner. I remembered the broken, blighted family that used to live there. The strong, hard face of the mother, with its wilderness of hair, rose before me. She had driven her husband away, and while I taught school a strange man lived there, big and jovial, and people talked. I felt sure that Ben and 'Tildy would come to naught from such a home. But this is an odd world; for Ben is a busy farmer in Smith County, "doing well, too," they say, and he had cared for little 'Tildy until last spring, when a lover married her. A hard life the lad had led, toiling for meat, and laughed at because he was homely and crooked. There was Sam Carlon, an impudent old skinflint, who had definite notions about niggers, and hired Ben a summer and would not pay him. Then the hungry boy gathered his sacks together, and in broad daylight went into Carlon's corn; and when the hard- fisted farmer set upon him, the angry boy flew at him like a beast. Doc Burke saved a murder and a lynching that day.

The story reminded me again of the Burkes, and an impatience seized me to know who won in the battle, Doc or the seventy-five acres. For it is a hard thing to make a farm out of nothing, even in fifteen years. So I hurried on, thinking of the Burkes. They used to have a certain magnificent barbarism about them that I liked. They were never vulgar, never immoral, but rather rough and primitive, with an unconventionality that spent itself in loud guffaws, slaps on the back, and naps in the corner. I hurried by the cottage of the misborn Neill boys. It was empty, and they were grown into fat, lazy farm hands. I saw the home of the Hickmans, but Albert, with his stooping shoulders, had passed from the world. Then I came to the Burkes' gate and peered through; the inclosure looked rough and untrimmed, and yet there were the same fences around the old farm save to the left, where lay twenty-five other acres. And lo! the cabin in the hollow had climbed the hill and swollen to a half-finished six-room cottage.

The Burkes held a hundred acres, but they were still in debt. Indeed, the gaunt father who toiled night and day would scarcely be happy out of debt, being so used to it. Some day he must stop, for his massive frame is showing decline. The mother wore shoes, but the lionlike physique of other days was broken. The children had grown up. Rob, the image of his father, was loud and rough with laughter. Birdie, my school baby of six, had grown to a picture of maiden beauty, tall and tawny. "Edgar is gone," said the mother, with head half bowed,—"gone to work in Nashville; he and his father couldn't agree."

Little Doc, the boy born since the time of my school, took me horseback down the creek next morning toward Farmer Dowell's. The road and the stream were battling for mastery, and the stream had the better of it. We splashed and waded, and the merry boy, perched behind me, chattered and laughed. He showed me where Simon Thompson had bought a bit of ground and a home; but his daughter Lana, a plump, brown, slow girl, was not there. She had married a man and a farm twenty miles away. We wound on down the stream till we came to a gate that I did not recognize, but the boy insisted that it was "Uncle Bird's." The farm was fat with the growing crop. In that little valley was a strange stillness as I rode up; for death and marriage had stolen youth, and left age and childhood there. We sat and talked that night, after the chores were done. Uncle Bird was grayer, and his eyes did not see so well, but he was still jovial. We talked of the acres bought,—one hundred and twenty-five,—of the new guest chamber added, of Martha's marrying. Then we talked of death: Fanny and Fred were gone; a shadow hung over the other daughter, and when it lifted she was to go to Nashville to school. At last we spoke of the neighbors, and as night fell Uncle Bird told me how, on a night like that, 'Thenie came wandering back to her home over yonder, to escape the blows of her husband. And next morning she died in the home that her little bow-legged brother, working and saving, had bought for their widowed mother.

My journey was done, and behind me lay hill and dale, and Life and Death. How shall man measure Progress there where the dark-faced Josie lies? How many heartfuls of sorrow shall balance a bushel of wheat? How hard a thing is life to the lowly, and yet how human and real! And all this life and love and strife and failure,—is it the twilight of nightfall or the flush of some faint-dawning day?

Thus sadly musing, I rode to Nashville in the Jim Crow car.

Source: Atlantic Monthly, New York, 1899, Volume 83: pp. 99–104. Copyright © 1999, by the Rector and Visitors of the University of Virginia. Courtesy of The University of Virginia Library.

64. A prayer: words by B. G. Brawley, music by Arthur Hilton Ryder, 1899

B.G. Brawley, a student at Atlanta Baptist College, composed this short prayer in response to racial troubles in Georgia in 1899.

With dignity.

1. Lord God, to whom our fathers pray'd
To whom they did not pray in vain,
And who for them assurance made,
Though oft repeated their refrain.
Hope of our race, again we cry.
Draw near and help us, lest we die.

2 The battle rages fierce and long,
The wicked seem to triumph still;
Yet all things to the Lord belong,
And all must bow beneath His will.
Lord God of old, again we cry,
Draw near and help us, lest we die.

3 If brooding o'er the wrongs we grieve,
Our hearts forget to turn to Thee;
Or if they e'er do not believe
That Thou in time hear our plea,
Hope of our race, stand by us then.
And help us "quit ourselves like men."

4 As now we bend before Thy throne,
Upon us send Thy truth and light;

From us all other hopes are flown-
We pray Thee, help us in the right.
Father of lights, Thy mercy send
Upon us, as we lowly bend.

5 Lord God, we pray Thee help us all
To live in harmony and peace;
Help us to listen to Thy call,
And from all evil-doing cease.
Hope of our people, hear our cry;
Draw near and help us, lest we die.

Source: Atlanta: Atlanta Baptist College Press, 1899. Library of Congress, Rare Book and Special Collections Division, Daniel A.P. Murray Pamphlets Collection.

65. The Hardwick Bill: an interview in the Atlanta Constitution, 1900
BOOKER T. WASHINGTON

This interview of Booker T. Washington in the Atlanta Constitution illustrates Washington's eloquent demeanor in his response to the defeat of the Hardwick Bill, a bill that would have allowed the disenfranchisement of Negroes. He respectfully addresses the intellect of all Southerners, black and white in this brief interview.

The Hardwick Bill was a measure introduced in the Georgia legislature for the purpose of disfranchising the colored people. While this Bill was before the Legislature, Principal Booker T. Washington gave the following interview to the Atlanta Constitution. The Bill was defeated in the Legislature, receiving only 3 votes in its favor in the lower House where it was introduced and 137 votes being cast against it.

Professor Booker T. Washington, the head of the famous industrial school for colored youths at Tuskegee, and probably the foremost man of his race today, gave his views on the question of franchise restriction to a representative of the Constitution yesterday. Professor Washington spent the day in the city, having come here on business. When asked for an expression on the Hardwick bill, he said that he did not care to discuss that or any other specific measure, but on the subject of an educational qualification restricting the ballot to the intelligence of the country, he had very decided views.

"I dread the idea of seeming to intrude my views too often upon the public," said Professor Washington, "but I feel that I can speak very frankly upon this subject, because I am speaking to the south and southern people. It has been my experience that when our southern people are convinced that one speaks from the heart and tries to speak that which he feels is for the permanent good of both races, he is always accorded a respectful hearing. No possible influence could tempt me to say that which I thought would tend merely to stir up strife or to induce my own people to return to the old time method of political agitation rather than give their time, as most of them are now doing, to the more fundamental principles of citizenship, education, industry and prosperity.

"The question of the rights and elevation of the negro is not left almost wholly to the south, as it has been long pleaded should be done," added Professor Washington. "The south has over and over said to the north and her representatives have repeated it in congress, that if the north and the federal government would hands off, the south would deal justly and fairly with the negro. The prayer of the south has been almost wholly answered. The world is watching the south as it has never done before. "Not only have the north and the federal congress practically agreed to leave the matter of the negro's citizenship in the hands of the south, but many conservative and intelligent negroes in recent years have advised the negro to cast his lot more closely with the southern white man and to cease a continued senseless opposition to his interests. This policy has gained ground to such an extent that the white man controls practically every state and every country and township in the south.

"There is a feeling of friendship and mutual confidence growing between the two races that is most encouraging. But in the midst of this condition of things one is surprised and almost astounded at the measures being introduced and passed by the various law-making bodies of the southern states. What is the object of the election laws? Since there is white domination throughout the south, there can be but one object in the passing of these laws—to disfranchise the negro. At the present time the south has a great opportunity as well as responsibility. Will she shirk this opportunity or will she look matters in the face and grapple with it bravely, taking the negro by the hand and seeking to lift him up to the point where he will be prepared for citizenship? None of the laws passed by any southern state, or that are now pending, will do this. These new laws will simply change the form of the present bad election system and widen the breach between the two races, when we might, by doing right, cement the friendship between them.

"To pass an election law with an understanding clause simply means that some individual will be tempted to perjure his soul and degrade his whole life by deciding in too many cases that the negro does not "understand" the constitution and that a white man, even though he be an ignorant white foreigner with but recently acquired citizenship does "understand" it. In a recent article President Hadley, of Yale university, covers the whole truth when he says "We cannot make a law which shall allow the right exercise of a discretionary power and prohibit its wrong use." The 'understanding' clause may serve to keep negroes from voting, but the time will come when it will also be used to keep white men from voting if any number of them disagree with the election officer who holds the discretionary power. "While discussing this matter, it would be unfair to the white people of the south and to my race if I were not perfectly frank. What interpretation does the outside world and the negro put upon these 'understanding' clauses? Either that they are meant to leave a loophole so that the ignorant white man can vote or to prevent the educated negro from voting. If this interpretation is correct in either case the law is unjust. It is unjust to the white man because it takes away from him the incentive to prepared himself to become an intelligent voter. It is unjust to the negro because it makes him feel that no matter how well he prepared himself in education for voting he will be refused a vote through the operation of the 'understanding' clause.

"And what is worse this treatment will keep alive in the negro breast the feeling that he is being wrongfully treated by the southern white man and therefore he ought to vote against him, whereas with just treatment the years will not be many before a large portion of the colored people will be willing to vote with the southern white people. "Then again I believe that such laws put our southern white people in a false position. I cannot think that there is any large number of white people in the south who are so ignorant or so poor that they cannot get education and property enough that will enable them to stand the test by the side of the negro in these respects. I do not believe that these white people want it continually advertised to the world that some special law must be passed by which they will seem to be given an unfair advantage over the negro by reason of their ignorance or poverty. "It is unfair to blame the negro for not preparing himself for citizenship by acquiring intelligence and then when he does get education and property to pass a law that can be so operated as to prevent him from being a citizen even though he may be a large tax payer. The southern white people have reached the point where they can afford to be just and generous; where there will be nothing to hide and nothing to explain. It is an easy matter, requiring little thought, generosity or statesmanship to push a weak man down when he is struggling to get up. Any one can do that. Greatness, generosity, statesmanship are shown in stimulating, encouraging every individual in the body politic to make of himself the most useful, intelligent and patriotic citizen possible. Take from the negro all incentive to make himself and children useful property-holding citizens and can any one blame him for becoming a beast capable of committing any crime?

"I have the greatest sympathy with the south in its efforts to find a way out of present difficulties, but I do not want to see the south tie its self to a body a of death. No form of repression will help matters. Spain tried that for 400 years and was the loser. There is one, and but one way out of our present difficulties and that is the right way. All else but right will fail. We must face the fact that the tendency of the world is forward and not backward. That all civilized countries are growing in the direction of giving liberty to their citizens, not withholding it. Slavery ceased because it was opposed to the progress of both races and so all form of repression, will fail-must fail-in the long run. Whenever a change is thought necessary to be made in the fundamental law of the states, as Governor Candler says in his recent message: "The man who is virtuous and intelligent, however poor or humble; or of whatever race or color, may be safely intrusted with the ballot."

"And as the recent industrial convention at Huntsville, Ala., composed of the best brains of the white south puts it: "To move the race problem from the domain of politics, where it has so long and seriously vexed the industrial progress of the south, we recommend to the several states of the south the adoption of an intelligent standard of citizenship that will equally apply to black and white alike.' We must depend upon the mental, industrial and moral elevation of all the people to bring relief. The history of the world proves that there is no other safe cure. We may find a way to stop the negro from selling his vote, but what about the conscience of the man who buys his vote? We must go to the bottom of the evil.

"Our southern states cannot afford to have suspicion of evil intention resting upon them. It not only will hurt them morally, but financially.

"In conclusion let me add that the southern states owe it to themselves not to pass unfair election laws because it is against the constitution of the United States and each state is under a solemn obligation that every citizen, regardless of color, shall be given the full protection of the laws. No state can make a law that can be so interpreted to mean one thing when applied to the black man and another when applied to a white man, without disregarding the constitution of the United States. In the second place, unfair election laws in the long run, I repeat, will injure the white man more than the negro, such laws will not only disfranchise the negro, but the white man as well.

"The history of the country shows that in those states where the election laws are most just, there you will find the most wealth, the most intelligence and the smallest percentage of crime. The best element of white people in the south are not in favor of oppressing the negro, they want to help him up, but they are sometimes mistaken as to the best method of doing this. "While I have spoken very plainly, I do not believe that any one will misinterpret my motives. I am not in politics per se, nor do I intend to be, neither would I encourage my people to become mere politicians, but the question I have been discussing strikes at the very fundamental principles of citizenship."—Atlanta Constitution

Source: Tuskegee, Ala.: Tuskegee Institute Steam Print., 1900. Library of Congress, Rare Book and Special Collections Division, Daniel A.P. Murray Pamphlets Collection.

66. Nineteenth annual report of the principal of the Tuskegee Normal and Industrial Institute, Tuskegee, Alabama, for the year ending May 31, 1900, submitted by Booker T. Washington

In this annual report, founder Booker T. Washington provided information on the national figures that had been involved with the Tuskegee Institute[GIVE DESCRIPTOR]. He stated that "the chief value of industrial education is to give to the students habits of industry, thrift, economy, and an idea of the dignity of labour."

FORM OF BEQUEST

I give and devise to the Trustees of the Tuskegee Normal and Industrial Institute, Tuskegee, Alabama, the sum of dollars, payable, etc.

To The Trustees Of The Tuskegee Normal And Industrial Institute:

Gentlemen.—there has not been a year since freedom came to the Negro, that has witnessed such widespread discussion, both North and South, of all phases of his condition, as the present one. I cannot rid myself of the feeling that much, if not all of this discussion, is going to prove most helpful to the Negro's education and general development.

I am of the opinion that there is more thoughtful interest in the Negro at the present time, than has ever existed. The mere spasmodic and sentimental interest in him has been, in a large degree, replaced by the more substantial, thoughtful kind, based upon a comprehension of the facts.

One is often surprised at the misleading and unfounded statements made regarding the progress of the Negro, but these very exaggerations serve a good purpose in causing individuals to seek facts for themselves.

The Value and For example, I have recently seen a statement going Purpose of going the rounds of the press, to the effect that out of Industrial of 1,200 students educated at industrial schools, only twelve Education. were farming, and three working at the trades for which they were educated. Whether the Tuskegee Institute was included in this list, I do not know.

It is to be regretted that those who presume to speak with authority on the advancement of the Negro, do not in more cases actually visit him, where they can see his better life. Few of the people who make discouraging statements regarding him, have ever taken the trouble to inspect his home life, his school life, his church life, or his business or industrial life. It is always misleading to judge any race or community by its worst. The Negro race should, like other races, be judged by its best types, rather than by its worst.

Any one who judges of the value of industrial education by the mere number who actually follow the industry or trade learned at a school, makes a mistake. One might as well judge of the value of arithmetic by the number of people who spend their time after leaving school, in working out problems in arithmetic.

The chief value of industrial education is to give to the students habits of industry, thrift, economy and an idea of the dignity of labour. But in addition to this, in the present economic condition of the colored people, it is most important that a very large proportion of those trained in such institutions as this, actually spend their time at industrial occupations. Let us value the work of Tuskegee by this test: On January 10th of this school year, we dedicated the Slater-Armstrong Memorial Trades' Building. This building is in the form of a double Greek cross and, in its main dimension, is 283 × 315 feet, and is two stories high. The plans of this building were drawn by our instructor in mechanical drawing, a colored man. Eight hundred thousand bricks were required to construct it, and every one of them was manufactured by our students, while learning the trade of brickmaking. All the bricks were laid into the building by students who were being taught the trade of brickmasonry. The plastering, carpentry work, painting and tin-roofing, were done by students while learning these trades. The whole number of students who received training on this building alone was about one hundred and ninety-six. It is to be lighted by electricity and all the electric fixtures are being put in by students who are learning electrical engineering. The power to operate the machinery in this building comes from a one hundred and twenty-five horse power engine and a seventy-five horse-power boiler. All this machinery is not only operated by students who are learning the trade of steam engineering, but was installed by students under the guidance of their instructor.

Let us take another example, that of agriculture: Our students actually cultivate every day, seven hundred acres of land, while studying agriculture. The students studying dairying, actually milk and care for seventy-five milch cows daily. Besides, they, of course, take care of the dairy products. All of this is done while learning the industry of dairying. The whole number of students receiving instruction in the divisions of Agriculture and Dairying the past year, is one hundred and forty-two.

The students who are receiving training in farming, have cared for six hundred and nineteen head of hogs this year, and so, I could go on and give not theory, nor hearsay, but actual facts, gleaned from all the departments of the school.

It does not look reasonable that, of all the large number of graduate students engaged upon the farms and in the diary, only about one per cent, should make any practical use of their trades. But this is not the fact. The best place to get a true estimate of an individual is at his home. The same is true of an institution. Let us take for example, Macon Country, Alabama, in which the Tuskegee Institute is located. By a careful investigation, it is found that there are not less than thirty-five graduates and former students in Macon Country and the town of Tuskegee alone who are working at trades or industries which they learned at this institution. At the present time, a large, two-story brick building is going up in the town of Tuskegee that is to be used as a store. In the first place, the store is owned by a graduate of this institution. From the making of the brick to the completion of all the details of this building, the work is being done by graduates or former students of this school; and so the examples could be multiplied. Following the graduates and former students into the outer world, the record is as follows: A careful examination shows that at least three-fourths of them are actually using ... the industrial knowledge which they gained here. Even those who do not use this knowledge in making a living, use it as housekeepers in their private homes, and those who teach in the public schools, either directly or indirectly, use it in helping their pupils.

Aside from all that I have said, it must be kept in mind that the whole subject of industrial training on any large and systematic scale is new, and besides, is confined to a very few institutions in the South. Industrial training could not be expected to revolutionize the progress of a race within ten or fifteen years. At the present time the call for graduates from this institution to take positions as instructors of industries in other smaller institutions, as well as in city schools, is so urgent and constant that many of our graduates who would work independently at their trades, are not permitted to do so. In fact, one of the most regretful things in connection with our whole work, is that the calls for our graduates are so many more than we can supply. As the demand for instructors in industrial branches of various schools becomes supplied, a still larger percentage of graduates will use their knowledge of the trades in independent occupations.

The one thing which every Negro institution should seek ... is the giving of such training as will result in creating an influence in the rural districts. This should be done both in the interest of the white man and in the interest of the Negro, himself.

Every land-owner needs every laborer he can secure. The Negro is not so much in demand in cities as in the country. The colored man is at his best in the rural districts, where he is kept away from the demoralizing influences of city life, and besides, in most cases, the competition in the cities is too severe for him. The only way to keep the colored man in the rural districts and away from the cities, is to give him first-class agricultural training, to the extent that he will not consider farming a drudgery and a degradation, but will see in farm life dignity and beauty ...

The demand for the introduction of industrial or of industrial manual training into the public schools of both the cities training into and the country, has become so wide-spread throughout the public schools that this institution is constantly appealed to for information and help. Besides numerous letters from school officials, we are having visits from school superintendents and boards of education, seeking such information as will enable them to introduce our methods into their schools. In connection with this subject however, I wish it thoroughly understood that I do not advocate the lowering of the mental standard as I understand is proposed by the public school boards of one, or two of our Southern cities. No race can be elevated till its mind is awakened and strengthened. In order that we may meet these demands in the best manner, we ought to have an addition to our present industrial department for the older students, a model primary school that will serve as an object lesson to those who want to get information as to the manner of introducing manual and industrial training into the public schools. The present primary school of 176 pupils, which is taught upon the grounds, will serve as a foundation. To carry out the plan that I have mentioned, we should have a new and larger building and the location should be where there is plenty of land that can be used for their purpose of teaching, among other things, simple lessons in gardening, to the small children. In addition to the usual class rooms, such a building should contain space for teaching kindergarten, mechanical drawing, carpentry, sewing, cooking and laundering. There should also be a place for bathing. Such a building, well equipped, would cost about $2000. I urge this as one of our most pressing needs. Few things would so much extend the influence for good in all parts of the South as the securing of this building.

Attendance and The average attendance for the school year has been Growth of 1,083; 321 young women, and 762 young men. The total the School enrollment has been 1,231; 359 young women and 872 young men. Nine-tenths of the number have boarded and slept on the school grounds.

In all the departments, including officers, clerks and instructors, 103 persons are in the employ of the school. Counting students, officers and teachers, together with their families, the total number of persons constantly upon the school grounds, is about 1,200. Students have come to us from 27 States and territories, from Africa, Porto Rico, Cuba, Jamaica and Barbadoes. There are 12 students from Cuba alone.

During the present school year students have been trained in the following 28 industries, in addition to the religious and academic training: Agriculture, Dairying, Horticulture, Stock raising, Blacksmithing, Brickmasonry, Carpentry, Carriage Trimming, Cooking, Architectural, Freehand and Mechanical Drawing, Plain Sewing, Plastering, Plumbing, Printing, Sawmilling, Founding, Housekeeping, Harnessmaking, Electrical Engineering, Laundering, Machinery, Mattress-making, Millinery, Nurse Training, Painting, Shoemaking, Tailoring, Tinning and Wheelwrighting.

This year we have made progress in the matter of training young women in outdoor occupations. Beginning with this school year, we are now giving a number of girls training in poultry raising, bee culture, dairying, gardening, fruit growing, etc. In this climate there is no reason why women should not be trained in such industries, and thereby get a knowledge which will command a good living and enable them to live at the same time out in the open fresh air. A large hennery is now being built, and it will be almost wholly under the supervision of our girls. The electric lighting has been extended to the point where about one-half the buildings are now lighted by electricity.

Notwithstanding the stress put upon industrial training, we are not in any degree neglecting normal training for those who are to teach in the public schools. The number of graduates this year from all the departments is 51. In addition to religious and academic training, each one of these graduates has had training at some trade or industry. In considering the number that go out each year, account should be taken of those who are well trained, but who are unable to remain long enough to graduate. Our graduates and former students are now scattered all over the South, and wherever they can, they not only help the colored people, but use their influence in cultivating friendly relations between the races.

While our work is not sectarian, it is thoroughly Christian, and the growth in the religious tone of the school is most gratifying. We have had more visits this year than ever from Southern white people, who are more and more showing their interest in our effort.

Financial. The total cash receipts for the year, including endowment, beneficiary and building funds, as well as for current expenses, have been $236,163.40. The current expenses for the year have been $75,992.59. The bulk of the remainder of the cash receipts went into Endowment Fund and into the permanent improvement of the plant, in the way of buildings, machinery, etc. As to the details of the financial condition of the institution, I refer you to the report of the treasurer, Mr. Warren Logan.

The main sources of income of the institution are as follows:
State of Alabama $ 4,500 00.
John F. Slater Fund 11,000 00.
Peabody Fund 1,500 00.
Frothingham Fund 700 00.
Society for Propagating the Gospel 500 00.
Entrance Fees paid by students 1,234 00.
Interest from Endowment Funds 3,530 98.

The other portion of the funds necessary to carry on the work of the school comes mainly from individuals, Sunday Schools, missionary societies and churches.

An especial effort in which ex-President Grover Cleveland took special interest, has been made during the past year to secure a partial endowment fund of at least $500,000. I am glad to say that, counting a gift of 50 bonds from Mr. and Mrs. C. P. Huntington, the Endowment Fund has now been increased to $152,232.49.

The Temporary Relief Fund of $50,000 referred to in my last report, which some friends in Boston began raising two years ago at the suggestion of Mr. H. A. Wilder, has proved most helpful in relieving the Principal in some degree from the daily strain of collecting money.

Friends in New York who do not permit their names to be known, have given us through one of our Trustees, Mr. W. H. Baldwin, Jr., $9,717.13 to be used in meeting special needs. The bulk of this money is being used to enlarge the hennery, to erect a dairy house, and a large dairy barn.

Every possible means are used to keep the expenses of the school down to the lowest possible point. During the present year circumstances have forced us to make some additions to the plant, for which we did not have the money, but I believe that the wisdom of these expenditures will appear in reduced expenditures in the future. The smallpox, which appeared two years ago, compelled the destruction of cabins which had to be replaced by new barracks. Aside from this, we found it necessary to erect two small buildings to be used in case of contagious diseases. Added to this was the erection of a teacher's cottage, the enlargement of the dining room, the introduction of steam heating and electric lighting into several buildings, and the putting of new machinery into the laundry, and cooking apparatus into the kitchen. All of these were expenses which could not be avoided, and for which there were no funds. Next year there will be little reason, I think, for departing from the principle to contract no debts for improvements till the money is in hand to make payment.

The erection of the following buildings, for which funds have been secured, is now proceeding in a satisfactory manner: Huntington Hall, the Girls' Industrial Building, the Hennery, the Dairy House and Dairy barn.

The life of this school depends upon small gifts which carry with them the good will and active interest of hundreds of the best people throughout the country. In addition to the smaller gifts, we have received during the year among other donations, the following:

TOWARDS THE ENDOWMENT FUND.
Mrs. Alfred T. White $1,000 00.
Mrs. J. B. Ames 500 00.
A Friend, Columbus, Ohio 25,000 00.
Mrs. George Faulkner 1,000 00.
Mrs. E.P. Stillman and daughter 1,000 00.
Friends in memory of Mrs. Elizabeth C. Lewis 1,000 00
A Friend, Philadelphia, Pa. 5,000 00.
Mrs. Harriet A. Soutworth and daughter 1,000 00.
Miss Emily Howland 1,000 00.
Mrs. Leroy King 2,000 00.
Mrs. A. M. Harris 1,000 00.
Mr. John E. Parsons 500 00.
Mr. George Foster Peabody 1,000 00.
Miss H. W. Kendall 500 00
Mr. H. W. Maxwell 500 00.
Mr. Oswald Offendorfer 500 00.
Hon. Seth Low 1,000 00.
Estate of Mrs. Mary M. Brown 1,805 10.

Besides those mentioned above, Mr. and Mrs. C. P. Huntington have given $50,000 toward the Endowment Fund.

For general and special purposes, aside from endowment, the following amounts are among the principal ones given during the year:
Estate of Mr. Robert C. Billings $ 8,000 00.
Estate of Mr. H. E. Hecox 500 00.

Mr. John D. Rockefeller 12,500 00.

Mrs. Julia Billings 1,000 00.

Mrs. Eleanor C. Morris 1,000 00.

Mr. and Mrs. Wm. E. Dodge 2,000 00.

Friends, through Mr. Wm. H. Baldwin, Jr., 9,717 00

Hon. W. Bourke Cockran 500 00.

Mr. H. A. Wildner, for Painting Buildings 600 00.

The gift of a large 75 horse-power boiler and 125 horse-power engine, also given by Mr. C. P. Huntington, of New York, has added much to the efficiency of our industrial department.

We are also indebted to Mr. Wm. E. Dodge for an outfit for our shoemaking division.

Needs. I repeat what I have often said, that it is very necessary that every thing at this institution be done in the very best manner, because so many look to us for example.

Among our greatest needs at present are:

$2,000 for Model School building, as already described.

$10,000 for better equipment of industrial departments.

$4,000 for hospital building.

$20,000 for Library and Administration building.

$15,000 for dormitory for young men.

$40,000 for steam heating.

$348,000 to bring the endowment up to $500,000.

Five teachers' cottages, cost $1,200 each.

In closing this report, I would say that my feeling grows stronger each year that the main thing that we want to be sure of is that Negro is making progress day by day. With constant, tangible, visible, indisputable progress being made evident, all the minor details regarding the adjustment of our position in the body politic will, in a natural way, settle themselves.

Respectfully Submitted:

Booker T. Washington,

Principal.

Tuskegee, Ala., May 30, 1900.

Source: Tuskegee, Ala.: Tuskegee Institute Steam Print, 1900. Library of Congress, Rare Book and Special Collections Division, Daniel A.P. Murray Pamphlets Collection.

67. Paths of Hope for the Negro: Practical Suggestions of a Southerner, 1900

JEROME DOWD

In this article, *Century Magazine* contributor Jerome Dowd explained in detail the possible opportunities available for African Americans living in the southern United States. He explained that education of the black man needed to be practical and inclusive of the arts in order to promote literacy, self-esteem, and empowerment.

It is too late in the day to discuss whether it would have been better had the Negro never been brought into the Southern States. If his presence here has been beneficial, or is ever to prove so, the price of the benefit has already been dearly paid for. He was the occasion of the deadliest and most expensive war in modern times. In the next place, his presence has corrupted politics and has limited statesmanship to a mere question of race supremacy. Great problems concerning the political, industrial, and moral life of the people have been subordinated or overshadowed, so that, while important strides have been made elsewhere in the investigation of social conditions and in the administration of State and municipal affairs, in civil-service reform, in the management of penal and charitable institutions, and in the field of education, the South has lagged behind.

On the charts of illiteracy and crime the South is represented by an immense black spot. Such are a few items of the account. It will require millions more of dollars and generations more of earnest work before the total cost is met of bringing the black man to this side of the globe. But the debt has been incurred and must be liquidated.

The welfare of the Negro is bound up with that of the white man in many important particulars:

First, the low standard of living among the blacks keeps down the wages of all classes of whites. So long as the Negroes are content to live in miserable huts, wear rags, and subsist upon hog fat and cow-pease, so long must the wages of white people in the same kind of work be pressed toward the same level. The higher we raise the standard of living among the Negroes, the higher will be the wages of the white people in the same occupations. The low standard of the Negroes is the result of low productive power. The less intelligent and skilled the Negroes are, the less they can produce, whether working for themselves or others, and hence, the less will be the total wealth of the country.

But it may be asked, When the standard of living of the Negroes is raised, will not wages go up, and will not that be a drawback? Certainly wages will go up, because the income of all classes will be increased. High wages generally indicate high productive power and general wealth, while low wages indicate the opposite. Only benefits can arise from better wages.

In the next place, the Negro's propensity to crime tends to excite the criminal tendencies of the white man. The South enjoys the distinction of having the highest percentage of crime in all the civilized world, and the reason is that the crimes of the one race provoke counter-crimes in the other.

The physical well-being of the one race has such a conspicuous influence upon that of the other that the subject requires no elaboration. The uncleanliness of person and habits of the Negroes in their homes and in the homes of their employers tends to propagate diseases, and thus impairs the health and increases the death-rate of the whole population.

Again, the lack of refinement in intellect, manners, and dress among the Negroes is an obstacle to the cultivated life of the whites. Ignorance and the absence of taste and self-respect in servants result in badly kept homes and yards, destruction of furniture and ware, ill-prepared food, poor table service, and a general lowering of the standard of living. Furthermore, the corrupt, coarse, and vulgar language of the Negroes is largely responsible for the jumbled and distorted English spoken by many of the Southern whites.

Seeing that the degradation of the Negro is an impediment to the progress and civilization of the white man, how may we effect an improvement in his condition?

First, municipalities should give more attention to the streets and alleys that traverse Negro settlements. In almost every town in the South there are settlements, known by such names as "New Africa," "Haiti," "Log Town," "Smoky Hollow," or "Snow Hill," exclusively inhabited by Negroes.

These settlements are often outside the corporate limits. The houses are built along narrow, crooked, and dirty lanes, and the community is without sanitary regulations or oversight. These quarters should be brought under municipal control, the lanes widened into streets and cleaned, and provision made to guard against the opening of similar ones in the future.

In the next place, property-owners should build better houses for the Negroes to live in. The weakness in the civilization of the Negroes is most pronounced in their family life. But improvement in this respect is not possible without an improvement in the character and the comforts of the houses they live in. Bad houses breed bad people and bad neighborhoods. There is no more distinctive form of crime than the building and renting of houses unfit for human habitation.

Scarcely second in importance to improvements in house architecture is the need among Negroes of more time to spend with their families. Employers of Negro labor should be less exacting in the number of hours required for a day's work. Many domestic servants now work from six in the morning until nine and ten o'clock at night. The Southern habit of keeping open shopping-places until late at night encourages late suppers, retains cooks, butlers, and nurses until bedtime, and robs them of all home life. If the merchants would close their shops at six o'clock, as is the custom in the North, the welfare of both races would be greatly promoted.

Again, a revolution is needed in the character of the Negro's religion. At present it is too largely an affair of the emotions. He needs to be taught that the religious life is something to grow into by the perfection of personality, and not to be jumped into or sweated into at camp-meetings. The theological seminaries and the graduate preachers should assume the task of grafting upon the religion of the Negro that much sanity at least.

A reform is as much needed in the methods and aims of Negro education. Up to the present Negro education has shared with that of the white man the fault of being top-heavy. Colleges and universities have developed out of proportion to, and at the expense of, common schools. Then, the kind of education afforded the Negro has not been fitted to his capacities and needs. He has been made to pursue courses of study parallel to those prescribed for the whites, as though the individuals of both races had to fill the same positions in life. Much of the Negro's education has had nothing to do with his real life-work. It has only made him discontented and disinclined to unfold his arms. The survival of the Negroes in the race for existence depends upon their retaining possession of the few bread-winning occupations now open to them. But instead of better qualifying themselves for these occupations they have been poring over dead languages and working problems in mathematics. In the meantime the Chinaman and the steam-laundry have abolished the Negro's wash-tub, trained white "tonsorial artists" have taken away his barber's chair, and skilled painters and plasterers and mechanics have taken away his paint-brushes and tool-chests. Every year the number of occupations open to him becomes fewer because of his lack of progress in them. Unless a radical change takes place in the scope of his education, so that he may learn better how to do his work, a tide of white immigration will set in and force him out of his last stronghold, domestic service, and limit his sphere to the farm.

All primary schools for the Negroes should be equipped for industrial training in such work as sewing, cooking, laundering, carpentry, and house-cleaning, and, in rural districts, in elementary agriculture.

Secondary schools should add to the literary courses a more advanced course in industrial training, so as to approach as nearly as possible the objects and methods of the Tuskegee and Hampton Industrial and Normal Schools. Too much cannot be said in behalf of the revolution in the life of the Negro which the work of these schools promises and, in part, has already wrought. The writer is fully aware that education has a value aside from and above its bread-winning results, and he would not dissuade the Negro from seeking the highest culture that he may be capable of; but it is folly for him to wing his way through the higher realms of the intellect without some acquaintance with the requirements and duties of life.

Changes are needed in the methods of Negro education as well as in its scope. Educators should take into account, more than they have yet done, the differences in the mental characteristics of the two races. It is a well-established fact that, while the lower races possess marked capacity to deal with simple, concrete ideas, they lack power of generalization, and soon fatigue in the realm of the abstract. It is also well known that the inferior races, being deficient in generalization, which is a subjective process, are absorbed almost entirely in the things that are objective. They have strong and alert eyesight, and are susceptible to impressions through the medium of the eye to an extent that is impossible to any of the white races. This fact is evidenced in the great number of pictures found in the homes of the Negroes. In default of anything better, they will paper their walls with advertisements of the theater and the circus, and even with pictures from vicious newspapers. They delight in street pageantry, fancy costumes, theatrical performances, and similar spectacles. Factories employing Negroes generally find it necessary to suspend operations on "circus day." They love stories of adventure and any fiction that gives play to their imaginations. All their tastes lie in the realm of the objective and the concrete.

Hence, in the school-room stress should be laid on those studies that appeal to the eye and the imagination. Lessons should be given in sketching, painting, drawing, and casting. Reprints of the popular works of art should be placed before the Negroes, that their love for art may be gratified and their taste cultivated at the same time. Fancy needlework, dress-making, and home decorations should also have an important place. These studies, while not contributing directly to bread-winning, have a refining and softening influence upon character, and inspire efforts to make the home more attractive. The more interest we can make the Negro take in his personal appearance and in the comforts of his home, the more we shall strengthen and promote his family life and raise the level of his civilization.

The literary education of the Negro should consist of carefully selected poems and novels that appeal to his imagination and produce clear images upon his mind, excluding such literature as is in the nature of psychological or moral research. Recitations and dialogues should be more generally and more frequently required. In history emphasis should be given to what is picturesque, dramatic, and biographical.

Coming to the political phase of the Negro problem, there is a general agreement among white men that the Southern States cannot keep pace with the progress of the world as long as they are menaced by Negro domination, and that, therefore, it is necessary to eliminate the Negro vote from politics. When the Negroes become intelligent factors in society, when they become thrifty and accumulate wealth, they will find the way to larger exercise of citizenship. They can never sit upon juries to pass upon life and property until they are property-owners themselves, and they can never hold the reins of government by reason of mere superiority of numbers. Before they can take on larger political responsibilities they must demonstrate their ability to meet them.

The Negroes will never be allowed to control State governments so long as they vote at every election upon the basis of color, without regard whatever to political issues or private convictions. If the Negroes would divide their votes according to their individual opinions, as the lamented Charles Price, one of their best leaders, advised, there would be no danger of Negro domination and no objection to their holding offices which they might be competent to fill. But as there is no present prospect of their voting upon any other basis than that of color, the white people are forced to accept the situation and protect themselves accordingly. Years of bitter and costly experience have demonstrated over and over again that Negro rule is not only incompetent and corrupt, but a menace to civilization. Some people imagine that there is something anomalous, peculiar, or local in the race prejudice that binds all Negroes together; but this clan spirit is a characteristic of all savage and semi-civilized peoples.

It should be well understood by this time that no foreign race inhabiting this country and acting together politically can dominate the native whites. To permit an inferior race, holding less than one tenth of the property of the community, to take the reins of government in its hands, by reason of mere numerical strength, would be to renounce civilization. Our national government, in making laws for Hawaii, has carefully provided for white supremacy by an educational qualification for suffrage that excludes the semi-civilized natives. No sane man, let us hope, would think of placing Manila under the control of a government of the Philippine Islands based upon universal suffrage. Yet the problem in the South and the problem in the Philippines and in Hawaii differ only in degree.

The only proper safeguard against Negro rule in States where the blacks outnumber or approximate in number the whites lies in constitutional provisions establishing an educational test for suffrage applicable to black and white alike. If the suffrage is not thus limited it is necessary for the whites to resort to technicalities and ballot laws, to bribery or intimidation. To set up an educational test with a "grandfather clause," making the test apply for a certain time to the blacks only, seems to an outsider unnecessary, arbitrary, and unjust. The reason for such a clause arises from the belief that no constitutional amendment could ever carry if it immediately disfranchised the illiterate whites, as many property-holding whites belong to that class. But the writer does not believe in the principle nor in the necessity for a "grandfather clause." If constitutional amendments were to be submitted in North Carolina and Virginia applying the educational test to both races alike after 1908, the question would be lifted above the level of party gain, and would receive the support of white men of all parties and the approbation of the moral sentiment of the American people. A white man who would disfranchise a Negro because of his color or for mere party advantage is himself unworthy of the suffrage. With the suffrage question adjusted upon an educational basis the Negroes would have the power to work out their political emancipation, the white people having made education necessary and provided the means for attaining it.

When the question of Negro domination is settled, the path of progress of both races will be very much cleared. Race conflicts will then be less frequent and race feeling less bitter. With more friendly relations growing up, and with more concentration of energy on the part of the Negroes in industrial lines, the opportunities for them will be widened and the task of finding industrial adjustment in the struggle for life made easier. The wisest and best leaders among the Negroes, such as Booker Washington and the late Charles Price, have tried to turn the attention of the Negroes from politics to the more profitable pursuits of industry, and if the professional politician would cease inspiring the Negroes to seek salvation in political domination over the whites, the race issue would soon cease to exist.

The field is broad enough in the South for both races to attain all that is possible to them. In spite of the periodic political conflicts and occasional local riots and acts of individual violence, the relations between the races, in respect to nine tenths of the population, are very friendly. The general condition has been too often judged by the acts of a small minority. The Southern people understand the Negroes, and feel a real fondness for those that are thrifty and well behaved. When fairly treated the Negro has a strong affection for his employer. He seldom forgets a kindness, and is quick to forget a wrong. If he does not stay long at one place, it is not that he dislikes his employer so much as that he has a restless temperament and craves change. His disposition is full of mirth and sunshine, and not a little of the fine flavor of Southern wit and humor is due to his influence. His nature is plastic, and while he is easily molded into a monster, he is also capable of a high degree of culture. Many Negroes are thoroughly honest, notwithstanding their bad environment and hereditary disposition to steal. Negro servants are trusted with the keys to households to an extent that, probably, is not the case among domestics elsewhere in the civilized world.

It is strange that two races working side by side should possess so many opposite traits of character. The white man has strong will and convictions and is set in his ways. He lives an indoor, monotonous life, restrains himself like a Puritan, and is inclined to be melancholy. The prevalence of Populism throughout the South is nothing but the outcome of this morbid tendency. Farmers and merchants are entirely absorbed in their business, and the women, especially the married women, contrast with the women of France, Germany, and even England, in their indoor life and disinclination to mingle with the world outside. Public parks and public concerts, such as are found in Europe, which call out husband, wife, and children for a few hours of rest and communion with their friends, are almost unknown in the South. The few entertainments that receive sanction generally exclude all but the well-to-do by the cost of admission. The life of the poor in town and country is bleak and bare to the last degree.

Contrasting with this tendency is the free-and-easy life of the blacks. The burdens of the present and the future weigh lightly upon their shoulders. They love all the worldly amusements; in their homes, they are free entertainers, and in their fondness for conversation and love of street life, they are equal to the French or Italians.

May we not hope that the conflict of these two opposite races is working out some advantages to both, and that the final result will justify all that the conflict has cost?

Source: *Century Magazine*, Volume 61. New York: 1900. Copyright © 1999, by the Rector and Visitors of the University of Virginia. Courtesy of The University of Virginia Library.

68. The Freedmen's Bureau, March 1901
W. E. BURGHARDT DuBOIS

W. E. B DuBois first became famous through writing in which he declared the single most important question America would face during the twentieth century would be the problem of race relations. It was race, DuBois wrote, that caused the Civil War;

when the war ended, an old question cloaked in new words emerged: What shall be done with slaves? A bureaucracy called the Freedmen's Bureau was created in March of 1865 to solve this new problem.

In this essay, DuBois both praised and critizized the Bureau's work. Its chief success, DuBois argued, was the founding and operating of hundreds of free public schools for African Americans. Its primary failure, DuBois claimed, was in not being powerful enough to overcome the tyranny of the local courts, which maintained the superior position of whites, especially former slave owners.

Peremptory military commands, this way and that, could not answer the query; the Emancipation Proclamation seemed but to broaden and intensify the difficulties; and so at last there arose in the South a government of men called the Freedmen's Bureau, which lasted, legally, from 1865 to 1872, but in a sense from 1861 to 1876, and which sought to settle the Negro problems in the United States of America.

It is the aim of this essay to study the Freedmen's Bureau,—the occasion of its rise, the character of its work, and its final success and failure,—not only as a part of American history, but above all as one of the most singular and interesting of the attempts made by a great nation to grapple with vast problems of race and social condition.

No sooner had the armies, east and west, penetrated Virginia and Tennessee than fugitive slaves appeared within their lines. They came at night, when the flickering camp fires of the blue hosts shone like vast unsteady stars along the black horizon: old men, and thin, with gray and tufted hair; women with frightened eyes, dragging whimpering, hungry children; men and girls, stalwart and gaunt,—a horde of starving vagabonds, homeless, helpless, and pitiable in their dark distress. Two methods of treating these newcomers seemed equally logical to opposite sorts of minds. Said some, "We have nothing to do with slaves."

"Hereafter," commanded Halleck, "no slaves should be allowed to come into your lines at all; if any come without your knowledge, when owners call for them, deliver them." But others said, "We take grain and fowl; why not slaves?" Whereupon Fremont, as early as August, 1861, declared the slaves of Missouri rebels free. Such radical action was quickly countermanded, but at the same time the opposite policy could not be enforced; some of the black refugees declared themselves freemen, others showed their masters had deserted them, and still others were captured with forts and plantations. Evidently, too, slaves were a source of strength to the Confederacy, and were being used as laborers and producers.

"They constitute a military resource," wrote the Secretary of War, late in 1861; "and being such, that they should not be turned over to the enemy is too plain to discuss." So the tone of the army chiefs changed, Congress forbade the rendition of fugitives, and Butler's "contrabands" were welcomed as military laborers. This complicated rather than solved the problem; for now the scattering fugitives became a steady stream, which flowed faster as the armies marched.

Then the long-headed man, with care-chiseled face, who sat in the White House, saw the inevitable, and emancipated the slaves of rebels on New Year's, 1863. A month later Congress called earnestly for the Negro soldiers whom the act of July, 1862, had half grudgingly allowed to enlist. Thus the barriers were leveled, and the deed was done. The stream of fugitives swelled to a flood, and anxious officers kept inquiring: "What must be done with slaves arriving almost daily? Am I to find food and shelter for women and children?"

It was a Pierce of Boston who pointed out the way, and thus became in a sense the founder of the Freedmen's Bureau. Being specially detailed from the ranks to care for the freedmen at Fortress Monroe, he afterward founded the celebrated Port Royal experiment and started the Freedmen's Aid Societies. Thus, under the timid Treasury officials and bold army officers, Pierce's plan widened and developed. At first, the able-bodied men were enlisted as soldiers or hired as laborers, the women and children were herded into central camps under guard, and "superintendents of contrabands" multiplied here and there. Centres of massed freedmen arose at Fortress Monroe, Va., Washington, D. C., Beaufort and Port Royal, S. C., New Orleans, La., Vicksburg and Corinth, Miss., Columbus, Ky., Cairo, Ill., and elsewhere, and the army chaplains found here new and fruitful fields.

Then came the Freedmen's Aid Societies, born of the touching appeals for relief and help from these centres of distress. There was the American Missionary Association, sprung from the Amistad, and now full grown for work, the various church organizations, the National Freedmen's Relief Association, the American Freedmen's Union, the Western Freedmen's Aid Commission,—in all fifty or more active organizations, which sent clothes, money, school-books, and teachers southward. All they did was needed, for the destitution of the freedmen was often reported as "too appalling for belief," and the situation was growing daily worse rather than better. And daily, too, it seemed more plain that this was no ordinary matter of temporary relief, but a national crisis; for here loomed a labor problem of vast dimensions. Masses of Negroes stood idle, or, if they worked spasmodically, were never sure of pay; and if perchance they received pay, squandered the new thing thoughtlessly. In these and in other ways were camp life and the new liberty demoralizing the freedmen. The broader economic organization thus clearly demanded sprang up here and there as accident and local conditions determined. Here again Pierce's Port Royal plan of leased plantations and guided workmen pointed out the rough way. In Washington, the military governor, at the urgent appeal of the superintendent, opened confiscated estates to the cultivation of the fugitives, and there in the shadow of the dome gathered black farm villages. General Dix gave over estates to the freedmen of Fortress Monroe, and so on through the South. The government and the benevolent societies furnished the means of cultivation, and the Negro turned again slowly to work. The systems of control, thus started, rapidly grew, here and there, into strange little governments, like that of General Banks in Louisiana, with its 90,000 black subjects, its 50,000 guided laborers, and its annual budget of $100,000 and more. It made out 4000 pay rolls, registered all freedmen, inquired into grievances and redressed them, laid and collected taxes, and established a system of public schools. So too Colonel Eaton, the superintendent of Tennessee and Arkansas, ruled over 100,000, leased and cultivated 7000 acres of cotton land, and furnished food for 10,000 paupers. In South Carolina was General Saxton, with his deep interest in black folk. He succeeded Pierce and the Treasury officials, and sold forfeited estates, leased abandoned plantations, encouraged schools, and received from Sherman, after the terribly picturesque march to the sea, thousands of the wretched camp followers.

Three characteristic things one might have seen in Sherman's raid through Georgia, which threw the new situation in deep and shadowy relief: the Conqueror, the Conquered, and the Negro. Some see all significance in the grim front of the destroyer, and some in the bitter sufferers of the lost cause. But to me neither soldier nor fugitive speaks with so deep a meaning as that dark and human cloud that clung like remorse on the rear of those swift columns, swelling at times to half their size, almost engulfing and choking them. In vain were they ordered back, in vain were bridges hewn from beneath their feet; on they trudged and writhed and surged, until they rolled into Savannah, a starved and naked horde of tens of thousands. There too came the characteristic military remedy:

"The islands from Charleston south, the abandoned rice fields along the rivers for thirty miles back from the sea, and the country bordering the St. John's River, Florida, are reserved and set apart for the settlement of Negroes now made free by act of war." So read the celebrated field order.

All these experiments, orders, and systems were bound to attract and perplex the government and the nation. Directly after the Emancipation Proclamation, Representative Eliot had introduced a bill creating a Bureau of Emancipation, but it was never reported.

The following June, a committee of inquiry, appointed by the Secretary of War, reported in favor of a temporary bureau for the "improvement, protection, and employment of refugee freedmen," on much the same lines as were afterward followed. Petitions came in to President Lincoln from distinguished citizens and organizations, strongly urging a comprehensive and unified plan of dealing with the freedmen, under a bureau which should be "charged with the study of plans and execution of measures for easily guiding, and in every way judiciously and humanely aiding, the passage of our emancipated and yet to be emancipated blacks from the old condition of forced labor to their new state of voluntary industry."

Some half-hearted steps were early taken by the government to put both freedmen and abandoned estates under the supervision of the Treasury officials. Laws of 1863 and 1864 directed them to take charge of and lease abandoned lands for periods not exceeding twelve months, and to "provide in such leases or otherwise for the employment and general welfare" of the freedmen. Most of the army officers looked upon this as a welcome relief from perplexing "Negro affairs;" but the Treasury hesitated and blundered, and although it leased large quantities of land and employed many Negroes, especially along the Mississippi, yet it left the virtual control of the laborers and their relations to their neighbors in the hands of the army.

In March, 1864, Congress at last turned its attention to the subject, and the House passed a bill, by a majority of two, establishing a Bureau for Freedmen in the War Department. Senator Sumner, who had charge of the bill in the Senate, argued that freedmen and abandoned lands ought to be under the same department, and reported a substitute for the House bill, attaching the Bureau to the Treasury Department. This bill passed, but too late for action in the House. The debate wandered over the whole policy of the administration and the general question of slavery, without touching very closely the specific merits of the measure in hand.

Meantime the election took place, and the administration, returning from the country with a vote of renewed confidence, addressed itself to the matter more seriously. A conference between the houses agreed upon a carefully drawn measure which contained the chief provisions of Charles Sumner's bill, but made the proposed organization a department independent of both the War and Treasury officials. The bill was conservative, giving the new department "general superintendence of all freedmen." It was to "establish regulations" for them, protect them, lease them lands, adjust their wages, and appear in civil and military courts as their "next friend." There were many limitations attached to the powers thus granted, and the organization was made permanent. Nevertheless, the Senate defeated the bill, and a new conference committee was appointed. This committee reported a new bill, February 28, which was whirled through just as the session closed, and which became the act of 1865 establishing in the War Department a "Bureau of Refugees, Freedmen, and Abandoned Lands."

This last compromise was a hasty bit of legislation, vague and uncertain in outline. A Bureau was created, "to continue during the present War of Rebellion, and for one year thereafter," to which was given "the supervision and management of all abandoned lands, and the control of all subjects relating to refugees and freedmen," under "such rules and regulations as may be presented by the head of the Bureau and approved by the President." A commissioner, appointed by the President and Senate, was to control the Bureau, with an office force not exceeding ten clerks. The President might also appoint commissioners in the seceded states, and to all these offices military officials might be detailed at regular pay. The Secretary of War could issue rations, clothing, and fuel to the destitute, and all abandoned property was placed in the hands of the Bureau for eventual lease and sale to ex-slaves in forty-acre parcels.

Thus did the United States government definitely assume charge of the emancipated Negro as the ward of the nation. It was a tremendous undertaking. Here, at a stroke of the pen, was erected a government of millions of men,—and not ordinary men, either, but black men emasculated by a peculiarly complete system of slavery, centuries old; and now, suddenly, violently, they come into a new birthright, at a time of war and passion, in the midst of the stricken, embittered population of their former masters. Any man might well have hesitated to assume charge of such a work, with vast responsibilities, indefinite powers, and limited resources. Probably no one but a soldier would have answered such a call promptly; and indeed no one but a soldier could be called, for Congress had appropriated no money for salaries and expenses.

Less than a month after the weary emancipator passed to his rest, his successor assigned Major General Oliver O. Howard to duty as commissioner of the new Bureau. He was a Maine man, then only thirty-five years of age. He had marched with Sherman to the sea, had fought well at Gettysburg, and had but a year before been assigned to the command of the Department of Tennessee. An honest and sincere man, with rather too much faith in human nature, little aptitude for systematic business and intricate detail, he was nevertheless conservative, hard-working, and, above all, acquainted at first-hand with much of the work before him. And of that work it has been truly said, "No approximately correct history of civilization can ever be written which does not throw out in bold relief, as one of the great landmarks of political and social progress, the organization and administration of the Freedmen's Bureau."

On May 12, 1865, Howard was appointed, and he assumed the duties of his office promptly on the 15th, and began examining the field of work. A curious mess he looked upon: little despotisms, communistic experiments, slavery, peonage, business speculations, organized charity, unorganized almsgiving,—all reeling on under the guise of helping the freedman, and all enshrined in the smoke and blood of war and the cursing and silence of angry men. On May 19 the new government—for a government it really was—issued its constitution; commissioners were to be appointed in each of the seceded states, who were to take charge of "all subjects relating to refugees and freedmen," and all relief and rations were to be given by their consent alone. The Bureau invited continued cooperation with benevolent societies, and declared, "It will be the object of all commissioners to introduce practicable systems of compensated labor," and to establish schools. Forthwith nine assistant commissioners were appointed. They were to hasten to their fields of work; seek gradually to close relief establishments, and make the destitute self-supporting; act as courts of law where there were no courts, or where Negroes were not recognized in them as free; establish the institution of marriage among ex-slaves, and keep records; see that freedmen were free to choose their employers, and help in making fair contracts for them; and finally, the circular said, "Simple good faith, for which we hope on all hands for those concerned in the passing away of slavery, will especially relieve the assistant commissioners in the discharge of their duties toward the freedmen, as well as promote the general welfare."

No sooner was the work thus started, and the general system and local organization in some measure begun, than two grave difficulties appeared which changed largely the theory and outcome of Bureau work. First, there were the abandoned lands of the South. It had long been the more or less definitely expressed theory of the North that all the chief problems of emancipation might be settled by establishing the slaves on the forfeited lands of their masters,—a sort of poetic justice, said some. But this poetry done into solemn prose meant either wholesale confiscation of private property in the South, or vast appropriations. Now Congress had not appropriated a cent, and no sooner did the proclamations of general amnesty appear than the 800,000 acres of abandoned lands in the hands of the Freedmen's Bureau melted quickly away. The second difficulty lay in perfecting the local organization of the Bureau throughout the wide field of work. Making a new machine and sending out officials of duly ascertained fitness for a great work of social reform is no child's task; but this task was even harder, for a new central organization had to be fitted on a heterogeneous and confused but already existing system of relief and control of ex-slaves; and the agents available for this work must be sought for in an army still busy with war operations,—men in the very nature of the case ill fitted for delicate social work,—or among the questionable camp followers of an invading host. Thus, after a year's work, vigorously as it was pushed, the problem looked even more difficult to grasp and solve than at the beginning. Nevertheless, three things that year's work did, well worth the doing: it relieved a vast amount of physical suffering; it transported 7000 fugitives from congested centres back to the farm; and, best of all, it inaugurated the crusade of the New England school ma'am.

The annals of this Ninth Crusade are yet to be written, the tale of a mission that seemed to our age far more quixotic than the quest of St. Louis seemed to his. Behind the mists of ruin and rapine waved the calico dresses of women who dared, and after the hoarse mouthings of the field guns rang the rhythm of the alphabet. Rich and poor they were, serious and curious. Bereaved now of a father, now of a brother, now of more than these, they came seeking a life work in planting New England schoolhouses among the white and black of the South. They did their work well. In that first year they taught 100,000 souls, and more. Evidently, Congress must soon legislate again on the hastily organized Bureau, which had so quickly grown into wide significance and vast possibilities. An institution such as that was well-nigh as difficult to end as to begin. Early in 1866 Congress took up the matter, when Senator Trumbull, of Illinois, introduced a bill to extend the Bureau and enlarge its powers. This measure received, at the hands of Congress, far more thorough discussion and attention than its predecessor. The war cloud had thinned enough to allow a clearer conception of the work of emancipation. The champions of the bill argued that the strengthening of the Freedmen's Bureau was still a military necessity; that it was needed for the proper carrying out of the Thirteenth Amendment, and was a work of sheer justice to the ex-slave, at a trifling cost to the government. The opponents of the measure declared that the war was over, and the necessity for war measures past; that the Bureau, by reason of its extraordinary powers, was clearly unconstitutional in time of peace, and was destined to irritate the South and pauperize the freedmen, at a final cost of possibly hundreds of millions. Two of these arguments were unanswered, and indeed unanswerable: the one that the extraordinary powers of the Bureau threatened the civil rights of all citizens; and the other that the government must have power to do what manifestly must be done, and that present abandonment of the freedmen meant their practical enslavement. The bill which finally passed enlarged and made permanent the Freedmen's Bureau. It was promptly vetoed by President Johnson, as "unconstitutional," "unnecessary," and "extrajudicial," and failed of passage over the veto. Meantime, however, the breach between Congress and the President began to broaden, and a modified form of the lost bill was finally passed over the President's second veto, July 16.

The act of 1866 gave the Freedmen's Bureau its final form,—the form by which it will be known to posterity and judged of men. It extended the existence of the Bureau to July, 1868; it authorized additional assistant commissioners, the retention of army officers mustered out of regular service, the sale of certain forfeited lands to freedmen on nominal terms, the sale of Confederate public property for Negro schools, and a wider field of judicial interpretation and cognizance. The government of the un-reconstructed South was thus put very largely in the hands of the Freedmen's Bureau, especially as in many cases the departmental military commander was now made also assistant commissioner. It was thus that the Freedmen's Bureau became a full-fledged government of men. It made laws, executed them and interpreted them; it laid and collected taxes, defined and punished crime, maintained and used military force, and dictated such measures as it thought necessary and proper for the accomplishment of its varied ends. Naturally, all these powers were not exercised continuously nor to their fullest extent; and yet, as General Howard has said, "scarcely any subject that has to be legislated upon in civil society failed, at one time or another, to demand the action of this singular Bureau."

To understand and criticize intelligently so vast a work, one must not forget an instant the drift of things in the later sixties: Lee had surrendered, Lincoln was dead, and Johnson and Congress were at loggerheads; the Thirteenth Amendment was adopted, the Fourteenth pending, and the Fifteenth declared in force in 1870. Guerrilla raiding, the ever present flickering after-flame of war, was spending its force against the Negroes, and all the Southern land was awakening as from some wild dream to poverty and social revolution. In a time of perfect calm, amid willing neighbors and streaming wealth, the social uplifting of 4,000,000 slaves to an assured and self-sustaining place in the body politic and economic would have been an Herculean task; but when to the inherent difficulties of so delicate and nice a social operation were added the spite and hate of conflict, the Hell of War; when suspicion and cruelty were rife, and gaunt Hunger wept beside Bereavement,—in such a case, the work of any instrument of social regeneration was in large part foredoomed to failure. The very name of the Bureau stood for a thing in the South which for two centuries and better men had refused even to argue,—that life amid free Negroes was simply unthinkable, the maddest of experiments. The agents which the Bureau could command varied all the way from unselfish philanthropists to narrow-minded busybodies and thieves; and even though it be true that the average was far better than the worst, it was the one fly that helped to spoil the ointment. Then, amid all this crouched the freed slave, bewildered between friend and foe. He had emerged from slavery: not the worst slavery in the world, not a slavery that made all life unbearable,—rather, a slavery that had here and there much of kindliness, fidelity, and happiness,—but withal slavery, which, so far as human aspiration and desert were concerned, classed the black man and the ox together. And the Negro knew full well that, whatever their deeper convictions may have been, Southern men had fought with desperate energy to perpetuate this slavery, under which the black masses, with half-articulate thought, had writhed and shivered. They welcomed freedom with a cry. They fled to the friends that had freed them. They shrank from the master who still strove for their chains. So the cleft between the white and black South grew. Idle to say it never should have been; it was as inevitable as its results were pitiable. Curiously incongruous elements were left arrayed against each other: the North, the government, the carpetbagger, and the slave, here; and there, all the South that was white, whether gentleman or vagabond, honest man or rascal, lawless murderer or martyr to duty.

Thus it is doubly difficult to write of this period calmly, so intense was the feeling, so mighty the human passions, that swayed and blinded men. Amid it all two figures ever stand to typify that day to coming men: the one a gray-haired gentleman, whose fathers had quit themselves like men, whose sons lay in nameless graves, who bowed to the evil of slavery because its abolition boded untold ill to all; who stood at last, in the evening of life, a blighted, ruined form, with hate in his eyes. And the other, a form hovering dark and mother-like, her awful face black with the mists of centuries, had aforetime bent in love over her white master's cradle, rocked his sons and daughters to sleep, and closed in death the sunken eyes of his wife to the world; ay, too, had laid herself low to his lust and borne a tawny man child to the world, only to see her dark boy's limbs scattered to the winds by midnight marauders riding after Damned Niggers. These were the saddest sights of that woeful day; and no man clasped the hands of these two passing figures of the present-past; but hating they went to their long home, and hating their children's children live to-day.

Here, then, was the field of work for the Freedmen's Bureau; and since, with some hesitation, it was continued by the act of 1868 till 1869, let us look upon four years of its work as a whole. There were, in 1868, 900 Bureau officials scattered from Washington to Texas, ruling, directly and indirectly, many millions of men. And the deeds of these rulers fall mainly under seven heads,—the relief of physical suffering, the overseeing of the beginnings of free labor, the buying and selling of land, the establishment of schools, the paying of bounties, the administration of justice, and the financiering of all these activities. Up to June, 1869, over half a million patients had been treated by Bureau physicians and surgeons, and sixty hospitals and asylums had been in operation. In fifty months of work 21,000,000 free rations were distributed at a cost of over $4,000,000,—beginning at the rate of 30,000 rations a day in 1865, and discontinuing in 1869. Next came the difficult question of labor. First, 30,000 black men were transported from the refuges and relief stations back to the farms, back to the critical trial of a new way of working. Plain, simple instructions went out from Washington,—the freedom of laborers to choose employers, no fixed rates of wages, no peonage or forced labor. So far so good; but where local agents differed in capacity and character, where the personnel was continually changing, the outcome was varied. The largest element of success lay in the fact that the majority of the freedmen were willing, often eager, to work. So contracts were written—50,000 in a single state,—laborers advised, wages guaranteed, and employers supplied. In truth, the organization became a vast labor bureau; not perfect, indeed,—notably defective here and there,—but on the whole, considering the situation, successful beyond the dreams of thoughtful men. The two great obstacles which confronted the officers at every turn were the tyrant and the idler: the slave-holder, who believed slavery was right, and was determined to perpetuate it under another name; and the freedman, who regarded freedom as perpetual rest. These were the Devil and the Deep Sea.

In the work of establishing the Negroes as peasant proprietors the Bureau was severely handicapped, as I have shown. Nevertheless, something was done. Abandoned lands were leased so long as they remained in the hands of the Bureau, and a total revenue of $400,000 derived from black tenants. Some other lands to which the nation had gained title were sold, and public lands were opened for the settlement of the few blacks who had tools and capital. The vision of landowning, however, the righteous and reasonable ambition for forty acres and a mule which filled the freedmen's dreams, was doomed in most cases to disappointment. And those men of marvelous hind-sight, who to-day are seeking to preach the Negro back to the soil, know well, or ought to know, that it was here, in 1865, that the finest opportunity of binding the black peasant to the soil was lost. Yet, with help and striving, the Negro gained some land, and by 1874, in the one state of Georgia, owned near 350,000 acres.

The greatest success of the Freedmen's Bureau lay in the planting of the free school among Negroes, and the idea of free elementary education among all classes in the South. It not only called the schoolmistress through the benevolent agencies, and built them schoolhouses, but it helped discover and support such apostles of human development as Edmund Ware, Erastus Cravath, and Samuel Armstrong. State superintendents of education were appointed, and by 1870 150,000 children were in school. The opposition to Negro education was bitter in the South, for the South believed an educated Negro to be a dangerous Negro. And the South was not wholly wrong; for education among all kinds of men always has had, and always will have, an element of danger and revolution, of dissatisfaction and discontent. Nevertheless, men strive to know. It was some inkling of this paradox, even in the unquiet days of the Bureau, that allayed an opposition to human training, which still to-day lies smouldering, but not flaming. Fisk, Atlanta, Howard, and Hampton were founded in these days, and nearly $6,000,000 was expended in five years for educational work, $750,000 of which came from the freedmen themselves.

Such contributions, together with the buying of land and various other enterprises, showed that the ex-slave was handling some free capital already. The chief initial source of this was labor in the army, and his pay and bounty as a soldier. Payments to Negro soldiers were at first complicated by the ignorance of the recipients, and the fact that the quotas of colored regiments from Northern states were largely filled by recruits from the South, unknown to their fellow soldiers. Consequently, payments were accompanied by such frauds that Congress, by joint resolution in 1867, put the whole matter in the hands of the Freedmen's Bureau. In two years $6,000,000 was thus distributed to 5000 claimants, and in the end the sum exceeded $8,000,000. Even in this system, fraud was frequent; but still the work put needed capital in the hands of practical paupers, and some, at least, was well spent.

The most perplexing and least successful part of the Bureau's work lay in the exercise of its judicial functions. In a distracted land where slavery had hardly fallen, to keep the strong from wanton abuse of the weak, and the weak from gloating insolently over the half-shorn strength of the strong, was a thankless, hopeless task. The former masters of the land were peremptorily ordered about, seized and imprisoned, and punished over and again, with scant courtesy from army officers. The former slaves were intimidated, beaten, raped, and butchered by angry and revengeful men. Bureau courts tended to become centres simply for punishing whites, while the regular civil courts tended to become solely institutions for perpetuating the slavery of blacks. Almost every law and method ingenuity could devise was employed by the legislatures to reduce the Negroes to serfdom—to make them the slaves of the state, if not of individual owners; while the Bureau officials too often were found striving to put the "bottom rail on top," and give the freedmen a power and independence which they could not yet use. It is all well enough for us of another generation to wax wise with advice to those who bore the burden in the heat of the day. It is full easy now to see that the man who lost home, fortune, and family at a stroke, and saw his land ruled by "mules and niggers," was really benefited by the passing of slavery. It is not difficult now to say to the young freedman, cheated and cuffed about, who has seen his father's head beaten to a jelly and his own mother namelessly assaulted, that the meek shall inherit the earth. Above all, nothing is more convenient than to heap on the Freedmen's Bureau all the evils of that evil day, and damn it utterly for every mistake and blunder that was made.

All this is easy, but it is neither sensible nor just. Some one had blundered, but that was long before Oliver Howard was born; there was criminal aggression and heedless neglect, but without some system of control there would have been far more than there was. Had that control been from within, the Negro would have been reenslaved, to all intents and purposes. Coming as the control did from without, perfect men and methods would have bettered all things; and even with imperfect agents and questionable methods, the work accomplished was not undeserving of much commendation. The regular Bureau court consisted of one representative of the employer, one of the Negro, and one of the Bureau. If the Bureau could have maintained a perfectly judicial attitude, this arrangement would have been ideal, and must in time have gained confidence; but the nature of its other activities and the character of its personnel prejudiced the Bureau in favor of the black litigants, and led without doubt to much injustice and annoyance. On the other hand, to leave the Negro in the hands of Southern courts was impossible.

What the Freedmen's Bureau cost the nation is difficult to determine accurately. Its methods of bookkeeping were not good, and the whole system of its work and records partook of the hurry and turmoil of the time. General Howard himself disbursed some $15,000,000 during his incumbency; but this includes the bounties paid colored soldiers, which perhaps should not be counted as an expense of the Bureau. In bounties, prize money, and all other expenses, the Bureau disbursed over $20,000,000 before all of its departments were finally closed. To this ought to be added the large expenses of the various departments of Negro affairs before 1865; but these are hardly extricable from war expenditures, nor can we estimate with any accuracy the contributions of benevolent societies during all these years.

Such was the work of the Freedmen's Bureau. To sum it up in brief, we may say: it set going a system of free labor; it established the black peasant proprietor; it secured the recognition of black freemen before courts of law; it founded the free public school in the South. On the other hand, it failed to establish good will between ex-masters and freedmen; to guard its work wholly from paternalistic methods that discouraged self- reliance; to make Negroes landholders in any considerable numbers. Its successes were the result of hard work, supplemented by the aid of philanthropists and the eager striving of black men. Its failures were the result of bad local agents, inherent difficulties of the work, and national neglect. The Freedmen's Bureau expired by limitation in 1869, save its educational and bounty departments. The educational work came to an end in 1872, and General Howard's connection with the Bureau ceased at that time. The work of paying bounties was transferred to the adjutant general's office, where it was continued three or four years longer.

Such an institution, from its wide powers, great responsibilities, large control of moneys, and generally conspicuous position, was naturally open to repeated and bitter attacks. It sustained a searching congressional investigation at the instance of Fernando Wood in 1870. It was, with blunt discourtesy, transferred from Howard's control, in his absence, to the supervision of Secretary of War Belknap in 1872, on the Secretary's recommendation. Finally, in consequence of grave intimations of wrongdoing made by the Secretary and his subordinates, General Howard was court-martialed in 1874. In each of these trials, and in other attacks, the commissioner of the Freedmen's Bureau was exonerated from any willful misdoing, and his work heartily commended. Nevertheless, many unpleasant things were brought to light: the methods of transacting the business of the Bureau were faulty; several cases of defalcation among officials in the field were proven, and further frauds hinted at; there were some business transactions which savored of dangerous speculation, if not dishonesty; and, above all, the smirch of the Freedmen's Bank, which, while legally distinct from, was morally and practically a part of the Bureau, will ever blacken the record of this great institution. Not even ten additional years of slavery could have done as much to throttle the thrift of the freedmen as the mismanagement and bankruptcy of the savings bank chartered by the nation for their especial aid. Yet it is but fair to say that the perfect honesty of purpose and unselfish devotion of General Howard have passed untarnished through the fire of criticism. Not so with all his subordinates, although in the case of the great majority of these there were shown bravery and devotion to duty, even though sometimes linked to narrowness and incompetency.

The most bitter attacks on the Freedmen's Bureau were aimed not so much at its conduct or policy under the law as at the necessity for any such organization at all. Such attacks came naturally from the border states and the South, and they were summed up by Senator Davis, of Kentucky, when he moved to entitle the act of 1866 a bill "to promote strife and conflict between the white and black races ... by a grant of unconstitutional power." The argument was of tremendous strength, but its very strength was its weakness. For, argued the plain common sense of the nation, if it is unconstitutional, unpracticable, and futile for the nation to stand guardian over its helpless wards, then there is left but one alternative: to make those wards their own guardians by arming them with the ballot. The alternative offered the nation then was not between full and restricted Negro suffrage; else every sensible man, black and white, would easily have chosen the latter. It was rather a choice between suffrage and slavery, after endless blood and gold had flowed to sweep human bondage away. Not a single Southern legislature stood ready to admit a Negro, under any conditions, to the polls; not a single Southern legislature believed free Negro labor was possible without a system of restrictions that took all its freedom away; there was scarcely a white man in the South who did not honestly regard emancipation as a crime, and its practical nullification as a duty. In such a situation, the granting of the ballot to the black man was a necessity, the very least a guilty nation could grant a wronged race. Had the opposition to government guardianship of Negroes been less bitter, and the attachment to the slave system less strong, the social seer can well imagine a far better policy: a permanent Freedmen's Bureau, with a national system of Negro schools; a carefully supervised employment and labor office; a system of impartial protection before the regular courts; and such institutions for social betterment as savings banks, land and building associations, and social settlements. All this vast expenditure of money and brains might have formed a great school of prospective citizenship, and solved in a way we have not yet solved the most perplexing and persistent of the Negro problems.

That such an institution was unthinkable in 1870 was due in part to certain acts of the Freedmen's Bureau itself. It came to regard its work as merely temporary, and Negro suffrage as a final answer to all present perplexities. The political ambition of many of its agents and proteges led it far afield into questionable activities, until the South, nursing its own deep prejudices, came easily to ignore all the good deeds of the Bureau, and hate its very name with perfect hatred. So the Freedmen's Bureau died, and its child was the Fifteenth Amendment.

The passing of a great human institution before its work is done, like the untimely passing of a single soul, but leaves a legacy of striving for other men. The legacy of the Freedmen's Bureau is the heavy heritage of this generation. Today, when new and vaster problems are destined to strain every fibre of the national mind and soul, would it not be well to count this legacy honestly and carefully? For this much all men know: despite compromise, struggle, war, and struggle, the Negro is not free. In the backwoods of the Gulf states, for miles and miles, he may not leave the plantation of his birth; in well-nigh the whole rural South the black farmers are peons, bound by law and custom to an economic slavery, from which the only escape is death or the penitentiary. In the most cultured sections and cities of the South the Negroes are a segregated servile caste, with restricted rights and privileges. Before the courts, both in law and custom, they stand on a different and peculiar basis. Taxation without representation is the rule of their political life. And the result of all this is, and in nature must have been, lawlessness and crime. That is the large legacy of the Freedmen's Bureau, the work it did not do because it could not.

I have seen a land right merry with the sun; where children sing, and rolling hills lie like passioned women, wanton with harvest. And there in the King's Highway sat and sits a figure, veiled and bowed, by which the traveler's footsteps hasten as they go. On the tainted air broods fear. Three centuries' thought has been the raising and unveiling of that bowed human heart, and now, behold, my fellows, a century new for the duty and the deed. The problem of the twentieth century is the problem of the color line.

Source: The Atlantic Monthly, March 1901, Volume 87, No. 519: pages 354–365.

69. The Free Colored People of North Carolina, 1902
CHARLES WADDELL CHESNUTT

This essay by writer Charles W. Chesnutt addresses the transformative lifestyle of individuals living in the South after the Civil War. He discusses the movement of industry to the northern states and the need for young blacks to seek education in the industrial trades to ensure financial stability, self-esteem, and a better lifestyle.

IN our generalizations upon American history—and the American people are prone to loose generalization, especially where the Negro is concerned—it is ordinarily assumed that the entire colored race was set free as the result of the Civil War. While this is true in a broad, moral sense, there was, nevertheless, a very considerable technical exception in the case of several hundred thousand free people of color, a great many of whom were residents of the Southern States. Although the emancipation of their race brought to these a larger measure of liberty than they had previously enjoyed, it did not confer upon them personal freedom, which they possessed already. These free colored people were variously distributed, being most numerous, perhaps, in Maryland, where, in the year 1850, for example, in a state with 87,189 slaves, there were 83,942 free colored people, the white population of the State being 515,918; and perhaps least numerous in Georgia, of all the slave states, where, to a slave population of 462,198, there were only 351 free people of color, or less than three-fourths of one percent, as against the about fifty per cent. in Maryland. Next to Maryland came Virginia, with 58,042 free colored people, North Carolina with 30,463, Louisiana with 18,647, (of whom 10,939 were in the parish of New Orleans alone), and South Carolina with 9,914. For these statistics, I have of course referred to the census reports for the years mentioned. In the year 1850, according to the same authority, there were in the state of North Carolina 553,028 white people, 288,548 slaves, and 27,463 free colored people. In 1860, the white population of the state was 631,100, slaves 331,059, free colored people, 30,463.

These figures for 1850 and 1860 show that between nine and ten per cent. of the colored population, and about three per cent. of the total population in each of those years, were free colored people, the ratio of increase during the intervening period being inconsiderable. In the decade preceding 1850 the ratio of increase had been somewhat different. From 1840 to 1850 the white population of the state had increased 14.05 per cent., the slave population 17.38 per cent., the free colored population 20.81 per cent. In the long period from 1790 to 1860, during which the total percentage of increase for the whole population of the state was 700.16, that of the whites was 750.30 per cent., that of the free colored people 720.65 per cent., and that of the slave population but 450 per cent., the total increase in free population being 747.56 per cent.

It seems altogether probable that but for the radical change in the character of slavery, following the invention of the cotton-gin and the consequent great demand for laborers upon the far Southern plantations, which turned the border states into breeding-grounds for slaves, the forces of freedom might in time have overcome those of slavery, and the institution might have died a natural death, as it already had in the Northern States, and as it subsequently did in Brazil and Cuba. To these changed industrial conditions was due, in all probability, in the decade following 1850, the stationary ratio of free colored people to slaves against the larger increase from 1840 to 1850. The gradual growth of the slave power had discouraged the manumission of slaves, had resulted in legislation curtailing the rights and privileges of free people of color, and had driven many of these to seek homes in the North and West, in communities where, if not warmly welcomed as citizens, they were at least tolerated as freemen.

This free colored population was by no means evenly distributed throughout the state, but was mainly found along or near the eastern seaboard, in what is now known as the "black district" of North Carolina. In Craven county, more than one-fifth of the colored population were free; in Halifax county, where the colored population was double that of the whites, one-fourth of the colored were free. In Hertford county, with 3,947 whites and 4,445 slaves, there were 1,112 free colored. In Pasquotank county, with a white and colored population almost evenly balanced, one-third of the colored people were free. In some counties, for instance in that of Jackson, a mountainous county in the west of the state, where the Negroes were but an insignificant element, the population stood 5,241 whites, 268 slaves, and three free colored persons.

The growth of this considerable element of free colored people had been due to several causes. In the eighteenth century, slavery in North Carolina had been of a somewhat mild character. There had been large estates along the seaboard and the water-courses, but the larger part of the population had been composed of small planters or farmers, whose slaves were few in number, too few indeed to be herded into slave quarters, but employed largely as domestic servants, and working side by side with their masters in field and forest, and sharing with them the same rude fare. The Scotch-Irish Presbyterian strain in the white people of North Carolina brought with it a fierce love of liberty, which was strongly manifested, for example, in the Mecklenburg declaration of independence, which preceded that at Philadelphia; and while this love of liberty was reconciled with slavery, the mere prejudice against race had not yet excluded all persons of Negro blood from its benign influence. Thus, in the earlier history of the state, the civil status of the inhabitants was largely regulated by condition rather than by color. To be a freeman meant to enjoy many of the fundamental rights of citizenship. Free men of color in North Carolina exercised the right of suffrage until 1835, when the constitution was amended to restrict this privilege to white men. It may be remarked, in passing, that prior to 1860, Jews could not vote in North Carolina. The right of marriage between whites and free persons of color was not restricted by law until the year 1830, though social prejudice had always discouraged it.

The mildness of slavery, which fostered kindly feelings between master and slave, often led to voluntary manumission. The superior morality which characterized the upper ranks of white women, so adequately protected by slavery, did not exist in anything like the same degree among the poorer classes, and occasional marriages, more or less legal, between free Negroes and slaves and poor white women, resulted in at least a small number of colored children, who followed the condition of their white mothers. I have personal knowledge of two free colored families of such origin, dating back to the eighteenth century, whose descendants in each case run into the hundreds. There was also a considerable Quaker element in the population, whose influence was cast against slavery, not in any fierce polemical spirit, but in such a way as to soften its rigors and promote gradual emancipation. Another source of free colored people in certain counties was the remnant of the Cherokee and

Tuscarora Indians, who, mingling with the Negroes and poor whites, left more or less of their blood among the colored people of the state. By the law of *partitus sequitur ventrem*, which is a law of nature as well as of nations, the child of a free mother was always free, no matter what its color or the status of its father, and many free colored people were of female Indian ancestry.

One of these curiously mixed people left his mark upon the history of the state— a bloody mark, too, for the Indian in him did not passively endure the things to which the Negro strain rendered him subject. Henry Berry Lowrey was what was known as a "Scuffletown mu-latto" Scuffletown being a rambling community in Robeson county, N. C., inhabited mainly by people of this origin. His father, a prosperous farmer, was impressed, like other free Negroes, during the Civ-il War, for service upon the Confederate public works. He resisted and was shot to death with several sons who were assisting him. A younger son, Henry Berry Lowrey, swore an oath to avenge the injury, and a few years later carried it out with true Indian persistence and ferocity. During a career of murder and robbery extending over several years, in which he was aided by an organized band of desperadoes who rendezvoused in inaccessible swamps and terrorized the county, he killed every white man concerned in his father's death, and incidentally several others who interfered with his plans, making in all a total of some thirty killings. A body of romance grew up about this swarthy Robin Hood, who, armed to the teeth, would freely walk into the towns and about the railroad stations, knowing full well that there was a price upon his head, but relying for safety upon the sympathy of the blacks and the fears of the whites. His pretty yellow wife, "Rhody," was known as "the queen of Scuffletown." Northern reporters came down to write him up. An astute Boston detective who penetrated, under false colors, to his stronghold, is said to have been put to death with savage tortures. A state official was once conducted, by devious paths, under Lowrey's safeguard, to the outlaw's camp, in order that he might see for himself how difficult it would be to dislodge them. A dime novel was founded upon his exploits. The state offered ten thousand, the Federal government, five thousand dollars for his capture, and a regiment of Federal troops was sent to subdue him, his career resembling very much that of the picturesque Italian bandit who has recently been captured after a long career of crime. Lowrey only succumbed in the end to a bullet from the hand of a treacherous comrade, and there is even yet a tradition that he escaped and made his way to a distant state. Some years ago these mixed Indians and Negroes were recognized by the North Carolina legislature as "Croatan Indians," being supposed to have descended from a tribe of that name and the whites of the lost first white colony of Virginia. They are allowed, among other special privileges conferred by this legislation, to have separate schools of their own, being placed, in certain other respects, upon a plane somewhat above that of the Negroes and a little below that of the whites.

I may add that North Carolina was a favorite refuge for runaway slaves and indentured servants from the richer colonies north and south of it. It may thus be plainly seen how a considerable body of free colored people sprang up within the borders of the state.

The status of these people, prior to the Civil War, was anomalous but tenable. Many of them, perhaps most of them, were as we have seen, persons of mixed blood, and received, with their dower of white blood, an intellectual and physical heritage of which social prejudice could not entirely rob them, and which helped them to prosperity in certain walks of life. The tie of kinship was sometimes recognized, and brought with it property, sympathy and opportunity which the black did not always enjoy. Many free colored men were skilled mechanics. The State House at Raleigh was built by colored workmen, under a foreman of the same race. I am acquainted with a family now living in the North, whose Negro grandfather was the leading tailor, in Newbern, N. C. He owned a pew on the ground floor of the church which he attended, and was buried in the cemetery where white people were laid to rest. In the town where I went to live when a child, just after the Civil War, nearly all the mechanics were men of color. One of these, a saddler by trade, had himself been the owner, before the war, of a large plantation and several slaves. He had been constrained by force of circumstances to invest in Confederate bonds, but despite this loss, he still had left a considerable tract of land, a brick store, and a handsome town residence, and was able to send one of his sons, immediately after the war, to a Northern school, where he read law, and returning to his native state, was admitted to the bar and has ever since practiced his profession. This was an old free family, descended from a free West Indian female ancestor. For historical reasons, which applied to the whole race, slave and free, these families were, before the war, most clearly traceable through the female line.

The principal cabinet-maker and undertaker in the town was an old white man whose workmen were colored. One of these practically inherited what was left of the business after the introduction of factory-made furniture from the North, and has been for many years the leading undertaker of the town. The tailors, shoemakers, wheelwrights and blacksmiths were men of color, as were the carpenters, bricklayers and plasterers.

It is often said, as an argument for slavery, by the still numerous apologists for that institution, that these skilled artisans have not passed on to the next generation the trades acquired by them under, if not in, slavery. This failure is generally ascribed to the shiftlessness of the race in freedom, and to the indisposition of the younger men to devote themselves to hard work. But the assumption is not always correct; there are still many competent colored mechanics in the South. In the town of which I have spoken, for instance, colored men are still the barbers, blacksmiths, masons and carpenters. And while there has been such a falling off, partly due to the unsettled conditions resulting from emancipation and inseparable from so sudden and radical a change, another reason for it exists in the altered industrial conditions which confront mechanics all over the country, due mainly to the growth of manufactures and the increased ease and cheapness of transportation. The shoes which were formerly made by hand are now manufactured in Massachusetts and sold, with a portrait of the maker stamped upon the sole, for less money than the most poorly paid mechanic could afford to make them for by hand. The buggies and wagons, to produce which kept a large factory, in the town where I lived, in constant operation, are now made in Cincinnati and other Northern cities, and delivered in North Carolina for a price prohibitive of manufacture by hand. Furniture is made at Grand Rapids, coffins in one place, and clothing in still another. The blacksmith buys his horseshoe ready made, in assorted sizes, and has merely to trim the hoof and fasten them on with machine-made nails. The shoemaker has degenerated into the cobbler; the tinner merely keeps a shop for the sale of tinware; the undertaker merely embalms the dead and conducts funerals, and tombstones are sold by catalogue with blanks for the insertion of names and dates before delivery. In some of the new industries which have sprung up in the South, such, for instance, as cotton-milling, Negroes are not employed. Hence, in large part through the operation of social forces beyond any control on their part, they have lost their hereditary employments, and these have only in part been replaced by employment in tobacco factories and in iron mines and mills.

The general decline of the apprenticeship system which has affected black and white alike, is also in some degree responsible for the dearth of trained mechanics in the South. Even in Northern cities the finer grades of stone-cutting, bricklaying, carpentry and cabinet work, and practically all the mosaic and terra-cotta work and fine interior decorating, is done by workmen of foreign birth and training.

Many of the younger colored people who might have learned trades, have found worthy employment as teachers and preachers; but the servile occupations into which so many of the remainder have drifted by following the line of least resistance, are a poor substitute for the independent position of the skilled mechanic. The establishment, for the colored race, of such institutions as Hampton and Tuskegee, not only replaces the apprenticeship system, but fills a growing industrial want. A multiplication of such agencies will enable the "free colored people" of the next generation, who now embrace the whole race and will number some ten millions or more, to regain these lost arts, and through them, by industry and thrift, under intelligent leadership, to win that equality of citizenship of which they are now grasping, perhaps, somewhat more than the shadow but something less than the substance.

Source: The Southern Workman, volume 31, number 3: pp. 136–141. Hampton Institute, Hampton, VA. Copyright © 1999, by the Rector and Visitors of the University of Virginia. Courtesy of The University of Virginia Library.

70. Of the Training of Black Men, September 1902
W. E. B. DuBOIS

In the fall of 1902, W.E.B. DuBois wrote an article in *The Atlantic* where he argued against the then-popular idea of training young black men as tradesmen for economic purposes alone. This approach of teaching black men trades alone was a shallow solution to a deeper problem faced by all blacks in America—assimilation into mainstream American life. Merely training them to work as carpenters, masons, and other tradesmen belittled them in their own eyes and in the eyes of the world. DuBois wrote that better race relations required broader education of young black men so that America would be populated by two self-respecting, cultured, and educated races, not one elite and the other a resentful minority.

From the shimmering swirl of waters where many, many thoughts ago the slave-ship first saw the square tower of Jamestown have flowed down to our day three streams of thinking: one from the larger world here and over-seas, saying, the multiplying of human wants in culture lands calls for the world-wide co-operation of men in satisfying them. Hence arises a new human unity, pulling the ends of earth nearer, and all men, black, yellow, and white. The larger humanity strives to feel in this contact of living nations and sleeping hordes a thrill of new life in the world, crying, If the contact of Life and Sleep be Death, shame on such Life. To be sure, behind this thought lurks the afterthought of force and dominion,—the making of brown men to delve when the temptation of beads and red calico cloys.

The second thought streaming from the death-ship and the curving river is the thought of the older South: the sincere and passionate belief that somewhere between men and cattle God created a tertium quid, and called it a Negro,—a clownish, simple creature, at times even lovable within its limitations, but straitly foreordained to walk within the Veil. To be sure, behind the thought lurks the afterthought,—some of them with favoring chance might become men, but in sheer self-defense we dare not let them, and build about them walls so high, and hang between them and the light a veil so thick, that they shall not even think of breaking through.

And last of all there trickles down that third and darker thought, the thought of the things themselves, the confused half-conscious mutter of men who are black and whitened, crying Liberty, Freedom, Opportunity—vouchsafe to us, O boastful World, the chance of living men! To be sure, behind the thought lurks the afterthought: suppose, after all, the World is right and we are less than men? Suppose this mad impulse within is all wrong, some mock mirage from the untrue?

So here we stand among thoughts of human unity, even through conquest and slavery; the inferiority of black men, even if forced by fraud; a shriek in the night for the freedom of men who themselves are not yet sure of their right to demand it. This is the tangle of thought and afterthought wherein we are called to solve the problem of training men for life.

Behind all its curiousness, so attractive alike to sage and dilettante, lie its dim dangers, throwing across us shadows at once grotesque and awful. Plain it is to us that what the world seeks through desert and wild we have within our threshold;—a stalwart laboring force, suited to the semi-tropics; if, deaf to the voice of the Zeitgeist, we refuse to use and develop these men, we risk poverty and loss. If, on the other hand, seized by the brutal afterthought, we debauch the race thus caught in our talons, selfishly sucking their blood and brains in the future as in the past, what shall save us from national decadence? Only that saner selfishness which, Education teaches men, can find the rights of all in the whirl of work.

Source: The Atlantic Monthly, September 1902, Volume 90, No. 539: pages 289–297.

71. The Negro Development and Exposition Company of the U.S.A., An address to the American Negro, 1907

This is an address to the American Negro written by the Negro Development and Exposition Company of the U.S.A. and delivered at an annual exhibition held in Virginia to consolidate and promote Negro thrift, progress, and commerce after emancipation.

To the Ten Million Negroes of the United States, Greeting ...

Whereas a large number of representative men and women of the race secured, under the laws of Virginia, a charter for the Negro Development and Exposition Company of the United States of America, on the 13th day of August, 1903, which company was organized for the purpose of holding a separate exhibit on the occasion of the 300th anniversary of the landing of the first English speaking people of this country at Jamestown. Va., but before the incorporation of this company, there was organized and chartered the Jamestown Exposition Company, under the laws of Virginia, for the purpose of celebrating the said 300th anniversary, by holding a land and naval exhibition at or near Hampton Roads, Va.

This last company is officered, owned and operated by the white people of this country.

The Negro felt that in as much as there was to be a celebration of the said event by the white race, it would be a fit and opportune time for the Negro to come upon the scenes and there present to the nations of the earth, the evidence of his thrift and progress, by putting upon exhibition the articles and things made and invented, created and produced by the race since its emancipation, and that in accordance with the uncertain and unsatisfactory conditions now existing as to the Negro in this country, that a creditable exhibit of his industrial capacities would result in untold good to the entire race, that the Negro question has been and is being discussed all over this country, some taking a favorable view of the situation, others taking different views, leaving him in an unsatisfactory position as to his relation to the government and the country in which he lives. A creditable exhibit would have a tendency to show just what the Negro can do, what he has done, and what he is doing in the solution of the much talked of question, or problem. That in this particular time, such an exhibit would be productive of great results from every point of view. The fact that the nations of the earth have been invited by the President of the United States to participate in the said exposition, is another evidence that such and exhibit would be of untold benefit to the Negro. It would also be stimulating to the Negro to see for himself what he can do, as such an exhibit would bring together the entire race with its exhibits to be thus viewed, which under no other circumstances it could have done.

After the incorporation of the said Negro Development and Exposition Company, its executive officers conferred with the Jamestown Company and secured concessions to hold a separate and distinct exhibit on the occasion of the great national and international exposition to enable the Negro to produce the results above referred to. The concessions were in every way satisfactory and agreeable to both the Negro Development and Exposition Company and the Jamestown Exposition Company. After this concession, the said Negro Development and Exposition Company proceeded to present its claim for a special exhibit on account of the race to the American people regardless of race or color. Its first effort was for the endorsement of the National Negro Business League, of which Dr. Booker T. Washington is president. Its second effort was to secure the endorsement and support of the National Negro Baptist Convention at its session in the city of Chicago on the 27th day of October 1905, which endorsement was unanimously received. It received the endorsement of a number of the State Baptist Conventions, and of the State A. M. E. Conferences including that of Virginia. It received the endorsement of the State Baptist Conventions of North Carolina, South Carolina and a number of district and other conventions of the race in the various States of the Union. Among them were the Florida State Negro Business League, and the Mississippi State Negro Business League. We carried the cause from State to State. We have had resolutions adopted endorsing our efforts in nearly every State of the Union, where the race population justified the adoption of such resolutions. We have spoken and received the endorsement in mass meetings assembled in the cities in the North and West.

The company's authorized capital stock was fixed at $800,000 at the par value of $10 each. We saw that the money could not be raised in time to have the desired result by the sale of the capital stock among the members of our own race. We, therefore, appealed to the governors of the different States, where the colored people were in large numbers of the colored population justified asking that they recommend to their legislatures the appropriation of an amount of money, justified by the numbers of Negroes, to aid and assist the Negro of their respective States in uniting with their brethren in Virginia in making a creditable exhibit of their achievements from their said States. From them we received favorable response. A large number of the governors recommended such an appropriation, and in a number of States appropriations have been made for the said State's participation in the Jamestown Exposition. We have appealed to the State commissioners, appointed by their respective governors, asking that a proportion of the appropriation thus made, be set apart to assist the Negro of that State in the part he desires to take in connection with the Negro exhibit at the Jamestown Exposition.

We have appeared before the committees of several legislatures. We have presented the cause of the Negroes and asked the legislatures to provide for them. Then, for fear that the States might not act as promptly as we hoped to or as satisfactorily as we hoped they would, we appealed to the president of the United States, and asked for the influence of his good office in securing an appropriation from the national government. The mere calling the President's attention to the situation secured his immediate endorsement and his pledge of support in our effort to get governmental aid in this laudable enterprise. To emphasize his position in the matter on the occasion of his visit in the South in passing through Richmond, Va., on the 18th day of October, 1905, President Roosevelt stopped the procession that was escorting him through the city of Richmond when it reached the head-quarters of the Negro Development and Exposition Company, and there called for Giles B. Jackson, the Director General of the said company, and addressing him, said in part; "Mr. Jackson, I congratulate you and your people on the magnificient showing you have made in your development. I am with you. I assure you and your people that you have my hearty support in the efforts you are making to have a creditable exhibit of the achievements of your race and I commend you in the effort you are making for the betterment of the condition of your race."

Having thus received the public commendation of the President of the United States, we proceeded to Washington with a bill in hand prepared with pains and asking for the appropriation of $250,000 by the Congress of the United States to the Negro Development and Exposition Company, to aid him in his exhibit. This bill was referred to the committee on Industrial Arts and Expositions and after several meetings of the committee once in the city of Norfolk and on other occasions in the city of Washington, it was agreed to recommend the appropriation of $100,000 in the aid of the Negro Development and Exposition Company. This bill was likewise reported by the committee in the senate, and on the 30th day of June, it passed both houses of Congress and was signed by the president and there upon became the law of the land.

It is needless for us to say that we had quite a difficult task in getting this appropriation. We had to fight those whom we had expected would be our friends, and those whom we had expected to meet in compact in opposition to this appropriation, were those who came to our rescue.

We mean there was not a single white man in congress to raise his voice against us. It passed congress with only one vote against us and that was so faint one could not discover the one who said it. He did not mean it. If he had, he would have made himself heard and his identity known, therefore, we regard it regard it that the bill, appropriating this $100,000 to aid the Negro, was passed without a single voice against it. But, strange as it may appear, there were those among our own race, who wrote letters to congress protesting against governmental aid of the Negro Development and Exposition Company, and these were men of learning, as we are told, but their effort was so preposterous that it made friends for us in congress. The white man saw that any Negro who opposed such an appropriation was an enemy to himself and his race, hence, the opposition of the few, simply made friends for us. We have not an unkind word to say against them or anybody else. The fact that the government has put its seal of approval upon the effort of the Negro Development and Exposition Company and its officers by making the appropriation to aid it in its work, is sufficient to commend the said company to the entire Negro race and to the American people. It does commend it, and in no uncertain tone, for when the government of the United States passes an act appropriating $1,000,000, it puts its commendation upon it. When the Congress of the United States passes an act appropriating $1.00 to any cause, it carries with it its commendation to the world. The committee on Industrial Arts and Expositions investigated everything pertaining to the Negro Development and Exposition Company. They had meetings after meetings, and Negro after Negro appeared before them, either in writing or otherwise, and tried to throw cold water upon the efforts of the Negro in Virginia, but every step they made redowned to the benefit of the Negro Development and Exposition Company. The harder the Negro fought it the better faith the white man had in it, because the Negro could not make the argument sufficiently strong against the appropriation to convince an illiterate man, much less a member of congress, that the Negro exhibit was not the thing to be had.

The fact that there was a Negro department at the Atlanta Exposition, which was supported by governmental aid, and the fact that there was a Negro department at the Charleston Exposition, which was supported by governmental aid, and the fact that the Negro exhibit was gathered together by the authorities of the national government and carried to Paris, and there put upon exhibition, all three of which exhibitions were declared a success, have caused our opposers to abandon all opposition, and to unite with the Negro Development and Exposition Company to make the desired success of the exposition. They were the pride of the Negro race. This alone was argument in favor of the Negro exhibit at the Jamestown Exposition, and left no room for the opposers to make a stand.

Now that all of this has happened and the Negro Development and Exposition Company is still marching to the front with the aid of the government, and is planning to have a gigantic exhibit at the Jamestown Exposition, and that the government of the United States, by its act has removed all doubt as to the success of the exhibit and has declared its faith in the management of the Negro Development and Exposition Company, the thing now to do is for the whole race, even those who differ with us, to unite as one and carry forward the great work of creating the gigantic exhibit on behalf of the Negro race of this country at the Jamestown Exposition.

The argument that the Negro exhibit was a Jim Crow affair, has been knocked out by the act of the government and by the act of the Negro Development and Exposition Company.

The fact that the company is owned and officered by the Negro himself and was made and created on his motion, removed any taint of Jim Crowism. If the Negro

Development and Exposition Company is a Jim Crow affair, then every institution of learning, owned and officered by Negroes, is likewise a Jim Crow affair; every church, in which Negroes worship and over which our bishops preside, is a Jim Crow affair. If one is a Jim Crow affair, then the others is. We say neither is. The Negro Development and Exposition Company, and the church, and the institution of learning, owned and operated by Negroes, each is a separate institution for the benefit of the Negro exhibit at the Jamestown Exposition.

Argument has been produced against the exhibit because of the Jim Crow car laws, that exist in the Southern States. This we deplore, and our position is known. We were so much opposed to the law, that Giles B. Jackson, the Director General of this company, appeared before the legislative committee on roads and internal navigation of the Virginia legislature, and opposed the enactment of this law. With all his vim, oratory, force , and effect. He made it possible for a committee, that was headed by Dr. Atkins, of Hampton, Va., to appear before the said committee and enter a solemn protest, but after all the bill was enacted. It was only in keeping with all the Southern States. It is now the law, and as law-abiding citizens, we are compelled to bow in humble submission. If the State is insufficient to compel us to obey the law, the United States government, under the constitution, would have to intervene until we were subjected under the laws of the State. Then, too, is it not the proper thing for us to do to make the best terms we can with railroads since they have the power to give equal accommodation to both races, that being the law of different Southern States that the races should be separated that no distinction should be made as to accommodation? It is incumbent on the Negro to stop kicking and quarreling, and go to the law and to the heads of the authorities of the States and ask that the railroads be required to give equal accommodation for the colored passengers, and this will be done. But whether the citizens of the different States do it or not, the Negro Development and Exposition Company, having in charge the Negro exhibit at Jamestown, will see to it that equal and good accommodations will be afforded to the Negro travelers, to and from the exposition. The Negro Development and Exposition Company is making itself busy in looking after this part of the program. It will take up the matter with the heads of the railroad companies. In fact, it has already done so with some of the companies and they have pledged their word and honor that good, clean and satisfactory accommodations will be given to the Negro travelers from the North, South, East and West. That they shall have no reason to complain, other than the fact that they will not be riding with the white folks. They will be riding together in clean, decent and respectable cars with efficient service. Those traveling, who find any fault with the management, will please report the same to Giles B. Jackson, the Director General and the general counsel for the Negro Development and Exposition Company, of U. S. A., and he will take the matter up immediately with the railroad companies and see to it that there shall not be any other occasion for complaint. Col. Jackson is on good terms with the railroad companies, but if they fail to do their duty, the aid of the corporation commission, having charge of the overseeing of all the railroads of Virginia, will adjust matters. This commission was made and created under the constitution of Virginia for the purpose of enforcing the laws, and its aid will be invoked whenever the occasion requires, but it is hoped and believed that the occasion will not require it. The railroad and steamboat companies will make special effort to avoid any complaint from any travelers on all lines and roads.

We issue this address that the members of our race may thoroughly understand the true condition of affairs and that they may not be afraid to come to the exposition. The fact that there will be crowds of people coming from all over the country to the exposition will make it convenient for the reunion of families, that have been separated for ten, twenty, yes, thirty years. The opportunity will be afforded for the meeting of our friends, whom we have not seen since the war. The opportunity will be afforded for the meeting of our kin-folks and relatives, whom we have not seen since our emancipation. Every car coming will bring lots of our race, every boat will be loaded down. On every day there will be those who have not seen each other for years.

Source: Richmond, Va.: The Negro Development and Exposition Company of the U.S.A., 1907. Library of Congress, Rare Book and Special Collections Division, Daniel A.P. Murray Pamphlets Collection.

72. The Negro Development and Exposition Company of the U.S.A., An address to the American Negro on "Separate but Equal" doctrines, 1907

Written by the Negro Development and Exposition Company, this essay was of particular interest to Negroes who found navigating their surroundings and everyday life difficult in a society where "separate but equal" was not only unjust law, but not even a reality. The essay focused on the difficult task of using public accommodations.

Board and lodging will be the same as it is now. No one will be allowed to charge more than the usual price. Board and lodging can be secured in the families and hotels in Norfolk, Hampton, Phoebus, Newport News and the surrounding towns …

Ample accommodations will be made by which persons can reach the exposition grounds in twenty-five minutes. Street facilities and bus lines will be in abundance. The colored people in the city of Norfolk are now organizing a transportation line with the view of running carriages of all kinds and busses into the grounds.

The Jamestown Exposition Company will issue their proclamation calling upon the people to do justice between man and man. The authorities of Virginia will see to it that no man will be put to inconvenience or prosecuted unless he is proven guilty of violating the laws of the land. The law is not made to punish the just and law abiding citizens but it is made to punish the offenders of the law, and it is made to protect the just and those who come under its protection. There are those among both races whom the law was made to subdue. It will not allow them to predominate or to obstruct the law abiding members of any race, who shall come upon the soil of Virginia. The judges of our courts are conservative. We speak from our own knowledge of practice before the bar for twenty years. No man will be unfairly dealt with, but he must obey the law. We mean the rowdy and shiftless element that might drift among us. They will find the white and black men united to suppress them, if they commence to evade the law or hinder others in their pursuit of happiness. The Negro will have no complaint to make when he comes to the exposition. We vouch for it that the first carload that comes here will go back with such good news and glad tidings that many more will be anxious to come. This remains to be seen, that we understand the situation and predict this as the result of careful study of the situation.

Source: Richmond, Va.: The Negro Development and Exposition Company of the U.S.A., 1907. Library of Congress, Rare Book and Special Collections Division, Daniel A.P. Murray Pamphlets Collection.

73. The Flat Hunters: a Musical Satire on Moving Day, 1914
JUNIE McCREE

This is an excerpt from a stage production of Negro theater by a group who called themselves "The Flat Hunters." It is housed in historical archives about the American variety stage and vaudeveille.

Introduction: Cast: Henry Fish ... Nahitabel Fish (his wife) Scarletina (Her sister)
Enter Nahitabel and Scarletine, carrying hat boxes neatly ribboned etc. Henry carries a long trunk, two chairs fastened to each end, bird cage with bird inside and other junk he decided to carry. To make it funny and look as though he was carrying the entire furnishings of a flat. The girls enter first—he follows and remains R. They go centre.

SCENE—STREET

SONG— "Moving Day"
Verse
(Nahitabel and Scarletina)
We've been hunting flats now since the middle of September,
And to carry such a burden calls for spunk
Henry
(set trunk and junk down)
The only burden carried now as far as I remember
Is you made me carry both this bird and trunk
N & S
We're looking for a flat unfurnished five rooms and a bath,
The bath is most essential to console
HENRY
The reason that the bath is really such a consolation
It's the most essential place to keep our coal
CHORUS
N&S
(Pretty song and dance moves)
Moving Day, Moving Day
Made by woman first of each October,
HENRY
I must say that moving day,
Was never made by man if he was sober
N&S
We know that movin' day is just like play
It's simple exercise for any man.
HENRY
But his bones just ache him,
When they take him

From a moving van

(Girls go into soft dance, music is very soft, during dance, following dialogue, Henry remains on the trunk watching the dancers.)

N.

I love to dance, don't you?

SCARLETINE

I adore it.

HENRY

If yo' all had toted this trunk around for ten hours your terpsichorean affection would lose some of its ardor.

SCARLETINE

I feel so light on my feet.

HENRY

I hope you light on yore head.

SCARLETINE

If you had your choice, which would you rather have, a tangoist or a turkey trotter to carry through life?

HENRY

I'd rather have an express wagon to carry this trunk.

Source: Library of Congress, Rare Book and Special Collections Division.

74. The Negro Genius, May 1915
BENJAMIN BRAWLEY

In this book excerpt, Benjamin Brawley, dean of Morehouse College in Atlanta, Georgia, discusses the genius within each individual regardless of racial history.

In his lecture on "The Poetic Principle," in leading down to his definition of poetry, Edgar Allan Poe has called attention to the three faculties, intellect, feeling, and will, and shown that poetry, that the whole realm of aesthetics in fact, is concerned primarily and solely with the second of these. Does it appeal to a sense of beauty? This is his sole test of a poem or of any work of art, the aim being neither to appeal to the intellect by satisfying the reason or inculcating truth, nor to appeal to the will by satisfying the moral sense or inculcating duty.

This standard has often been criticized as narrow; yet it embodies a large and fundamental element of truth. If, now, we study the races that go to make up our cosmopolitan American life we shall find that the three which most distinctively represent the faculties, intellect, feeling, and will, are respectively the Anglo-Saxon, the Negro, and the Jewish. Whatever achievement has been made by the Anglo-Saxon has been primarily in the domain of pure intellect. In religion, in business, in invention, in pure scholarship, the same principle holds; and examples are found in Jonathan Edwards, J. Pierpont Morgan, Thomas A. Edison, and in such scholars as Royce and Kittredge of the Harvard of today. Similarly the outstanding race in the history of the world for emphasis on the moral or religious element of life has been the Jewish. Throughout the Old Testament the heart of Israel cries out to Jehovah, and through the law given on Sinai, the songs of the Psalmist, and the prophecies of Isaiah, the tradition of Israel has thrilled and inspired the entire human race.

With reference now to the Negro two things are observable. One is that any distinction so far won by a member of the race in America has been almost always in some one of the arts; and the other is that any influence so far exerted by the Negro on American civilization has been primarily in the field of esthetics. A man of science like Benjamin Banneker is the exception. To prove the point we may refer to a long line of beautiful singers, to the fervid oratory of Douglass, to the sensuous poetry of Dunbar, to the picturesque style of Du Bois, to the impressionism of the paintings of Tanner, and to the elemental sculpture of Meta Warrick Fuller. Even Booker Washington, most practical of Americans, proves the point, the distinguishing qualities of his speeches being anecdote and brilliant concrete illustration.

Everyone must have observed the radical difference in the appearance of the homes of white people and Negroes of the peasant class in the South. If the white man is not himself cultivated, and if he has not been able to give to his children the advantages of culture, his home is most likely to be a bare, blank abode with no pictures and no flowers. Such is not the case with the Negro. He is determined to have a picture, and if nothing better is obtainable he will paste a circus poster or a flaring advertisement on the walls. The instinct for beauty insists upon an outlet; and there are few homes of Negroes of the humbler class that will not have a geranium on the windowsill or a rose-bush in the garden. If, too, we look at the matter conversely, we shall find that those things which are most picturesque make to the Negro the readiest appeal. Red is his favorite color, simply because it is the most pronounced of all colors. Goethe's "Faust" can hardly be said to be a play designed primarily for the galleries. In general it might be supposed to rank with "Macbeth" or "She Stoops to Conquer" or "Richelieu." One never sees it fail, however, that in any Southern city "Faust" will fill the gallery with the so-called lower class of Negro people, who would never dream of going to see one of the other plays just mentioned; and the applause never leaves one in doubt as to the reasons for Goethe's popularity. It is the suggestiveness of the love scenes, the red costume of Mephistopheles, the electrical effects, and the rain of fire, that give the thrill desired—all pure melodrama of course. "Faust" is a good show as well as a good play.

In some of our communities Negroes are frequently known to "get happy" in church. Now a sermon on the rule of faith or the plan of salvation is never known to awaken such ecstacy. This rather accompanies a vivid portrayal of the beauties of heaven, with its walls of jasper, the angels with palms in their hands, and (*summum bonum!*) the feast of milk and honey. And just here is the dilemma faced by the occupants of a great many pulpits in Negro churches. Do the Negroes want scholarly training? Very frequently the cultured preacher will be inclined to answer in the negative. Do they want rant and shouting? Such a standard fails at once to satisfy the ever-increasing intelligence of the audience itself. The trouble is that the educated Negro minister too often leaves out of account the basic psychology of his audience. That preacher who will ultimately be the most successful with the Negro congregation will be the one who to scholarship and culture can join brilliant imagination and fervid rhetorical expression. When all of these qualities are brought together in their finest proportion the effect is irresistible. Some distinguished white preachers, who to their deep spirituality have joined lively rhetorical expression, have never failed to succeed with a Negro audience as well as with an Anglo-Saxon one. Noteworthy examples within recent years have been Dr. P. S. Henson and Dr. R. S. MacArthur.

Gathering up the threads of our discussion so far, we find that there is constant striving on the part of the Negro for beautiful or striking effect, that those things which are most picturesque make the readiest appeal to his nature, and that in the sphere of religion he receives with most appreciation those discourses which are most imaginative in quality. In short, so far as the last point is concerned, it is not too much to assert that the Negro is thrilled, not so much by the moral as by the artistic and pictorial elements in religion.

But there is something deeper than the sensuousness of beauty that makes for the possibilities of the Negro in the realm of the arts, and that is the soul of the race. The wail of the old melodies and the plaintive quality that is ever present in the Negro voice are but the reflection of a background of tragedy. No race can rise to the greatest heights of art until it has yearned and suffered. The Russians are a case in point. Such has been their background in oppression and striving that their literature and art today are marked by an unmistakable note of power. The same future beckons to the American Negro. There is something very elemental about the heart of the race, something that finds its origin in the African forest, in the sighing of the night-wind, and in the falling of the stars. There is something grim and stern about it all too, something that speaks of the lash, of the child torn from its mother's bosom, of the dead body riddled with bullets and swinging all night from a limb by the roadside.

What does all this mean but that the Negro is a thorough-going romanticist? The philosophy, the satires, the conventionalities of the age of reason mean little to him; but the freedom, the picturesqueness, the moodiness of Wordsworth's day mean much. In his wild, weird melodies we follow once more the wanderings of the Ancient Mariner. In the fervid picture of the New Jerusalem we see the same emphasis on the concrete as in "To a Skylark" or the "Ode to the West Wind;" and under the spell of the Negro voice at its best we once more revel in the sensuousness of "The Eve of St. Agnes."

All of this of course does not mean that the Negro cannot rise to distinction in any sphere other than the arts, any more than it means that the Anglo-Saxon has not produced great painting and music. It does mean, however, that every race has its peculiar genius, and that, so far as we are at present able to judge, the Negro, with all of his manual labor, is destined to reach his greatest heights in the field of the artistic. But the impulse needs to be watched. Romanticism very soon becomes unhealthy. The Negro has great gifts of voice and ear and soul; but so far much of his talent has not soared above the vaudeville stage. This is due mostly largely of course, to economic instability. It is the call of patriotism, however, that America should realize that the Negro has peculiar gifts which need all possible cultivation, and which will one day add to the glory of the country. Already his music is recognized as the most distinctive that the United States has yet produced. The possibilities of the race in literature and oratory, in sculpture and painting, are illimitable.

Source: The Southern Workman, Volume 44. Hampton: Press of The Hampton Normal and Agricultural Institute, May, 1915. Copyright © 1999, by the Rector and Visitors of the University of Virginia. Courtesy of The University of Virginia Library.

75. Excerpt from the Marcus Garvey and Universal Negro Improvement Association (UNIA) Papers, 1919

Marcus Garvey and the Universal Negro Improvement Association (UNIA) formed a critical link in black America's centuries-long struggle for freedom, justice, and equality. As the leader of the largest organized mass movement in black history, Garvey is now best remembered as a champion of the back-to-Africa movement. In his own time he was hailed as a redeemer, a "Black Moses." Much of history has labeled Garvey as a fool and worse, a hustler who took advantage of his own people. That history is tainted by the scourge of systemic racism throughout history that has plagued black leaders who were hunted by slave catchers or, more officially, by the Justice Department and men like J. Edgar Hoover. The victims of these sanctioned witch hunts of black leaders included men such as slaves like Nat Turner and Dred Scott. In the twentieth century, these probes labeled leaders such as Garvey, the Dr. Martin Luther King, Jr., and Malcolm X as public enemies. Garvey was deported. King and Malcolm were assassinated.

Though he failed to realize all his objectives, Garvey's movement represents a liberation from the psychological bondage of racial inferiority.

Garvey was born on August 17, 1887 in St. Ann's Bay, Jamaica. He left school at 14, worked as a printer, joined Jamaican nationalist organizations, toured Central America, and spent time in London. Content at first with accommodation, on his return to Jamaica, he aspired to open a Tuskegee-type industrial training school. In 1916 he came to America at Booker T. Washington's invitation, but arrived just after Washington died.

Garvey arrived in America at the dawn of the "New Negro" era. Black discontent, punctuated by East St. Louis's bloody race riots in 1917 and intensified by postwar disillusionment, peaked in 1919's Red Summer. Shortly after arriving, Garvey embarked upon a period of travel and lecturing. When he settled in New York City, he organized a chapter of the UNIA, which he had earlier founded in Jamaica as a fraternal organization. Drawing on a gift for oratory, he melded Jamaican peasant aspirations for economic and cultural independence with the American gospel of success to create a new gospel of racial pride. "Garveyism" eventually evolved into a religion of success, inspiring millions of black people worldwide who sought relief from racism and colonialism

To enrich and strengthen his movement, Garvey envisioned a great shipping line to foster black trade, to transport passengers between America, the Caribbean, and Africa, and to serve as a symbol of black grandeur and enterprise. The UNIA incorporated the Black Star Line in 1919. The line's flagship, the S.S. Yarmouth, made its maiden voyage in November and two other ships joined the line in 1920. The Black Star Line became a powerful recruiting tool for the UNIA, but it was ultimately sunk by expensive repairs, discontented crews, and top-level mismanagement and corruption.

By 1920 the UNIA had hundreds of chapters worldwide; it hosted elaborate international conventions and published the Negro World, a widely disseminated weekly that was soon banned in many parts of Africa and the Caribbean. Over the next few years, however, the movement began to unravel under the strains of internal dissension, opposition from black critics, and government harassment. In 1922 the federal government indicted Garvey on mail fraud charges stemming from Black Star Line promotional claims and he suspended all BSL operations. (Two years later, the UNIA created another line, the Black Cross Navigation and Trading Co., but it, too, failed.) Garvey was sentenced to prison. The government later commuted his sentence, only to deport him back to Jamaica in November 1927. He never returned to America.

In Jamaica Garvey reconstituted the UNIA and held conventions there and in Canada, but the heart of his movement stumbled on in America without him.

While he dabbled in local politics, he remained a keen observer of world events, writing voluminously in his own papers. His final move was to London, in 1935. He settled there shortly before Fascist Italy invaded Ethiopia and his public criticisms of Haile Selassie's behavior after the invasion alienated many of his own remaining followers. In his last years he slid into such obscurity that he suffered the final indignity of reading his own obituaries a month before his death on June 10, 1940.

Source: Copyright © 1995–2008 The Marcus Garvey and UNIA Papers Project, UCLA.

76. A Century of Negro Migration, Chapter 10
CARTER GOODWIN WOODSON

The interstate movements of blacks after slavery created a perplexing problem for a country that was unprepared to grant them political and civil rights. According to noted historian Carter Goodwin Woodson, this nominal equality for blacks had been forced on the South. Woodson said it was not an uncommon belief that the two races could not live as equals, and some advocated segregating blacks to specific regions in the south.

Speaking more plainly to the point, the editor of the Philadelphia North American said that the true interest of the South was to accommodate itself to changed conditions and that the duty of the freedmen lies in making themselves worth more in the development of the South than they were as chattels. Although recognizing the disabilities and hardships of the South both to the whites and the blacks, he could not believe that the elimination of the Negroes would, if practicable, give relief. The *Boston Herald* inquired whether it was worth while to send away a laboring population in the absence of whites to take its place and referred to the misfortunes of Spain which undertook to carry out such a scheme. Speaking the real truth, The Milwaukee Journal said that no one needed to expect any appreciable decrease in the black population through any possible emigration, no matter how successful it might be. "The Negro," said the editor, "is here to stay and our institutions must be adapted to comprehend him and develop his possibilities." The Colored American, then the leading Negro organ of thought in the United States, believed that the Negroes should be thankful to Senator Morgan for his attitude on emigration, because he might succeed in deporting to Africa those Negroes who affect to believe that this is not their home and the more quickly we get rid of such foolhardy people the better it will be for the stalwart of the race.

A number of Negroes, however, under the inspiration of leaders like Bishop H.M. Turner, did not feel that the race had a fair chance in the United States. A few of them emigrated to Wapimo, Mexico; but, becoming dissatisfied with the situation there, they returned to their homes in Georgia and Alabama in 1895. The coming of the Negroes into Mexico caused suspicion and excitement. A newspaper, El Tiempo, which had been denouncing lynching in the United States, changed front when these Negroes arrived in that country.

Going in quest of new opportunities and desiring to reenforce the civilization of Liberia, 197 other Negroes sailed from Savannah, Georgia, for Liberia, March 19, 1895. Commending this step, the Macon Telegraph referred to their action as a rebellion against the social laws which govern all people of this country. This organ further said that it was the outcome of a feeling which has grown stronger and stronger year by year among the Negroes of the Southern States and which will continue to grow with the increase of education and intelligence among them. The editor conceded that they had an opportunity to better their material condition and acquire wealth here but contended that they had no chance to rise out of the peasant class. The Memphis Commercial Appeal urged the building of a large Negro nation in Africa as practicable and desirable, for it was "more and more apparent that the Negro in this country must remain an alien and a disturber," because there was "not and can never be a future for him in this country." The Florida Times Union felt that this colonization scheme, like all others, was a fraud. It referred to the Negro's being carried to the land of plenty only to find out that there, as everywhere else in the world, an existence must be earned by toil and that his own old sunny southern home is vastly the better place.

Only a few intelligent Negroes, however, had reached the position of being contented in the South. The Negroes eliminated from politics could not easily bring themselves around to thinking that they should remain there in a state of recognized inferiority, especially when during the eighties and nineties there were many evidences that economic as well as political conditions would become worse. The exodus treated in the previous chapter was productive of better treatment for the Negroes and an increase in their wages in certain parts of the South but the migration, contrary to the expectations of many, did not become general. Actual prosperity was impossible even if the whites had been willing to give the Negro peasants a fair chance. The South had passed through a disastrous war, the effects of which so blighted the hopes of its citizens in the economic world that their land seemed to pass, so to speak, through a dark age. There was then little to give the man far down when the one to whom he of necessity looked for employment was in his turn bled by the merchant or the banker of the larger cities, to whom he had to go for extensive credits.

Southern planters as a class, however, had not much sympathy for the blacks who had once been their property and the tendency to cheat them continued, despite the fact that many farmers in the course of time extricated themselves from the clutches of the loan sharks. There were a few Negroes who, thanks to the honesty of certain southern gentlemen, succeeded in acquiring considerable property in spite of their handicaps. They yielded to the white man's control in politics, when it seemed that it meant either to abandon that field or die, and devoted themselves to the accumulation of wealth and the acquisition of education.

This concession, however, did not satisfy the radical whites, as they thought that the Negro might some day return to power. Unfortunately, therefore, after the restoration of the control of the State governments to the master class, there swept over these commonwealths a wave of hostile legislation demanded by the poor white uplanders determined to debase the blacks to the status of the free Negroes prior to the Civil War. The Negroes have, therefore, been disfranchised in most reconstructed States, deprived of the privilege of serving in the State militia, segregated in public conveyances, and excluded from public places of entertainment. They have, moreover, been branded by public opinion as pariahs of society to be used for exploitation but not to be encouraged to expect that their status can ever be changed so as to destroy the barriers between the races in their social and political relations.

This period has been marked also by an effort to establish in the South a system of peonage not unlike that of Mexico, a sort of involuntary servitude in that one is considered legally bound to serve his master until a debt contracted is paid. Such laws have been enacted in Florida, Alabama, Georgia, Mississippi, North Carolina and South Carolina. No such distinction in law has been able to stand the constitutional test of the United States courts as was evidenced by the decision of the Supreme Court in 1911 declaring the Alabama law unconstitutional. But the planters of the South, still a law unto themselves, have maintained actual slavery in sequestered; districts where public opinion against peonage is too weak to support federal authorities in exterminating it. The Negroes themselves dare not protest under penalty of persecution and the peon concerned usually accepts his lot like that of a slave. Some years ago it was commonly reported that in trying to escape, the persons undertaking it often fail and suffer death at the hands of the planter or of murderous mobs, giving as their excuse, if any be required, that the Negro is a desperado or some other sort of criminal.

Unfortunately this reaction extended also to education. Appropriations to public schools for Negroes diminished from year to year and when there appeared practical leaders with their sane plan for industrial education, the South ignorantly accepted this scheme as a desirable subterfuge for seeming to support Negro education and at the same time directing the development of the blacks in such a way that they would never become the competitors of the white people. This was not these educators' idea but the South so understood it and in effecting the readjustment, practically left the Negroes out of the pale of the public school systems. Consequently, there has been added to the Negroes' misfortunes, in the South, that of being unable to obtain liberal education at public expense, although they themselves, as the largest consumers in some parts, pay most of the taxes appropriated to the support of schools for the youth of the other race.

The South, moreover, has adopted the policy of a more general intimidation of the Negroes to keep them down. The lynching of the blacks, at first for assaults on white women and later for almost any offense, has rapidly developed as an institution. Within the past fifty years there have been lynched in the South about 4,000 Negroes, many of whom have been publicly burned in the daytime to attract crowds that usually enjoy such feats as the tourney of the Middle Ages. Negroes who have the courage to protest against this barbarism have too often been subjected to indignities and in some cases forced to leave their communities or suffer the fate of those in behalf of whom they speak. These crimes of white men were at first kept secret but during the last two generations the culprits have become known as heroes, so popular has it been to murder Negroes. It has often been discovered also that the officers of these communities take part in these crimes and the worst of all is that politicians like Tillman, Blease and Vardaman glory in recounting the noble deeds of those who deserve so well of their countrymen for making the soil red with the Negroes' blood rather than permit the much feared Africanization of southern institutions.

In this harassing situation the Negro has hoped that the North would interfere in his behalf, but, with the reactionary Supreme Court of the United States interpreting this hostile legislation as constitutional in conformity with the demands of prejudiced public opinion, and with the leaders of the North inclined to take the view that after all the factions in the South must be left alone to fight it out, there has been nothing to be expected from without. Matters too have been rendered much worse because the leaders of the very party recently abandoning the freedmen to their fate, aggravated the critical situation by first setting the Negroes against their former masters, whom they were taught to regard as their worst enemies whether they were or not.

The last humiliation the Negroes have been forced to submit to is that of segregation. Here the effort has been to establish a ghetto in cities and to assign certain parts of the country to Negroes engaged in farming. It always happens, of course, that the best portion goes to the whites and the least desirable to the blacks, although the promoters of the segregation maintain that both races are to be treated equally. The ultimate aim is to prevent the Negroes of means from figuring conspicuously in aristocratic districts where they may be brought into rather close contact with the whites. Negroes see in segregation a settled policy to keep them down, no matter what they do to elevate themselves. The southern white man, eternally dreading the miscegenation of the races, makes the life, liberty and happiness of individuals second to measures considered necessary to prevent this so-called evil that this enviable civilization, distinctly American, may not be destroyed. The United States Supreme Court in the decision of the Louisville segregation case recently declared these segregation measures unconstitutional.

These restrictions have made the progress of the Negroes more of a problem in that directed toward social distinction, the Negroes have been denied the helpful contact of the sympathetic whites. The increasing race prejudice forces the whites to restrict their open dealing with the blacks to matters of service and business, maintaining even then the bearing of one in a sphere which the Negroes must not penetrate. The whites, therefore, never seeing the blacks as they are, and the blacks never being able to learn what the whites know, are thrown back on their own initiative, which their life as slaves could not have permitted to develop. It makes little difference that the Negroes have been free a few decades. Such freedom has in some parts been tantamount to slavery, and so far as contact with the superior class is concerned, no better than that condition; for under the old regime certain slaves did learn much by close association with their masters.

For these reasons there has been since the exodus to the West a steady migration of Negroes from the South to points in the North. But this migration, mainly due to political changes, has never assumed such large proportions as in the case of the more significant movements due to economic causes, for, as the accompanying map shows, most Negroes are still in the South. When we consider the various classes migrating, however, it will be apparent that to understand the exodus of the Negroes to the North, this longer drawn out and smaller movement must be carefully studied in all its ramifications. It should be noted that unlike some of the other migrations it has not been directed to any particular State. It has been from almost all Southern States to various parts of the North and especially to the largest cities.

What classes then have migrated? In the first place, the Negro politicians, who, after the restoration of Bourbon rule in the South, found themselves thrown out of office and often humiliated and impoverished, had to find some way out of the difficulty. Some few have been relieved by sympathetic leaders of the Republican party, who secured for them federal appointments in Washington. These appointments when sometimes paying lucrative salaries have been given as a reward to those Negroes who, although dethroned in the South, remain in touch with the remnant of the Republican party there and control the delegates to the national conventions nominating candidates for President. Many Negroes of this class have settled in

Washington. In some cases, the observer witnesses the pitiable scene of a man once a prominent public functionary in the South now serving in Washington as a messenger or a clerk.

The well-established blacks, however, have not been so easily induced to go. The Negroes in business in the South have usually been loath to leave their people among whom they can acquire property, whereas, if they go to the North, they have merely political freedom with no assurance of an opportunity in the economic world. But not a few of these have given themselves up to unrelenting toil with a view to accumulating sufficient wealth to move North and live thereafter on the income from their investments. Many of this class now spend some of their time in the North to educate their children. But they do not like to have these children who have been under refining influences return to the South to suffer the humiliation which during the last generation has been growing more and more aggravating. Endeavoring to carry out their policy of keeping the Negro down, southerners too often carefully plan to humiliate the progressive and intelligent blacks and in some cases form mobs to drive them out, as they are bad examples for that class of Negroes whom they desire to keep as menials.

There are also the migrating educated Negroes. They have studied history, law and economics and well understand what it is to get the rights guaranteed them by the Constitution. The more they know the more discontented they become. They cannot speak out for what they want. No one is likely to second such a protest, not even the Negroes themselves, so generally have they been intimidated. The more outspoken they become, moreover, the more necessary is it for them to leave, for they thereby destroy their chances to earn a livelihood. White men in control of the public schools of the South see to it that the subserviency of the Negro teachers employed be certified beforehand. They dare not complain too much about equipment and salaries even if the per capita appropriation for the education of the Negroes be one fourth of that for the whites.

In the higher institutions of learning, especially the State schools, it is exceptional to find a principal who has the confidence of the Negroes. The Negroes will openly assert that he is in the pay of the reactionary whites, whose purpose is to keep the Negro down; and the incumbent himself will tell his board of regents how much he is opposed by the Negroes because he labors for the interests of the white race. Out of such sycophancy it is easily explained why our State schools have been so ineffective as to necessitate the sending of the Negro youth to private institutions maintained by northern philanthropy. Yet if an outspoken Negro happens to be an instructor in a private school conducted by educators from the North, he has to be careful about contending for a square deal; for, if the head of his institution does not suggest to him to proceed conservatively, the mob will dispose of the complainant. Physicians, lawyers and preachers, who are not so economically dependent as teachers can exercise no more freedom of speech in the midst of this triumphant rule of the lawless.

A large number of educated Negroes, therefore, have on account of these conditions been compelled to leave the South. Finding in the North, however, practically nothing in their line to do, because of the proscription by race prejudice and trades unions, many of them lead the life of menials, serving as waiters, porters, butlers and chauffeurs. While in Chicago, not long ago, the writer was in the office of a graduate of a colored southern college, who was showing his former teacher the picture of his class. In accounting for his classmates in the various walks of life, he reported that more than one third of them were settled to the occupation of Pullman porters.

The largest number of Negroes who have gone North during this period, however, belong to the intelligent laboring class. Some of them have become discontented for the very same reasons that the higher classes have tired of oppression in the South, but the larger number of them have gone North to improve their economic condition. Most of these have migrated to the large cities in the East and Northwest, such as Philadelphia, New York, Indianapolis, Pittsburgh, Cleveland, Columbus, Detroit and Chicago. To understand this problem in its urban aspects, the accompanying diagram showing the increase in the Negro population of northern cities during the first decade of this century will be helpful.

Some of these Negroes have migrated after careful consideration; others have just happened to go north as wanderers; and a still larger number on the many excursions to the cities conducted by railroads during the summer months. Sometimes one excursion brings to Chicago two or three thousand Negroes, two thirds of whom never go back. They do not often follow the higher pursuits of labor in the North but they earn more money than they have been accustomed to earn in the South. They are attracted also by the liberal attitude of some whites, which, although not that of social equality, gives the Negroes a liberty in northern centers which leads them to think that they are citizens of the country.

This shifting in the population has had an unusually significant effect on the black belt. Frederick Douglass advised the Negroes in 1879 to remain in the South where they would be in sufficiently large numbers to have political power, but they have gradually scattered from the black belt so as to diminish greatly their chances ever to become the political force they formerly were in this country. The Negroes once had this possibility in South Carolina, Georgia, Alabama, Mississippi and Louisiana and, had the process of Africanization prior to the Civil War had a few decades longer to do its work, there would not have been any doubt as to the ultimate preponderance of the Negroes in those commonwealths. The tendencies of the black population according to the censuses of the United States and especially that of 1910, however, show that the chances for the control of these State governments by Negroes no longer exist except in South Carolina and Mississippi. It has been predicted, therefore, that, if the same tendencies continue for the next fifty years, there will be even few counties in which the Negroes will be in a majority. All of the Southern States except Arkansas showed a proportionate increase of the white population over that of the black between 1900 and 1910, while West Virginia and Oklahoma with relatively small numbers of blacks showed, for reasons stated elsewhere, an increase in the Negro population. Thus we see coming to pass something like the proposed plan of Jefferson and other statesmen who a hundred years ago advocated the expansion of slavery to lessen the evil of the institution by distributing its burdens.

The migration of intelligent blacks, however, has been attended with several handicaps to the race. The large part of the black population is in the South and there it will stay for decades to come. The southern Negroes, therefore, have been robbed of their due part of the talented tenth. The educated blacks have had no constituency in the North and, consequently, have been unable to realize their sweetest dreams of the land of the free. In their new home the enlightened Negro must live with his light under a bushel. Those left behind in the South soon despair of seeing a brighter day and yield to the yoke. In the places of the leaders who were wont to speak for their people, the whites have raised up Negroes who accept favors offered them on the condition that their lips be sealed up forever on the rights of the Negro.

This emigration too has left the Negro subject to other evils. There are many first-class Negro business men in the South, but although there were once progressive men of color, who endeavored to protect the blacks from being plundered by white sharks and harpies, there have arisen numerous unscrupulous Negroes who have for a part of the proceeds from such jobbery associated themselves with ill-designing white men to dupe illiterate Negroes. This trickery is brought into play in marketing their crops, selling them supplies, or purchasing their property. To carry out this iniquitous plan the persons concerned have the protection of the law, for while Negroes in general are imposed upon, those engaged in robbing them have no cause to fear.

Source: Chapter 10: pp.149–166. Copyright © 1918 by Carter Godwin Woodson.

77. The Soul of White Folks, 1920
W. E. B. DuBOIS

Scholar and activist W. E. B. DuBois began writing a series of scholarly papers, books, and newspaper and magazine articles early in the twentieth century to explore the esoteric varieties of life from the perspective of a black man in America. Many were published in various magazines and journals, including *The Atlantic*, *The Independent*, *The Crisis*, and *The Journal of Race Development*. DuBois' works on race were among the first such articles widely circulated to a largely white audience. This is an essay from a collection of his essays.

These are the things of which men think, who live: of their own selves and the dwelling place of their fathers; of their neighbors; of work and service; of rule and reason and women and children; of Beauty and Death and War. To this thinking I have only to add a point of view:

I have been in the world, but not of it. I have seen the human drama from a veiled corner, where all the outer tragedy and comedy have reproduced themselves in microcosm within. From this inner torment of souls the human scene without has interpreted itself to me in unusual and even illuminating ways. For this reason, and this alone, I venture to write again on themes on which great souls have already said greater words, in the hope that I may strike here and there a half-tone, newer even if slighter, up from the heart of my problem and the problems of my people.

Between the sterner flights of logic, I have sought to set some little alightings of what may be poetry. They are tributes to Beauty, unworthy to stand alone; yet per-versely, in my mind, now at the end, I know not whether I mean the Thought for the Fancy—or the Fancy for the Thought, or why the book trails off to playing, rather than standing strong on unanswering fact. But this is alway—is it not?—the Riddle of Life.

High in the tower, where I sit above the loud complaining of the human sea, I know many souls that toss and whirl and pass, but none there are that intrigue me more than the Souls of White Folk.

Of them I am singularly clairvoyant. I see in and through them. I view them from unusual points of vantage. Not as a foreigner do I come, for I am native, not foreign, bone of their thought and flesh of their language. Mine is not the knowledge of the traveler or the colonial composite of dear memories, words and wonder. Nor yet is my knowledge that which servants have of masters, or mass of class, or capitalist of artisan. Rather I see these souls undressed and from the back and side. I see the working of their entrails. I know their thoughts and they know that I know. This knowledge makes them now embarrassed, now furious.

They deny my right to live and be and call me misbirth! My word is to them mere bitterness and my soul, pessimism. And yet as they preach and strut and shout and threaten, crouching as they clutch at rags of facts and fancies to hide their nakedness, they go twisting, flying by my tired eyes and I see them ever stripped,—ugly, human.

The discovery of personal whiteness among the world's peoples is a very modern thing,—a nineteenth and twentieth century matter, indeed. The ancient world would have laughed at such a distinction. The Middle Age regarded skin color with mild curiosity; and even up into the eighteenth century we were hammering our national manikins into one, great, Universal Man, with fine frenzy which ignored color and race even more than birth. Today we have changed all that, and the world in a sudden, emotional conversion has discovered that it is white and by that token, wonderful!

This assumption that of all the hues of God whiteness alone is inherently and obviously better than brownness or tan leads to curious acts; even the sweeter souls of the dominant world as they discourse with me on weather, weal, and woe are continually playing above their actual words an obligato of tune and tone, saying:

"My poor, un-white thing! Weep not nor rage. I know, too well, that the curse of God lies heavy on you. Why? That is not for me to say, but be brave! Do your work in your lowly sphere, praying the good Lord that into heaven above, where all is love, you may, one day, be born—white!"

I do not laugh. I am quite straight-faced as I ask soberly:

"But what on earth is whiteness that one should so desire it?" Then always, somehow, some way, silently but clearly, I am given to understand that whiteness is the ownership of the earth forever and ever, Amen!

Now what is the effect on a man or a nation when it comes passionately to believe such an extraordinary dictum as this? That nations are coming to believe it is manifest daily. Wave on wave, each with increasing virulence, is dashing this new religion of whiteness on the shores of our time. Its first effects are funny: the strut of the Southerner, the arrogance of the Englishman amuck, the whoop of the hoodlum who vicariously leads your mob. Next it appears dampening generous enthusiasm in what we once counted glorious; to free the slave is discovered to be tolerable only in so far as it freed his master! Do we sense somnolent writhings in black Africa or angry groans in India or triumphant banzais in Japan? "To your tents, O Israel!" These nations are not white!

After the more comic manifestations and the chilling of generous enthusiasm come subtler, darker deeds. Everything considered, the title to the universe claimed by White Folk is faulty. It ought, at least, to look plausible. How easy, then, by emphasis and omission to make children believe that every great soul the world ever saw was a white man's soul; that every great thought the world ever knew was a white man's thought; that every great deed the world ever did was a white man's deed; that every great dream the world ever sang was a white man's dream. In fine, that if from the world were dropped everything that could not fairly be attributed to White Folk, the world would, if anything, be even greater, truer, better than now. And if all this be a lie, is it not a lie in a great cause?

Here it is that the comedy verges to tragedy. The first minor note is struck, all unconsciously, by those worthy souls in whom consciousness of high descent brings burning desire to spread the gift abroad,—the obligation of nobility to the ignoble. Such sense of duty assumes two things: a real possession of the heritage and its frank appreciation by the humble-born. So long, then, as humble black folk, voluble with thanks, receive barrels of old clothes from lordly and generous whites, there is much mental peace and moral satisfaction. But when the black man begins to dispute the white man's title to certain alleged bequests of the Fathers in wage and position, authority and training; and when his attitude toward charity is sullen anger rather than humble jollity; when he insists on his human right to swagger and swear and waste,—then the spell is suddenly broken and the philanthropist is ready to believe that Negroes are impudent, that the South is right, and that Japan wants to fight America.

After this the descent to Hell is easy. On the pale, white faces which the great billows whirl upward to my tower I see again and again, often and still more often, a writing of human hatred, a deep and passionate hatred, vast by the very vagueness of its expressions. Down through the green waters, on the bottom of the world, where men move to and fro, I have seen a man—an educated gentleman—grow livid with anger because a little, silent, black woman was sitting by herself in a Pullman car. He was a white man. I have seen a great, grown man curse a little child, who had wandered into the wrong waiting-room, searching for its mother: "Here, you damned black—" He was white. In Central Park I have seen the upper lip of a quiet, peaceful man curl back in a tigerish snarl of rage because black folk rode by in a motor car. He was a white man. We have seen, you and I, city after city drunk and furious with ungovernable lust of blood; mad with murder, destroying, killing, and cursing; torturing human victims because somebody accused of crime happened to be of the same color as the mob's innocent victims and because that color was not white! We have seen,—Merciful God! in these wild days and in the name of Civilization, Justice, and Motherhood,—what have we not seen, right here in America, of orgy, cruelty, barbarism, and murder done to men and women of Negro descent.

Up through the foam of green and weltering waters wells this great mass of hatred, in wilder, fiercer violence, until I look down and know that today to the millions of my people no misfortune could happen,—of death and pestilence, failure and defeat— that would not make the hearts of millions of their fellows beat with fierce, vindictive joy! Do you doubt it? Ask your own soul what it would say if the next census were to report that half of black America was dead and the other half dying.

Unfortunate? Unfortunate. But where is the misfortune? Mine? Am I, in my blackness, the sole sufferer? I suffer. And yet, somehow, above the suffering, above the shackled anger that beats the bars, above the hurt that crazes there surges in me a vast pity,—pity for a people imprisoned and enthralled, hampered and made miserable for such a cause, for such a phantasy!

Conceive this nation, of all human peoples, engaged in a crusade to make the "World Safe for Democracy"! Can you imagine the United States protesting against Turkish atrocities in Armenia, while the Turks are silent about mobs in Chicago and St. Louis; what is Louvain compared with Memphis, Waco, Washington,

Dyersburg, and Estill Springs? In short, what is the black man but America's Belgium, and how could America condemn in Germany that which she commits, just as brutally, within her own borders?

A true and worthy ideal frees and uplifts a people; a false ideal imprisons and lowers. Say to men, earnestly and repeatedly: "Honesty is best, knowledge is power; do unto others as you would be done by." Say this and act it and the nation must move toward it, if not to it. But say to a people: "The one virtue is to be white," and the people rush to the inevitable conclusion, "Kill the 'nigger'!"

Is not this the record of present America? Is not this its headlong progress? Are we not coming more and more, day by day, to making the statement "I am white," the one fundamental tenet of our practical morality? Only when this basic, iron rule is involved is our defense of right nation-wide and prompt. Murder may swagger, theft may rule and prostitution may flourish and the nation gives but spasmodic, intermittent and lukewarm attention. But let the murderer be black or the thief brown or the violator of womanhood have a drop of Negro blood, and the righteousness of the indignation sweeps the world. Nor would this fact make the indignation less justifiable did not we all know that it was blackness that was condemned and not crime.

In the awful cataclysm of World War, where from beating, slandering, and murdering us the white world turned temporarily aside to kill each other, we of the Darker Peoples looked on in mild amaze.

Among some of us, I doubt not, this sudden descent of Europe into hell brought unbounded surprise; to others, over wide area, it brought the Schaden Freude of the bitterly hurt; but most of us, I judge, looked on silently and sorrowfully, in sober thought, seeing sadly the prophecy of our own souls.

Here is a civilization that has boasted much. Neither Roman nor Arab, Greek nor Egyptian, Persian nor Mongol ever took himself and his own perfectness with such disconcerting seriousness as the modern white man. We whose shame, humiliation, and deep insult his aggrandizement so often involved were never deceived. We looked at him clearly, with world-old eyes, and saw simply a human thing, weak and pitiable and cruel, even as we are and were.

These super-men and world-mastering demi-gods listened, however, to no low tongues of ours, even when we pointed silently to their feet of clay. Perhaps we, as folk of simpler soul and more primitive type, have been most struck in the welter of recent years by the utter failure of white religion. We have curled our lips in something like contempt as we have witnessed glib apology and weary explanation. Nothing of the sort deceived us. A nation's religion is its life, and as such white Christianity is a miserable failure.

Nor would we be unfair in this criticism: We know that we, too, have failed, as you have, and have rejected many a Buddha, even as you have denied Christ; but we acknowledge our human frailty, while you, claiming super-humanity, scoff endlessly at our shortcomings.

The number of white individuals who are practising with even reasonable approximation the democracy and unselfishness of Jesus Christ is so small and unimportant as to be fit subject for jest in Sunday supplements and in Punch, Life, Le Rire, and Fliegende Blaetter. In her foreign mission work the extraordinary self-deception of white religion is epitomized: solemnly the white world sends five million dollars worth of missionary propaganda to Africa each year and in the same twelve months adds twenty-five million dollars worth of the vilest gin manufactured. Peace to the augurs of Rome!

We may, however, grant without argument that religious ideals have always far outrun their very human devotees. Let us, then, turn to more mundane matters of honor and fairness. The world today is trade. The world has turned shopkeeper; history is economic history; living is earning a living. Is it necessary to ask how much of high emprise and honorable conduct has been found here? Something, to be sure. The establishment of world credit systems is built on splendid and realizable faith in fellow-men. But it is, after all, so low and elementary a step that sometimes it looks merely like honor among thieves, for the revelations of highway robbery and low cheating in the business world and in all its great modern centers have raised in the hearts of all true men in our day an exceeding great cry for revolution in our basic methods and conceptions of industry and commerce.

We do not, for a moment, forget the robbery of other times and races when trade was a most uncertain gamble; but was there not a certain honesty and frankness in the evil that argued a saner morality? There are more merchants today, surer deliveries, and wider well-being, but are there not, also, bigger thieves, deeper injustice, and more calloused selfishness in well-being? Be that as it may,—certainly the nicer sense of honor that has risen ever and again in groups of forward-thinking men has been curiously and broadly blunted. Consider our chiefest industry,—fighting. Laboriously the Middle Ages built its rules of fairness—equal armament, equal notice, equal conditions. What do we see today? Machine-guns against assegais; conquest sugared with religion; mutilation and rape masquerading as culture,—all this, with vast applause at the superiority of white over black soldiers!

War is horrible! This the dark world knows to its awful cost. But has it just become horrible, in these last days, when under essentially equal conditions, equal armament, and equal waste of wealth white men are fighting white men, with surgeons and nurses hovering near?

Think of the wars through which we have lived in the last decade: in German Africa, in British Nigeria, in French and Spanish Morocco, in China, in Persia, in the Balkans, in Tripoli, in Mexico, and in a dozen lesser places—were not these horrible, too? Mind you, there were for most of these wars no Red Cross funds.

Behold little Belgium and her pitiable plight, but has the world forgotten Congo? What Belgium now suffers is not half, not even a tenth, of what she has done to black Congo since Stanley's great dream of 1880. Down the dark forests of inmost Africa sailed this modern Sir Galahad, in the name of "the noble-minded men of several nations," to introduce commerce and civilization. What came of it? "Rubber and murder, slavery in its worst form," wrote Glave in 1895.

Harris declares that King Leopold's regime meant the death of twelve million natives, "but what we who were behind the scenes felt most keenly was the fact that the real catastrophe in the Congo was desolation and murder in the larger sense. The invasion of family life, the ruthless destruction of every social barrier, the shattering of every tribal law, the introduction of criminal practices which struck the chiefs of the people dumb with horror—in a word, a veritable avalanche of filth and immorality overwhelmed the Congo tribes."

Yet the fields of Belgium laughed, the cities were gay, art and science flourished; the groans that helped to nourish this civilization fell on deaf ears because the world round about was doing the same sort of thing elsewhere on its own account.

As we saw the dead dimly through rifts of battlesmoke and heard faintly the cursings and accusations of blood brothers, we darker men said: This is not Europe gone mad; this is not aberration nor insanity; this is Europe; this seeming Terrible is the real soul of white culture—back of all culture,—stripped and visible today. This is where the world has arrived,—these dark and awful depths and not the shining and ineffable heights of which it boasted. Here is whither the might and energy of modern humanity has really gone.

But may not the world cry back at us and ask: "What better thing have you to show? What have you done or would do better than this if you had today the world rule? Paint with all riot of hateful colors the thin skin of European culture,—is it not better than any culture that arose in Africa or Asia?"

It is. Of this there is no doubt and never has been; but why is it better? Is it better because Europeans are better, nobler, greater, and more gifted than other folk? It is not. Europe has never produced and never will in our day bring forth a single human soul who cannot be matched and over-matched in every line of human endeavor by Asia and Africa. Run the gamut, if you will, and let us have the Europeans who in sober truth over-match Nefertari, Mohammed, Rameses and Askia, Confucius, Buddha, and Jesus Christ. If we could scan the calendar of thousands of lesser men, in like comparison, the result would be the same; but we cannot do this because of the deliberately educated ignorance of white schools by which they remember Napoleon and forget Sonni Ali.

The greatness of Europe has lain in the width of the stage on which she has played her part, the strength of the foundations on which she has builded, and a natural, human ability no whit greater (if as great) than that of other days and races. In other words, the deeper reasons for the triumph of European civilization lie quite outside and beyond Europe,—back in the universal struggles of all mankind.

Why, then, is Europe great? Because of the foundations which the mighty past have furnished her to build upon: the iron trade of ancient, black Africa, the religion and empire-building of yellow Asia, the art and science of the "dago" Mediterranean shore, east, south, and west, as well as north. And where she has builded securely upon this great past and learned from it she has gone forward to greater and more splendid human triumph; but where she has ignored this past and forgotten and sneered at it, she has shown the cloven hoof of poor, crucified humanity,—she has played, like other empires gone, the world fool!

If, then, European triumphs in culture have been greater, so, too, may her failures have been greater. How great a failure and a failure in what does the World War betoken? Was it national jealousy of the sort of the seventeenth century? But Europe has done more to break down national barriers than any preceding culture. Was it fear of the balance of power in Europe? Hardly, save in the half-Asiatic problems of the Balkans. What, then, does Hauptmann mean when he says: "Our jealous enemies forged an iron ring about our breasts and we knew our breasts had to expand,—that we had to split asunder this ring or else we had to cease breathing. But Germany will not cease to breathe and so it came to pass that the iron ring was forced apart."

Whither is this expansion? What is that breath of life, thought to be so indispensable to a great European nation? Manifestly it is expansion overseas; it is colonial aggrandizement which explains, and alone adequately explains, the World War. How many of us today fully realize the current theory of colonial expansion, of the relation of Europe which is white, to the world which is black and brown and yellow? Bluntly put, that theory is this: It is the duty of white Europe to divide up the darker world and administer it for Europe's good.

This Europe has largely done. The European world is using black and brown men for all the uses which men know. Slowly but surely white culture is evolving the theory that "darkies" are born beasts of burden for white folk. It were silly to think otherwise, cries the cultured world, with stronger and shriller accord. The supporting arguments grow and twist themselves in the mouths of merchant, scientist, soldier, traveler, writer, and missionary: Darker peoples are dark in mind as well as in body; of dark, uncertain, and imperfect descent; of frailer, cheaper stuff; they are cowards in the face of mausers and maxims; they have no feelings, aspirations, and loves; they are fools, illogical idiots,—"half-devil and half-child."

Such as they are civilization must, naturally, raise them, but soberly and in limited ways. They are not simply dark white men. They are not "men" in the sense that Europeans are men. To the very limited extent of their shallow capacities lift them to be useful to whites, to raise cotton, gather rubber, fetch ivory, dig diamonds,—and let them be paid what men think they are worth—white men who know them to be well-nigh worthless.

Such degrading of men by men is as old as mankind and the invention of no one race or people. Ever have men striven to conceive of their victims as different from the victors, endlessly different, in soul and blood, strength and cunning, race and lineage. It has been left, however, to Europe and to modern days to discover the eternal world-wide mark of meanness,—color!

Such is the silent revolution that has gripped modern European culture in the later nineteenth and twentieth centuries. Its zenith came in Boxer times: White supremacy was all but world-wide, Africa was dead, India conquered, Japan isolated, and China prostrate, while white America whetted her sword for mongrel Mexico and mulatto South America, lynching her own Negroes the while. Temporary halt in this program was made by little Japan and the white world immediately sensed the peril of such "yellow" presumption! What sort of a world would this be if yellow men must be treated "white"? Immediately the eventual overthrow of Japan became a subject of deep thought and intrigue, from St. Petersburg to San Francisco, from the Key of Heaven to the Little Brother of the Poor.

The using of men for the benefit of masters is no new invention of modern Europe. It is quite as old as the world. But Europe proposed to apply it on a scale and with an elaborateness of detail of which no former world ever dreamed. The imperial width of the thing,—the heaven-defying audacity—makes its modern newness.

The scheme of Europe was no sudden invention, but a way out of long-pressing difficulties. It is plain to modern white civilization that the subjection of the white working classes cannot much longer be maintained. Education, political power, and increased knowledge of the technique and meaning of the industrial process are destined to make a more and more equitable distribution of wealth in the near future. The day of the very rich is drawing to a close, so far as individual white nations are concerned. But there is a loophole. There is a chance for exploitation on an immense scale for inordinate profit, not simply to the very rich, but to the middle class and to the laborers. This chance lies in the exploitation of darker peoples. It is here that the golden hand beckons. Here are no labor unions or votes or questioning onlookers or inconvenient consciences. These men may be used down to the very bone, and shot and maimed in "punitive" expeditions when they revolt. In these dark lands "industrial development" may repeat in exaggerated form every horror of the industrial history of Europe, from slavery and rape to disease and maiming, with only one test of success,—dividends!

This theory of human culture and its aims has worked itself through warp and woof of our daily thought with a thoroughness that few realize. Everything great, good, efficient, fair, and honorable is "white"; everything mean, bad, blundering, cheating, and dishonorable is "yellow"; a bad taste is "brown"; and the devil is "black." The changes of this theme are continually rung in picture and story, in newspaper heading and moving-picture, in sermon and school book, until, of course, the King can do no wrong,—a White Man is always right and a Black Man has no rights which a white man is bound to respect.

There must come the necessary despisings and hatreds of these savage half-men, this unclean canaille of the world—these dogs of men. All through the world this gospel is preaching. It has its literature, it has its secret propaganda and above all— it pays!

There's the rub,—it pays. Rubber, ivory, and palm-oil; tea, coffee, and cocoa; bananas, oranges, and other fruit; cotton, gold, and copper—they, and a hundred other things which dark and sweating bodies hand up to the white world from pits of slime, pay and pay well, but of all that the world gets the black world gets only the pittance that the white world throws it disdainfully.

Small wonder, then, that in the practical world of things-that-be there is jealousy and strife for the possession of the labor of dark millions, for the right to bleed and exploit the colonies of the world where this golden stream may be had, not always for the asking, but surely for the whipping and shooting. It was this competition for the labor of yellow, brown, and black folks that was the cause of the World War. Other causes have been glibly given and other contributing causes there doubtless were, but they were subsidiary and subordinate to this vast quest of the dark world's wealth and toil.

Colonies, we call them, these places where "niggers" are cheap and the earth is rich; they are those outlands where like a swarm of hungry locusts white masters may settle to be served as kings, wield the lash of slave-drivers, rape girls and wives, grow as rich as Croesus and send homeward a golden stream. They belt the earth, these places, but they cluster in the tropics, with its darkened peoples: in Hong Kong and Anam, in Borneo and Rhodesia, in Sierra Leone and Nigeria, in Panama and Havana—these are the El Dorados toward which the world powers stretch itching palms.

Germany, at last one and united and secure on land, looked across the seas and seeing England with sources of wealth insuring a luxury and power which Germany could not hope to rival by the slower processes of exploiting her own peasants and workingmen, especially with these workers half in revolt, immediately built her navy and entered into a desperate competition for possession of colonies of darker peoples. To South America, to China, to Africa, to Asia Minor, she turned like a hound quivering on the leash, impatient, suspicious, irritable, with blood-shot eyes and dripping fangs, ready for the awful word. England and France crouched watchfully over their bones, growling and wary, but gnawing industriously, while the blood of the dark world whetted their greedy appetites. In the background, shut out from the highway to the seven seas, sat Russia and Austria, snarling and snapping at each other and at the last Mediterranean gate to the El Dorado, where the Sick Man enjoyed bad health, and where millions of serfs in the Balkans, Russia, and Asia offered a feast to greed well-nigh as great as Africa.

The fateful day came. It had to come. The cause of war is preparation for war; and of all that Europe has done in a century there is nothing that has equaled in energy, thought, and time her preparation for wholesale murder. The only adequate cause of this preparation was conquest and conquest, not in Europe, but primarily among the darker peoples of Asia and Africa; conquest, not for assimilation and uplift, but for commerce and degradation. For this, and this mainly, did Europe gird herself at frightful cost for war.

The red day dawned when the tinder was lighted in the Balkans and Austro-Hungary seized a bit which brought her a step nearer to the world's highway; she seized one bit and poised herself for another. Then came that curious chorus of challenges, those leaping suspicions, raking all causes for distrust and rivalry and hatred, but saying little of the real and greatest cause.

Each nation felt its deep interests involved. But how? Not, surely, in the death of Ferdinand the Warlike; not, surely, in the old, half-forgotten revanche for Alsace-Lorraine; not even in the neutrality of Belgium. No! But in the possession of land overseas, in the right to colonies, the chance to levy endless tribute on the darker world,—on coolies in China, on starving peasants in India, on black savages in Africa, on dying South Sea Islanders, on Indians of the Amazon—all this and nothing more.

Even the broken reed on which we had rested high hopes of eternal peace,—the guild of the laborers—the front of that very important movement for human justice on which we had builded most, even this flew like a straw before the breath of king and kaiser. Indeed, the flying had been foreshadowed when in Germany and America "international" Socialists had all but read yellow and black men out of the kingdom of industrial justice. Subtly had they been bribed, but effectively: Were they not lordly whites and should they not share in the spoils of rape? High wages in the United States and England might be the skilfully manipulated result of slavery in Africa and of peonage in Asia.

With the dog-in-the-manger theory of trade, with the determination to reap inordinate profits and to exploit the weakest to the utmost there came a new imperialism,—the rage for one's own nation to own the earth or, at least, a large enough portion of it to insure as big profits as the next nation. Where sections could not be owned by one dominant nation there came a policy of "open door," but the "door" was open to "white people only." As to the darkest and weakest of peoples there was but one unanimity in Europe,—that which Hen Demberg of the German Colonial Office called the agreement with England to maintain white "prestige" in Africa,—the doctrine of the divine right of white people to steal.

Thus the world market most wildly and desperately sought today is the market where labor is cheapest and most helpless and profit is most abundant. This labor is kept cheap and helpless because the white world despises "darkies." If one has the temerity to suggest that these workingmen may walk the way of white workingmen and climb by votes and self-assertion and education to the rank of men, he is howled out of court. They cannot do it and if they could, they shall not, for they are the enemies of the white race and the whites shall rule forever and forever and everywhere. Thus the hatred and despising of human beings from whom Europe wishes to extort her luxuries has led to such jealousy and bickering between European nations that they have fallen afoul of each other and have fought like crazed beasts. Such is the fruit of human hatred.

But what of the darker world that watches? Most men belong to this world. With Negro and Negroid, East Indian, Chinese, and Japanese they form two-thirds of the population of the world. A belief in humanity is a belief in colored men. If the uplift of mankind must be done by men, then the destinies of this world will rest ultimately in the hands of darker nations.

What, then, is this dark world thinking? It is thinking that as wild and awful as this shameful war was, it is nothing to compare with that fight for freedom which black and brown and yellow men must and will make unless their oppression and humiliation and insult at the hands of the White World cease. The Dark World is going to submit to its present treatment just as long as it must and not one moment longer.

Let me say this again and emphasize it and leave no room for mistaken meaning: The World War was primarily the jealous and avaricious struggle for the largest share in exploiting darker races. As such it is and must be but the prelude to the armed and indignant protest of these despised and raped peoples. Today Japan is hammering on the door of justice, China is raising her half-manacled hands to knock next, India is writhing for the freedom to knock, Egypt is sullenly muttering, the Negroes of South and West Africa, of the West Indies, and of the United States are just awakening to their shameful slavery. Is, then, this war the end of wars? Can it be the end, so long as sits enthroned, even in the souls of those who cry peace, the despising and robbing of darker peoples? If Europe hugs this delusion, then this is not the end of world war,—it is but the beginning!

We see Europe's greatest sin precisely where we found Africa's and Asia's,—in human hatred, the despising of men; with this difference, however: Europe has the awful lesson of the past before her, has the splendid results of widened areas of tolerance, sympathy, and love among men, and she faces a greater, an infinitely greater, world of men than any preceding civilization ever faced.

It is curious to see America, the United States, looking on herself, first, as a sort of natural peacemaker, then as a moral protagonist in this terrible time. No nation is less fitted for this role. For two or more centuries America has marched proudly in the van of human hatred,—making bonfires of human flesh and laughing at them hideously, and making the insulting of millions more than a matter of dislike,— rather a great religion, a world war-cry: Up white, down black; to your tents, O white folk, and world war with black and parti-colored mongrel beasts!

Instead of standing as a great example of the success of democracy and the possibility of human brotherhood America has taken her place as an awful example of its pitfalls and failures, so far as black and brown and yellow peoples are concerned. And this, too, in spite of the fact that there has been no actual failure; the Indian is not dying out, the Japanese and Chinese have not menaced the land, and the experiment of Negro suffrage has resulted in the uplift of twelve million people at a rate probably unparalleled in history. But what of this? America, Land of Democracy, wanted to believe in the failure of democracy so far as darker peoples were concerned. Absolutely without excuse she established a caste system, rushed into preparation for war, and conquered tropical colonies. She stands today shoulder to shoulder with Europe in Europe's worst sin against civilization. She aspires to sit among the great nations who arbitrate the fate of "lesser breeds without the law" and she is at times heartily ashamed even of the large number of "new" white people whom her democracy has admitted to place and power. Against this surging forward of Irish and German, of Russian Jew, Slav and "dago" her social bars have not availed, but against Negroes she can and does take her unflinching and immovable stand, backed by this new public policy of Europe. She trains her immigrants to this despising of "niggers" from the day of their landing, and they carry and send the news back to the submerged classes in the fatherlands.

Source: Darkwater: Voices from Within the Veil. New York: Harcourt, Brace & Co., 1920.

78. Declaration of Rights of the Negro Peoples of the World, 1920

This a final version of a declaration first drafted and adopted at a convention held in New York in 1920 of the Universal Negro Improvement Association (UNIA), over which Marcus Garvey presided as chairman, and at which he was elected Provisional President of Africa. The use of the word "Africa" most likely denotes his claims as a world leader of black men and women everywhere, rather than an official leader of the vast continent of Africa. Although this document was drafted in 1920, it was not officially notarized and recorded with the New York County Clerk until two years later.

PREAMBLE

Be it Resolved, That the Negro people of the world, through their chosen representatives in convention assembled in Liberty Hall, in the City of New York and United States of America, from August 1 to August 31, in the year of our Lord, one thousand nine hundred and twenty, protest against the wrongs and injustices they are suffering at the hands of their white brethren, and state what they deem their fair and just rights, as well as the treatment they propose to demand of all men in the future.

We complain:

I. That nowhere in the world, with few exceptions, are black men accorded equal treatment with white men, although in the same situation and circumstances, but, on the contrary, are discriminated against and denied the common rights due to human beings for no other reason than their race and color.

We are not willingly accepted as guests in the public hotels and inns of the world for no other reason than our race and color.

II. In certain parts of the United States of America our race is denied the right of public trial accorded to other races when accused of crime, but are lynched and burned by mobs, and such brutal and inhuman treatment is even practiced upon our women.

III. That European nations have parcelled out among themselves and taken possession of nearly all of the continent of Africa, and the natives are compelled to surrender their lands to aliens and are treated in most instances like slaves.

IV. In the southern portion of the United States of America, although citizens under the Federal Constitution, and in some states almost equal to the whites in population and are qualified land owners and taxpayers, we are, nevertheless, denied all voice in the making and administration of the laws and are taxed without representation by the state governments, and at the same time compelled to do military service in defense of the country.

V. On the public conveyances and common carriers in the Southern portion of the United States we are jim-crowed and compelled to accept separate and inferior accommodations and made to pay the same fare charged for first-class accommodations, and our families are often humiliated and insulted by drunken white men who habitually pass through the jim-crow cars going to the smoking car.

VI. The physicians of our race are denied the right to attend their patients while in the public hospitals of the cities and states where they reside in certain parts of the United States. Our children are forced to attend inferior separate schools for shorter terms than white children, and the public school funds are unequally divided between the white and colored schools.

VII. We are discriminated against and denied an equal chance to earn wages for the support of our families, and in many instances are refused admission into labor unions, and nearly everywhere are paid smaller wages than white men.

VIII. In Civil Service and departmental offices we are everywhere discriminated against and made to feel that to be a black man in Europe, America and the West Indies is equivalent to being an outcast and a leper among the races of men, no matter what the character and attainments of the black man may be.

IX. In the British and other West Indian Islands and colonies, Negroes are secretly and cunningly discriminated against, and denied those fuller rights in government to which white citizens are appointed, nominated and elected.

X. That our people in those parts are forced to work for lower wages than the average standard of white men and are kept in conditions repugnant to good civilized tastes and customs.

XI. That the many acts of injustice against members of our race before the courts of law in the respective islands and colonies are of such nature as to create disgust and disrespect for the white man's sense of justice.

XII. Against all such inhuman, unchristian and uncivilized treatment we here and now emphatically protest, and invoke the condemnation of all mankind. In order to encourage our race all over the world and to stimulate it to a higher and grander destiny, we demand and insist on the following Declaration of Rights:

1. Be it known to all men that whereas, all men are created equal and entitled to the rights of life, liberty and the pursuit of happiness, and because of this we, the duly elected representatives of the Negro peoples of the world, invoking the aid of the just and Almighty God, do declare all men women and children of our blood throughout the world free citizens, and do claim them as free citizens of Africa, the Motherland of all Negroes.

2. That we believe in the supreme authority of our race in all things racial; that all things are created and given to man as a common possession; that their should be an equitable distribution and apportionment of all such things, and in consideration of the fact that as a race we are now deprived of those things that are morally and legally ours, we believe it right that all such things should be acquired and held by whatsoever means possible.

3. That we believe the Negro, like any other race, should be governed by the ethics of civilization, and, therefore, should not be deprived of any of those rights or privileges common to other human beings.

4. We declare that Negroes, wheresoever they form a community among themselves, should be given the right to elect their own representatives to represent them in legislatures,

courts of law, or such institutions as may exercise control over that particular community.

5. We assert that the Negro is entitled to even-handed justice before all courts of law and equity in whatever country he may be found, and when this is denied him on account of his race or color such denial is an insult to the race as a whole and should be resented by the entire boy of Negroes.

6. We declared it unfair and prejudicial to the rights of Negroes in communities where they exist in considerable numbers to be tried by a judge and jury composed entirely of an alien race, but in all such cases members of our race are entitled to representation on the jury.

7. We believe that any law or practice that tends to deprive any African of his land or the privileges of free citizenship within his country is unjust and immoral, and no native should respect any such law or practice.

8. We declare taxation without representation unjust and tyrannous, and there should be no obligation on the part of the Negro to obey the levy of a tax by any law-making body from which he is excluded and denied representation on account of his race and color.

9. We believe that any law especially directed against the Negro to his detriment and singling him out because of his race or color is unfair and immoral, and should not be respected.

10. We believe all men entitled to common human respect, and that our race should in no way tolerate any insults that may be interpreted to mean disrespect to our color.

11. We deprecate the use of the term "nigger" as applied to Negroes, and demand that the word "Negro" be written with a capital "N."

12. We believe that the Negro should adopt every means to protect himself against barbarous practices inflicted upon him because of color.

13. We believe in the freedom of Africa for the Negro people of the world, and by the principle of Europe for the Europeans and Asia for the Asiatics; we also demand Africa for the Africans at home and abroad.

14. We believe in the inherent right of the Negro to possess himself of Africa, and that his possession of same shall not be regarded as an infringement on any claim or purchase made by any race or nation.

15. We strongly condemn the cupidity of those nations of the world who, by open aggression or secret schemes, have seized the territories and inexhaustible natural wealth of Africa, and we place on record our most solemn determination to reclaim the treasures and possession of the vast continent of our forefathers.

16. We believe all men should live in peace one with the other, but when races and nations provoke the ire of other races and nations by attempting to infringe upon their rights, war becomes inevitable, and the attempt in any way to free one's self or protect one's rights or heritage becomes justifiable.

17. Whereas, the lynching, by burning, hanging or any other means, of human beings is a barbarous practice, and a shame and disgrace to civilization, we therefore declared any country guilty of such atrocities outside the pale of civilization.

18. We protest against the atrocious crime of whipping, flogging and overworking of the native tribes of Africa and Negroes everywhere. These are methods that should be abolished, and all means should be taken to prevent a continuance of such brutal practices.

19. We protest against the atrocious practice of shaving the heads of Africans, especially of African women or individuals of Negro blood, when placed in prison as a punishment for crime by an alien race.

20. We protest against segregated districts, separate public conveyances, industrial discrimination, lynchings and limitations of political privileges of any Negro citizen in any part of the world on account of race, color, or creed, and will exert our full influence and power against all such.

21. We protest against any punishment inflicted upon a Negro with severity, as against lighter punishment inflicted upon another of an alien race for like offense, as an act of prejudice injustice, and that should be resented by the entire race.

22. We protest against the system of education in any country where Negroes are denied the same privileges and advantages as other races.

23. We declare it inhuman and unfair to boycott Negroes from industries and labor in any part of the world.

24. We believe in the doctrine of the freedom of the press, and we therefore emphatically protest against the suppression of Negro newspapers and periodicals in various parts of the world, and call upon Negroes everywhere to employ all available means to prevent such suppression.

25. We further demand free speech universally for all men.

26. We hereby protest against the publication of scandalous and inflammatory articles by an alien press tending to create racial strife and the exhibition of picture films showing the Negro as a cannibal.

27. We believe in the self-determination of all peoples.

28. We declare for the freedom religious worship.

29. With the help of Almighty God, we declare ourselves the protectors of the honor and virtue of our women and children, and pledge our lives for their protection and defense everywhere, and under all circumstances from wrongs and outrages.

30. We demand the right of unlimited and unprejudiced education for ourselves and our posterity forever.

31. We declare that the teaching in any school by alien teachers to our boys and girls, that the alien race is superior to the Negro race, is an insult to the Negro people of the world.

32. Where Negroes form a part of the citizenry of any country, and pass the civil service examination of such country, we declare them entitled to the same consideration as other citizens as to appointments in such civil service.

33. We vigorously protest against the increasingly unfair and unjust treatment accorded Negro travelers on land and sea by the agents and employees of railroad and steamship companies and insist that for equal fare we receive equal privileges with travelers of other races.

34. We declare it unjust for any country, State or nation to enact laws tending to hinder and obstruct the free immigration of Negroes on account of their race and color.

35. That the right of the Negro to travel unmolested throughout the world be not abridged by any person or persons, and all Negroes are called upon to give aid to a fellow Negro when thus molested.

36. We declare that all Negroes are entitled to the same right to travel over the world as other men.

37. We hereby demand that the governments of the world recognize our leader and his representatives chosen by the race to look after the welfare of our people under such governments.

38. We demand complete control of our social institutions without interference by any alien race or races.

39. That the colors, Red, Black and Green, be the colors of the Negro race.

40. Resolved, That the anthem "Ethiopia, Thou Land of Our Fathers," etc., shall be the anthem of the Negro race.

41. We believe that any limited liberty which deprives one of the complete rights and prerogatives of full citizenship is but a modified form of slavery.

42. We declare it an injustice to our people and a serious impediment to the health of the race to deny to competent licensed Negro physicians the right to practice in the public hospitals of the communities in which they reside, for no other reason than their race and color.

43. We call upon the various governments of the world to accept and acknowledge Negro representatives who shall be sent to the said governments to represent the general welfare of the Negro peoples of the world.

44. We deplore and protest against the practice of confining juvenile prisoners in prisons with adults, and we recommend that such youthful prisoners be taught gainful trades under humane supervision.

45. Be it further resolved, that we as a race of people declare the League of Nations null and void as far as the Negro is concerned, in that it seeks to deprive Negroes of their liberty.

46. We demand of all men to do unto us as we would do unto them, in the name of justice; and we cheerfully accord to all men all the rights we claim herein for ourselves.

47. We declare that no Negro shall engage himself in battle for an alien race without first obtaining the consent of the leader of the Negro people of the world, except in a matter of national self-defense.

48. We protest against the practice of drafting Negroes and sending them to war with alien forces without proper training, and demand in all cases that Negro soldiers be given the same training as the aliens.

49. We demand that instructions given Negro children in schools include the subject of "Negro History," to their benefit.

50. We demand a free and unfettered commercial intercourse with all the Negro people of the world.

51. We declare for the absolute freedom of the seas for all peoples.

52. We demand that our duly accredited representatives be given proper recognition in all leagues, conferences, conventions or courts of international arbitration wherever human rights are discussed.

53. We proclaim the 31st day of August of each year to be an international holiday to be observed by all Negroes.

54. We want all men to know we shall maintain and contend for the freedom and equality of every man, woman and child of our race, with our lives, our fortunes and our sacred honor.

These rights we believe to be justly ours and proper for the protection of the Negro race at large, and because of this belief we, on behalf of the four hundred million Negroes of the world, do pledge herein the sacred blood of the race in defense, and we hereby subscribe our names as a guarantee of the truthfulness and faithfulness hereof in the presence of Almighty God, on the 13th day of August, in the year of our Lord one thousand nine hundred and twenty.

Marcus Garvey, et al.

Source: John Bayne, Notary Public, New York County, County Clerk's No. 378, New York Register's No. 12102. © 1998 Copyright UNIA-ACL. All Rights Reserved.

79. The Eruption of Tulsa, June 29, 1921
WALTER WHITE

In one of the most chilling events in the entire history of race tensions in the United States, the Tulsa race riots reversed generations of economic, social, and political gains made by African Americans in the city. Beginning on Memorial Day in 1921, a well-armed white mob, some of them deputized by the police department, targeted Tulsa's prosperous black neighborhood, Greenwood—"The black Wall Street," which had become one of the most vibrant centers of African American life in the country. Eventually, the white mob razed thirty-six square blocks, burned to the ground more than 3,000 homes and killed as many as 300 people, many of whom were buried in mass graves or simply dumped anonymously into the Arkansas River. By the end of the onslaught, Tulsa's thriving black community, which had numbered 15,000 people and rivaled New York City as a national center of urban black life, was destroyed. This document, published in the NAACP's Crisis magazine, laments the episode.

A hysterical white girl related that a nineteen-year-old colored boy attempted to assault her in the public elevator of a public office building of a thriving town of 100,000 in open daylight. Without pausing to find out whether or not the story was true, without bothering with the slight detail of investigating the character of the woman who made the outcry (as a matter of fact, she was of exceedingly doubtful reputation), a mob of 100-percent Americans set forth on a wild rampage that cost the lives of fifty white men; of between 150 and 200 colored men, women and children; the destruction by fire of $1,500,000 worth of property; the looting of many homes; and everlasting damage to the reputation of the city of Tulsa and the State of Oklahoma.

Walter White, President of the NAACP

This, in brief, is the story of the eruption of Tulsa on the night of May 31 and the morning of June 1, 1921. One could travel far and find few cities where the likelihood of trouble between the races was as little thought of as in Tulsa. Her reign of terror stands as a grim reminder of the grip mob violence has on the throat of America, and the ever-present possibility of devastating race conflicts where least expected.

Tulsa is a thriving, bustling, enormously wealthy town of between 90,000 and 100,000. In 1910 it was the home of 18,182 souls, a dead and hopeless outlook ahead. Then oil was discovered. The town grew amazingly. On December 29, 1920, it had bank deposits totaling $65,449,985.90; almost $1,000 per capita when compared with the Federal Census figures of 1920, which gave Tulsa 72,075. The town lies in the center of the oil region and many are the stories told of the making of fabulous fortunes by men who were operating on a shoe-string. Some of the stories rival those of the "forty-niners" in California. The town has a number of modern office buildings, many beautiful homes, miles of clean, well-paved streets, and aggressive and progressive businessmen who well exemplify Tulsa's motto of "The City with a Personality."

So much for the setting. What are the causes of the race riot that occurred in such a place?

First, the Negro in Oklahoma has shared in the sudden prosperity that has come to many of his white brothers, and there are some colored men there who are wealthy. This fact has caused a bitter resentment on the part of the lower order of whites, who feel that these colored men, members of an "inferior race," are exceedingly presumptuous in achieving greater economic prosperity than they who are members of a divinely ordered superior race. There are at least three colored persons in Oklahoma who are worth a million dollars each; J.W. Thompson of Clearview is worth $500,000; there are a number of men and women worth $100,000; and many whose possessions are valued at $25,000 and $50,000 each. This was particularly true of Tulsa, where there were two colored men worth $150,000 each; two worth $100,000; three $50,000; and four who were assessed at $25,000. In one case where a colored man owned and operated a printing plant with $25,000 worth of printing machinery in it, the leader of a mob that set fire to and destroyed the plant was a linotype operator employed for years by the colored owner at $48 per week. The white man was killed while attacking the plant. Oklahoma is largely populated by pioneers from other States. Some of the white pioneers are former residents of Mississippi, Georgia, Tennessee, Texas, and other States more typically Southern than Oklahoma. These have brought with them their anti-Negro prejudices. Lethargic and unprogressive by nature, it sorely irks them to see Negroes making greater progress than they themselves are achieving.

One of the charges made against the colored men in Tulsa is that they were "radical." Questioning the whites more closely regarding the nature of this radicalism, I found it means that Negroes were uncompromisingly denouncing "Jim-Crow" cars, lynching, peonage; in short, were asking that the Federal constitutional guaranties of "life, liberty, and the pursuit of happiness" be given regardless of color. The Negroes of Tulsa and other Oklahoma cities are pioneers; men and women who have dared, men and women who have had the initiative and the courage to pull up stakes in other less-favored States and face hardship in a newer one for the sake of eventual progress. That type is ever less ready to submit to insult. Those of the whites who seek to maintain the old white group control naturally do not relish seeing Negroes emancipating themselves from the old system.

A third cause was the rotten political conditions in Tulsa. A vice ring was in control of the city, allowing open operation of houses of ill fame, of gambling joints, the illegal sale of whiskey, the robbing of banks and stores, with hardly a slight possibility of the arrest of the criminals, and even less of their conviction. For fourteen years Tulsa has been in the absolute control of this element. Most of the better element, and there is a large percentage of Tulsans who can properly be classed as such, are interested in making money and getting away. They have taken little or no interest in the election of city or county officials, leaving it to those whose interest it was to secure officials who would protect them in their vice operations. About two months ago the State legislature assigned two additional judges to Tulsa County to aid the present two in clearing the badly clogged dockets. These judges found more than six thousand cases awaiting trial. Thus in a county of approximately 100,000 population, six out of every hundred citizens were under indictment for some sort of crime, with little likelihood of trial in any of them.

Last July a white man by the name of Roy Belton, accused of murdering a taxicab driver, was taken from the county jail and lynched. According to the statements of many prominent Tulsans, local police officers directed traffic at the scene of the lynching, trying to afford every person present an equal chance to view the event. Insurance companies refuse to give Tulsa merchants insurance on their stocks; the risk is too great. There have been so many automobile thefts that a number of companies have canceled all policies on cars in Tulsa. The net result of these conditions was that practically none of the citizens of the town, white or colored, had very much respect for the law.

Source: The Nation 112 (June 29, 1921): 909–910.

80. The Autobiography of Marcus Garvey, 1923

In June of 1923, civil rights leader Marcus Garvey was arrested and incarcerated in the Tombs Prison in New York City where he stayed to await the outcome of an appeal for bail. He had been convicted mail fraud related to selling what the government deemed to be illegal securities or stock in companies related to his back-to-Africa movement. While in jail, Garvey wrote the most extensive autobiographical statement of his career, and the first written for the American public.

Garvey attempted to meet two objectives with his statement: to present a brief account of his background and to answer the attacks of his critics. The excerpted essay thus represents Garvey as he wanted the public to view him during a critical phase of his career as an author and the founder of the Universal Negro Improvement Association.

I was born in the Island of Jamaica, British West Indies, on Aug. 17, 1887. My parents were black Negroes. My father was a man of brilliant intellect and dashing courage. He was unafraid of consequences. He took human chances in the course of life, as most bold men do, and he failed at the close of his career. He once had a fortune; he died poor. My mother was a sober and conscientious Christian, too soft and good for the time in which she lived. She was the direct opposite of my father. He was severe, firm, determined, bold and strong, refusing to yield even to superior forces if he believed he was right. My mother, on the other hand, was always willing to return a smile for a blow, and ever ready to bestow charity upon her enemy. Of this strange combination I was born thirty-six years ago, and ushered into a world of sin, the flesh an[d] the devil.

I grew up with other black and white boys. I was never whipped by any, but made them all respect the strength of my arms. I got my education from many sources— through private tutors, two public schools, two grammar or high schools and two colleges. My teachers were men and women of varied experiences and abilities; four of them were eminent preachers. They studied me and I studied them. With some I became friendly in after years, others and I drifted apart, because as a boy they wanted to whip me, and I simply refused to be whipped. I was not made to be whipped. It annoys me to be defeated; hence to me, to be once defeated is to find cause for an everlasting struggle to reach the top.

I became a printer's apprentice at an early age, while still attending school. My apprentice master was a highly educated and alert man. In the affairs of business and the world he had no peer. He taught me many things before I reached twelve, and at fourteen I had enough intelligence and experience to manage men. I was strong and manly, and I made them respect me. I developed a strong and forceful character, and have maintained it still.

To me, at home in my early days, there was no difference between white and black. One of my father's properties, the place where I lived most of the time, was adjoining that of a white man. He had three girls and two boys; the Wesleyan minister, another white man whose church my parents attended, also had property adjoining ours. He had three girls and one boy. All of us were playmates. We romped and were happy children playmates together. The little white girl whom I liked most knew no better than I did myself. We were two innocent fools who never dreamed of a race feeling and problem. As a child, I went to school with white boys and girls, like all other negroes. We were not called negroes then. I never heard the term negro used once until I was about fourteen.

At fourteen my little white playmate and I parted. Her parents thought the time had come to separate us and draw the color line. They sent her and another sister to Edinburgh, Scotland, and told her that she was never to write or try to get in touch with me, for I was a "nigger." It was then that I found for the first time that there was some difference in humanity, and that there were different races, each having its own separate and distinct social life. I did not care about the separation after I was told about it, because I never thought all during our childhood association that the girl and the rest of the children of her race were better than I was; in fact, they used to look up to me. So I simply had no regrets. I only thought them "fresh."

After my first lesson in race distinction, I never thought of playing with white girls any more, even if they might be next door neighbors. At home my sister's company was good enough for me, and at school I made friends with the colored girls next to me. White boys and I used to frolic together. We played cricket and baseball, ran races and rode bicycles together, took each other to the river and to the sea beach to learn to swim, and made boyish efforts while out in deep water to drown each other, making a sprint for shore crying out "shark, shark, shark." In all our experiences, however, only one black boy was drowned. He went under on a Friday afternoon after school hours, and his parents found him afloat half eaten by sharks on the following Sunday afternoon. Since then we boys never went back to sea.

"YOU ARE BLACK"

At maturity the black and white boys separated, and took different courses in life. I grew up then to see the difference between the races more and more. My school-mates as young men did not know or remember me any more. Then I realized that I had to make a fight for a place in the world, that it was not so easy to pass on to office and position. Personally, however, I had not much difficulty in finding and holding a place for myself, for I was aggressive. At eighteen I had an excellent position as manager of a large printing establishment, having under my control several men old enough to be my grandfathers. But I got mixed up with public life. I started to take an interest in the politics of my country, and then I saw the injustice done to my race because it was black, and I became dissatisfied on that account. I went traveling to South and Central America and parts of the West Indies to find out if it was so elsewhere, and I found the same situation. I set sail for Europe to find out if it was different there, and again I found the same stumbling-block—"You are black." I read of the conditions in America. I read "Up From Slavery," by Booker T. Washington, and then my doom—if I may so call it—of being a race leader dawned upon me in London after I had traveled through almost half of Europe.

I asked, "Where is the black man's Government?" "Where is his King and his kingdom?" "Where is his President, his country, and his ambassador, his army, his navy, his men of big affairs?" I could not find them, and then I declared, "I will help to make them."

Becoming naturally restless for the opportunity of doing something [for] the advancement of my race, I was determined that the black man would not continue to be kicked about by all the other races and nations of the world, as I saw it in the West Indies, South and Central America and Europe, and as I read of it in America. My young and ambitious mind led me into flights of great imagination. I saw before me then, even as I do now, a new world of black men, not peons, serfs, dogs and slaves, but a nation of sturdy men making their impress upon civilization and causing a new light to dawn upon the human race. I could not remain in London any more. My brain was afire. There was a world of thought to conquer. I had to start ere it became too late and the work be not done. Immediately I boarded a ship at

Southampton for Jamaica, where I arrived on July 15, 1914. The Universal Negro Improvement Association and African Communities (Imperial) League was founded and organized five days after my arrival, with the program of uniting all the negro peoples of the world into one great body to establish a country and Government absolutely their own.

Where did the name of the organization come from? It was while speaking to a West Indian negro who was a passenger with me from Southampton, who was returning home to the West Indies from Basutoland with his Basuto wife, that I further learned of the horrors of native life in Africa. He related to me in conversation such horrible and pitiable tales that my heart bled within me. Retiring from the conversation to my cabin, all day and the following night I pondered over the subject matter of that conversation, and at midnight, lying flat on my back, the vision and thought came to me that I should name the organization the Universal Negro Improvement Association and African Communities (Imperial) League. Such a name I thought would embrace the purpose of all black humanity. Thus to the world a name was born, a movement created, and a man became known.

I really never knew there was so much color prejudice in Jamaica, my own native home, until I started the work of the Universal Negro Improvement Association. We started immediately before the war. I had just returned from a successful trip to Europe, which was an exceptional achievement for a black man. The daily papers wrote me up with big headlines and told of my movement. But nobody wanted to be a negro. "Garvey is crazy; he has lost his head," "Is that the use he is going to make of his experience and intelligence?"—such were the criticisms passed upon me. Men and women as black as I, and even more so, had believed themselves white under the West Indian order of [society]. I was simply an impossible man to use openly the term "negro;" yet every one beneath his breath was calling the black man a negro.

I had to decide whether to please my friends and be one of the "black-whites" of Jamaica, and be reasonably prosperous, or come out openly and defend and help improve and protect the integrity of the black millions and suffer. I decided to do the latter, hence my offence against "colored-black-white" society in the colonies and America. I was openly hated and persecuted by some of these colored men of the island who did not want to be classified as negroes, but as white. They hated me worse than poison. They opposed me at every step, but I had a large number of white friends, who encouraged and helped me. Notable among them were the then Governor of the Colony, the Colonial Secretary and several other prominent men. But they were afraid of offending the "colored gentry" that were passing for white. Hence my fight had to be made alone. I spent hundreds of pounds (sterling) helping the organization to gain a footing. I also gave up all my time to the promulgation of its ideals. I became a marked man, but I was determined that the work should be done.

The war helped a great deal in arousing the consciousness of the colored people to the reasonableness of our program, especially after the British at home had rejected a large number of West Indian colored men who wanted to be officers in the British army. When they were told that negroes could not be officers in the British army they started their own propaganda, which supplemented the program of the Universal Negro Improvement Association. With this and other contributing agencies a few of the stiff-necked colored people began to see the reasonableness of my program, but they were firm in refusing to be known as negroes. Furthermore, I was a black man and therefore had absolutely no right to lead; in the opinion of the "colored" element, leadership should have been in the hands of a yellow or a very light man. On such flimsy prejudices our race has been retarded. There is more bitterness among us negroes because of the caste of color than there is between any other peoples, not excluding the people of India.

I succeeded to a great extent in establishing the association in Jamaica with the assistance of a Catholic Bishop, the Governor, Sir John Pringle, the Rev. William Graham, a Scottish clergyman, and several other white friends. I got in touch with Booker Washington and told him what I wanted to do. He invited me to America and promised to speak with me in the Southern and other States to help my work. Although he died in the Fall of 1915, I made my arrangements and arrived in the United States on March 23, 1916.

Here I found a new and different problem. I immediately visited some of the then so-called negro leaders, only to discover, after a close study of them, that they had no program, but were mere opportunists who were living off their so-called leadership while the poor people were groping in the dark. I traveled through thirty-eight States and everywhere found the same condition. I visited Tuskegee and paid my respects to the dead hero, Booker Washington, and then returned to New York, where I organized the New York division of the Universal Negro Improvement Association. After instructing the people in the aims and objects of the association, I intended returning to Jamaica to perfect the Jamaica organization, but when we had enrolled about 800 or 1,000 members in the Harlem district and had elected the officers, a few negro politicians began trying to turn the movement into a political club.

POLITICAL FACTION FIGHT

Seeing that these politicians were about to destroy my ideals, I had to fight to get them out of the organization. There it was that I made by first political enemies in Harlem. They fought me until they smashed the first organization and reduced its membership to about fifty. I started again and in two months built up a new organization of about 1,500 members. Again the politicians came and divided us into two factions. They took away all the books of the organization, its treasury and all its belongings. At that time I was only an organizer, for it was not then my intention to remain in America, but to return to Jamaica. The organization had its proper officers elected, and I was not an officer of the New York division, but President of the Jamaica branch.

On the second split in Harlem thirteen of the members conferred with me and requested me to become President for a time of the New York organization so as to save them from the politicians. I consented and was elected President. There then sprung up two factions, one led by the politicians with the books and the money, and the other led by me. My faction had no money. I placed at their disposal what money I had, opened an office for them, rented a meeting place, employed two women secretaries, went on the streets of Harlem at night to speak for the movement. In three weeks more than 2,000 new members joined. By this time I had the association incorporated so as to prevent the other faction using the name, but in two weeks the politicians had stolen all the people's money and had smashed up their faction.

The organization under my Presidency grew by leaps and bounds. I started The Negro World. Being a journalist, I edited this paper free of cost for the association, and worked for them without pay until November, 1920. I traveled all over the country for the association at my own expense, and established branches until in 1919 we had about thirty branches in different cities. By my writings and speeches we were able to build up a large organization of over 2,000,000 by June, 1919, at which time we launched the program of the Black Star Line.

To have built up a new organization, which was not purely political, among negroes in America was a wonderful feat, for the negro politician does not allow any other kind of organization within his race to thrive. We succeeded, however, in making the Universal Negro Improvement Association so formidable in 1919 that we encountered more trouble from our political brethren. They sought the influence of the District Attorney's office of the County of New York to put us out of business. Edwin P. Kilroe, at that time an Assistant District Attorney, on the complaint of the negro politicians, started to investigate us and the association. Mr. Kilroe would constantly and continuously call me to his office for investigation on extraneous matters without coming to the point. The result was that after the eight or ninth time I wrote an article in our newspaper, The Negro World, against him. This was interpreted as criminal libel, for which I was indicted and arrested, but subsequently dismissed on retracting what I had written.

During my many tilts with Mr. Kilroe, the question of the Black Star Line was discussed. He did not want us to have a line of ships. I told him that even as there was a White Star Line, we would have, irrespective of his wishes, a Black Star Line. On June 27, 1919, we incorporated the Black Star Line of Delaware, and in September we obtained a ship.

The following month (October) a man by the name of Tyler came to my office at 56 West 135th Street, New York City, and told me that Mr. Kilroe had sent him to "get me," and at once fired four shots at me from a .38-calibre revolver. He wounded me in the right leg and the right side of my scalp. I was taken to the Harlem Hospital, and he was arrested. The next day it was reported that he committed suicide in jail just before he was to be taken before a City Magistrate.

RECORD-BREAKING CONVENTION

The first year of our activities for the Black Star Line added prestige to the Universal Negro Improvement Association. Several hundred thousand dollars worth of shares were sold. Our first ship, the steamship Yarmouth, had made two voyages to the West Indies and Central America. The white press had flashed the news all over the world. I, a young Negro, as President of the corporation, had become famous. My name was discussed on five continents. The Universal Negro Improvement Association gained millions of followers all over the world. By August, 1920, over 4,000,000 persons had joined the movement. A convention of all the negro peoples of the world was called to meet in New York that month. Delegates came from all parts of the known world. Over 25,000 persons packed the Madison Square Garden on Aug. 1 to hear me speak to the first International Convention of Negroes. It was a record-breaking meeting, the first and the biggest of its kind. The name of Garvey had become known as a leader of his race.

Such fame among negroes was too much for other race leaders and politicians to tolerate. My downfall was planned by my enemies. They laid all kinds of traps for me. They scattered their spies among the employes of the Black Star Line and the

Universal Negro Improvement Association. Our office records were stolen. Employes started to be openly dishonest; we could get no convictions against them; even if on complaint they were held by a Magistrate, they were dismissed by the Grand Jury. The ships' officers started to pile up thousands of dollars of debts against the company without the knowledge of the officers of the corporation. Our ships were damaged at sea, and there was a general riot of wreck and ruin. Officials of the Universal Negro Improvement Association also began to steal and be openly dishonest. I had to dismiss them. They joined my enemies, and thus I had an endless fight on my hands to save the ideals of the association and carry out our program for the race. My negro enemies, finding that they alone could not destroy me, resorted to misrepresenting me to the leaders of the white race, several of whom, without proper investigation, also opposed me.

With robberies from within and from without, the Black Star Line was forced to suspend active business in December, 1921. While I was on a business trip to the West Indies in the Spring of 1921, the Black Star Line received the blow from which it was unable to recover. A sum of $25,000 was paid by one of the officers of the corporation to a man to purchase a ship, but the ship was never obtained and the money was never returned. The company was defrauded of a further sum of $11,000. Through such actions on the part of dishonest men in the shipping business, the Black Star Line received its first setback. This resulted in my being indicted for using the United States mails to defraud investors in the company. I was subsequently convicted and sentenced to five years in a Federal penitentiary. My trial is a matter of history. I know I was not given a square deal, because my indictment was the result of a "frame-up" among my political and business enemies. I had to conduct my own case in court because of the peculiar position in which I found myself. I had millions of friends and a large number of enemies. I wanted a colored attorney to handle my case, but there was none I could trust. I feel that I have been denied justice because of prejudice. Yet I have an abundance of faith in the courts of America, and I hope yet to obtain justice on my appeal.

ASSOCIATION'S 6,000,000 MEMBERSHIP

The temporary ruin of the Black Star Line in no way affected the larger work of the Universal Negro Improvement Association, which now has 900 branches with an approximate membership of 6,000,000. This organization has succeeded in organizing the negroes all over the world and we now look forward to a renaissance that will create a new people and bring about the restoration of Ethiopia's ancient glory.

Being black, I have committed an unpardonable offense against the very light colored negroes in America and the West Indies by making myself famous as a negro leader of millions. In their view, no black man must rise above them, but I still forge ahead determined to give to the world the truth about the new Negro who is determined to make and hold for himself a place in the affairs of men. The Universal Negro Improvement Association has been misrepresented by my enemies. They have tried to make it appear that we are hostile to other races. This is absolutely false. We love all humanity. We are working for the peace of the world which we believe can only come about when all races are given their due.

We feel that there is absolutely no reason why there should be any differences between the black and white races, if each stop to adjust and steady itself. We believe in the purity of both races. We do not believe the black man should be encouraged in the idea that his highest purpose in life is to marry a white woman, but we do believe that the white man should be taught to respect the black woman in the same way as he wants the black man to respect the white woman. It is a vicious and dangerous doctrine of social equality to urge, as certain colored leaders do, that black and white should get together, for that would destroy the racial purity of both.

We believe that the black people should have a country of their own where they should be given the fullest opportunity to develop politically, socially and industrially. The black people should not be encouraged to remain in white people's countries and expect to be Presidents, Governors, Mayors, Senators, Congressmen, Judges and social and industrial leaders. We believe that with the rising ambition of the negro, if a country is not provided for him in another 50 or 100 years, there will be a terrible clash that will end disastrously to him and disgrace our civilization. We desire to prevent such a clash by pointing the negro to a home of his own. We feel that all well disposed and broad minded white men will aid in this direction. It is because of this belief no doubt that my negro enemies, so as to prejudice me further in the opinion of the public, wickedly state that I am a member of the Ku Klux Klan, even though I am a black man.

I have been deprived of the opportunity of properly explaining my work to the white people of America through the prejudice worked up against me by jealous and wicked members of my own race. My success as a[n] organizer was much more than rival negro leaders could tolerate. They, regardless of consequences, either to me or to the race, had to destroy me by fair means or foul. The thousands of anonymous and other hostile letters written to the editors and publishers of the white press by negro rivals to prejudice me in the eyes of public opinion are sufficient evidence of the wicked and vicious opposition I have had to meet from among my own people, especially among the very lightly colored. But they went further than the press in their attempts to discredit me. They organized clubs all over the United States and the West Indies, and wrote both open and anonymous letters to city, State and Federal officials of this and other Governments to induce them to use their influence to hamper and destroy me. No wonder, therefore, that several Judges, District Attorneys and other high officials have been against me without knowing me. No wonder, therefore, that the great white population of this country and of the world has a wrong impression of the aims and objects of the Universal Negro Improvement Association and of the work of Marcus Garvey.

THE STRUGGLE OF THE FUTURE

Having had the wrong education as a start in his racial career, the negro has become his own greatest enemy. Most of the trouble I have had in advancing the cause of the race has come from negroes. Booker Washington aptly described the race in one of his lectures by stating that we were like crabs in a barrel, that none would allow the other to climb over, but on any such attempt all would continue to pull back into the barrel the one crab that would make the effort to climb out. Yet, those of us with vision cannot desert the race, leaving it to suffer and die.

Looking forward a century or two, we can see an economic and political death struggle for the survival of the different race groups. Many of our present-day national centres will have become overcrowded with vast surplus populations. The fight for bread and position will be keen and severe. The weaker and unprepared group is bound to go under. That is why, visionaries as we are in the Universal Negro Improvement Association, we are fighting for the founding of a negro nation in Africa, so that there will be no clash between black and white and that each race will have a separate existence and civilization all its own without courting suspicion and hatred or eyeing each other with jealousy and rivalry within the borders of the same country.

White men who have struggled for and built up their countries and their own civilizations are not disposed to hand them over to the negro or any other race without let or hindrance. It would be unreasonable to expect this. Hence any vain assumption on the part of the negro to imagine that he will one day become President of the Nation, Governor of the State, or Mayor of the city in the countries of white men, is like waiting on the devil and his angels to take up their residence in the Realm on High and direct there the affairs of Paradise.

Source: Copyright © 1995–2008 The Marcus Garvey and UNIA Papers Project, UCLA.

81. Harlem, March 1925
ALAIN LOCKE

In March 1925 *Survey Graphic* magazine commissioned scholar Alain Locke to oversee a landmark collection of studies, reports, and essays, all dedicated to what seemed like the emergence of a renaissance—a cultural flowering of black life—in Harlem.

If we were to offer a symbol of what Harlem has come to mean in the short span of twenty years, it would be another statue of liberty on the landward side of New York. It stands for a folk-movement which in human significance can be compared only with the pushing back of the western frontier in the first half of the last century, or the waves of immigration which have swept in from overseas in the last half. Numerically far smaller than either of these movements, the volume of migration is such none the less that Harlem has become the greatest Negro community the world has known—without counterpart in the South or in Africa. But beyond this, Harlem represents the Negro's latest thrust towards Democracy.

The special significance that today stamps it as the sign and center of the renaissance of a people lies, however, layers deep under the Harlem that many know but few have begun to understand. Physically Harlem is little more than a note of sharper color in the kaleidoscope of New York. The metropolis pays little heed to the shifting crystallizations of its own heterogeneous millions. Never having experienced permanence, it has watched, without emotion or even curiosity, Irish, Jew, Italian, Negro, a score of other races drift in and out of the same colorless tenements.

So Harlem has come into being and grasped its destiny with little heed from New York. And to the herded thousands who shoot beneath it twice a day on the subway, or the comparatively few whose daily travel takes them within sight of its fringes or down its main arteries, it is a black belt and nothing more. The pattern of delicatessen store and cigar shop and restaurant and undertaker's shop which repeats itself a thousand times on each of New York's long avenues is unbroken through Harlem. Its apartments, churches and storefronts antedated the Negroes and, for all

New York knows, may outlast them there. For most of New York, Harlem is merely a rough rectangle of common-place city blocks, lying between and to east and west of Lenox and Seventh Avenues, stretching nearly a mile north and south—and unaccountably full of Negroes.

Another Harlem is savored by the few—a Harlem of racy music and racier dancing, of cabarets famous or notorious according to their kind, of amusement in which abandon and sophistication are cheek by jowl—a Harlem which draws the connoisseur in diversion as well as the undiscriminating sightseer. This Harlem is the fertile source of the "shuffling" and "rollin'" and "runnin' wild" revues that establish themselves season after season in "downtown" theaters. It is part of the exotic fringe of the metropolis.

Beneath this lies again the Harlem of the newspapers—a Harlem of monster parades and political flummery, a Harlem swept by revolutionary oratory or draped about the mysterious figures of Negro "millionaires," a Harlem pre-occupied with naive adjustments to a white world—a Harlem, in short, grotesque with the distortions of journalism.

YET in final analysis, Harlem is neither slum, ghetto, resort or colony, though it is in part all of them. It is—or promises at least to be—a race capital. Europe seething in a dozen centers with emergent nationalities, Palestine full of a renascent Judaism—these are no more alive with the spirit of a racial awakening than Harlem; culturally and spiritually it focuses a people. Negro life is not only founding new centers, but finding a new soul. The tide of Negro migration, northward and city-ward, is not to be fully explained as a blind flood started by the demands of war industry coupled with the shutting off of foreign migration, or by the pressure of poor crops coupled with increased social terrorism in certain sections of the South and Southwest. Neither labor demand, the boll-weevil nor the Ku Klux Klan is a basic factor, however contributory any or all of them may have been. The wash and rush of this human tide on the beach line of the northern city centers is to be explained primarily in terms of a new vision of opportunity, of social and economic freedom of a spirit to seize, even in the face of an extortionate and heavy toll, a chance for the improvement of conditions. With each successive wave of it, the movement of the Negro migrant becomes more and more like that of the European waves at their crests, a mass movement toward the larger and the more democratic chance—in the Negro's case a deliberate flight not only from countryside to city, but from medieaval America to modern.

The secret lies close to what distinguishes Harlem from the ghettos with which it is sometimes compared. The ghetto picture is that of a slowly dissolving mass, bound by ties of custom and culture and association, in the midst of a freer and more varied society. From the racial standpoint, our Harlems are themselves crucibles. Here in Manhattan is not merely the largest Negro community in the world, but the first concentration in history of so many diverse elements of Negro life. It has attracted the African, the West Indian, the Negro American; has brought together the Negro of the North and the Negro of the South; the man from the city and the man from the town and village; the peasant, the student, the business man, the professional man, artist, poet, musician, adventurer and worker, preacher and criminal, exploiter and social outcast. Each group has come with its own separate motives and for its own special ends, but their greatest experience has been the finding of one another. Proscription and prejudice have thrown these dissimilar elements into a common area of contact and interaction. Within this area, race sympathy and unity have determined a further fusing of sentiment and experience ... Hitherto, it must be admitted that American Negroes have been a race more in name than in fact, or to be exact, more in sentiment than in experience. The chief bond between them has been that of a common condition rather than a common consciousness; a problem in common rather than a life in common. In Harlem, Negro life is seizing upon its first chances for group expression and self-determination. That is why our comparison is taken with those nascent centers of folk-expression and self-determination which are playing a creative part in the world today. Without pretense to their political significance, Harlem has the same role to play for the New Negro as Dublin has had for the New Ireland or Prague for the New Czechoslovakia.

It is true the formidable centers of our race life, educational, industrial, financial, are not in Harlem, yet here, nevertheless, are the forces that make a group known and felt in the world. The reformers, the fighting advocates, the inner spokesmen, the poets, artists and social prophets are here, and pouring in toward them are the fluid ambitious youth and pressing in upon them the migrant masses. The professional observers, and the enveloping communities as well, are conscious of the physics of this stir and movement, of the cruder and more obvious facts of a ferment and a migration. But they are as yet largely unaware of the psychology of it, of the galvanizing shocks and reactions, which mark the social awakening and internal reorganization which are making a race out of its own disunited elements.

A railroad ticket and a suitcase, like a Baghdad carpet, transport the Negro peasant from the cotton-field and farm to the heart of the most complex urban civilization. Here in the mass, he must and does survive a jump of two generations in social economy and of a century and more in civilization. Meanwhile the Negro poet, student, artist, thinker, by the very move that normally would take him off at a tangent from the masses, finds himself in their midst, in a situation concentrating the racial side of his experience and heightening his race-consciousness. These moving, half-awakened newcomers provide an exceptional seed-bed for the germinating contacts of the enlightened minority. And that is why statistics are out of joint with fact in Harlem, and will be for a generation or so.

HARLEM, I grant you, isn't typical—but it is significant, it is prophetic. No sane observer, however sympathetic to the new trend, would contend that the great masses are articulate as yet, but they stir, they move, they are more than physically restless. The challenge of the new intellectuals among them is clear enough—the "race radicals" and realists who have broken with the old epoch of philanthropic guidance, sentimental appeal and protest. But are we after all only reading into the stirrings of a sleeping giant the dreams of an agitator? The answer is in the migrating peasant. It is the "man farthest down" who is most active in getting up. One of the most characteristic symptoms of this is the professional man himself migrating to recapture his constituency after a vain effort to maintain in some Southern corner what for years back seemed an established living and clientele. The clergyman following his errant flock, the physician or lawyer trailing his clients, supply the true clues. In a real sense it is the rank and file who are leading, and the leaders who are following. A transformed and transforming psychology permeates the masses.

When the racial leaders of twenty years ago spoke of developing race-pride and stimulating race-consciousness, and of the desirability of race solidarity, they could not in any accurate degree have anticipated the abrupt feeling that has surged up and now pervades the awakened centers. Some of the recognized Negro leaders and a powerful section of white opinion identified with "race work" of the older order have indeed attempted to discount this feeling as a "passing phase," an attack of "race nerves," so to speak, an "aftermath of the war," and the like. It has not abated, however, if we are to gage by the present tone and temper of the Negro press, or by the shift in popular support from the officially recognized and orthodox spokesmen to those of the independent, popular, and often radical type who are unmistakable symptoms of a new order. It is a social disservice to blunt the fact that the Negro of the Northern centers has reached a stage where tutelage, even of the most interested and well-intentioned sort, must give place to new relationships, where positive self-direction must be reckoned with in ever increasing measure.

As a service to this new understanding, the contributors to this Harlem number have been asked, not merely to describe Harlem as a city of migrants and as a race center, but to voice these new aspirations of a people, to read the clear message of the new conditions, and to discuss some of the new relationships and contacts they involve. First, we shall look at Harlem, with its kindred centers in the Northern and Mid-Western cities, as the way mark of a momentous folk movement; then as the center of a gripping struggle for an industrial and urban foothold. But more significant than either of these, we shall also view it as the stage of the pageant of contemporary Negro life. In the drama of its new and progressive aspects, we may be witnessing the resurgence of a race; with our eyes focused on the Harlem scene we may dramatically glimpse the New Negro. A.L.

Source: The Survey Graphic Harlem Number, Vol. VI, No. 6, March, 1925. Survey Associates, Inc.

82. Enter the New Negro, March 1925
ALAIN LOCKE

In or around 1915, a new segment of American society—a culture of African Americans—began to gradually make itself evident. The newness was not due to the presence of African Americans, but rather the flowering of a self-conscious "New Negro." It was an evolution that probably began the minute after the first group of slaves arrived in Jamestown; when the first slave revolt occurred or when the first slave escaped bondage anywhere in America and began the trek towards self discovery.

Regardless of when this liberation movement began, what it flowered was finally recognized in the decade between 1915 and 1925 as "something beyond the watch and guard of statistics ... in the life of the American Negro." Scholar Alain Locke said these changes went unnoticed by sociologists, philanthropists, and others because this emerging cultural wing of mainstream America seemed to defy any "formulae." A "younger generation is vibrant with a new psychology; the new spirit is awake in the masses, and under the very eyes of the professional observers is transforming what has been a perennial problem into the progressive phases of contemporary Negro life," Locke said. In "Enter the New Negro," Locke explains the unprecedented transformation of black culture in America.

The Old Negro had long become more of a myth than a man. The Old Negro, we must remember, was a creature of moral debate and historical controversy. His has been a stock figure perpetuated as an historical fiction partly in innocent sentimentalism, partly in deliberate reactionism. The Negro himself has contributed his share to this through a sort of protective social mimicry forced upon him by the adverse circumstances of dependence. So for generations in the mind of America, the Negro has been more of a formula than a human being—a something to be argued about, condemned or defended, to be "kept down," or "in his place," or "helped up," to be worried with or worried over, harassed or patronized, a social bogey or a social burden. The thinking Negro even has been induced to share this same general attitude, to focus his attention on controversial issues, to see himself in the distorted perspective of a social problem. His shadow, so to speak, has been more real to him than his personality. Through having had to appeal from the unjust stereotypes of his oppressors and traducers to those of his liberators, friends and benefactors, he has subscribed to the traditional positions from which his case has been viewed. Little true social or self-understanding has or could come from such a situation.

But while the minds of most of us, black and white, have thus burrowed in the trenches of the Civil War and Reconstruction, the actual march of development has simply flanked these positions, necessitating a sudden reorientation of view. We have not been watching in the right direction; set worth and South on a sectional axis, eve have not noticed the East till the sun has us blinking.

Recall how suddenly the Negro spirituals revealed themselves; suppressed for generations under the stereotypes of Wesleyan hymn harmony, secretive, half-ashamed, until the courage of being natural brought them out—and behold, there was folk-music. Similarly the mind of the Negro seems suddenly to have slipped from under the tyranny of social intimidation and to be shaking off the psychology of imitation and implied inferiority. By shedding the old chrysalis of the Negro problem we are achieving something like a spiritual emancipation. Until recently, lacking self understanding, we have been almost as much of a problem to ourselves as we still are to others. But the decade that found us with a problem has left us with only a task. The multitude perhaps feels as yet only a strange relief and a new vague urge, but the thinking few know that in the reaction the vital inner grip of prejudice has been broken.

With this renewed self-respect and self-dependence, the life of the Negro community is bound to enter a new dynamic phase, the buoyancy from within compensating for whatever pressure there may be of conditions from without. The migrant masses, shifting from countryside to city, hurdle several generations of experience at a leap, but more important, the same thing happens spiritually in the life-attitudes and self-expression of the Young Negro, in his poetry, his art, his education and his new outlook, with the additional advantage, of course, of the poise and greater certainty of knowing what it is all about. From this comes the promise and warrant of a new leadership. As one of them has discerningly put it:

We have tomorrow
Bright before us
Like a flame.

Yesterday, a night-gone thing
A sun-down name.

And dawn today
Broad arch above the road we came.
We march!

This is what, even more than any "most creditable record of fifty years of freedom," requires that the Negro of today be seen through other than the dusty spectacles of past controversy. The day of "aunties," "uncles" and "mammies" is equally gone. Uncle Tom and Sambo have passed on, and even the "Colonel" and "George" play barnstorm roles from which they escape with relief when the public spotlight is off. The popular melodrama has about played itself out, and it is time to scrap the fictions, garret the bogeys and settle down to a realistic facing of facts.

First we must observe some of the changes which since the traditional lines of opinion were drawn have rendered these quite obsolete. A main change has been, of course, that shifting of the Negro population which has made the Negro problem no longer exclusively or even predominantly Southern. Why should our minds remain sectionalized, when the problem itself no longer is? Then the trend of migration has not only been toward the North and the Central Midwest, but city-ward and to the great centers of industry—the problems of adjustment are new, practical, local and not peculiarly racial. Rather they are an integral part of the large industrial and social problems of our present-day democracy. And finally, with the Negro rapidly in process of class differentiation, if it ever was warrantable to regard and treat the Negro en masse it is becoming with every day less possible, more unjust and more ridiculous.

The Negro too, for his part, has idols of the tribe to smash. If on the one hand the white man has erred in making the Negro appear to be that which would excuse or extenuate his treatment of him, the Negro, in turn, has too often unnecessarily excused himself because of the way he has been treated. The intelligent Negro of today is resolved not to make discrimination an extenuation for his shortcomings in performance, individual or collective; he is trying to hold himself at par, neither inflated by sentimental allowances nor depreciated by current social discounts. For this he must know himself and be known for precisely what he is, and for that reason he welcomes the new scientific rather than the old sentimental interest. Sentimental interest in the Negro has ebbed. We used to lament this as the falling off of our friends; now we rejoice and pray to be delivered both from self-pity and condescension. The mind of each racial group has had a bitter weaning, apathy or hatred on one side matching disillusionment or resentment on the other; but they face each other today with the possibility at least of entirely new mutual attitudes.

It does not follow that if the Negro were better known, he would be better liked or better treated. But mutual understanding is basic for any subsequent cooperation and adjustment. The effort toward this will at least have the effect of remedying in large part what has been the most unsatisfactory feature of our present stage of race relationships in America, namely the fact that the more intelligent and representative elements of the two race groups have at so many points got quite out of vital touch with one another.

The fiction is that the life of the races is separate and increasingly so. The fact is that they have touched too closely at the unfavorable and too lightly at the favorable levels.

While inter-racial councils have sprung up in the South, drawing on forward elements of both races, in the Northern cities manual laborers may brush elbows in their everyday work, but the community and business leaders have experienced no such interplay or far too little of it. These segments must achieve contact or the race situation in America becomes desperate. Fortunately this is happening. There is a growing realization that in social effort the cooperative basis must supplant long-distance philanthropy, and that the only safeguard for mass relations in the future must be provided in the carefully maintained contacts of the enlightened minorities of both race groups. In the intellectual realm a renewed and keen curiosity is replacing the recent apathy; the Negro is being carefully studied, not just talked about and discussed. In art and letters, instead of being wholly caricatured, he is being seriously portray eel and painted.

To all of this the New Negro is keenly responsive as an augury of a new democracy in American culture. He is contributing his share to the new social understanding. But the desire to be understood would never in itself have been sufficient to have opened so completely the protectively closed portals of the thinking Negro's mind. There is still too much possibility of being snubbed or patronized for that. It was rather the necessity for fuller, truer, self-expression, the realization of the unwisdom of allowing social discrimination to segregate him mentally, and a counter-attitude to cramp and fetter his own living—and so the "spite-wall" that the intellectuals built over the "color-line" has happily been taken down. Much of this reopening of intellectual Contacts has Entered in New York and has been richly fruitful not merely in the enlarging of personal experience, but in the definite enrichment of American art and letters and in the clarifying of our common vision of the social tasks ahead.

The particular significance in the reestablishment of contact between the more advanced and representative classes is that it promises to offset some of the unfavorable reactions of the past, or at least to re-surface race contacts somewhat for the future. Subtly the conditions that are moulding a New Negro are moulding a new American attitude.

However, this new phase of things is delicate; it will call for less charity but more justice; less help, but infinitely closer understanding. This is indeed a critical stage of race relationships because of the likelihood, if the new temper is not understood, of engendering sharp group antagonism and a second crop of more calculated prejudice. In some quarters, it has already done so. Having weaned the Negro, public opinion cannot continue to paternalize. The Negro today is inevitably moving forward under the control largely of his own objectives. What are these objectives? Those of his outer life are happily already well and finally formulated, for they are none other than the ideals of American institutions and democracy. Those of his inner life are yet in process of formation, for the new psychology at present is more of a consensus of feeling than of opinion, of attitude rather than of program. Still some points seem to have crystallized.

UP to the present one may adequately describe the Negro's "inner objectives" as an attempt to repair a damaged group psychology and reshape a warped social perspective. Their realization has required a new mentality for the American Negro. And as it matures we begin to see its effects; at first, negative, iconoclastic, and then positive and constructive. In this new group psychology we note the lapse of sentimental appeal, then the development of a more positive self-respect and self-reliance; the repudiation of social dependence, and then the gradual recovery from hyper-sensitiveness and "touchy" nerves, the repudiation of the double standard of judgment with its special philanthropic allowances and then the sturdier desire for objective and scientific appraisal; and finally the rise from social disillusionment to race pride, from the sense of social debt to the responsibilities of social contribution, and offsetting the necessary working and commonsense acceptance of restricted conditions, the belief in ultimate esteem and recognition. Therefore the Negro today wishes to be known for what he is, even in his faults and shortcomings, and scorns a craven and precarious survival at the price of seeming to be what he is not. He resents being spoken for as a social ward or minor, even by his own, and to being regarded a chronic patient for the sociological clinic, the sick man of American Democracy. For the same reasons he himself is through with those social nostrums and panaceas, the so-called "solutions" of his "problem," with which he and the country have been so liberally dosed in the past. Religion, freedom, education, money—in turn, he has ardently hoped for and peculiarly trusted these things; he still believes in them, but not in blind trust that they alone will solve his life-problem.

Each generation, however, will have its creed and that of the present is the belief in the efficacy of collective efforts in race cooperation. This deep feeling of race is at present the mainspring of Negro life. It seems to be the outcome of the reaction to proscription and prejudice; an attempt, fairly successful on the whole, to convert a defensive into an offensive position, a handicap into an incentive. It is radical in tone, but not in purpose and only the most stupid forms of opposition, misunderstanding or persecution could make it otherwise. Of course, the thinking Negro has shifted a little toward the left with the world-trend, and there is an increasing group who affiliate with radical and liberal movements. But fundamentally for the present the Negro is radical on race matters, conservative on others, in other words, a "forced radical," a social protestant rather than a genuine radical. Yet under further pressure and injustice iconoclastic thought and motives will inevitably increase. Harlem's quixotic radicalisms call for their ounce of democracy today lest tomorrow they be beyond cure.

The Negro mind reaches out as yet to nothing but American wants, American ideas. But this forced attempt to build his Americanism on race values is a unique social experiment, and its ultimate success is impossible except through the fullest sharing of American culture and institutions. There should be no delusion about this. American nerves in sections unstrung with race hysteria are often fed the opiate that the trend of Negro advance is wholly separatist, and that the effect of its operation will be to encyst the Negro as a benign foreign body in the body politic. This cannot be—even if it were desirable. The racialism of the Negro is no limitation or reservation with respect to American life; it is only a constructive effort to build the obstructions in the stream of his progress into an efficient dam of social energy and power. Democracy itself is obstructed and stagnated to the extent that any of its channels are closed. Indeed they cannot be selectively closed. So the choice is not between one way for the Negro and another way for the rest, but between American institutions frustrated on the one hand and American ideals progressively fulfilled and realized on the other.

There is, of course, a warrantably comfortable feeling in being on the right side of the country's professed ideals. We realize that we cannot be undone without America's undoing. It is within the gamut of this attitude that the thinking Negro faces America, but the variations of mood in connection with it are if anything more significant than the attitude itself. Sometimes we have it taken with the defiant ironic challenge of McKay:

Mine is the future grinding down today
Like a great landslip moving to the sea,

Bearing its freight of debris far away
Where the green hungry waters restlessly
Heave mammoth pyramids and break and roar
Their eerie challenge to the crumbling shore.

Sometimes, perhaps more frequently as yet, in the fervent and almost filial appeal and counsel of Weldon Johnson's:

O Southland, dear Southland!
Then why do you still cling
To an idle age and a musty page,
To a dead and useless thing.

But between defiance and appeal, midway almost between cynicism and hope, the prevailing mind stands in the mood of the same author's To America, an attitude of sober query and stoical challenge:

How would you have us, as we are?
Or sinking heath the load we bear,
Our eyes fixed forward on a star,
Or gazing empty at despair?

Rising or falling? Men or things?
With dragging pace or footsteps fleet?
Strong, willing sinews in your wings,
Or tightening chains about your feet?

More and more, however, an intelligent realization of the great discrepancy between the American social creed and the American social practice forces upon the Negro the taking of the moral advantage that is his. Only the steadying and sobering effect of a truly characteristic gentleness of spirit prevents the rapid rise of a definite cynicism and counter-hate and a defiant superiority feeling. Human as this reaction would be, the majority still deprecate its advent, and would gladly see it forestalled by the speedy amelioration of its causes. We wish our race pride to be a healthier, more positive achievement than a feeling based upon a realization of the shortcomings of others. But all paths toward the attainment of a sound social attitude have been difficult; only a relatively few enlightened minds have been able as the phrase puts it "to rise above" prejudice. The ordinary man has had until recently only a hard choice between the alternatives of supine and humiliating submission and stimulating but hurtful counter-prejudice. Fortunately from some inner, desperate resourcefulness has recently sprung up the simple expedient of fighting prejudice by mental passive resistance, in other words by trying to ignore it. For the few, this manna may perhaps be effective, but the masses cannot thrive on it.

FORTUNATELY there are constructive channels opening out into which the balked social feelings of the American Negro can flow freely.

Without them there would be much more pressure and danger than there is. These compensating interests are racial but in a new and enlarged way. One is the consciousness of acting as the advance-guard of the African peoples in their contact with Twentieth Century civilization; the other, the sense of a mission of rehabilitating the race in world esteem from that loss of prestige for which the fate and conditions of slavery have so largely been responsible. Harlem, as we shall see, is the center of both these movements; she is the home of the Negro's "Zionism." The pulse of the Negro world has begun to beat in Harlem. A Negro newspaper carrying news material in English, French and Spanish, gathered from all quarters of America, the West Indies and Africa has maintained itself in Harlem for over five years. Two important magazines, both edited from New York, maintain their news and circulation consistently on a cosmopolitan scale. Under American auspices and backing, three pan-African congresses have been held abroad for the discussion of common interests, colonial questions and the future cooperative development of Africa. In terms of the race question as a world problem, the Negro mind has leapt, so to speak, upon the parapets of prejudice and extended its cramped horizons. In so doing it has linked up with the growing group consciousness of the dark-peoples and is gradually learning their common interests. As one of our writers has recently put it: "It is imperative that we understand the white world in its relations to the non-white world." As with the Jew, persecution is making the Negro international.

As a world phenomenon this wider race consciousness is a different thing from the much asserted rising tide of color. Its inevitable causes are not of our making. The consequences are not necessarily damaging to the best interests of civilization. Whether it actually brings into being new Armadas of conflict or argosies of cultural exchange and enlightenment can only be decided by the attitude of the dominant races in an era of critical change. With the American Negro his new internationalism is primarily an effort to recapture contact with the scattered peoples of African derivation. Garveyism may be a transient, if spectacular, phenomenon, but the possible role of the American Negro in the future development of Africa is one of the most constructive and universally helpful missions that any modern people can lay claim to.

Constructive participation in such causes cannot help giving the Negro valuable group incentives, as well as increased prestige at home and abroad. Our greatest rehabilitation may possibly come through such channels, but for the present, more immediate hope rests in the revaluation by white and black alike of the Negro in terms of his artistic endowments and cultural contributions, past and prospective. It must be increasingly recognized that the Negro has already made very substantial contributions, not only in his folk-art, music especially, which has always found appreciation, but in larger, though humbler and less acknowledged ways. For generations the Negro has been the peasant matrix of that section of America which has most undervalued him, and here he has contributed not only materially in labor and in social patience, but spiritually as well. The South has unconsciously absorbed the gift of his folk-temperament. In less than half a generation it will be easier to recognize this, but the fact remains that a leaven of humor, sentiment, imagination and tropic nonchalance has gone into the making of the South from a humble, unacknowledged source. A second crop of the Negro's gifts promises still more largely. He now becomes a conscious contributor ... beneficiary and ward for that of a collaborator and participant in American civilization. The great social gain in this is the releasing of our talented group from the arid fields of controversy and debate to the productive fields of creative expression. The especially cultural recognition they win should in turn prove the key to that revaluation of the Negro which must precede or accompany any considerable further betterment of race relationships. But whatever the general effect, the present generation will have added the motives of self-expression and spiritual development to the old and still unfinished task of making material headway and progress. No one who understandingly faces the situation with its substantial accomplishment or views the new scene with its still more abundant promise can be entirely without hope. And certainly, if in our lifetime the Negro should not be able to celebrate his full initiation into American democracy, he can at least, on the warrant of these things, celebrate the attainment of a significant and satisfying new phase of group development, and with it a spiritual Coming of Age.

Source: The Survey Graphic Harlem Number, Vol. VI, No. 6, March, 1925. Survey Associates, Inc.

83. African Fundamentalism, 1925
MARCUS GARVEY

Activist Marcus Garvey wrote "African Fundamentalism," an editorial and one of his most famous essays, at the peak of the fundamentalist revival that swept America following World War I. In his essay, Garvey played on the social Darwinist issues that were publicly highlighted by the Scopes trial and gave them an ironic twist. He adopted elements of the evolutionary theory of the secularists and of the strong nativist strain of the fundamentalists and utilized them both as premises to support his own counterargument. He presented black people in northern Africa as representatives of a higher form of life and culture than their white counterparts in Europe. He thus reversed the popular contemporary claims of white eugenicists, who applied evolutionary theory to society, associating people of African heritage with the slow development of the apes and offering their results as "proof" of white racial superiority. Garvey's essay not only refutes this notion, but turns it completely on its head.

Fellow Men of the Negro Race, Greeting:
The time has come for the Negro to forget and cast behind him his hero worship and adoration of other races, and to start out immediately, to create and emulate heroes of his own.

Marcus Garvey

We must canonize our own saints, create our own martyrs, and elevate to positions of fame and honor black men and women who have made their distinct contributions to our racial history. Sojourner Truth is worthy of the place of sainthood alongside of Joan of Arc; Crispus Attucks and George William Gordon are entitled to the halo of martyrdom with no less glory than that of the martyrs of any other race. Toussaint L'Ouverture's brilliancy as a soldier and statesman outshone that of a Cromwell, Napoleon and Washington; hence, he is entitled to the highest place as a hero among men. Africa has produced countless numbers of men and women, in war and in peace, whose lustre and bravery outshine that of any other people. Then why not see good and perfection in ourselves?

THE RIGHT TO OUR DOCTRINE

We must inspire a literature and promulgate a doctrine of our own without any apologies to the powers that be. The right is ours and God's. Let contrary sentiment and cross opinions go to the winds. Opposition to race independence is the weapon of the enemy to defeat the hopes of an unfortunate people. We are entitled to our own opinions and not obligated to or bound by the opinions of others.

A PEEP AT THE PAST

If others laugh at you, return the laughter to them; if they mimic you, return the compliment with equal force. They have no more right to dishonor, disrespect and disregard your feeling and manhood than you have in dealing with them. Honor them when they honor you; disrespect and disregard them when they vilely treat you. Their arrogance is but skin deep and an assumption that has no foundation in morals or in law. They have sprung from the same family tree of obscurity as we have; their history is as rude in its primitiveness as ours; their ancestors ran wild and naked, lived in caves and in the branches of trees, like monkeys, as ours; they made human sacrifices, ate the flesh of their own dead and the raw meat of the wild beast for centuries even as they accuse us of doing; their cannibalism was more prolonged than ours; when we were embracing the arts and sciences on the banks of the Nile their ancestors were still drinking human blood and eating out of the skulls of their conquered dead; when our civilization had reached the noonday of progress they were still running naked and sleeping in holes and caves with rats, bats and other insects and animals. After we had already unfathomed the mysteries of the stars and reduced the heavenly constellations to minute and regular calculus they were still backwoodsmen, living in ignorance and blatant darkness.

WHY BE DISCOURAGED?

The world today is indebted to us for the benefits of civilization. They stole our arts and sciences from Africa. Then why should we be ashamed of ourselves? Their MODERN IMPROVEMENTS are but DUPLICATES of a grander civilization that we reflected thousands of years ago, without the advantage of what is buried and still hidden, to be resurrected and reintroduced by the intelligence of our generation and our prosperity. Why should we be discouraged because somebody laughs at us today? Who to tell what tomorrow will bring forth? Did they not laugh at Moses, Christ and Mohammed? Was there not a Carthage, Greece and Rome? We see and have changes every day, so pray, work, be steadfast and be not dismayed.

NOTHING MUST KILL THE EMPIRE URGE

As the Jew is held together by his RELIGION, the white races by the assumption and the unwritten law of SUPERIORITY, and the Mongolian by the precious tie of BLOOD, so likewise the Negro must be united in one GRAND RACIAL HIERARCHY. Our UNION MUST KNOW NO CLIME, BOUNDARY, or NATIONALITY. Like the great Church of Rome, Negroes the world over MUST PRACTICE ONE FAITH, that of Confidence in themselves, with One God! One Aim! One Destiny! Let no religious scruples, no political machination divide us, but let us hold together under all climes and in every country, making among ourselves a Racial Empire upon which "the sun shall never set."

ALLEGIANCE TO SELF FIRST

Let no voice but your own speak to you from the depths. Let no influence but your own raise you in time of peace and time of war. Hear all, but attend only that which concerns you.

Your first allegiance shall be to your God, then to your family, race and country. Remember always that the Jew in his political and economic urge is always first a Jew; the white man is first a white man under all circumstances, and you can do no less than being first and always a Negro, and then all else will take care of itself. Let no one inoculate you for their own conveniences. There is no humanity before that which starts with yourself. "Charity begins at home." First to thyself be true, and "thou canst not then be false to any man."

WE ARE ARBITERS OF OUR OWN DESTINY

God and Nature first made us what we are, and then out of our own creative genius we make ourselves what we want to be. Follow always that great law. Let the sky and God be our limit, and Eternity our measurement. There is no height to which we cannot climb by using the active intelligence of our own minds. Mind creates, and as much as we desire in Nature we can have through the creation of our own minds. Being at present the scientifically weaker race, you shall treat others only as they treat you; but in your homes and everywhere possible you must teach the higher development of science to your children; and be sure to develop a race of scientists par excellence, for in science and religion lies our only hope to withstand the evil designs of modern materialism. Never forget your God. Remember, we live, work and pray for the establishing of a great and binding RACIAL HIERARCHY, the rounding of a RACIAL EMPIRE whose only natural, spiritual and political limits shall be God and "Africa, at home and abroad."

Source: Editorial, *Negro World*, 1925. Copyright © 1995–2008 The Marcus Garvey and UNIA Papers Project, UCLA.

84. A Piece of Saw, May 1929
THEODORE LEDYARD BROWNE

DeWitt Clinton High School in the Bronx, New York, had over 10,000 students in the 1930s. Over the years, this New York City school produced more than its share of writers and artists, many of whom were first published in *The Magpie*, the school's literary magazine.

One of these esteemed writers was James Baldwin, who wrote at least fourteen short stories for the magazine. His work was published along with the poetry and prose of many others who, together, told the wider story of life during the depression years in America. These students included photographer Richard Avedon, film critic Stanley Kauffmann, cultural critic Robert Warshow, and cartoonists Teddy Shearer and Mel Casson. The influence of the Harlem Renaissance can also be found in illustrations by Robert Blackburn used in *The Magpie* and in the writing of Theodore Browne, who later became a writer, actor, and director for the Negro Theatre of the Work Progress Administration's Federal Theatre Project. Browne was a student at DeWitt Clinton High School in New York and a regular contributor to "The

Magpie," the literary magazine of the legendary school in the Bronx. This piece
appeared in the magazine in 1929.

The "Deep Evening" poolroom pulsated with its usual gathering of factory hands,
mill owners and low characters. It was six o'clock. Amid the stench of tobacco smoke
and body odor, black men played pool, shot crap, argued and frequently came to blows.

In a corner near the bootblack stand, Candy had isolated himself from the rest of
the crowd and was absorbed in watching a game of pool, when he was suddenly
slapped on the back.

Turning around, he met the broad grin of Shorty Stevens, whom he had met that
morning after his release from jail.

"You'se a confidenshul friend of mine, Candy," he said slowly, "en lemme tell
yuh something right now. Take a fool's advice, boy, and keep yo eyes glued on Buck
Gardner."

At the mention of Buck's name, Candy's oily, black face hardened into an ugly
scowl. To him no name was more odious than Buck Gardner's.

"Whut de hell I car 'bout Buck Gardner? He ain't no more'n a meat-man lak
myself. I sho ain't 'fraid of 'im," he declared boastfully. "Tell de truth, I ain't afraid
of no man on Gawd's earth."

"T'ain't a mattuh o' being 'fraid o' nobody. I jes wanna warn yuh. While you was
cooped up in jail, I'se seed Madge wid Buck several times. Dey done got mighty
close since you wus away.

"Madge ain't caring nothing 'bout 'im," said Candy, with rather half-heated
attempt at a smile. She's jes fooling 'im long. I ain't fraid of 'im taking my gal.
Madge's got sense. "She ain't 'some-timey' lak dese other wild-headed gals 'round
heah. I been going wid huh fuh two years; I oughta know."

"You caint be too sho' bout any of 'em, boy," said Shorty skeptically. "Dese wim-
men folks is pow'ful tricky. De very time you figures you're in power, cat's de very
time she's steading how to trick yuh."

Suddenly, there came a racket from the outside, a blowing of tin horns, inter-
mingled with noisy chatter. The clangor subsided, struck up again and then a sooty,
black, robust figure burst into the poolroom, garbed in red and white ginghams, with
a red and white bandanna around the head.

"Halloween!" cried Shorty. "Bless if dat ain't ole Zack dressed up like A'nt Dinah."

A torrent of gay masqueraders poured into the poolroom, women dressed in men's
clothes among them. For awhile shouts and laughter filled the room.

"Let's celebrate," cried Shorty fervently. "Dere's a dance at the Elk's Hall; let's go!"

Candy capitulated and they jostled their way to the street. They found the hall
already thronged with drunken revelers and decided to remain outside for a while
listening to the noisy jazz band. An unpleasant thought came to Candy as he stood
there. He wondered why it had come to him just then. Could Madge be inside "carrying on" with Buck?

The door opened and two besotted couples left the place. It opened a second
time and Candy's eyes settled upon Madge. She was alone. Why had he not thought
of Hallowe'en before? Madge always depended upon him to take her this night.

But things did not turn out as he expected. Madge ignored his stare and spitefully
engaged in a talk with the door keeper.

Candy, heated with jealousy, went over to Madge, took her by the arm. and to
the amusement of the chubby doorkeeper, roughly drew her aside.

Madge looked beautiful that night. She was dressed in a circus rider's costume, the snowy whiteness of which became her bronze colored skin, and made her seem like some dark water nymph.

"Whut you mean by trying to act so'dicty' tonight?" he asked gruffly.

The girl hesitated before replying.

"I mought as well tell you now," she said, "I'm tired of you. I lak a man who 'puts out' sometimes. Cain't nobody live offern love alone nowadays. Hit's high time you foun' dat out."

For a moment, Candy was rendered speechless. He stood staring at her blankly, out of the whiteness of his big, round eyes, frozen mute by what she had told him.

Finally speech came to him, but it was feeble and harsh. "Don't I put out when I'se got hit?"

"When you'se got hit!" she sneered mockingly.

Anger possessed him. He clutched her bare shoulders with both hands. His piercing gaze met her unmoved one.

"Whut you think I went to jail fuh?"

"Selling likker, I reckon," she answered coolly.

"You reckon! You knows whut I went dare fuh—you—dam hit—fuh yo sake!"

"Youse a lie!" Madge retorted hotly. "You jes wonted t' git some easy money fuh yosef. You ain't never gin me nothing—but a lotta hot air."

She struggled in vain to free her shoulders, for he held them with a vise-like grip.

"You knows I tried t' git money so you could buy dat fur coat. But I wus caught, dat's whut, en put in jail. Now you wonts t' disown hit."

He withdrew one tremblin hand and before he realized it, had struck her a blow in the face. She screamed. Then Candy felt Shorty's hand upon his shoulder.

"Leave huh 'lone, boy. Ain't no use getting in trouble over no woman. C'mon, let's go home," he coaxed.

But Candy still held Madge while she fought to release her self. He seemed uncertain what to do.

"Turn me loose!" she was shrieking and cursing.

Finally, obeying Shorty's entreaties, Candy released his grip, and was about to take leave when Buck appeared in the doorway.

"Whut you raising de debbil fuh? Dat corn likker giving you all dat hell?" he inquired of Madge.

He was so drunk that he could hardly stand. He did not see Candy. The latter swore wrathfully and made an effort to reach his enemy, but was restrained by a friend.

Candy returned home that night, a disillusioned, beaten man, rejected and wronged by one from whom he least expected injury. It was a painful rejection.

The next day, while at the poolroom he was told that some one was waiting for him outside. Leaving the game, he went to the door.

"C'mon out! Don't be 'fraid! T'aint nobody but me, honey," he heard a familiar voice say. It was Madge.

"Whut you come heah to me fuh?" he asked.

Candy had made up his mind to deal severely with Madge, to impress her with the fact that he could live content without her. But that playful smile so characteristic of her seemed to drown his severity and weaken him.

"Fuh Gawd's sakes, man, don't look at me lak dat!" she laughed, and, changing to a serious tone, she said, "Aw don't pay whut happened last night no mind. T'wont my fault. T'wus dat bad likker made se say dem things. I don't know whut de debbil I wus saying. Hit's de truth! Oh, let's forget hit, honey." Madge took his big, rough hand and, squeezing it coaxingly, looked up into his face and smiled.

"Lissen, baby! Wanna make some easy money?"

"Doing whut? Stealing? Ef dat's whut youse gotta say, you mought ez well save yo' breath."

"Who said anything 'bout stealing? Gimme time to say what I has t say."

He shrugged his shoulders, making a gesture of indifference with his hands.

"Go haid," he told her. "Ain't nobody stoppin' yuh from saying."

"Barton wont's yuh t' run his still down at Elephant's Falls tonight and tomorrow night. Said he'd gi' yuh sixteen dollars. He wonts de likker fuh de white folk's fair next week. You'd betuh grab hit."

"Lak hell I'll take hit. I jes came out o' jail, en I ain't planning no early trip back. Damn a likker job, en—" he was about to say "you too," but he checked himself. "Furthermo', I'm going t' work Monday at de saw mill."

But Madge knew Candy's nature too well to give up coaxing, him.

"Dese cops ain't pecking on no white man, specially ef he relays dem off. Hit's only dese nigguh bootleggers dey grabs."

Won over by this second thought he became the dupe of Madge's project. Two night's work. Sixteen dollars. Of course he would take it.

Startling news swept through the crowded poolroom the following evening and dulled the hilarity that usually infested the place. A whiskey still at Elephant's Falls had been raided, and Candy had been caught and was now in jail.

One early morning, a month later, a train of negro prisoners, single file, and linked together by a chain around each ankle, plodded alongside a wry-faced white man at whose side hung a heavy revolver. On their shoulders, the "chain gang' carried pick axes to dig a ditch they had started.

The rising of the sun from behind the hills transformed the surrounding heavens into a crudely beautiful painting, such as a gifted child artist might unconsciously have painted with his water colors.

The sight was beautiful to behold, but its beauty hardly seemed to arouse the convicts. They went about their work of digging the ditch indifferent to the colorful panorama that was about them. Instead, as they broke the earth with their pickaxes, they filled the fresh, morning air with song:

"Trouble, trouble
I has hit all my days,
Hit seems lak trouble's
Going last me to my grave.
"Tell me high yallar,
How long I has t' wait?
Kin I get you now,
Or mus' I hesitate?"

But upon the face of one there was a look of suffering and worry.

"I gut a lettuh from home," he told the short man at his side. "Sis said muh wus bad off sick, en heah I is far way from huh. Sis said she keeps asking fuh me." He gulped as though his grief were choking him, then shook his head remorsefully. The short man shook his head too, and looked with eyes of hopeless pity at his friend.

"Huh heart's bad-leaking heart," he muttered.

"Boy, I feels damn sorry fuh you. I ain't kering bout mu self, 'cause I ain't gut no sick mudder t' wurry bout. Hit's tough! Tough! In a way, boy, I'se mighty glad dey sent me up heah. I gut even wid my nigguh. I tried t' bust his skull open. Dirty scoundrel! I'd gi muh life t' see you git even wid de nigguh dat framed you."

There was a look of astonishment on the gloomy man's face.

"Whut you mean Shorty?" he asked. "Who—who dat framed me?"

"Ain't you know who t'wus?"

"Swear fo' Gawd, man! Tell me! Quick, Shorty! Tell me!"

"Buck! He's de cause of yo' being heah on this 'chain gang'. He was a 'stool pigeon' for ole police Sargeant Brinkley. You know he ain't nevah laked Barton, who you was working fuh. Buck know'd dat too, en got you de job, so he could frame you."

Candy's eyes grew bigger. He gritted his teeth and looked about him madly, as though anticipating an escape. Looking down he saw the chain—the thing which held him from his dying mother. He cursed it under his breath.

He raised his chained leg, and to his utter amazement, discovered a piece of saw used for cutting iron. He had noticed before the iron foundry nearby. He had also noticed a wooden box and pair of baby carriage wheels near the ditch. Perhaps children had gotten the saw from the trash pile in back of the foundry, and had made a toy wagon.

Candy clutched the saw to his chest and a look of grave deliberation swept over his face.

"Boy," he said to his bewildered comrades who continued to dig at the ground to keep from attracting the guard's attention, "de Lawd mus be wid me. He mus 'tend fuh me t' kill dat nigguh!"

Off and on for three hours, Candy stole moments when the guard was not watching, to saw away his bonds. It was pains taking, scrupulous work, but at length he succeeded.

Word was whispered to the other convicts to keep quiet. The ditch meandered past a big tree. He would crawl until he reached the tree, then would run quickly across the open lot to the railroad tracks, and there board a freight train.

While the guard had his attention attracted by a cart and horse passing in the distance, Candy made up mind to flee. Through the muddy water in the ditch, he waded until he reached the tree. He looked about carefully. The guard was still watching the cart and horse. Now he would make his way across the field to the tracks, for he saw a train approaching in the distance.

As he ran, he heard shouts behind him. Could it be that he was trapped? He became sick with fear, but dared not stop.

"Halt! Halt!"—he heard the words distinctly. There was another sound, like the discharge of a gun.

Candy felt holes being bored into his head and back. Some thing hot, denser than perspiration, ran in streams down his face. He rubbed his face with his hands, looked at them. Blood! He shut both eyes tightly. Blood! Everything was blood. What on earth had happened?

"Muh! Muh!" he shrieked. He was too weak to go further, and sank helplessly down on the grass covered earth. "Hep me! Muh! I'm dying! Some water, Muh! Quick! Oh, Gawd, have mercy! Hit's all over!"

"I bet he's dead, too," one of the convicts said to another.

"Damn right," agreed the other. "I know he is. Po' boy, I feels fuh 'im. En now he won't git even wid dat hell cat en Buck."

Source: *The Magpie*, DeWitt Clinton High School literary magazine, May 1929, p.51. The New Deal Network.

85. The South Speaks, April 26, 1933
JOHN HENRY HAMMOND, JR.

The nation watched in 1933 as an all-white judge and jury sentenced to death black men who had been wrongly accused of raping a white woman. The accused were members of the Scottsboro boys, nine black youth, aged twelve to twenty, accused of raping two white women in Scottsboro, Alabama. These trials were landmark cases that gained widespread national attention. This story in *The Nation* magazine helped to spread the story of Haywood Patterson's death sentence throughout America. The exposure allowed many people to witness these proceedings and condemn Alabama. This kind of coverage of a Negro trial in the deep south was unprecedented.

AGAIN fear has driven an Alabama jury to condemn to death one of the Scottsboro boys. It matters little how flimsy the evidence was against Haywood Patterson; a white woman had accused a Negro of raping her, and in this matter a white woman's word is law.

The Scottsboro case has slowly attained world-wide publicity owing to the efforts of the International Labor Defense, which fought the case successfully before the United States Supreme Court and won a new trial in Alabama. The nine Negroes, accused of assaulting two white girl hobos on a freight train two years ago, were granted a change of venue from seething Scottsboro to the comparatively peaceful town of Decatur, seventy miles away. The defense made the best possible fight, but it was hopeless from the start. The boys could hardly have had an abler attorney than Samuel Leibowitz, with an almost perfect record of acquittals in criminal cases. Nor could they have been tried before a fairer man than Judge James E. Horton, who astounded skeptical Northerners by his tolerance and poise. But Southern prejudice was more than a match for a fair judge, lack of evidence against the Negroes, and a jury above the community's average in intelligence.

At the beginning of the trial Decatur was a quiet Alabama town, perhaps a little busier than the average. Its twenty thousand inhabitants used to find employment in several hosiery mills and a steel and iron foundry employing something like two thousand men. The mills are running full time, with slashed wages, but the foundry is practically shut down. The town does not belong to the old South; its houses are modern and nondescript, as are its public buildings. Its upper class is not of the "aristocracy."

There was little bitterness evident at first. The prevailing feeling was one of annoyance at the expense of the trial. The townsfolk were fully aware of the fact that the schools of Scottsboro and Jackson County had been shut down by the cost of the original trial and appeal. The defendants, of course, were guilty. The average Southerner firmly believes that Negroes desire above everything to have intercourse with white women. But there was little animosity shown the prisoners. They would be found guilty and duly executed. The penalty for rape in Alabama is anything from ten years to death. The Negro faces death.

By the most adroit of maneuverings the defense forced the court to produce the secret jury rolls of Morgan County, after failing to get so much as a peep into Scottsboro's records. To the surprise and dismay of Attorney-General Tom Knight, Judge Horton ruled that the defense had made a prima facie case that no Negroes were on the rolls; that it was up to the prosecution to prove that there were. Of course Negroes do not sit on Southern juries, nor do their names appear on panels. But the matter was never so thoroughly threshed out as in Decatur. Leibowitz collected a list of highly intelligent property-holding Negroes, most of them possessing college degrees. These men appeared in court to prove that they possessed every qualification for jury duty under the Alabama statutes. In doing so they performed a most courageous act. Although the defense lost its motion for a mistrial on the ground that the jury panel contained no names of Negroes, it laid the base for an appeal to the federal courts.

To many the choice of Samuel Leibowitz seemed a grievous error for the defense. Here, they argued, was a Northerner, a Jew, with a long record for defending gangsters and getting them off; a man who would make the worst possible impression on a Southern community. But Leibowitz is a master showman. And the court is the principal place of diversion for the Southern citizen. There were often gasps of unwilling admiration for this outsider who could outsmart their own Tom Knight.

It was Leibowitz's first trip South. He was surprisingly ignorant of the relationship between black and white. So when he first brought forward John Sanford of Scottsboro as a worthy applicant for jury duty, he was shocked at the treatment his witness received at the hands of the Attorney-General. After protesting twice at the bullying Sanford was receiving, he rose in a rage and shouted: "Now listen, Mr. Attorney-General, I've warned you twice about your treatment of my witness. For the last time now, stand back, take your finger out of his eye, and call him mister." Leibowitz had the courage to do what no Southerner could have done—challenge the South's whole jury system. Without this the case could never be appealed to the federal courts. And it is extremely doubtful if even the highest court in Alabama would set these prisoners free, no matter what the weight of evidence in their favor.

Although Leibowitz took care to lay all possible bases for appeal, he was confident of an acquittal. He had never tried a case in which a frame-up was more apparent, and as he said in his initial courtroom speech at Decatur, he had full confidence in the integrity and fairness of the South. His thoroughness was astonishing. He produced in court the conductor and fireman of the freight train on which the attack was supposed to have taken place, witnesses who never were called at the original trial. From the railroad he obtained the exact line-up of the cars on the train and had them reproduced in miniature. He found Lester Carter, one of the white boys who accompanied the two girls on the train and provided for the defense its star witness. By competent witnesses found in Chattanooga it was possible to trace the girls' movements the night before the fatal trip and puncture completely their sworn testimony.

In the conduct of this case the International Labor Defense was making an experiment. It concentrated on the legal side of defense rather than on mass pressure. As a result, there were no traces of Communist literature in Decatur, no demonstrations, and no telegrams with demands to the judge until the lives of the defendants appeared to be in actual danger. Contrary to popular belief communism had little if anything to do with the verdict of guilty.

There appeared to be a veritable battery of prosecutors, but Attorney-General Tom Knight did all the work. Knight is only thirty-four, the son of the Alabama Supreme Court Justice who wrote the court's decision affirming the verdict in the trials two years ago. He is a small, nervous man. Even in court he had little control of himself. His behavior was that of a small and enthusiastic child. But Tom Knight is exceptionally clever. He knows his courtroom gallery and all its prejudices. He successfully counteracted all of Leibowitz's many plays to the jury. He is a bad cross-examiner and seems not too sure of himself, but he is well versed in legal procedure. Out of court he is quite affable and charming, "one of the boys" to the newspaper fraternity. During the trial he became so excited that he seldom slept more than two hours a night. Out of court he insisted that he wanted to give the defendants a scrupulously fair trial. Of course, said he, the niggers were guilty, but if Leibowitz could convince him that there had been a miscarriage of justice, then he would publicly announce his conversion and have the indictments quashed. Inside the courthouse it was a different story. He browbeat Negro witnesses with all the thoroughness of a county solicitor. When Leihowitz announced that he would prove that Victoria Price had been arrested often for adultery and lewdness, Knight cried out: "I don't care how often you prove she was convicted as long as you can't prove she had anything to do with niggers."

Knight had a match, however, in the first defendant, Haywood Patterson. After grilling Patterson severely in an attempt to shake his story, the prosecutor finally asked in desperation: "Well, were you tried two years ago in Scottsboro?" "No suh," said Patterson calmly, "I was framed two years ago in Scottsboro."

Knight's chief assistants were Solicitor Bailey of Scottsboro and Wade Wright, a solicitor of Morgan County, who made the now-famous Jew-baiting summary to the jury. Bailey is quite without importance—hard-boiled and soft-spoken. But Wright is a huge individual, blustering and bullying, a perfect barometer of the less enlightened Decatur opinion. When he speaks his face becomes purple and he imparts his frenzy to the court hangers-on. Until Wright spoke, many of the newspapermen felt that there was an outside chance for acquittal, at least a hung jury. But Wright registered to perfection the repressed feelings and prejudices of the twelve good men. From then on the defense was helpless.

Without a doubt the most unexpected element in the trial was the attitude of Judge Horton. Much has been written about him. Most of it is true. Courteous, generous, and scrupulous according to his own lights, he made an admirable presiding officer. The defense could have had no fairer treatment from a Southerner. Judge Horton allowed the defense to introduce evidence showing that Victoria Price, the State's star witness, was a perjurer, prostitute, and consorted with Negroes—heinous crime in the South. (In the original trials no evidence concerning the moral character of either girl was admitted.) He allowed the defense to put Negroes on the stand to refute white witnesses, and himself asked questions of witnesses which proved beneficial to the case of the defendants. But this really honorable man made dubious rulings against the defense on many important points. After allowing the International Labor Defense to prove systematic exclusion of Negroes from jury duty, he denied the motion for a mistrial. He failed to stop Wade Wright's appeal to bigotry and fear, and refused a change of venue to a more cosmopolitan environment after it had become evident that hysteria had gripped the good people of Decatur.

Decatur was quiet when the trial began. But it was not long before latent prejudices flared up. During the first day of the actual trial a menacing band of fifty came into the courthouse from Scottsboro "out of curiosity." Leibowitz's method of questioning pure Southern womanhood had aroused their resentment, and they made no bones about it. Organized mobs began to form outside of Decatur. Farmers from surrounding towns held protest meetings. Hadn't an outsider dared to call a black man "mister" in court and demanded that the Attorney-General do the same? Wasn't the defense advocating racial equality, and wasn't there danger of these Northerners arousing the niggers?

The effect of the trial on the three thousand Negroes of Decatur was enlightening. At first there was no appreciable difference in behavior. But after the most respectable members of their community—doctors, Sunday-school teachers, school principals, ministers, and storekeepers—got up in court to show that they were the equals of whites, the working Negro acquired confidence. Faces which had been expressionless in the courtroom took on smiles, and a few whispered exclamations were to be heard when Leibowitz made a point. Decatur whites took notice of this. In no time at all the local hardware stores were completely sold out of guns and ammunition, and they were not selling to Negroes. No one entered "niggertown" without some kind of weapon. The black folk were also taking due precautions. At first it was hard for these colored people to believe that a fight was being waged for them. But when they saw the defense treat Negroes as equals in court they were convinced.

Alabama's Negroes are not the only ones aroused. Colored people throughout the land who have been determinedly apathetic to the appeals of the I. L. D. and the Communists are thoroughly enraged by the verdict. In Harlem, Baltimore, Richmond, Virginia, Washington, Chicago, and scores of other cities real protest meetings are being held. The churches are stepping up as never before; collections are being taken for the defense of the prisoners. Theaters and dance halls arc staging benefits; newspapers are formulating plans for a protest march of 50,000 to Washington. The South has only to repeat the verdicts in the cases of the other boys to find the Negroes organizing into militant groups.

During the second day of the trial one of my neighbors in court began to talk to me. After learning that I was a correspondent from the North he introduced himself as a merchant who had been born and bred in Decatur. He asked me what I thought of the trial. I told him that Judge Horton seemed one of the fairest jurists I had ever encountered.

"This judge here is a fine man," he said, "but he's prejudiced. All of us Southerners is prejudiced. You know, I'm beginning to think that those niggers was framed. That girl Victoria made a bad impression. But that doctor [Dr. Bridges of Scottsboro, who testified that he had examined the girls less than two hours after the alleged attack, had found their pulse and temperature normal, and could detect no sign of hysteria] sure cinched the case for them niggers."

He turned around and asked his friends in the row behind what they thought. All seven of them were convinced that there was something wrong somewhere. Two of the more daring also ventured the opinion that it looked like a frame-up. But all this was before the prosecution made its final successful appeal to the passions and fears of the jury.

Source: The Nation, Vol. 135, No. 3538, p.465. April 26, 1933. The New Deal Network.

86. The Pullman Porters Win, August 21, 1935
EDWARD BERMAN

Working-class Negroes won a decisive victory on July 1, 1935, when the National Mediation Board certified the Brotherhood of Sleeping Car Porters, the first all-black union, as the duly authorized representative of the porters and maids employed by the Pullman Company. "Pullman Porters Win" was the headline in *The Nation* on August 21, 1935.

Working-class Negroes won a decisive victory on July 1 when the National Mediation Board certified the Brotherhood of Sleeping Car Porters as the duly authorized representative of the porters and maids employed by the Pullman Company. This certification and the election which preceded it were the climax in a courageous struggle for labor organization and collective bargaining which has been carried on for more than a decade against great odds.

Aggressive attempts to organize the Pullman porters in an independent union attracted public attention about 1920. Toward the end of that year the Pullman Company countered with the usual device of company unionism. From that time on the efforts of the porters to make the employee-representation scheme function effectively in the workers' interest or to organize an independent union were met by the whole barrage of opposition which employers developed so effectively in the decade of the twenties. In February, 1921, the company established its Pullman Porters' Benefit Association to provide sickness, incapacity, and death benefits. As early as 1914 it had put into effect a pension plan for aged employees. In February, 1926, it introduced an employee stock-ownership plan. It also put into operation an extensive scheme of welfare work, with a newspaper for employees, as well as workers' choruses, bands and orchestras.

The porters and their leaders at first attempted to use these devices for the purpose of improving the lot of the workers. The company countered by employing spies and discharging porters who were too active in the interest of their fellows. The leaders finally realized that the condition of the workers could be improved only by organizing an absolutely independent union not subject to the influence of the Pullman Company, and on August 25, 1925, steps were taken to establish the Brotherhood of Sleeping Car Porters. Its officers, with one exception, were porters of long standing in the company's service. They gave up their jobs to become leaders of the union or were soon discharged for their activities. The one exception was A. Philip Randolph, a prominent publicist and leader among Negroes. Since 1925 all the officers have stayed with the organization, generally without salaries of any kind, eking out an often precarious living for themselves and their families by engaging in various small business enterprises.

The organization of the independent union led to increased opposition by the Pullman Company. Spying became more intense and effective, and discharges of active unionists became common. Porters many years in the service found themselves let out for reasons which were mere subterfuges. It came to be worth a man's job to show an active interest in the new union. Yet hundreds of porters continued to pay dues and to attend meetings.

In 1926 the union tried unsuccessfully to get consideration from the Interstate Commerce Commission on the question of wages. From 1930 to the beginning of

1934 it attempted with equal lack of success to get an injunction against the company under the terms of the Railway Labor Act of 1926. Meanwhile in 1933 the Railway Emergency Act had been passed. Among its provisions was one which had the effect of outlawing the company unions. Unfortunately, however, whether by oversight or otherwise, the act made no reference to the Pullman Company or to the express companies. In the autumn of 1933 the Brotherhood of Sleeping Car Porters began a campaign of publicity to have the Pullman Company brought within the scope of the act. With the aid of Coordinator Eastman, who included proposals to this effect in his recommendations to Congress, an act was passed in June, 1934, correcting the defects in the previous legislation. The porters could now appeal to the National Mediation Board for the right to be recognized as the official agency of the porters for the purposes of collective bargaining. In preparation for the test it knew was coming, the Pullman Company, in October, 1934, reorganized its company union. The grosser forms of company influence were not so apparent in the new constitution. Presumably the organization was to be financed exclusively by the employees themselves, but it was specified that its officers should be employees of the company.

The fight between the new company union and the Brotherhood to secure official recognition from the National Mediation Board began late in 1934. At the direction of the board an election to enable the porters and maids to express their preference was conducted from May 27 to June 27. It resulted in an overwhelming victory for the Brotherhood. Of a total of 8,316 eligible votes, the Brotherhood captured 5,931 and the company union only 1,422. In only three cities, Louisville, Memphis, and Atlanta, did the company union receive a majority of the eligible votes. The Brotherhood won majorities in 25 cities; it also received the overwhelming majority of votes cast by mail. The Brotherhood has already taken steps to initiate negotiations with the Pullman Company. The real fruits of victory will not be realized until a collective agreement is secured, but the chances for such an agreement are excellent.

The reason for the porters' long and determined fight for an independent union is to be found of course in wages that are unbelievably low and conditions of work that most unskilled white workers would consider intolerable. The Pullman porter is regarded as an aristocrat by the workers of his race. The Pullman Company itself not only depends upon him to furnish courteous and efficient service to its patrons, but frankly acknowledges that the opinion which the traveling public has of the Pullman service largely depends upon him. It imposes upon him an enormous variety of tasks, skilled and unskilled; and the traveling public knows how well he performs those tasks.

It is one of the ironies of the status of the Negro in American life, however, that the Pullman porter is one of the worst-exploited workers in the country. A survey covering the year from March, 1934, to February, 1935, shows that the annual income of all porters covered by the sample investigation was $880. Porters on regular assignment received in that year $1,056, while those on extra service received $624. (Since extra porters must constantly hold themselves in readiness for duty, they have no opportunity to earn additional income.) This income was received only in part from the company. The average wage received by all porters directly from the company was $879; the sum of $237 was received in tips, but $236 was spent for occupational expenses. The weekly income of all porters covered in the survey was only $16.92, that of porters on regular assignment $20.30, and that of extra porters only $12. Obviously the common impression that porters get large sums in tips is erroneous. Some do, but on the average the amount is about offset by the sum which goes for occupational expenses. The status of the porter is well indicated by the nature and extent of these expenses. He is compelled to furnish his own brushes and shoe-polishing materials. He must pay for his uniforms until he has been in service for ten years. He must eat his meals from the dining car, paying half price for what he gets—and the middle-class American of small income knows that even half-price on a Pullman diner is too much. Moreover, he must sleep at night in the smoking compartment of his car unless a certain upper berth near that compartment happens to be vacant. He does not retire until the occupants of the smoking compartment go to bed. He is subject to call at every moment of the day or night while on service.

As against an average weekly income for the porters of $16.02, the average wage of all workers in manufacturing industries in the United States in 1934 was $19.12, in New York State $23.19, in Illinois $20.50, and in Wisconsin $18.29. Against the porters' annual average income of $880 may be set the "minimum comfort budget" calculated by Professor Ogburn for the War Labor Board for a family of five, which would have cost $1,516 in 1934. Against it may also be set the "minimum American standard budget" for a family of four established by an employers' organization, the National Industrial Conference Board. In a small city such as Marion, Ohio, this would have cost $1,129 in 1934. In New York City (and it should be remembered that most porters live in large cities) it would have cost $1,299.

But this is not the whole story. Hours of service are barbarously long. The porters are paid on a mileage basis, the basic wage being earned when they have traveled 11,000 miles per month. But they work before and after the trains get into motion, and for this "preparatory" and "terminal" time, as it is called, they get no pay. A survey made at the beginning of the present year indicates that on regular runs the porters put in an average of 9.2 percent of their working time in getting cars ready for occupancy and receiving passengers, and 3.5 per cent in arranging cars after the train has arrived at its terminal. These hours of service are required by the company. Not infrequently, more than the stated time is required after a car has reached the terminal. The variations among individual porters are great. Some put in more than 50 per cent of all their service in the form of preparatory and terminal time. For example, there was the case of a porter required to put in 14 hours and 52 minutes of preparatory time and 3 hours and 5 minutes of terminal time out of a total service period per round trip of 26 hours and 30 minutes. Such cases are not uncommon. The important point is that an average of 12.7 per cent of all the time the porters spend in service is not paid for.

Investigation shows that in 1934 porters on regular runs worked an average of 317 hours per month, or over 73 hours per week. Contrast this figure with the fact that in the year 1934 workers in all manufacturing industries in the United States averaged just under 35 hours per week. The average net income for porters on regular assignment for the year from March, 1934, to February, 1935, was 27.8 cents an hour. In 1934 workers in all manufacturing industries received an average of 54.8 cents; and workers on federal public works projects, 57.8 cents per hour.

Here then is a group of skilled workers receiving an average annual income of $880, an average weekly income of $16.92, and an working hourly income, if they work regularly, of 27.8 cents. While many hundreds of thousands of their fellow-workers remain partly or wholly unemployed, they work 317 hours per month under conditions which are little short of disgraceful They work, moreover, for a company which has consistently made large profits.

After many years of struggle and persistent devotion, the porters have succeeded in obtaining recognition of their union. It marks a most important step in their fight for decent working conditions. Their victory should give courage to the Negro working class.

Source: *The Nation*, Vol. 141, No. 3659, p. 217. August 21, 1935. The New Deal Network.

87. Deadhead: A Pullman Porter Steps Out of Character, August 1935
JESSIE CARTER

A union of Negro trainmen eventually became the force behind the creation of the first Negro union in the United States, the Brotherhood of Sleeping Car Porters. These men worked long shifts catering to passengers of railroads that carted long trains fitted with sleeping cars built and maintained by the Pullman company. From coast to coast, passengers generically referred to these porters all by a single name. They were called "George," a term that was used to describe all porters by white passengers, made these valets on wheels invisible in a country where discrimination and racism were widespread. This story in *Opportunity Magazine* tells the story of one man who helped organize that union.

SILENT Bumbry was a Pullman porter who operated a sleeping car out of the New York Central district when Richtmyer was Superintendent of the Pullman Company in that district. Bumbry was the prototype employee usually seen complementing the Pullman exhibits in metropolitan terminals—tall, of angular frame, high cheek-boned and the color of boiled coffee.

The most complete account that any one of his fellow workers could have given about Bumbry was hearsay; for he walked from the subway, swinging in a deliberate long stride to the yards. No one knew him well; none had been to his home, many doubted that he had a home because they concluded that he must be a bachelor because he still wore the first suit of clothes he had ever purchased, or its pattern and ravels belied its chronological conception. They also guessed that Bumbry was from the South originally because he elongated his vowels and elided his consonants in speaking. When he left the yards, they watched the subway swallow him from whence he emerged placidly when he reported for his next regular run.

The porters liked Silent, and they supposed that the officials liked him for they had never heard of a single insubordination, nor noted an infrequent absence due to a book suspension; nor had they ever seen his name on the board or in the order book. He was their most frequent personnel topic for discussion, but each admired, yea, coveted Bumbry's solitude so they endearingly named him, not without admiration, Silent Bumbry.

The speculation about Bumbry increased when organization came to the Pullman porter group in the early twenties, for on one hand was Simmon's inside Employee Representation Plan, sponsored and maintained by the Company; on the other was Randolph's outside Brotherhood of Sleeping Car Porters, a bona fide trade union affiliated with the American Federation of Labor.

All about the Pullman quarters and "sign-out" windows fell subtle suspicion, thick as train smoke and silence as heavy as seasonal runs. He who had formerly been a comrade in endeavor, had he at any time said, "If you want to ride this train, vote annually under and for the Employee Representation Plan" was blackballed as a stool pigeon, Uncle Tom or a handkerchief head; but should he query "Service or Servitude?" he was proscripted to the ranks of the predamned as an ingrate, a radical, or agitator.

Which side of the fence? was the implied inflection in the most casual conversation, Which side of the fence?

Behind the inflections were those less careful who openly rebelled, declaring loudly: "'Tis us who sell John Public, George Pullman. The sleeper is useless without the porter—we are the magic touch of labor which transforms any material into a saleable commodity. Fight or Be Slaves."

The other group advocated, "Don't bite the hand that's feeding you." Or "Work for either the Brotherhood or the Pullman Company."

Less silently, less subtly, the Pullman management overlords and underlords were firing over five hundred men for "monkeying" with outside union affiliation, firing them without recourse to hearing or firing them technically by suspending them until that day when they should come back whimpering, kneeling their way to tell the superintendent that they had seen the light at last, which pantomime would take place on the historically warped economic structure of race and bread ... black man ... fewer jobs ... last hired, first fired ... black skin ... Fight or be slaves.... Employee Representation Plan ... John Brown's Body, or did John Brown live in the days of Pullman Cars ... hunger is contagious and my family is mighty susceptible.... Simmons ... job ... bread ... For Whom are you working? ... violated seniority ... preparatory time ... Randolph ... good porter ... black skin, aw, what the hell!

Silent's name was on the black board and in the order book when his train pulled into the yards from the West one golden autumn day and the porters looked knowingly at each other and shuddered. They spoke not a word to each other, but knew that the superintendent would at last ferret through Silent's coveted complacency. He would be, in no uncertain rhetorical questioning, asked for whom he was working.

Order for Bumbry could mean nothing else, since he was adjudged too slow to be curt and too naive to be suspicious. The mystery around Bumbry grew more intricate as he took the subway uptown for the Superintendent's office, for although he had never been seen to vote for the Plan of Employee Representation, he had never been heard chanting that infectious quartette, "Fight or Be Slaves."

When Bumbry reported to the Pullman Company's offices, the pale, fragile-appearing blonde switchboard operator in the tight yellow blouse asked him what he wanted.

"Nothing," said Bumbry and he shrugged his shoulders. "Who do you want a see?" "Who me? No one." "Well, whatcha here for?" "Mr. Richtmyer wants to see me." "Oh, well, sit down, Porter. Sit down and wait."

Bumbry waited. He waited thirty-five minutes by the office clock on the exceedingly hard bench reserved impartially by the Company for its porters, whether faithful Company men or radical union agitators. Then she told him, "You can go in now."

Silently, awkwardly, Bumbry entered the Superintendent's office, deferentially twisting his misshapen hat and walking on tiptoe lest he interrupt the

Superintendent who seemed to be busy with the scattered diagrams on his mahogany desk. After a few fog-heavy seconds Richtmyer looked up from the technical diagrams, acknowledged Silent's presence with a curt nod, then returned his eyes to the diagrams before him and began to mumble the copyrighted, periodically aired, safety lecture phrases about The Pullman Family.

"You have been a good porter, Bumbry, considered by the management as one of the most reliable and congenial members of the Pullman Family in this district. As you know, there are more Negroes in The Pullman Service than in any other unit of industry in this chosen land, the United States of America; and truly it is a land of unexplored wealth and resource. This Company took your forefathers directly from slavery, illiterate and untaught, and has given them work, and the means wherewith to buy food, clothing and excellent shelter. It, The Company, is training this select group of workers into a school of thought that will make your children worthy of citizenship in the greatest republic on earth. And with what shall you repay the Pullman Company? Service is not enough. There must be loyalty."

As Richtmyer talked, his voice rising chromatically in a faulty crescendo, Bumbry punctured the monologue with a shift of the already battered hat in his angular hands. When he reached the psychological volume and pitch, Richtmyer yelled:

"Porter, are you a member of this Brotherhood of Sleeping Car Porters?" Bumbry shifted, then waited for the echo to die down in the silver pitcher marked Pullman on the table beside the massive, mahogany desk. Then he whispered in a half halting legato, a pitchless nasal tone:

"Mr. Richtmyer, Sir, do you belong to the Roman Catholic Church? The Masons? The Child Welfare Society, The Metropolitan Life Insurance Company, the Book of the Month Club, the Animal-"

"Porter, you're out of place and insubordinate. Have you forgotten that I am district superintendent of the Pullman Company? Why—why it's none of your business just what I belong to !"

"No sir, Mr. Richtmyer, I ain't forgot what you are, but your answer is exactly the same one I was going to give to the question you put to me!"

"What answer?" "That it ain't your business what I belong to, neither." Bumbry turned to leave. He walked slowly as if respectful of the high office; but the superintendent would not accept defeat at the hands of a dark menial so easily. He jumped to his feet and yelled in a voice like a trumpet:

"Now, Porter, I want you to be careful, do you understand!"

Bumbry turned, knowing that the questioning was not yet over, but fully aware that everything he uttered would be used against him. He then spoke in a voice more moderately thin than his previous one, shaking his head slowly from side to side:

"Mr. Superintendent of the Pullman Company, I got nothing to be careful for. I own enough houses in Brooklyn."

Bumbry quietly opened the office door and walked evenly through the main office, thinking back to those days in the oppressive South when some white folks had offered to buy his rock-strewn, infertile farm because they had discovered on it the graves of their ancestors, and they weren't particular about having niggers owning their flesh and blood. He thought of the then fabulous sum of money they had paid for their contempt of dark skin, then turned his thoughts to the snug row of houses in Brooklyn. Inwardly, he laughed at the impudence of the Superintendent who had pried in vain, and as he passed the mourner's bench with the half anxious, half defiant porters waiting to be admitted to the office, he felt inside his pocket and caressed with his long, angular fingers the membership card of the Brotherhood of Sleeping Car Porters.

Source: *Opportunity, Journal of Negro Life*, Vol. 13, No. 8, p. 242. August, 1935. National Urban League. The New Deal Network.

88. September Ghost Town—Almost: The Depression Hits a Negro Town, September 1935
ISABEL M. THOMPSON AND LOUISE T. CLARKE

Opportunity magazine, launched by the National Urban League, became the voice of a Negro population of migrants in the 1930s. By the early years of the twentieth century, millions of Negroes had begun migrating away from the rural south and created new lives for themselves in cities across America. This was particularly true in midwestern cities such as Detroit and Chicago. While mainstream publications occasionally covered issues relevant to this migrant population, publications like *Opportunity* and *The Crisis*, the publications started by the National Association of Colored People, were founded to cover racial issues. *Opportunity* covered a town called Nicodemus to clear up a myth that Nicodemus only existed in the minds of storytellers during the depression years.

What is Nicodemus? Myth or a reality?" The social-worker pondered this, as she viewed the report from the little town. "Population-76; number on relief-72"—these were the figures.

What of the stories that had flourished, concerning this all-Negro town—the only one of its kind ever established in the State of Kansas? Nicodemus! With all city government, churches, schools, banks, businesses controlled by Negroes. Nicodemus! With its valuable wheat lands. Nicodemus! Whose citizens were so influential in the state political organization.... Had this ever been fact? Was any of it true of the present-day town?

As the social-worker made her decision to visit Nicodemus, she was grateful for the new position that was enabling her to study past and present conditions in her native state.

Days later, she was viewing an almost-deserted village. There were three small stone buildings: a church, a hall, and a store, the latter very small and meagerly stocked. (Practically all marketing and trading are carried on at Bogue, about six miles distant.) The small frame buildings that could be seen were sadly in need of repair....

"Perhaps," thought the social-worker, "there has been gross exaggeration concerning the history of this town." But, someone was stating facts now—facts that were corroborated by dependable sources by black type in newspapers, by official records, by pictures, and by the living word of old-timers.... The desolate, weed-grown settlement receded, and live, hopeful figures marched before her. Nineteen thirty-five became eighteen seventy-six.

Eighteen seventy-six! The Negro population in the South is extremely restless. The Reconstruction Period, following the War Between the States, has failed to bring them the freedom, equality, and prosperity so long anticipated. They are poverty-stricken, debt-ridden, starving. Many have already left for the North. Many times that many are hesitating—wanting to go, but fearing the perils of unknown country. Families in the backwoods of Kentucky and Tennessee listen eagerly to the tales of one W. R. Hill who describes a sparsely settled territory with abundant wild game and wild horses that can be easily tamed. But sweetest of all to the ears of former slaves is the statement that they can become land-owners through the home-steading process. Hill, originally from Covington, Indiana, has already taken three Negro men—Zack Fletcher, the Reverend Roundtree, and another named Smith—to a location in northwestern Kansas. Fifteen miles from Hill City, these men have established claims and made temporary quarters in dugouts. (The town Nicodemus was later built here.)

Hill's words have finally stirred some to action, and three-hundred eight tickets have been purchased to transport families to Ellis, Kansas, the nearest railroad point to the desired location. There are fifty-five miles farther to go! The serious problem of transportation confronts these penniless settlers who have only faith to sustain them. But independence is a prize worthy of struggle, and in September, 1877, they have reached the site. Within a month, the first Negro child is born in Graham County.

The social-worker shivered, as she learned of the adverse weather conditions, the privation and disappointment experienced by these pioneers newly-arrived from a warm, sunny land. She could almost hear a banjo strumming "My Old Kentucky Home," while a Kansas wind howled. She could see the founders of Nicodemus flinching, as, one by one, the myths of "milk and honey" were exploded. But these people stayed! And with spring came new hope, as they began the task of bringing a yield from the soil. Another colony came from the South, and the local government, headed by "President" Smith, was established.

For several years there was a steady influx of southerners, while the settlers were troubled by lack of funds for clothing and supplies and by a disastrous grasshopper plague. Through the efforts of the minister, contributions of money and clothing were obtained from the East. As for the plague—it could only be observed and regretted. No one returned to the South, however!

By eighteen-eighty, there were five hundred inhabitants in Nicodemus, which boasted a bank, two hotels, a newspaper, drug store, a number of "general stores," and several other business houses. An area of twelve square miles was being cultivated.

Now the settlers knew that the extension of a railroad to Nicodemus from Stockton, Kansas, would be an important step in the growth of the all-Negro town. Yet, when the offer was made, there was a disagreement concerning financial compensation; the railway company withdrew its offer and established Bogue, Kansas, as the nearest station. This left Nicodemus as an inland village and stopped the steady growth in population.

However, the state-wide political influence of the town flourished. Ed McKabe, a Negro land agent, took the first census, was later elected county clerk, and was finally sent to the capital to be the first Negro State Auditor of Kansas. The founding of Nicodemus seems well worthwhile when one learns that more Negroes have been elected to county offices in Graham County than in all of the other one-hundred four Kansas counties combined. Some of these men were: John DePrad, a pioneer who was county clerk; J. R. Hawkins, court clerk; J. E. Porter, court clerk; G. W. Jones, county clerk and district attorney; Dan Hickman, chairman of the board of county commissioners; W. L. Sayers, county attorney; John Q. Sayers, county attorney. The two Sayers brothers are now practicing attorneys in Hill City.

In 1928, the farmers of Nicodemus were cultivating from fifty to one thousand acres each. When the seasons were favorable, the lands frequently yielded more value in wheat than the actual sale value of the land.

Everyone knows what happened to business in 1929, and what subsequently happened to the farmer's prices. Almost all of the young people left Nicodemus during the financial upheaval. Further, nature has given a freak side-show of weather conditions in Western Kansas. Droughts of 1932, 1933, and 1934 were followed by destructive dust storms in the late winter and early spring of 1935. Entire families deserted this unproductive region.

"What is Nicodemus? And what has happened to it?" The social worker need ask these questions no longer.

What will happen to Nicodemus? Late spring and early summer rains were heavy in Kansas, and may help to repair some crop damage. Will favorable weather conditions definitely improve the financial status and revive interest in the town? Will the political influence of Nicodemus' citizens be maintained, lost, or increased? Will a railroad company ever again consider extending its lines to Kansas' all-Negro town?

The social worker wonders.

Source: *Opportunity, Journal of Negro Life*, Vol. 13, No. 9, p. 277. September, 1935. National Urban League. The New Deal Network.

89.　Harlem: Dark Weather-Vane, August 1936
ALAIN LOCKE

In 1925, *Survey Graphic* magazine announced the arrival of a "new Negro" and the onset of a "Negro renaissance" in Harlem. Eleven years later, that same Harlem, like the rest of America, was in the grip of the depression; moreover, Harlem was in the throes of social unrest that erupted in the Harlem riot of 1935. Scholar Alain Locke, sometimes referred to as the father of the Harlem Renaissance, said that the renaissance and the riot indicated a serious relapse and a premature setback in racial progress. In a special issue of *Survey Graphic*, he tells the story about the hard times in Harlem.

Just eleven brief years ago Harlem was full of the thrill and ferment of sudden progress and prosperity; and *Survey Graphic* sounded the tocsin of the emergence of a "new Negro" and the onset of a "Negro renaissance."

Today, we confront the sobering facts of a serious relapse and premature setback; indeed, find it hard to believe that the rosy enthusiasms and hopes of 1925 were more than bright illusions or a cruelly deceptive mirage. Yet after all there was a renaissance, with its poetic spurt of cultural and spiritual advance, vital with significant but uneven accomplishments; what we face in Harlem today is the first scene of the next act—the prosy ordeal of the reformation with its stubborn tasks of economic reconstruction and social and civic reform.

Curtain-raiser to the reformation was the Harlem riot of March 19 and 20, 1935; variously diagnosed as a depression spasm, a Ghetto mutiny, a radical plot and dress rehearsal of proletarian revolution. Whichever it was, like a revealing flash of light-ning it etched on the public mind another Harlem than the bright surface Harlem of the night clubs, cabaret tours and arty magazines, a Harlem that the social worker knew all along but had not been able to dramatize—a Harlem, too, that the radical press and street-corner orator had been pointing out but in all too incredible exag-gerations and none too convincing shouts.

In the perspective of time, especially if the situation is handled constructively, we shall be grateful for that lightning-flash which brought the first vivid realization of the actual predicament of the mass life in Harlem and for the echoing after-peals of thunder that have since broken our placid silence and Pollyanna complacency about it. For no cultural advance is safe without some sound economic underpin-ning, the foundation of a decent and reasonably secure average standard of living; and no emerging élite—artistic, professional or mercantile—can suspend itself in thin air over the abyss of a mass of unemployed stranded in an over-expensive, dis-ease- and crime-ridden slum. It is easier to dally over black Bohemia or revel in the hardy survivals of Negro art and culture than to contemplate this dark Harlem of semi-starvation, mass exploitation and seething unrest. But turn we must. For there is no cure or saving magic in poetry and art, an emerging generation of talent, or in international prestige and interracial recognition, for unemployment or precarious marginal employment, for high rents, high mortality rates, civic neglect, capitalistic exploitation on the one hand and radical exploitation on the other. Yet for some years now Harlem has been subject to all this deep undertow as against the surface advance of the few bright years of prosperity. Today instead of applause and public-ity, Harlem needs constructive social care, fundamental community development and planning, and above all statesman-like civic handling.

Immediately after the March riot, Mayor La Guardia appointed a representative bi-racial Commission of Investigation, headed by an esteemed Negro citizen, Dr. Charles H. Roberts. After 21 public and 4 closed hearings conducted with strategic liberality by Arthur Garfield Hays, and nearly a year's investigation by subcommis-sions on Health and Hospitalization, Housing, Crime and Delinquency and Police, Schools, the Social Services and Relief Agencies, a general report has been assembled under the direction of E. Franklin Frazier, professor of sociology at Howard University, which was filed with the Mayor March 31, 1936, just a few days after the first anniversary of the riots. A preliminary section on the causes of the riot has been published, and several other sections have found their way to publication, some regrettably in garbled form. The public awaits the full and official publication of what is, without doubt, an important document on the present state of Harlem. When published, the findings will shock the general public and all but the few social experts already familiar with the grave economic need and social adjustment in Har-lem and the inadequacies of short-sighted provisions in basic civic facilities of schools, hospitals, health centers, housing control and the like, a legacy of neglect from the venal, happy-go-lucky days of Tammany-controlled city government. Now with a socially-minded city and national government the prospects of Negro Harlem—and for that matter all handicapped sections—are infinitely brighter.

But there is evidence that the present city administration is losing no time in act-ing to improve the Harlem situation; partly no doubt upon the specific findings and recommendations of the recent investigation, but largely from previous plans, seri-ously delayed by lack of capital funds or federal subsidies such as are now financing some of the major items of the reform program. Within recent months, in some cases weeks, Harlem's urgent community needs have been recognized in the reconditioning of its sorely inadequate and formerly overcrowded municipal hospital, the completion and equipment of a long delayed woman's hospital pavilion approximately doubling the bed capacity of the Harlem Hospital, the remodeling of a temporary out-patient department, and the recommendation by the Commissioner of Hospitals of a new out-patient building and of plans for a new independent hospital plant. Similarly, in the school system's 1937 budget, two new school plants for Harlem have been incorporated. On June 20, the Mayor and the Secretary of the Interior spoke at the dedication of the foundations of the new Harlem River housing project, which will afford model housing for 574 low income families with also a nursery school, community playground, model recreation and health clinic facilities—a $4,700,000 PWA project. On June 24, the Mayor drove the last foundation piling for another PWA project, the. $240,000 district health clinic for the badly congested Central Harlem section, where the incidence of tuberculosis, social disease and infant mortality is alarmingly high, and announced the appointment of an experienced Negro physician as head officer It has been announced that a stipulation had been incorporated in the contract specifications for these new public works that Negro skilled labor was to have its fair share of consideration.

All this indicates a new and praiseworthy civic regard for Harlem welfare, contrasting sharply with previous long-standing neglect. The Commission in complaining of present conditions is careful to make plain that the present city administration has inherited most of them and that, therefore, they are not to be laid at its door. Yet they are on its doorstep, waiting immediate attention and all possible relief. The conditions are a reproach not only to previous politically minded municipal administrations but also to the apathy and lack of public-mindedness on the part of Harlem's Negro politicians and many professional leaders who either did not know or care about the condition of the masses.

Recent improvements will make some sections of the Commission's report contrary to present fact when it appears, but few will care to cavil about that. Yet, both for the record and for the sake of comparison, the situation as the Commission found it should be known. Harlem may not be disposed to look gift horses in the mouth, though a few professional agitators may. Clearly the present administration is now aware of Harlem's objective needs and is taking steps to meet some of them. Mayor La Guardia, speaking at the housing ceremony, said: "We cannot be expected to correct in a day the mistakes and omissions of the past fifty years. But we are going places and carrying out a definite program. While the critics have been throwing stones, I have been laying bricks." But admittedly the situation is still inadequately provided for even when present plans and immediate prospects are carried out; compounding the actual need is a swelling sense of grievance over past civic neglect and proscription. A long-range plan of civic improvements in low-cost housing, and slum clearance, in further hospital and health clinic facilities, recreation, library and adult education centers, auxiliary school agencies is imperatively necessary. And in certain city departments a clearer policy of fair play is needed, not so much with regard to the inclusion of Negroes in municipal posts—though that too is important—as in their consideration for executive and advisory appointments where they can constructively influence municipal policies and remedial measures for the Harlem constituency. One of the fatal gaps between good intentions and good performance is in this matter of local administrators, where often an executive policy officially promulgated gets short circuited into discrimination at the point of practical application. Negroes are often accused of race chauvinism in their almost fanatical insistence upon race representatives on executive boards and in councils of policy, but the principle of this vital safeguard is of manifest importance. Especially in situations of accumulated wrong and distrust, mere practical expediency requires public assurance and reassurance.

The riot itself might never have occurred had such imponderables been taken into consideration. Its immediate causes were trivial,—the theft of a ten-cent pocket-knife by a Negro lad of sixteen in Kresge's department store on 125 Street. It was rumored that the boy had been beaten in the basement by store detectives and was gravely injured or dead; by tragic coincidence an ambulance called to treat one of the Kresge employee, whose hand the boy had bitten, seemed to confirm the rumor and a hearse left temporarily outside its garage in an alley at rear of the store to corroborate this. As a matter of fact the boy had given back the stolen knife and had been released through the basement door. But it must be remembered that this store, though the bulk of its trade was with Negroes, has always discriminated against Negroes in employment. Shortly before the riot it had been the objective of a picketing campaign for the employment of Negro store clerks, had grudgingly made the concession of a few such jobs and then transferred the so-called "clerks" to service at the lunch counter. While the original culprit slept peacefully at home, a community of 200,000 was suddenly in the throes of serious riots through the night, with actual loss of life, many injuries to police and citizens, destruction of property, and a serious aftermath of public grievance and anger. The careful report of the Commission on this occurrence correctly places the blame far beyond the immediate precipitating incidents. It was not the unfortunate rumors, but the state of mind on which they fell; not the inflammatory leaflets issued several hours after the rioting had begun by the Young Liberators, a radical Negro defense organization, or the other broadside distributed a little later by the Young Communist League, but the sense of grievance and injustice that they could depend on touching to the quick by any recital of fresh wrong and injustice.

The report finds that the outbreak was spontaneous and unpremeditated; that it was not a race riot in the sense of physical conflict between white and colored groups; that it was not instigated by Communists, though they sought to profit by it and circulated a false and misleading leaflet after the riots were well underway; that the work of the police was by no means beyond criticism; and that this sudden breach of the public order was the result of a highly emotional situation among the colored people of Harlem, due in part to the nervous strain of years of unemployment and insecurity. "... Its distinguishing feature was an attack I upon property rather than persons, and resentment against whites who, while exploiting Negroes, denied them an opportunity to work." The report warns of possible future recurrences, offering as the only safe remedy the definite betterment of economic and civic conditions which, until improved, make Harlem a "fertile field for radical and other propaganda."

It is futile, [the report continues] to condemn the propagandists or to denounce them for fishing in troubled waters. The only answer is to eliminate the evils upon which they base their arguments. The blame belongs to a society that tolerates inadequate and often wretched housing, inadequate and inefficient schools and other public facilities, unemployment, unduly high rents, the lack of recreation grounds, discrimination in industry and the public utilities in the employment of colored people, brutality and lack of courtesy by police. As long as these conditions remain, the public order can not and will not be safe.

Despite this clear diagnosis, there are those even in official circles who insist upon a more direct connection between Harlem's restless temper and radical propaganda. To do so seriously misconstrues the situation by inverting the real order of cause and effect. Discrimination and injustice are the causes, not radicalism. But to neglect the symptoms, to ignore the grievances will be to spread radicalism. Violence will be an inevitable result. Eleven years ago, in the Harlem issue of *Survey Graphic*, the writer said:

"Fundamentally, for the present, the Negro is radical only on race matters, in other words, a forced radical, a social protestant rather than a genuine radical. Yet under further pressure and injustice iconoclastic thought and motives will inevitably increase. Harlem's quixotic radicalisms call for their ounce of democracy today lest tomorrow they be beyond cure.

That statement needs underscoring today, when aspects of discrimination, chronic through the years, become acute under the extra pressure of the depression. At such a time special—perhaps even heroic—remedy becomes necessary where preventive long term treatment should and could have been the scientific course. It follows that at this stage both the basic disease and its many complications as well must be treated. Obviously both long and short term measures are indicated, from the temporary palliative that allays inflamed public opinion to the long range community planning which requires years for development and application. The Commission report spreads its recommendations over just such a wide range. It is particularly wise and sound, even at the risk of appearing doctrinaire, in pointing to the Negro's economic exploitation through the employment policy of the whole community as the basic economic disease, anal to segregation as inducing the radical complications. Unlike many such reports this one does not overlook fundamentals, and in that respect renders a service of truly scientific and permanent value.

It follows then that Harlem's most acute problem is employment. Not mere job occupancy, but rather a lifting of its economic earning power through less discriminatory job distribution. A careful analysis of job categories and employment trends makes this clear and is the basis for the rather startling suggestion that the municipality grapple with the traditionally non-governmental problem of the right to work according to ability. Knowing of course that the city cannot directly control the private labor market, the report nevertheless suggests, as a long term policy, measures of indirect control. It suggests that the city enact an ordinance that no municipal contracts be given to firms or corporations that discriminate, racially or otherwise, against workers, and that in its contracts with the public utilities it make provisions and reservations which will prevent flagrant labor discrimination. It further suggests that the city itself as an employer set a good example, not merely by the number of Negroes employed but by widening the range of jobs filled by Negroes. This is a particularly pointed suggestion in view of the fact that the relatively small quota of Negroes in the New York city service, 2.2 percent in 1920 had fallen to 1.4 percent in 1930, the latest figure available. The PWA housing project for Harlem sets the proper but daring precedent of specifying that the employment of less than one third skilled Negro labor will constitute *prima facie* evidence of discrimination, and furnish grounds for disciplinary action against the contractor. Revolutionary as all this may seem, it goes to the economic roots of the race issue, and boldly carries the principle of the Fourteenth Amendment into the economic field. Typical is the report of the New York Edison Company with 65 Negroes in its employ out of 10,000 and the Fifth Avenue Coach Co. with 213 Negroes out of a total of 16,000 employee. It is such an industrial policy that brings, in the words of the report, "a certain retribution upon a community that discriminates against the Negro worker through the money it must spend upon him in the form of relief."

The common sense and logic of such a position become obvious when a community has to pay the indirect costs of labor discrimination in relief to the victims of insecure and marginal employment. Definite proof of this economic inequality is seen in the disproportionate number of Negroes on New York City relief rolls. Ten percent of the Negro population is on relief, over double its relative population of 4 percent. It has been further evidenced in the difficulties encountered by Negro workers with skilled vocational training and experience in securing work relief assignments except as unskilled laborers. Negroes did not receive their proportionate share of work relief jobs even in sections predominantly Negro, and in sections predominantly white, Negro home relief clients were not given their proportional share of referral assignments to work relief jobs. Many skilled Negro workers had either to accept places in the unskilled ranks or go back to the home relief rolls as "unemployables." Of the employables in New York City on relief the year preceding the riot, 14 percent or 58,950 were Negroes.

Most of the complaints of discrimination in the relief services have occurred in the work relief sections, where finally an advisory committee on Negro problems was appointed, and in the matter of personnel policies of the Emergency Relief Bureau itself. In home relief, the investigation found substantial fairness and little or no justifiable complaint. Negroes have been employed in the relief services at a ratio almost double their percentage in the city's population, incidentally affording indirect evidence of the disproportionate amount of unemployment among Negroes with relatively high grade qualifications. There was some complaint, according to the report, about their slow admission to higher administration grades, especially the strategic positions of occupational clerks, a type of position vital for initiating any broader policy of labor classification for Negro eligibles. Recently, Mayor La Guardia announced the appointment of Dr. John H. Johnson, rector of St. Martin's Episcopal Church, as the sixth member of the Emergency Relief Bureau.

Housing is the most serious special community problem of Harlem. The Negro's labor short dollar is further clipped by the exorbitant rentals characteristic of the segregated areas where most Negroes must reside. Whereas rents should approximate 20 percent of family income, and generally tend to do so, in Harlem they average nearly double or 40 percent. Model housing does not begin to touch the real mass need either as slum clearance or low cost housing until it brings the average rental down to $5 to $7 per room per month. The Dunbar Apartments, erected some years back with Rockefeller subsidy, could not meet this need, although at the time it gave middle-class Harlem a real lift in the direction of decent housing and neighborhood conditions. The new Harlem River Houses, to be erected with federal subsidy, will be the first model housing to reach the class that needs it most. The New York Housing Authority deserves great credit for initiation and for the principle of local Negro advice and promised Negro management which it has adopted. Harlem's appreciative response was clearly evident at the recent cornerstone-laying when Secretary Ickes, Mayor La Guardia and Commissioner Langdon Post of the Tenement House Department endorsed the principle of bringing modern housing to the congested sections of Harlem. Secretary Ickes said: "The record of American housing is proof positive of one thing. Private initiative cannot, unaided, properly house our low income families. It is simply not in the cards. It can mulct unenviable profits by housing our people badly; it cannot make money by housing them well." That holds *a fortiori* for the Negro. But when the federally aided scheme has demonstrated its social and humane objectives, cut the cost of crime and juvenile delinquency, exerted its remedial influence on other negative social forces, including racial discontent, the subsidizing of still larger scale projects by the state and municipality will be wisely charged off to their proper balances in the saner bookkeeping of an intelligently social-minded community. The Commission's subcommission on housing under Morris L. Ernst was very active in its advocacy of progressive housing legislation before the State Legislature, and considerable progress in condemning old-law tenements and in slum clearance projects is contemplated under the progressive state legislation for which the Harlem investigation housing commission was directly responsible.

Health is the second great problem and disease is the second grim link in the Ghetto chain which fetters Harlem life. Central Harlem's rate of infant mortality, tuberculosis, and venereal disease is expectedly high and in direct proportion to areas of congestion and poverty. Harlem's hospital and health facilities were handicapped over a period of years, directly by antiquated equipment, indirectly by political and racial feuds. Regrettable differences often brought the two professional organizations of Negro physicians in Harlem into conflict. Although these differences were often over divergent views as to the gains and losses of segregation, or of this or that tactic in securing the admission of Negroes to staff and internes' positions in the municipal hospitals, they were anything but conducive to the morale of Harlem Hospital or to any clear policy of the hospital authorities. It took years of agitation to get any Negroes on the staff and the governing medical board, and Negro internee were admitted to Harlem Hospital only within the last ten years. Until recently there was only one Negro on the Harlem Hospital Board, and one Negro physician of full staff rank. The situation both as to hospital facilities and staff personnel has shown material improvement recently under what promises to be a new and liberalized policy instituted by the present Commissioner of Hospitals, Dr. Goldwater. But that change was too recent to spare the Commissioner or his immediate subordinate in charge of the Harlem Hospital from adverse criticism by the Commission. Recent improvements offset some of the shocking and inadequate conditions that had existed for years.

On January 2 the opening of the new women's wing to Harlem Hospital increased its capacity from 325 to 665 beds. This pavilion, almost completed four years ago, had stood unfinished chiefly because of legal complications growing out of the failure of contractors. This relief from overcrowding, no doubt the basis for the most serious complaints as to previous maladministration, clears the way for remodeling and modernizing the older parts of the hospital, which is now proceeding under WPA grants. A new nurses' home has recently opened; plans for a new $1,500,000 outpatient department have been drawn, and an additional entirely new hospital has been recommended as an urgent item in the impending capital outlay for city hospitals. In the meantime, the Department of Hospitals has, with the assistance of the WPA, modernized a two-story building on the Harlem Hospital block, which will provide more than four times the space of the old clinic. These last projects are made necessary by the fact that the recently enlarged facilities of Harlem Hospital already are approaching a crowded condition at times.

Only incessant agitation brought staff appointments in municipal hospitals to Negro physicians. Recently, by a laudable departure in the direction of fairer play, five Negroes were given staff appointments to Queens' General Hospital and one to Sea View; and in the first six months of 1936 seven Negro physicians have been promoted from assistant to associate visiting rank, five from clinical assistants to assistant visiting rank, and seven new clinical appointments have been made. This, with three members of full attending rank and an increase of two members on the Medical Board of Harlem Hospital, represents a spectacular gain in comparison with the slow progress of former years. The Commission report, however, recommends "the admission of Negro physicians, internee and nurses to all city hospitals on merit in accordance with law, and the withholding of municipal financial aid from any institution refusing equal treatment to Negroes."

With the completion of the new health unit, there will no longer be ground for the present complaint that in the two health areas where Negroes are concentrated there is "conspicuous absence of the very agencies which deal with the major problems of Negro health—infant mortality and tuberculosis."

Similarly, the announcement of two new school buildings for Harlem in the 1937 Board of Education program corrects in prospect the major plant deficiencies complained of in the Commission's school report. It leaves for further consideration the plea for some special provisions to offset the effects of demoralized home and neighborhood conditions upon a considerable section of the Harlem school population. Primarily this is not a school function or responsibility, even though it gravely affects its work. Classes for deficient and delinquent children, special vocational guidance, supervised play are recommended, and also greater protection of school children from the demoralized elements of the adjacent neighborhoods by the police department. Logically and practically, however, it is obvious that only wide-scale slum clearance will reach the roots of such conditions.

One of the rare bright spots in the situation is the fine policy of the New York City school system of entirely disregarding race in the appointment and assignment of Negro school teachers, which policy should point a convincing precedent to other city departments and, for that matter, to other great municipalities.

No field of municipal government is more tied in with a problem such as underlies the Harlem riots than the police department. Even at that time a spirit of general antagonism toward the police was evident, and the fatal shooting of a sixteen-year-old high school student, Lloyd Hobbes, whom the police charge with looting during the riot (a charge which several witnesses dispute), did much to aggravate the bitterness. As the report aptly says, "A policeman who kills is prosecutor, judge and executioner." In fact a series of police shootings in Harlem, continuing down to two quite recent killings of children in the police pursuit of suspected criminals, has brought the community to the point of dangerous resentment toward the police. The frequent heavy mobilization of police forces in Harlem, however well based the fear or probability of public disorder and the recurrence of rioting, has the practical effect of stimulating the very thing it is meant to avert—tension, resentment, and disrespect for proper police authority. Every close student of the situation sympathizes with the police authorities in their difficult responsibilities, especially during the strenuous campaign against the vice and small-time racketeering which are all too prevalent in Harlem. But respect for and confidence in police authority are primary assets in such a housecleaning campaign, and the good-will and cooperation of the law-abiding, better class element are essential. Restored confidence and good-will are particularly vital in the situation, fraught with possible racial antagonisms.

Surprising and convincing reason for suspecting police brutality and intimidation is the fact that many in the Harlem community feel as much resentment toward Negro police as toward white police, and even toward the Negro police lieutenant, who sometime back was a popular hero and a proud community symbol. The Commission's recommendations, therefore, that the police be given instructions to use greater caution and tact in emergencies and show the strictest regard for citizens' rights, and that a bi-racial Citizens' Public Safety Committee be appointed as an advisory body to the Police Commissioner and to hear possible complaints and grievances against undue use of police power or claims of police brutality and intimidation, are of crucial and constructive importance in a somewhat critical situation. For without restored confidence and unbroken public order, Harlem's wound will not heal.

Dark as the Harlem situation has been, and in a lesser degree still is, the depression in general and the riot in particular have served a diagnostic purpose which, if heeded and turned into a program of constructive civic reform, will give us improvement and progress instead of revolution and anarchy. After all, in these days of economic crisis and reconstruction the Negro has more than racial import. As the man farthest down, he tests the pressure and explores the depths of the social and economic problem. In that sense he is not merely the man who shouldn't be forgotten; he is the man who cannot safely be ignored.

Yet, in addition, Harlem is racially significant as the Negro's greatest and formerly most favorable urban concentration in America. The same logic by which Harlem led the Negro renaissance dictates that it must lead the economic reconstruction and social reformation which we have been considering. There are some favorable signs from within and without that it will: from without, in terms of the promise of the new concern and constructive policy of the Mayor and a few progressive city authorities; from within, in terms of a new type and objective of Negro civic leadership. The latter is evidenced in part by the Mayor's Harlem Commission and its sustained activities, by the ever increasing advisory committees of leading and disinterested citizens, and recently, quite significantly, by the organization of the bi-racial All Peoples' Party in Harlem for independent political action to "rid Harlem of the corrupt political control of the two major parties and end the tyranny of political bosses." Recently 209 delegates from 89 social, civic and religious organizations organized with this objective of substituting civic organization and community welfare for political support and party spoils. A Harlem community-conscious and progressively cooperative is infinitely to be preferred to a Harlem racially belligerent and distempered. Contrast the Harlem of the recent WPA art festival, gaily and hopefully celebrating in a festival of music, art and adult education, dancing in Dorrance Brooks Square, with the Harlem of the riot, a bedlam of missiles, shattered plate glass, whacking night-sticks, mounted patrols, police sirens and police bullets;

and one can visualize the alternatives. It is to be hoped that Harlem's dark weather-vane of warning can be turned round to become a high index of constructive civic leadership and reform.

Source: *Survey Graphic*, Vol. 25, No. 8, p. 457. August, 1936. Survey Associates, Inc.

90. Twenty-one Negro Spirituals, Americana No. 3, Recorded by So. Carolina Project Workers, Effingham, South Carolina, 1937

America was plunged into the greatest economic depression in history in the early 1930s. Unemployment was widespread. In an attempt to put large numbers of Americans back to work and to raise spirits, the government launched what became commonly known as "The New Deal." The federal government poured millions of tax dollars into economic relief efforts. One of these was called the Work Progress Administration (WPA). Under this umbrella, a smaller program called the Federal Writer's Project was also started in at least 26 states. One of those projects was in South Carolina where writers interviewed residents about their daily lives. The lyrics of twenty-one Negro spirituals, ritual religious music, were recorded in Effington, South Carolina.

1

Jes' low down de chariot right easy
Right easy, right easy
Jes' low down de chariot right easy
An' bring God's servant home

Jes' tip eround my room right easy
Right easy, right easy
Jes' tip eround my room right easy
And bring God's servant home

Jes' move my pillow 'round right easy
Right easy, right easy
Jes' move my pillow 'round right easy
And bring God's servant home

Jes' turn de cover back right easy
Right easy, right easy
Jes' turn de cover back right easy
And bring God's servant home

Jes' tone de bell right easy
Right easy, right easy
Jes' tone de bell right easy
And bring God's servant home

2

God's settin' happy on His throne
De Angel dropped his wings en moan
I'm tired uv yo' wicked ways
I'm tired uv yo' wicked ways
God's gittin' tired uv yo' wicked ways

Go down, Angel, en bolt de do'
Dat time whut's been shan't be no mo'
I'm tired uv yo' wicked ways
I'm tired uv yo' wicked ways
God's gittin' tired uv yo' wicked ways

Walk en yo' room en fall on yo' knees
It's, Lord, have mercy ef you please
God's worryin' wid yo' wicked ways
God's worryin' wid yo' wicked ways
God's gittin' worried wid yo' wicked ways

Silver shall tinkle en gold shall ruin
God is gettin' worried wid yo' wicked coin'
God's worryin' wid yo' wicked ways
God's worryin' wid yo' wicked ways
God is gittin' worried wid yo' wicked ways

Go to church en weep en moan
Jes' well's ter plead as to stay at home
God's worryin' wid yo' wicked ways
God's worryin' wid yo' wicked ways
God is gittin' worried wid yo' wicked ways

3

Oh, when I am er dyin'
I don't want nobody to moan
All I want yer to do fer me
Is jes' give dat bell a tone

Den I'll be crossin' over
I'll be crossin' over
Den I'll be crossin' over
Jesus gonna make up my dyin' bed

4

If 'ligion was a thing money could buy
I ain't gonna lay my 'ligion down

Well, de rich would live, en de po' would die
I ain't gonna lay my 'ligion down

But I'm so glad God fixed it so
I ain't gonna lay my 'ligion down
Dat de rich must die as well as de po'
I ain't gonna lay my 'ligion down

Ef de rich don't pray, to Hell dey'll go
I ain't gonna lay my 'ligion down
En de devil gonna get 'em, I'm pretty sho'
I ain't gonna lay my 'ligion down

Want er know de reason I walk so bold?
I ain't gonna lay my 'ligion down
Well, I got Jesus all in my soul
I ain't gonna lay my 'ligion down

5

Time, Time, Time is windin' up
Time, Time, Time is windin' up
Oh, destruction is dis lan', God's done moved His han'
En Time is windin' up

6

Ole Satan is er liar en er conjurer too
Oh, de rock er my soul
Ef you don't mind he'll conjure you
Oh, de rock er my soul

Oh, rock er my soul in de bosom of Abraham
Rock er my soul in de bosom of Abraham
Rock er my soul in de bosom of Abraham
Oh, de rock er my soul

7

Oh, come on, Elders, let's go round de wall
En hit jes' suits me
Don't want ter stumble, don't want ter fall
En hit jes' suits me
Well, dis here religion is more'n a notion
It keeps your body in er workin' motion
En hit jes suits me

8

He's er gamberlin' all night long
He's er gamberlin' till break of day
He roll 'em on de gamberlin' floor
En he throwed dem cards away

Lord, I wonders where's dat gamberlin' man
Lord, I wonders where's he gone
Lord, I wonders where's dat gamberlin' man
Lord, I wonders where's he gone

9

Well, Death went over to dat gambler's home
"Gambler, come en go wid me
Come en go wid me
Come en go wid me"
Dat Gambler said: "I'm not willin' to go
Caze I got no traverlin' shoes"

Well, Death went over to de preacher's home
"Preacher, come en go wid me
Come en go
Come en go"
Dat preacher said: "I'm willin' to go
Caze I got on my traverlin' shoes
Got my, got my
Got on my traverlin' shoes"

10

When I gets to Heaven, set right down
Until de war is ended
Ax my Lord fer a starry crown
Until de war is ended

Oh, when I gets to Heaven, gonna talk en tell
'Til de war is ended
How I did shun dem gates uv Hell
'Til de war is ended

11

Took my sin en give me grace, give me grace
Took my sin en give me grace
Took my sin en give me grace
Took my feet out de mirin' clay, mirin' clay
Took my feet out de mirin' clay
Took my feet out de mirin' clay
Placed dem on de rocks of eternitay, eternitay

Oh, Jordan is so chilly en cold, chilly en cold
Oh, Jordan is so chilly en cold
Jordan is so chilly en cold, chilly en cold
I got Jesus in my sould

12

I been in de war so long, I ain't got tired yit
I been in de war so long, I ain't got tired yit
Well, my head been wet wid de midnight dew
The 'fo' day star was a witness too
I been in de war so long en I ain't got tired yit

My knees is acquainted wid de hillside clay
Ain't got tired yit
Feet placed on de rock of eternitay
Ain't got tired yit

Ole Satan is mad en I am glad
Ain't got tired yit
Missed a soul he thought he had
En I ain't got tired yit

Oh, been in de war so long, ain't got tired yit
Oh, been in de war so long, ain't got tired yit

13

Oh, de little black train is a-comin'
Hit'll git yo' bizness right
Better fix yo' house in order
Caze hit may be here tonight

Oh, de little black train is er comin'
Hit's comin' round de curve
Hit's puffin' en hit's blowin'
Hit's strainin' every nerve

14

Didn't you hear Heaven bells ringin'?
Yes, I heered Heaven bells ringin'
Didn't you hear Heaven bells ringin'?
Yes, I heered Heaven bells ringin'
Heaven bells ringin' in my soul
Heaven bells ringin' in my soul
Not a bit of evil in my soul
Not a bit of evil in my soul

Oh, didn't you hear dat turkle dove moan?
Yes, I heered dat turkle dove moan

Didn't you hear dat turkle dove moan?
Yes, I heered dat turkle dove moan
Turkle dove moanin' in my soul
Turkle dove moanin' in my soul
Not a bit of evil in my soul
Not a bit of evil in my soul

15

Oh, de hearse keep a-rollin' somebody to de grave-yard
Oh, de hearse keep a-rollin' somebody to de grave-yard
Oh, de hearse keep a-rollin' somebody to de grave-yard
Oh, Lord, I feel lak my time ain't long

Oh, de bell keep a-tonin' somebody is er dying
Oh, de bell keep a-tonin' somebody is er dying
Oh, de bell keep a-tonin' somebody is er dying
Oh, Lord, I feel lak my time ain't long

Oh, my mother outrun me en she gone on to glory
Oh, my mother outrun me en she gone on to glory
Oh, my mother outrun me en she gone on to glory
Oh, Lord, I feel lak my time ain't long

16

Ole John de Baptist, ole John Divine
Frogs an' de snakes gonna eat ole John so bad
God tole de angel: "Go down see 'bout John"
Angel flew frum de bottom uv de pit
Gathered de wind all in his fist
Gathered de stars all 'bout his wrist
Gathered de moon all 'round his waist
Cryin' "Holy," cryin' "Holy," cryin' "Holy, my Lord," cryin' "Holy"

17

One day, one day I was goin' to pray
Thank God A'mighty I'm free at las'
I met ole Satan on my way
Thank God A'mighty I'm free at las'
Whut you reckon, whut you reckon ole Satan had to say?
Thank God A'mighty I'm free at las'
Young man, young man, you's too young to pray
Thank God A'mighty I'm free at las'
Ef I'm too young to pray, I ain't too young ter die
Thank God A'mighty I'm free at las'

Thank God a'mighty I'm free at las'
I ain't been to Heaven, but I been told
Thank God A'mighty I'm free at las'

The streets is pearl en de gates is gold
Thank God A'mighty I'm free at las'
Whut you reckon, whut you reckon ole Satan had to say?
Thank God A'mighty I'm free at las'
That Jesus was dead and God gone away
Thank God A'mighty I'm free at las'

But Satan is a liar and a conjurer too
Thank God A'mighty I'm free at las'
An ef you doan mine, he'll conjure you
Thank God A'mighty I'm free at las'

18

Sinner man er you may run away er
But you gotta come back er at Judgment Day
You gotta go 'fore dem bars of God
The balance is dere er you must be weighed er
Says after you balance dem balance too low
Says down in Hell you er sho to go
My Lord, who built dis Ark? Nora, Nora
Who built dis Ark? Nora, Lord

Says, dig my grave er wid the silver spade
En the link er of chain fer to link er me down
Er en a windin' sheet fer to wind me up
In de lotion of friends all standin' round
Er de dirt come tumblin', en de coffin sound
Er en de creepin' things wuz on de ground
My Lord, who built de Ark? Nora, Nora
Oh, Lord, who built de Ark? Nora, Nora

19

Oh, you may be a white man
White as de dribberlin' snow
Ef yo' soul ain't ankeld* in Jesus
To hell you sho'ly go

20

I'm goin' to mumble up old Zion
Old Zion, Old Zion
I'm goin' to mumble up old Zion
Een muh h'art

21

Ezekial cried out: Dry bones!
Hear ye the Word of the Lawdl
Good Lawd! Dem bones, dry bones
Dem bones got to jumpin' around

Good Lawd! Dem bones, dry bones
Dem bones got to jumpin' around
Hear ye the Word of the Lawd!

Source: Guilds' Committee for Federal Writers' Publications, Inc., 1937.

91. Amateur Night in Harlem, "That's Why Darkies Were Born," 1938
DOROTHY WEST

The Apollo Theater in Harlem is legendary. Most African American performers started their musical or acting careers there or performed on this stage at some point. While the names of countless performers graced the stage of this sacred place, the audiences played a bigger role in wowing newcomers with thunderous applause, or booing so loud that stage clowns tugged them off stage, never to be seen or heard from again. Writer Dorothy West captured this place in the following piece and managed to deliver a poignant reminder that America outside the doors of this theater was less forgiving than even the most critical audience at the Apollo.

The second balcony is packed. The friendly, familiar usher who scowls all the time without meaning it, flatfoots up and down the stairs trying to find seats for the sweethearts. Through his tireless manipulation, separated couples are reunited, and his pride is pardonable.

The crowd has come early, for it is amateur night. The Apollo Theater is full to over-flowing. Amateur night is an institution. Every Wednesday, from eleven until midnight, the hopeful aspirants come to the mike, lift up their voices and sing, and retire to the wings for the roll call, when a fluttering piece of paper dangled above their heads comes to rest determined by the volume of applause to indicate to whom the prizes shall go.

The boxes are filled with sightseeing whites led in tow by swaggering blacks. The floor is chocolate liberally sprinkled with white sauce. But the balconies belong to the hardworking, holidaying Negroes, and the jitterbug whites are intruders, and their surface excitement is silly compared to the earthy enjoyment of the Negroes.

The moving picture ends. The screen shoots out of sight. The orchestra blares out the soul-ticking tune, "I think you're wonderful, I think you're grand." Spontaneously, feet and hands beat out the rhythm, and the show is on.

The regular stage show preceds Amateur Hour. Tonight an all-girls orchestra dominates the stage. A long black girl in flowing pink blows blue notes out of a clarinet. It is hot song, and the audience stomps its approval. A little yellow trumpeter swings out. She holds a high note, and it soars up solid. The fourteen pieces are in the groove.

The comedians are old-timers. Their comedy is pure Harlemese, and their proto-types are scattered throughout the audience. There is a burst of appreciative laughter and a round of applause when the redoubtable Jackie Mabley states that she is doing general housework in the Bronx and adds, with telling emphasis, "When you do housework up there, you really do housework." It is real Negro idiom when one comedian observes to-another who is carrying a fine fur coat for his girl, "Anytime I see you with something on your arm, somebody is without something."

The show moves on. The girls of sixteen varying shades dance without precision but with effortless joy . The best of their spontaneous steps will find their way downtown. A long brown boy who looks like Cab Calloway sings, "Papa Tree-Top Tall." The regular stage show comes to an end. The act file on stage. The chorus girls swing in the background. It is a free-for-all, and to the familiar "I think you're wonderful, I think you're grand", the black-face comic grabs the prettiest chorine and they truck on down. When the curtain descends, both sides of the house are having fun. A Negro show would rather have the plaudits of an Apollo audience than any other applause. For the Apollo is the hard, testing ground of Negro show business, and approval there can make or break an act.

It is eleven now. The house lights go up. The audience is restless and expectant. Somebody has brought a whistle that sounds like a wailing baby. The cry fills the theater and everybody laughs. The orchestra breaks into the theater's theme song again. The curtain goes up. A [WMCA?] announcer talks into a mike, explaining to his listeners that the three hundred and first broadcast of Amateur Hour at the Apollo is on the air. He signals to the audience and they obligingly applaud.

The emcee comes out of the wings. The audience knows him. He is Negro to his toes, but even Hitler would classify him as Aryan at first glance. He begins a steady patter of jive. When the audience is ready and mellow, he calls the first amateur out of the wings.

Willie comes out and, on his way to the mike, touches the Tree of Hope. For several years the original Tree of Hope stood in front of the Lafayette Theater on Seventh Avenue until the Commissioner of Parks tore it down. It was to bring good fortune to whatever actor touched it, and some say it was not Mr. Moses who had it cut down, but the steady stream of down-and-out actors since the depression who wore it out.

Willie sings "I surrender Dear" in a pure Georgia accent. "I can' mak' mah way," he moans. The audience hears him out and claps kindly. He bows and starts for the wings. The emcee admonishes, "You got to boogie-woogie off the stage, Willie." He boogie-woogies off, which is as much a part of established ritual as touching the Tree of Hope.

Vanessa appears. She is black and the powder makes her look purple. She is dressed [in black?], and is altogether unprepossessing. She is the kind of singer who makes faces and regards a mike as an enemy to be wrestled with. The orchestra sobs out her song. "I cried for you, now it's your turn to cry over me." Vanessa is an old-time "coon-shouter." She wails and moans deep blue notes. The audience give her their highest form of approval. They clap their hands in time with the music. She finishes to tumultous applause, and accepts their approval with proud self-confidence. To their wild delight, she flings her arms around the emcee, and boogie woogies off with him.

Ida comes out in a summer print to sing that beautiful lyric, "I Let a Song Go Out of My Heart," in a nasal, off-key whine. Samuel follows her. He is big and awkward, and his voice is very earnest as he promises, "I Won't Tell A Soul I love you." They are both so inoffensive and sincere that the audience lets them off with light applause.

Coretta steps to the mike. Her first note is so awful that the emcee goes to the Tree of Hope and touches it for her. The audience lets her sing the first bar, then bursts into cat- calls and derisive whistling. In a moment the familiar police siren is heard off-stage, and big, dark brown Porto Rico, who is part and parcel of amateur night, comes on stage with nothing covering his nakedness but a brassiere and panties and shoots twice at Coretta's feet. She hurriedly retires to the wings with Porto Rico switching after her, brandishing his gun.

A clarinetist, a lean dark boy, pours out such sweetness in "Body and Soul" that somebody rises and shouts, "Peace, brother!" in heartfelt approval. Margaret follows with a sour note. She has chosen to sing "Old Folks", and her voice quavers so from stage fright that her song becomes an unfortunate choice, and the audience stomps for Porto Rico who appears in a pink and blue ballet costume to run her off the stage.

David is next on the program. With mounting frenzy he sings the intensely pleading blues song, "Rock it for Me." He clutches his knees, rolls his eyes, sings away from the mike, and works himself up to a pitch of excitement that is only cooled by the appearance of Porto Rico in a red brassiere, an ankle-length red skirt, and an exaggerated picture hat. The audience goes wild. Ida comes out. She is a lumpy girl in a salmon pink blouse. The good-looking emcee leads her to the mike and pats her shoulder encouragingly. She snuggles up to him, and a female onlooker audibly snorts, "She sure wants to be hugged." A male spectator shouts, gleefully, "Give her something!"

Ida sings the plaintive, "My Reverie". Her accent is late West Indian and her voice is so bad that for a minute you wonder if it's an act. Instantly here are whistles, boos, and handclapping. The siren sounds off stage and Porto Rico rushed on in an old fashioned corset and a marabou-trimmed bed jacket. His shots leave her undisturbed. The audience tries to drown her out with louder applause and whistling. She holds to the mike and sings to the bitter end. It is Porto Rico who trots sheepishly after her when she walks unabashed from the stage.

James come to the mike and is reminded by the audience to touch the Tree of Hope. He hasn't forgotten. He tries to start his song, but the audience will not let him. The emcee explains to him that the Tree of Hope is a sacred emblem. The boy doesn't care, and begins his song again. He has been in New York two days, and the emcee cracks that he's been in New York two days too long. The audience refuses to let the lad sing, and the emcee banishes him to the wings to think it over.

A slight, young girl in a crisp white blouse and neat black shirt comes to the mike to sing "tisket tasket". She has lost her yellow-basket, and her listeners spontaneously inquire of her, "Was it red?" She shouts back dolefully, "No, no, no, no!"

"Was it blue?" No, it wasn't blue, either."

They go on searching together.

A chastened James reappears and touches the Tree of Hope. A woman states with grim satisfaction, "He teched de tree dat time." He has tried to upset a precedent, and the audience is against him from the start. They boo and whistle immediately. Porto Rico in red flannels and a floppy red hat happily shoots him off the stage.

A high school girl in middy blouse, jumper and socks rocks "Froggy Bottom." She is the youngest thing yet, and it doesn't matter how she sings. The house rocks with her. She winds up triumphantly with a tap dance, and boogie woogies confidently off the stage.

A frightened lad falls upon the mike. It is the only barrier between him and the murderous multitude. The emcee's encouragement falls on frozen ears. His voice starts down in his chest and stays here. The house roars for the kill, Porto Rico, in a baby's bonnet and a little girl's party frock, finishes him off with dispatch.

A white man comes out of the wings, but nobody minds. They have got accustomed to occasional white performers at the Apollo. There was a dancing act in the regular stage show which received deserved applause. The emcee announces the song, "That's Why——" he omits the next word "Were Born." He is a Negro emcee. He will not use the word "darky" in announcing a song a white man is to sing.

The white man begins to sing, "Someone had to plough the cotton, Someone had to plant the corn, Someone had to work while the white folks played, That's why darkies were born." The Negroes hiss and boo. Instantly the audience is partisan. The whites applaud vigorously. But the greater volume of hisses and boos drown out the applause. The singer halts. The emcee steps to the house mike and raises his hand for quiet. He does not know what to say, and says ineffectually that the song was written to be sung and urges that the singer be allowed to continue. The man begins again, and on the instant is booed down. The emcee does not know what to do. They are on a sectional hook-up—the announcer has welcomed Boston and Philadelphia to the program during the station break. The studio officials, the listening audience, largely white, has heard a Negro audience booing a white man. It is obvious that in his confusion the emcee has forgotten what the song connotes.

The Negroes are not booing the white man as such. They are booing him for his categorization of them. The song is not new. A few seasons ago they listened to it in silent resentment. Now they have learned to vocalize their bitterness. They cannot bear that a white man, as poor as themselves, should so separate himself from their common fate and sing paternally for a price of their predestined lot to serve.

For the third time the man begins, and now all the fun that has gone before is forgotten. There is resentment in every heart. The white man will not save the situation by leaving the stage, and the emcee steps again to the house mike with an impassioned plea. The Negroes know this emcee. He is as white as any white man. Now it is ironic that he should be so fair, for the difference between him and the amateur is too undefined. The emcee spreads out his arms and begins, "My people—."

He says without explanation that "his people" should be proud of the song. He begs "his people" to let the song be sung to show that they are ladies and gentlemen. He winds up with a last appeal to "his people" for fair-play. He looks for all the world like the plantation owner's yellow boy acting as buffer between the black and the big house.

The whole house breaks into applause, and this time the scattered hisses are drowned out. The amateur begins and ends in triumph. He is the last contestant, and in the line-up immediately following, he is overwhelmingly voted first prize. More of the black man's blood money goes out of Harlem.

The show is over. The orchestra strikes up, "I think you're wonderful, I think you're grand." The audience files out. They are quiet and confused and sad. It is twelve on the dot. Six hours of sleep and then back to the Bronx or up and down an elevator shaft. Yessir, Mr. White Man, I work all day while you-all play. It's only fair. That's why darkies were born.

Source: New York, NY, 1938. Library of Congress, Manuscript Division, WPA Federal Writers' Project Collection.

92. Temple of Grace, 1938
DOROTHY WEST

Writer Dorothy West covered the churches in Harlem, particularly that of a chrarismatic preacher, Marceline Manuel DaGraca, who called himself "Daddy Grace." Daddy Grace was a phenomenon who rose up in the 1930s to challenge the religious throne of a rival, George Baker, who called himself Father Divine.

Twenty West One Hundred and Fifteenth Street is the New York stomping ground of Daddy Grace, the self-styled rival of Father Divine. It was to this building that he came roaring out of Washington, with the as yet unfulfilled promise of dethroning the Father. Divine's lease on this property had expired, and at renewal time it was discovered that Daddy Grace had signed ahead of him.

Divine's prestige tottered briefly, for it was a test of faith to his followers to accept the forced removal of God from his heaven by a mundane piece of paper. However, through an act of a diviner God, the Father acquired Crum Elbow as well as a handsome property on West One Hundred and Twenty-Fourth Street, and it was Daddy Grace whose trimph was now scarcely more than hollow.

The grace Temple on One Hundred and Fifteenth Street, still surrounded by various flourishing business establishments of Father Divine, is a red-brick building plastered over with crude angelic drawings and pious exhortations. The entrance hall leads directly to a flight of descending stairs over which is the inscription Grace Kitchen, or across a narrow threshold into the auditorium. This auditorium is of good size, seating possibly two hundred people. The floor is plain, reverberating board. The seats appear new and are cushioned in red leather of good quality. The walls are blue, with gilt borders and two foot bases painted red. At the rear, to the right, are elevated rows of seats which the choir of fifteen lusty white-robed women occupy. On a platform above them is an upright piano.

At half-past seven the choir began to drift in, and until eight they sang unfamiliar hymns grouped around the piano. Occasionally the pianist quickened the tempo into swing, and the choir swayed and shuffled and beat out the rhythm with their hands and feet.

In the place occupied by the pulpit in the average church is an elevated, wooden enclosure, most nearly resembling the throne room of a maypole queen. Six graded steps lead up to it, and most of the incoming congregation knelt briefly at the foot of the stairs before settling in their seats. In the absence of Daddy Grace, who did not appear all evening, they made obeisance to the covered throne chair which stood center in the enclosure and was not uncovered at any time during the proceedings.

To the left of the throne room was orchestra space. There were a piano, a trombone, a drum, two sousaphones, and two trumpets. At half-past seven a child less that two was beating without reprimand on the drum. He played unceasingly until the orchestra members entered at past eight, and the drummer smilingly relieved him of the sticks.

The auditorium filled slowly In all there were about seventy-five people. Most of the congregation came singly or in groups from the dining room, and many continued to munch after they were seated.

There were at first no ushers. Toward the end of the evening a young man in a smart uniform with Captain lettered on an arm band and Grade Soldier lettered on his breast stood at stiff attention at the rear of the temple. His one duty was to admonish the half-dozen non-participants, a row of high-school boys, not to whisper. Oddly enough, at that time the place was bedlam.

The crowd gathered informally. There were as many young children as adults. The grown-ups visited with each other. The children played up and down the aisles. There was unchecked laughter. There were only two or three [lone?] men with poverty and disinterest in their faces, who spoke to no one and appeared to have come in to escape the cold.

In contrast to the Divinites who are for the most part somberly and shabbily dressed, the Grace cohorts, though apparently poor, follow their own fashion dictates. The older women were plainly and poorly costumed, but the younger women wore skillful make-up, cheap hats smartly tilted, intriguing veils, and spike heels. One young woman who came in street clothes disappeared down the stairs and returned in an ankle-length dinner dress of black taffeta. It was she who accepted the offerings which white-frocked women brought her after each collection.

At eight the choir took their proper seats, and for half an hour sang familiar hymns, with frequent interpolations of praise to Daddy Grace. The congregation meanwhile had settled and quieted. No one joined in the singing, but there was perfunctory applause at the conclusion of each song. Occasionally a member turned to look up at the choir with mild interest.

When the choir service ended, a slim light brown man in a business suit appeared. At his entrance the orchestra began to play an unfamiliar tune, a variation of four notes, in swing tempo. The man said there would be a short prayer. His voice rose in illiterate and incoherent prayer with frequent name coupling of God and Daddy Grace. At their mention, there were murmurs of "Amen" and "Praise Daddy."

The prayer concluded and the orchestra continued to play. Now the unchanging beat of the drum became insistent. Its steady monotone scraped the nerve center. The Africanesque beat went on … tom … tom … tom … tom … A woman in the front row rose. She flung out her arms. Her body was slim and strong and beautiful. Her delicate-featured dark face became ecstatic. She began to chant in a vibrant unmusical voice, "I love bread, sweet bread." She clapped her hands in 4/4 time. Presently she began to walk up and down before the throne, swaying from her hips, her feet shuffling in dance rhythm, singing over and over, "I love bread, sweet bread."

A man rose and flung his hands in the air, waving them from the wrists. He began to moan and writhe. The monotonous beat of the drum was the one dominant note now, though the other instruments continued to play. Others rose and went through the motions of the woman. Children rose, too, children of grade school age, their faces strained and searching. A six year old boy clapped and stomped until his dull, pale, yellow face was red and moist.

When a shouting, shuffling believer was struck by the spirit, his face assumed a look of idiocy, and he began to pivot slowly in a circle. Tender arms steadied him, and he was guided along by out-stretched hands until he reached the milling throng before the throne, where he whirled and danced and shrieked in the whirling, dancing, shrieking mob until he fell exhausted to the floor. When he revived, he weaved back unsteadily to his seat and helped to steer others to the throne.

Finally both drummer and dancers were weary. The space before the throne cleared. A big pompous dark man in a business suit who had been sitting in one of the elevated seats in the rear, looking on with quiet approval, descended and came down the aisle, mounted the stairs leading to the throne, walked to a table to the right of the throne, and put on a gilded crown with a five-pointed star in its center. He advanced to the front of the dais and read briefly from the Bible. The reading concluded, he began to address the congregation as "dear ones" and "beloved". His voice was oily, his expression crafty. His garbled speech played on the emotions. He spoke feelingly of the goodness of Daddy, of Daddy's great love for his flock. He called them Daddy's children and urged them to obey and trust Daddy, and reminded them that they were part of a United Kingdom of Prayer. When the swelling murmurs of "Amens" and "Praise Daddy" indicated their revived strength and ardor, he bent to the woman who had first started the singing and asked in his smooth voice, "Sister, will you start the singing again?"

She rose and began to moan and sway. The orchestra took up her tune, but this time the drum did not beat, and suddenly a tambourine was heard, then another, and then another, until their were four or five. The beat was the same as the drum's had been, steady, monotonous, insidious, and far more deafening. When the open palms and closed fists slapped the center of the tambourine, the little disks jangled and added to the maddening sound.

The crowd's frenzy mounted. Their hysteria was greater than it had been before. They crowded to the space before the throne and their jerking bodies and distorted faces made them appear like participants in a sex orgy. Their cries were animal. When the young girls staggered back to their seats, they lay exhausted against the chair backs, tearing at their hair, with uncontrollable shudders shaking their bodies.

The mad dance went on for forty minutes, twice as long and twice as terrible as the first had been. When the man in the gilded crown felt their frenzy had reached its peak, he came to the front of the platform and stood silently until their awareness of his big, overbearing presence slowed their pace, muted the tambourines, and finally hushed the auditorium.

When they returned exhausted to their seats, he immediately asked them if they loved Daddy enough to keep his temple going by the purchase of his various products. There was no attempt to gloss this bald question. When there were sufficient murmurs of "Amen" and "Praise Daddy", he blew a police whistle and up and down the aisles went the white-frocked women hawking "Daddy Grace" toothpaste, hair pomade, lotions, and toiletries of every kind. One young woman was selling the Grace Magazine, 15 for the current issue, and 5 for back numbers.

The sales were few, and the man in the gilded crown tried to encourage the buying by telling the congregation that soon Daddy Grace planned to open shops of every description all over Harlem, and there would be work for everybody. When the last purchase had been made, the pompous man asked the first spokesman to read the list of trinkets available for Christmas presents. The list included a cross bearing Daddy Grace's picture for $1.50, a combination pen and pencil for a like sum, other articles at various prices, most of them with Daddy's picture as special inducement. The devotees signified their promise to purchase these trinkets by fervent "Amens."

This business concluded, the oily tongue called for the tithe offerings. Those with tithe money were asked to form a line in the center aisle. Half of the congregation got in line. The oily tongue asked for a march. The orchestra struck up. The whistle blew, and the marchers advanced to the front of the throne where they dropped their tithe money in the proferred baskets.

The sum collected totaled only a dollar and some odd cents. The man in the gilded crown concluded that there were some who had tithes but were disinclined to march. Thereupon he dispatched the white-frocked women down the aisles with baskets. They bent over the rows, asking persuasively, "Help us with the offering, dear heart."

When they had returned to the throne, there was a short speech about pledge money, and they were dispatched again. Again they bent down, begging as persuasively as before, "Help us with the offering, dear heart."

When the copper and silver pledges were brought for his approval, the smooth tongue asked for offerings for the House of Prayer. His voice filled with entreaty. He talked of the Grace temples in other cities and implored the congregation to glad-den Daddy's heart by making this temple "the best of all." It could only be done with money, he said. His language was plain and his appeal was not garnished by an spiritual references. Rather, he fixed them with his eye and flatly informed them that the temple could not run without money, and it was money that he wanted. He then asked the pianist for a march. The pianist who was leaning indolently against the piano with his collar open and his tie loosed, said wearily, "I'm tired." One of the women in white ran down the aisle and returned with the man who had played for the choir. He obligingly swung into a march.

The police whistle blew. The people with pledges were asked to line up in the center aisle. Happily and proudly they lined up in double file. Their manner of marching was different now. It was a shuffling strut, and their arms were bent up at the elbows and held firmly against the side. The line marched down the center to the throne, then divided and in single file shuffled up the two side aisles, met again at the rear of the hall, and then one after one went down the center aisle again and placed their pledge money in the basket.

The man in the gilded crown announced that the offerings had reached the total of $5.06. He said that he did not want to take up their time by begging since the hour was growning late, but he wondered if there was anyone present who would raise the total to $5.25. A man came forward immediately. Thus encouraged, the pompous leader asked if there was another beloved heart who would increase the sum to $5.50. The woman who had led the singing promptly gave a quarter. The leader begged for another quarter for three or four minutes, but no one came forward. Abruptly he ended his plea and announced that he would now preach the sermon.

As he spoke a woman screamed, and her arm shot stiffly up into the air while her body grew rigid. Three women laid her on the floor in the aisle. She continued to scream and moan, and then began to talk unintelligibly in a high-pitched, unnatural voice.

The man in the gilded crown announced his text. His voice grew deep and stern.

"I'll tell my story about the cow and the sheep who told on the man." He paused, and then waved his arm dramatically at the prostrate woman. "Oh, my beloveds," he said, "sometimes I tremble in fear at the power, the wonderful, mysterious power."

He shook himself in semblance of terror, but it was not funny to the congregation. They stirred uneasily.

"You must fear the power, the wonderful power," he exhorted them. "You must fear and follow Daddy. You must have fear."

A man shot out of his seat and began to moan and sob, flinging his arms around in the air. Smooth tongue looked at him with satisfaction. The congregation strained forward, a concerted sigh escaping from them. Others began to scream and moan. In a few minutes half the flock was on its feet, beginning again that stupefying, tireless dance. In a few minutes more almost every man, woman, and child was dancing, this time without music but with a uniformity of shuffling step and weaving arms.

The man in the gilded crown retired to the rear of the platform, his performance over.

The crazy dance went on. In the street the sound was audible a half block away.

Source: New York, NY, 1938. Library of Congress, Manuscript Division, WPA Federal Writers' Project Collection.